When I first saw the title of Jeff Sheehan's new book, **There Are No Foreign Lands**, I was truly intrigued, because as a former diplomat who served as Philippine Ambassador to the United States of America, the term "foreign lands" was a standard term in diplomatic jargon and did not have any derogatory aspect. While I initially did not understand why Jeff used this title, I was eager to find out. As I started to read the book, I was astounded by Jeff's hypothesis "that there are universal values and predilections which are common to all humans and which are of far more importance than superficial characteristics such as language, culture, history, religion, and ethnicity." Based on his experience having met and interacted with 13,464 people from 85 countries, he suggests that "we can understand and find common ground with any other." I was very curious to find out how Jeff would validate or support his hypothesis which seemed incredible but so inspiring and encouraging, if in fact he was right.

I now find it amazing how Jeff has used his extensive research on the 17 special friends whom he has known personally for many years and whom he profiles in the book. After an intensive analysis of their value systems, personalities, ideologies, beliefs, religions, traditions, and spirituality, he concludes that "these friends share 13 characteristics that could be emulated by others hoping to spend their lives well and meaningfully."

As a former central bank governor, corporate CEO, and ambassador to the USA, I have always thought I was a knowledgeable and committed globalist. Jeff's book has made me rethink my concept of "foreign lands." He has persuaded me that there are no foreign lands.

    — **Jose L. Cuisia, Jr., Manila, Philippines**
        Former Governor, Central Bank of the Philippines
        Former CEO, Philippine-American Life Insurance Company
        Former Philippine Ambassador to the USA

A gem of a book! A true internationalist, Jeff Sheehan paints evocative images of transformational leaders from across the globe. His conclusions on the elements of greatness are both intriguing and inspiring. Jeff chronicles the leaders' drive to change the world, their ability to navigate significant challenges, and their inherent humility amidst great contributions. A thought-provoking set of stories – a pleasure to read and reflect upon.

    — **Harbir Singh, Philadelphia, Pennsylvania**
        Mack Professor and Professor of Management
        The Wharton School of the University of Pennsylvania

I have known Jeff for almost 30 years and had the privilege of sharing quite a few memorable experiences with him. Jeff is a unique character, one of a kind. Thanks to his curiosity, his empathy for people and his charisma, he has this unique ability to reach out to people of highly diverse cultures, religions, and social backgrounds, and to go behind the mirror to apprehend what makes them special. The manner in which he paints a riveting portrait of each individual is fascinating. Jeff is an incredible mind-reader and storyteller. He has the capacity to bring them to vivid life as we discover how each of them navigated through extraordinary inspiring trajectories. As he points out, we live on an interconnected global planet, multicultural, universal in many ways and yet the book shows how each individual remains deeply rooted. The 17 characters (some of whom I happen to know) are so unique and therefore so different from each other that no one would expect them to cross paths.Yet they have 13 things in common, namely the dispositions, values, and predilections that Jeff has identified. Readers of this anecdote-rich masterwork are in for a treat!

       — Frédéric Dubois, Paris, France
           President, Santé et Loisirs

Political national lines should have no role in the movement of products, services, people, and ideas. Jeff Sheehan proved this by flying 10 million miles around the world, implementing his international programs and meeting people that were very similar human beings, as proven beautifully by this book. We thank Jeff for his vision and promise to honor its spirit by remembering that there are no foreign lands.

       — Odemiro Fonseca. Rio de Janeiro, Brazil
           Co-Founder, Viena Rio Restaurantes Ltda.

Jeff Sheehan is truly an intercultural educator and diplomat who has never felt 'foreign' in his travels to more than 80 countries. Over the past three decades, I have had the pleasure of watching Jeff build personal relationships around the world as a genuine friend of all, who loves to offer his help. I am sure that you will find this book not only interesting but also inspiring.

       — Harvey H.W. Chang, Taipei, Taiwan
           Former President and Chief Executive Officer, Taiwan Mobile
           Former Chairman, TVBS Media, Inc.

There Are
No Foreign Lands

An Inquiry Concerning
Intercultural Communication

By

Jeffrey A. Sheehan

There Are
No Foreign Lands

Also by Jeffrey A. Sheehan

My Year of Living Adventurously
(2017)

There Are No Foreign Lands – in Chinese as 世界无界
(2019)

Flash the Lightnings, Weigh the Sun
(forthcoming)

To Truffle Sheehan
(2009-2021)

Who taught me all I need to know about
Infinite Compassion

Old age hath yet his honor and his toil.
Death closes all; but something ere the end,
Some work of noble note, may yet be done.

— *Alfred Lord Tennyson*

I want to start a virtuous cycle that will have no end.

— *Rosanna Ramos Velita*

Table of Contents

Table of Contents

There Are
No Foreign Lands

Preface

It was a beautiful, sunny September day. The heat of the summer had broken, and the day tasted as crisp as a ripe apple. I retired on that day after serving for 30 years as Associate Dean for International Relations at the Wharton School of the University of Pennsylvania. In anticipation of that occasion, I had rented an office and established a business which I named "Sheehan Advisory LLC" and which would serve as the cover story for any nefarious activities in which I would henceforth engage.

As I sat in my new office, I pondered what I would do next. A prize souvenir from my 30 years at Wharton was the collection of business cards I had accumulated in the course of travel to all the continents and sub-continents except Antarctica. In total, I had amassed 13,464 cards from individuals in 85 countries, as well as 10,943,568 miles on the American Airlines Frequent Flyer Program. The cards were carefully catalogued in card file boxes by country, by employer, and by name. If someone had changed jobs, I had stapled the new card to the old card(s), so in many cases I had a physical biography of that individual. I decided to go through the cards, one-by-one. This was originally an exercise in nostalgia; I had made many close friends over the years, and I thought it would be comforting to remember them.

However, as I started this task, which was not a quick process given the volume, I began removing from their designated spots the cards of those individuals for whom I had the greatest respect and affection. I had not established criteria to guide these choices; I just pulled cards when I was so moved. When I finished looking at all 13,464 cards, I examined the pile I had extracted – it numbered only 17. On closer inspection I observed that the 17 came from 17 countries, were engaged in 17 professions, spoke 13 mother tongues, were brought up in 11 spiritual traditions, and were not acquainted with one another. In short, they had nothing in common, other than my respect and affection. Or did they? At that moment, the idea for this book took shape. Why had I chosen these 17? What moved me to admire and love them? Were there characteristics that they shared? And if they did share characteristics, were there broader conclusions that could be drawn from that discovery? What follows is a long answer to these questions.

Introduction

Modernity and economic development are not the equivalents of culture and civilization, nor do the latter require the former as prerequisites. Today we say this without hesitation or skepticism, but this has not always been so. All through history, some groups "modernized" while others did not. Benedict Anderson argued that the concept of modernity was no more than a consequence of the creation of comparative history. In practical terms, this meant that the modernized societies invented weapons that killed more efficiently, mass-produced consumer goods along with the marketing that induced the unwitting populations to purchase these doodads, and invented "leisure time" with activities and objects designed to fill it. These modern societies were indisputably more powerful. However, they made the error of deducing that power was proof of the superiority of their cultures and civilizations. In fact, those who lacked these attributes of modernity were believed to lack any culture at all and were "uncivilized." Those who had modernized thought it was empirically evident. This was a dreadful mistake and led to untold suffering and misery.

The powerful invented more than war, consumerism, and indolence. They also invented slavery, colonialism, and imperialism, employing the assumption of their superiority as justification for mistreating their fellow humans. This justification was morally corrupt and ethically unsupportable, but the hypocrisy of the powerful only reinforced these behaviors.

Many books have documented these lamentable behaviors. Two representative examples will suffice for the purposes of this introduction. Just before the First Opium War broke out in 1839, the Duke of Wellington, speaking of the opium trade in China, pontificated that Parliament "cherished it, suggested its extension, and had deliberately looked for means of promoting it." On the other side of the Atlantic in 1857, Fred A. Ross, an Alabama Presbyterian minister, wrote that "Man, south of the Equator – in Asia, Australia, Oceania, America, especially Africa – is inferior to his northern brother... Slavery is of God, and [should] continue for the good of the slave, the good of the master, the good of the whole American family."

This arrogance of power evolved over time in what was commonly called the "West" before it started to dissipate. At first, most people believed that different "races" had separate and distinct ancestors and that some ancestors (and therefore, some races) were naturally superior to others. This was known as polygenism. In many cases, the powerful rationalized that those they mistreated were not "human." This belief was used as the justification for such blots on the conscience of humankind as the opium trade, slavery, colonialism, and imperialism already mentioned, and also Nazism, apartheid, genocide, the Chinese Exclusion Act of 1882, the eugenics movement, and other shameful episodes in world history.

A contrary idea led some scientists and others to rethink polygenism.. This new idea was based on something that Daniel J. Boorstin would later call the "latitudes of time" and Walter Benjamin would call "empty, homogenous time," a single concept that describes the separate but chronologically parallel paths which geographically separated humans with common ancestry have taken on their historical journeys. This was called monogenism. In order to take other people seriously, we must understand and accept that others have been doing identical (or at least similar) things at the same time that we have been doing these things. For example, turning sounds and thoughts into non-oral form – what we now call "writing" – happened virtually simultaneously in several widely disparate and distant sites. On the other hand, putting the northern hemisphere at the top and Europe at the center of maps are not astronomical, mathematical, scientific, or natural choices. Mercator's decision to show the north as "up" and Europe on top and in the center was both the product of Eurocentrism and a contribution to four centuries of cultural elitism.

A regrettable feature of this potentially valuable advance in thinking about human evolution was that these monogenists were also for the most part teleologists who believed that all humans must pass through the same sequence of behaviors, starting with "savagery," proceeding to "barbarism," and culminating with "civilization." Civilization was defined as the then-current state of affairs in North America and Western Europe. Native Americans were considered to be in the intermediate stage of barbarism. This hypothesis reserved the right – the duty – of "advanced," "civilized," people to subjugate, assimilate, and supervise savages and barbarians. Even Charles Darwin had ethnocentric and Eurocentric biases against sub-Saharan Africans which led him to his least scientific and most harmful assertions about race.

While this theory held out the possibility of primitive people eventually becoming civilized, it denied the possibility that so-called primitive people had civilizations and cultures. This hypothesis did not promote or enhance mutual respect. Lewis Henry Morgan, a nineteenth century American anthropologist, was one of its early exponents. Morgan based his theory on the study of Native American tribes, especially the Iroquois, as well as his admittedly ingenious global study of kinship systems. John Wesley Powell, the Director of the Bureau of Ethnology at the Smithsonian Institution from 1879 to 1902, was a follower of Morgan and had considerable influence on governmental policies promoting "acculturation" of Native Americans, by force if necessary. As with the previous approaches, the facts were made to fit the theory.

As arrogance became somewhat less respectable (or perhaps, more suspect), a new, quite revolutionary hypothesis emerged, this time based on empirical data from field work conducted by the pioneers in the academic discipline that became known as cultural anthropology. Franz Boas, and his coterie at Columbia University that included Margaret Mead, argued the novel proposition that all humans, at whatever stage of modernization and economic development, had cultures and must be considered civilized. No culture or civilization, they argued, was inherently superior to another. This, in turn, became known as cultural relativism. "The implications of the idea that we make our own agreed-upon truths was profound. It undermined the claim that social development is linear, running from allegedly primitive societies to so-called civilized ones." This new way of thinking faced some headwinds when it was introduced in the early years of the twentieth century. Regrettably, not all these headwinds have abated even one hundred years later.

After Boas, the standards of each civilization and the artifacts of each culture could henceforth be described simply as the imaginative creations of humans, none of which necessarily was better than any other. Boas argued that there was no ultimate stage of civilization toward which everyone had to strive. All civilizations were simply local adaptions, although all humans seemed to share certain behaviors. We owe respect to all humans, and must surrender our "rights" to enslave, colonize, dominate, and subjugate others whose only failing was to be economically and militarily less powerful. We were challenged by the cultural relativists to respect the cognitive equality, cultural integrity, and civilizational legitimacy of all human groups. This was a vital step forward in the history of intercultural communication – that essential but elusive ingredient in peaceful world affairs. The world was, and is, getting better.

But we are now well into the twenty-first century. War, intolerance, racism, injustice, bigotry, and discrimination, albeit at lower levels, still plague humans. Looking at the continuing problems from the perspective of the United States, it is instructive, if distressing, to consider a contemporary speech by an American politician. Former U.S. Senator Rick Santorum, in a speech on April 23, 2021, asserted that the culture of the United States is largely unchanged since it was birthed by Judeo-Christian values. "We came here and created a blank slate. We birthed a nation from nothing. I mean, there was nothing here. I mean yes, we have Native Americans, but candidly there isn't much Native American culture in American culture." Looking at the continuing problems from a global perspective, the UN High Commissioner for Refugees, in his 2019 annual report, noted that "By the end of the year, 70.8 million individuals were forcibly displaced worldwide as a result of persecution, conflict, violence, or human rights violations." We must not allow ourselves to conclude that we have reached the endpoint of our efforts to treat each other with empathy, respect, and compassion.

What can be done? Where do we go from here? We seem to be heading in the right direction, but we also have a long way to go. How do we take the next step in reconciling all those differences and in creating a world in which the "clash of civilizations" will be recognized as needless and will diminish? How do we as humans synchronize better our political, social, economic, and environmental efforts? And ultimately, how do we communicate better interculturally? This is the matter to which I will now turn, and from which I will form the hypothesis of this book.

My hypothesis is that there are humans today, representing a variety of cultures, civilizations, ethnicities, and spiritual traditions; speaking multiple languages; and following vastly different pursuits, who share what I believe are some common dispositions. I believe that these characteristics are not only praiseworthy in themselves but can also play a role in taking a next step in this long journey of *Homo sapiens* towards a world in which respectful and comprehensible intercultural communication promotes peace, equity, justice, tolerance, prosperity, and sustainability.

I say "a next step" because I am old enough to be realistic about the pace of progress. I also say "some common dispositions" because there are additional praiseworthy characteristics that are and will be needed. But I am proposing "some" dispositions and "a" next step because I have observed a remarkable congruity of characteristics among the seventeen people I extracted from my card files and who populate this book.

To phrase it slightly differently, the hypothesis of my book is that there are universal values and predilections which are common to all humans and which are of far more importance than the superficial characteristics of civilizations, such as language, cuisine, history, religion, and ethnicity. Based on my experience, which includes meeting with 13,464 people from 85 countries, I suggest that we can understand and find common ground with any other. There is no need for "foreign" lands. We are all brothers and sisters. The problem is that not everybody knows this yet. As a species, humans are still suffering from what Boorstin called an "illusion of knowledge" in regard to this topic.

In my book, I want to help curious world citizens to become more aware of the world in which they live and more proficient in intercultural communication. I intend to elucidate (not necessarily prove or validate, as I will explain soon) my hypothesis by recounting and comparing the lives, journeys, predilections, and values of the special people that I picked from my card files. Wildly dissimilar in every superficial way, they share characteristics that I believe collectively represent a good starting point through which most humans can find common ground and communicate with most other humans.

This is a book for readers from every nation, culture, religion, ethnicity, mother tongue, and profession who have an interest in how people can work together more collaboratively and productively, and how the world might be brought together for a better future. The book will be of particular interest to those who work alone or within organizations, as leaders or followers, scholars or schemers, loyalists or mutineers, and who wish to contribute to the success of a community of any size, or to achieve an idea or a dream that benefits more than themselves. It also draws on common sense conclusions collected from wisdom traditions around the world.

This is a book that takes as its primary sources the experiences of a lifetime spent at the intersection of cultures. I cannot call myself an expert in any culture other than the one into which I was born, but I have had ample opportunity to visit and learn from many other cultures. I will almost certainly be guilty of clumsy errors, embarrassing mistakes, and, probably, egregious misinterpretations. However, I share the perspective of Anne Fadiman, who wrote in the preface to her book about the clash of Hmong refugees with the American medical system: "I have always felt that the action most worth watching is not at the center of things but where edges meet…often, if you stand at the point of tangency, you can see both sides better than if you are in the middle of either one."

The title of this book reflects my deeply held belief that "foreign-ness" is an obsolete, destructive concept that I hope will die out from the face of the earth. I, for one, have never felt "foreign" in my travels because I have adopted each country I visited as my own, and attempted to understand the point of view of the people who lived there. I have noted that there are others who share this view, and I will quote many of them (including the seventeen whose biographies follow this Introduction) in this book.

How did I choose the people who populate this book? As noted in the Preface, it was not a scientific process. I simply chose people I have met and for whom I have the greatest affection and respect, based on their personal qualities and without a goal or quota. These are not casual acquaintances; I know them all well, in some cases for as long as 35 years.

I interviewed each of the individuals at length, in person, in dozens of cities around the world, logging hundreds of thousands of air miles. I also either met or interviewed by telephone their family members, friends, business associates, admirers, and even detractors to cross-check my observations and confirm my conclusions. I judge that each of these individuals is a heroine or a hero, not in the sense that any of them charged a mountain top to rescue fallen comrades amid a hail of bullets, but in the sense that they are ones who, in the words of Philip Zimbardo, "…are capable of resisting evil, of not giving in to temptations, of rising above mediocrity, and of heeding the call to action and to service when others fail to act." Each of the chapters describing the life of one of these individuals tells a heroic story according to this definition.

My conclusion, following this research, was that all these friends share thirteen characteristics, and that all of these characteristics could be emulated by others hoping to spend their lives well and meaningfully. I begin this book with biographical chapters of these individuals, organized into the groups to which I have assigned them. Part II consists of an exposition of the common characteristics. While my friends differ in virtually every superficial characteristic, the construction of a complex, although hypothetical, Venn Diagram reveals the thirteen common characteristics that populate the cell in which all seventeen sets overlap.

I hope, through examining the lives of these men and women, to share what I have learned about a life well spent, devoted to the enhancement of human flourishing. My vision of this kind of a life is a composite of the lives of these individuals, from whom I have learned so much. I feel profound gratitude to them for giving me "a continuous transfusion of courage." I hope that I can live up to their examples.

Two comments on methodology before I begin: First, my close friend and colleague Professor Jitendra Singh, former dean of the School of Business at the Hong Kong University of Science and Technology, was kind enough to read an early draft of this book. He pointed out an interesting challenge, namely that I needed to be careful about claiming that the qualities I had identified were the causes of the success of my heroes and heroines. Such a claim, he cautioned, would be difficult if not impossible to substantiate, and would require a much different book in which I would need to demonstrate (by an equally careful study of an equivalent group of people who did not exhibit these qualities) that the absence of these characteristics was clearly associated with a lack of success. That is not, as you will learn in the pages ahead, the book I have written.

Another good friend and colleague from the Wharton School, Professor John Zhang, said essentially the same thing after reading an early draft of the chapter on Yu Minhong, namely that establishing causality would require the determination that the characteristics these people have in common were not only sufficient but also necessary for the achievements of the people I profile.

Second, Jared Diamond (whom I have never met) artfully reminded me that success is quite often attained by avoiding the causes of failure rather than picking the reasons for success. As a consequence, I have attempted to avoid any suggestion that the 13 characteristics are the reasons why my friends have succeeded. In fact, my goal has been to avoid focusing on their successes. This has been a difficult goal to achieve because their successes are abundant. However, my intended focus has been on the common dispositions. The reader can make a personal judgment as to the relationship between these dispositions and the successes of the individuals I profile. My larger point is that the 13 characteristics are fully shared by everybody and I believe represent crucial but at the same time quite accessible keys to unlocking the door to meaningful intercultural communication.

And so, with thanks to Jitendra, John, and Jared for saving me from suggesting that I am doing something that I am not, I disclaim any pretensions to social science research. My sample is small, my methodology is qualitative rather than quantitative, and what is most important, I make no claim to having found pathways to anywhere. Are there universal human dispositions, some of which are values, others of which are predilections? Is the belief that different civilizations have different values false? I think so, but my book will not offer any proof. This is why I have sub-titled my book an "inquiry," not a theory or a truth, concerning intercultural communication. I am most probably describing, in aggregate, the person I aspire to be. If I have done my job well, you may develop the same aspiration.

Part I
The Heroines and Heroes

The Heroines and Heroes

I had envisioned listing my subjects alphabetically using the Roman alphabet, despite the fact that eight of the seventeen wrote in languages that did not use that particular alphabet. Even Romanization would not suffice, since four of them wrote in languages that used characters and not alphabets. The Romanization and transliteration of these names proved to be an interesting preview of a larger question about translation that would come to my attention in my discussions with James Kim Joo Jin (pages 201-202).

However, as I learned more about them, I came to the conclusion, organically, that they grouped themselves into categories that I had not planned or anticipated. I decided that there were six categories, and Part I of the book will tell their stories in these groups. All of them belong at least in part to more than one category, but I have placed each of them in the category that I believe best represents each person. There is no reason for the order in which I placed the categories. No category is more or less praiseworthy than another.

Devoted to the Commonweal

The "commonweal" is defined as the happiness, health, and harmony of all the people of a nation or other polity. There are three patriots who perfectly fit in the category of devotion to these desiderata. They are:

Luis Fernando Andrade Moreno – Colombia. Luis worked for 25 years for McKinsey & Co. in New York, São Paulo, and Bogota, and later served as President of the Colombian National Infrastructure Agency (ANI). Luis built roads to empower people.

Boediono – Indonesia. Boediono was the vice president of Indonesia from 2009 to 2014, elected with the greatest number of votes ever cast (as of that date) anywhere in the world in a free election, which totaled five million more than Barack Obama received in 2012. Boediono is disarmingly humble.

Chanthol Sun – Cambodia. Chanthol is a senior minister in the Government of the Kingdom of Cambodia. He served concurrently as Minister of Commerce and as Vice Chairman of the Council for the Development of Cambodia. Chanthol has no word for discouragement in Khmer, French, or English.

Compassionate Capitalists

There is a new breed of capitalist, whose members understand that investing need not separate positive impact from profitability. This type of capitalist is motivated by the opportunity to empower others to achieve financial security, more than the desire to add to their own private bank accounts. They are:

Dawn Hines – United States of America. Dawn is an entrepreneur who develops businesses and invests in West Africa, with a focus on Senegal. She is originally from Ann Arbor, Michigan. Dawn sees opportunities for wealth creation where others see despair and chaos.

Eric Kacou – Côte d'Ivoire. Eric is an author and consultant on "bottom of the pyramid" and post-conflict economic development. His roots are in a small village in the eastern part of the Côte d'Ivoire, but now he is a Citizen of the World. Eric uses his skills to help others to escape from survival traps and to change mind-sets.

Rosanna Ramos Velita – Peru. Rosanna is an entrepreneur with a passion for providing the financial means to enable previously marginalized and ignored communities to succeed. She owns and runs a micro-finance bank in a small town on the shore of Lake Titicaca. Rosanna has mud on her boots.

Durreen Shahnaz – Bangladesh. Durreen is the founder and chief executive officer of Impact Investment Exchange, the world's first social impact stock exchange, based in Singapore. Durreen survived a war, pernicious gender discrimination, and a variety of other challenges to emerge as a compassionate capitalist who is changing the world. She is a self-described "defiant optimist."

Stewards, Not the Owners of Their Wealth

Some people inherit money, position, or power through no fault of their own, and my group includes two individuals in this category. What makes them interesting is that they are using their inheritances for the good of more than just themselves. They are:

Shiv Khemka – India. Shiv is the fourth-generation leader of a principal investor and private equity fund manager active in Kazakhstan, Russia, Nigeria, and India. He was born and resides in New Delhi. Shiv is a teetotaler and a vegetarian who made a fortune brewing beer in a carnivorous country.

Jacob Wallenberg – Sweden. Jacob is the fifth-generation leader of a well-known Swedish commercial family, and serves as chairman of Investor AB, a publicly-traded holding company whose principal shareholder is the Knut and Alice Wallenberg Foundation. He is based in Stockholm. Jacob spends a substantial amount of his time explaining that he is a steward and not an owner.

The Long Legacy of Echo

In my first job out of college, I encountered a crusty gentleman named William Gwyer North who frowned more than he smiled, but who had wisdom that I have only recently started to appreciate. On June 3, 1972, at Dublin School in Dublin, New Hampshire, he gave a commencement address entitled "The Long Legacy of Echo," which was about tradition. These words accurately describe the lives and work of three of those whose biographies follow this introduction. They are:

Anthony Hamilton Russell – South Africa. Anthony is the second-generation proprietor of an eponymous vineyard in the Hemel-en-Aarde Valley, one of the most southerly wine estates in Africa. Anthony also has mud on his boots.

Keisuke Muratsu – Japan. Kei is the second-generation owner of a glass manufacturing business based in Osaka. He is also a semi-professional Katoubushi singer and an ardent amateur golfer. Kei has high standards and expectations that make everybody better.

Arantxa Ochoa – Spain. Arantxa was the Director of the School of Pennsylvania Ballet. She retired as Principal Dancer of the same company in 2012. Originally from Valladolid, she now lives in the United States. Arantxa has callouses on her toes and is infused with Spanish soul.

Breaking with Tradition

It is an irony of this book that those who embrace and protect tradition are so important, while at the same time those who break with tradition also represent an important and perfectly consistent theme. Some traditions, under certain circumstances, are life-affirming and vital. Other traditions, under different circumstances, beg to be broken. The tradition-breakers are:

Leslie C. Koo – Taiwan. Leslie was a leader of the current generation of a family with deep roots in the political and commercial history of Taiwan. He was Chairman and Chief Executive Officer of Taiwan Cement Corporation in Taipei. Leslie surprised everybody in Taiwan.

Vassily Sidorov – Russia. Vassily is a new-generation Russian who came of age during the breakup of the Union of Soviet Socialist Republics. Vassily is the harbinger of a Russia that will be a responsible member of the global community. He lives in Moscow.

Ebullient Survivors

While all my friends have met and overcome hardship, there are three whose travails were heart-breaking in their complexity and overwhelming in their difficulty but exhilarating in their denouements. They are:

Roberto Canessa – Uruguay. Roberto is a pediatric cardiologist in Montevideo. He is one of the survivors of an airplane crash in the Andes in 1972 that became the subject of many books and movies. Roberto never gives up on anybody or anything.

James Joo-Jin Kim – Korea. Jim is the second-generation chairman of a Korean-American company that is a global leader in semiconductor packaging and testing. He now resides in the United States. Jim survived unimaginable hardships as a child.

Yu Minhong – China. Michael is the founder and chairman of New Oriental Technology and Education Group, a company based in Beijing that offers training in English, test taking, and related fields. Michael has inspired tens of millions of young Chinese with the powerful exhortation, "You Can!"

Many people are well-acquainted with the men and women about whom you will read in the next seventeen chapters. They are all gregarious, other-directed "givers" who have had lasting impacts on many millions of people around the world. But nobody else, as far as I can tell, is well-acquainted with all of them. In fact, their circles of acquaintances are remarkable because they rarely, if ever, overlap. They grew up and spent their lives in isolation from each other and yet are excellent examples of the latitudes of time because of the fact that they are remarkably similar in moral and ethical beliefs as well as in dispositions and predilections. This is a key factor that makes this book unique. By reading the book, you are enlarging the circle of those who are acquainted with them and, I hope, will learn some of the same lessons that I have learned in getting to know them. It took me over 30 years and millions of air miles to do the research for this book. You have the advantage of being able to accomplish this journey from the comfort of your *fauteuil*.

Our first destination is Bogota, the capital of Colombia, situated on a plateau in the Andes Mountains, very close to the Equator. We will depart from Philadelphia, Pennsylvania, my Base Camp for the past thirty-eight years. We will need to stop in Miami, which is the connecting city for most flights to South America, to change planes. The flight will take about five and a half hours in total and will take us 2,434 miles almost due south. At the Equator, air temperature drops about 2 degrees Fahrenheit for every 500 feet of increase in altitude. At 8,675', Bogota is on average about 17 degrees cooler than a city at the same latitude but at Sea Level.

Bon voyage!

Devoted to the Commonweal

Luis Fernando Andrade Moreno

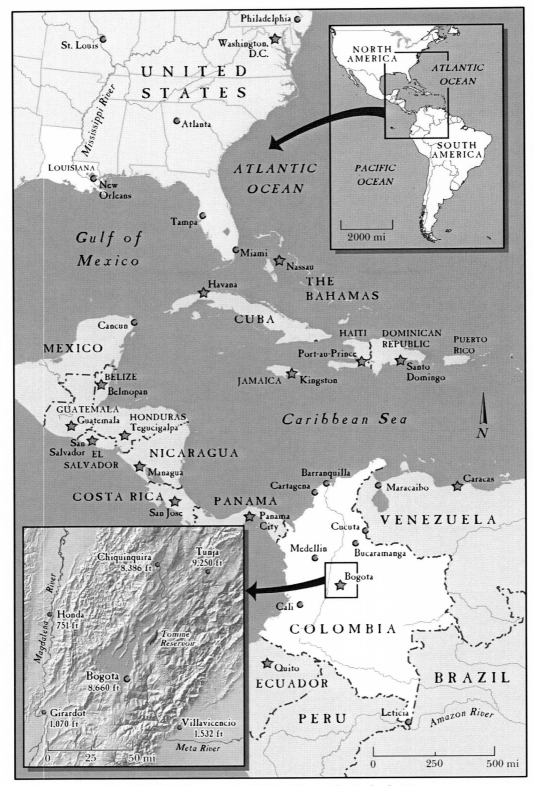

Devoted to the Commonweal: Luis Fernando Andrade Moreno

Gene Pools

At the beginning of their existence on earth, *Homo sapiens* were not particularly restless or curious. They tended to stay where they were, like honeybees, rhinoceroses, and even our cousins the chimpanzees. However, some geneticists speculate that about 60,000 years ago, a mutation in human DNA, poetically called DRD4-7r, created a human bias for movement, change, and adventure. Not everybody had or has this mutation. In the modern era, it is estimated that only 20% of the world's population has it. But those with this genetic mutation started to take more risks and to manifest the desire to explore new places. The consequence was migration out of Africa, the continent from which we all originated. It may have been the human break-out moment, and every human adventure, up to and including the current planning for a manned trip to Mars, may be a consequence of this glitch in the double-helix.

Indigenous means "produced, growing, living, or occurring natively or naturally in a particular region or environment." Strictly speaking, therefore, no inhabitants of the Americas are "indigenous" because the first Americans all came from Africa. Nobody came to the Americas during the Ice Age because sheets of ice did not support human life for travel. The Last Glacial Maximum (better known as the "LGM") started to recede around 19,000 years ago, opening up a passageway for humans to move from Northeast Asia (now called Russia) across the Bering Strait and down into what is now called the Americas. The generally accepted theory is that more or less 14,000 years ago, or 46,000 years after they left Africa, the first wave (in all probability more like a ripple) of humans crossed the Bering Strait and moved slowly but inexorably south. One may conclude with some degree of certainty that this group had inherited the DRD4-7r "wanderlust gene." Properly speaking, they were the "First Americans" or "Amerindians."

"My wife is interested in genetics, and she sent a sample of my saliva to a testing company," Luis laughed. "This test established that my gene pool is 7% Amerindian and 93% Spanish. The average for Colombians is around 30% Amerindian. The genetic testing also established that my Amerindian ancestors came to Colombia millennia ago from Siberia, via the Bering Strait when there was a land bridge."

The Spanish 93% of Luis arrived soon after Columbus traveled to the New World and inspired Vasco Núñez de Balboa to start his explorations. At the dawn of the sixteenth century, Balboa conquered several existing nations that spoke a common language called Chibchan and established the first European settlement on the mainland of the Americas in what is now southern Panama, very close to what is now northern Colombia. Ironically, Luis's Spanish gene pool also came from Africa but presumably reached Spain long before his Amerindian gene pool reached Colombia. One must assume that sufficient numbers of Spaniards also bore the DRD4-7r gene.

"Most of my ancestors were from Spain, but it is so long ago that it is irrelevant. My family has been Colombian since the 1600s on my mother's side and since the 1700s on my father's side. The Spanish colonized Colombia primarily for economic opportunity, making it different from the predominant reason for the English colonization in North America, which was mostly about religious freedom," he continued. "Nobody in Spain was fleeing the Catholic Church. On my mother's side, the family was involved in mining for gold. On my father's side, the family was involved with the civil service or the military. Most of the indigenous people were killed by disease unwittingly imported from Europe (smallpox, mumps, and measles being the primary culprits), not conquest. The Spanish conquerors and then colonizers were looking for subjects for their new empire, not an empty territory."

The Heritage of Alberto Lleras Camargo

The period of Spanish colonization lasted for several hundred years, but was eventually challenged by Simón Bolívar, born in Caracas in 1783, who is regarded as the greatest leader of Latin America's independence movement. One of the military and political leaders who fought alongside Bolivar during this period of upheaval was General Francisco de Paula Santander. Santander was an important figure in Colombia's war of independence and served as both the acting President (1819-1826) and then as the elected President (1832-1837.)

"My family's involvement in Colombian politics dates back to this era," recounted Luis. "Santander wanted to establish a country which respected and followed the rule of law, contracts, and property rights. His fundamental goal was to recreate what had happened in North America starting in 1776."

"Colombia has not succeeded very well despite its democratic intentions," Luis lamented. "But public service has been in my family's blood for many generations and in different formats. My father's family included government officials, and I learned about public service as I learned about the history of my family. I had a relative (a priest) who was a labor organizer (on the conservative, not the leftist, side). I learned from him about fighting for the rights of workers. This was also a new world for me."

General Santander had a follower, twenty years his junior, named Lorenzo Lleras. Lleras shared Santander's commitment to the ideal represented by the rule of law. Lorenzo's grandson, born in Bogota in 1906, was named Alberto Lleras Camargo. Alberto was a journalist and an important liberal (center-left) politician during the middle years of the twentieth century.

"At one point," resumed Luis, "the sitting president elected to resign when he was impeached. Alberto Lleras Camargo was appointed 'acting president' for one year (1945-46) with the single task of arranging an election for the next president. To the everlasting gratitude of the country, Alberto diligently and with great integrity planned and carried out a peaceful, fair election, which the opposition (conservative-right) won. This was a key moment for Colombia and for Alberto, because his respect for the constitution and the success of the democratic process won him the trust and respect not only of the people, but also of his political opponents."

Starting in 1948, Colombia endured a difficult period that is called "La Violencia," during which over 100,000 people died. It was essentially a civil war between the right and the left, a remnant of the battle between Fascists and Marxists in World War II. Despite the triumph of the democratic process engineered by Alberto Lleras in 1946, the elected conservative government decided that the civil strife in the country required a strong solution, and the government was handed over to a dictator, General Gustavo Rojas Pinilla, in 1953. The military then was given the task of suppressing the violence, which effort was pursued until 1957. Eventually the corruption, combined with the loss of civil liberties, caused increasing distress in the population.

Alberto Lleras once again rose to the challenge and organized a civil resistance movement to overthrow the dictator. A general strike effectively forced the resignation of the dictator and the re-establishment of democracy. A peace agreement was signed in 1957 between the Liberal and Conservative parties, ending the undeclared but deadly civil war that had been waged since 1948. Alberto was then elected President and served in the office from 1958 to 1962.

"Alberto's sister, Sofia Lleras, was my paternal grandmother," Luis concluded with a smile. "He served as a great inspiration to me, and his examples of diligence, love of country, integrity, and commitment to the rule of law have had an enormous influence on me."

The Early Years

Luis was born in New Orleans, Louisiana, on January 13, 1961, while his father was studying for his Ph.D. in biochemistry. Luis is his given name. Fernando is his "middle" name. Andrade is his father's family name. Moreno is his mother's family name. This is how Spaniards (and their diaspora) handle names. He goes by "Luis Andrade" so as not to confuse the gringos. His Colombian friends call him "Luis Fernando" because so many Colombians are also named Luis.

Luis resumed, "We moved back to our native Bogota after my father earned his doctoral degree. I and my family spent the next eleven years in Bogota. In 1976, when I was fifteen, my father's employer (Ralston Purina) transferred him to Miami. This meant that I attended high school in Florida. I attended college at the University of Florida and majored in Industrial Engineering."

"Following graduation, I was offered an engineering job with Westinghouse in Baltimore. I worked on a project that involved the development of new manufacturing technologies for radars for the defense industry, but it was a singularly academic environment. I enjoyed it very much."

"Nevertheless," he continued, "I felt constrained by the one-dimensional nature of my work. I soon learned that I wanted broader responsibilities and for this, I needed more knowledge and training. I applied to Wharton for the MBA program and started this next chapter in my education in the fall of 1983."

"Wharton," Luis said emphatically, "opened the world to me. Going to Wharton was one of the best decisions I have made. Wharton introduced me to the challenges of organizing, managing, and leading people. Very importantly, this is where I met my wife, Tere. She was a law student at Penn from Puerto Rico."

The McKinsey Years

"After I graduated from Wharton, I was offered a job with McKinsey. My first role as a consultant was to recommend the re-structuring of a company that was undergoing financial difficulties. One of the obvious answers was to lay off a number of employees. This particular recommendation was ethically complicated for me since I felt bad for the lives of those employees who may have served well and faithfully but would lose their jobs only to meet the financial goals of the shareholders."

"My big break occurred when I was offered the opportunity to re-open McKinsey's office in Brazil. At the time (1988), inflation was running at 20-30% per month, and the Brazilian economy was in chaos. By 1993, inflation was roughly 2,000% on an annual basis. I had never managed a business in Latin America or in a hyperinflationary environment, so my learning curve was steep in São Paulo. I learned a great deal about how things work in Latin America."

"By 1994," he observed triumphantly, "McKinsey decided to open an office in Colombia. I was ready and willing to take the assignment and I moved home to Bogota with Tere and our two daughters, Cristina and Patricia, to fulfill my duty to McKinsey and my birthright to my country. My son would be born in Bogota one-and-a-half years later. We named him after Great Uncle Alberto."

"Fundamentally, I was troubled by the poverty I saw everywhere in Colombia. I wanted to be an agent of change in the lives of poor Colombians. People were suffering. I also feared for the stability of the country because of the civil strife and drug culture. I also had the inspiration of Great Uncle Alberto to guide me."

"The next ten years were challenging in terms of public security. But things were not that bad," he stated, but not defensively. "We just had to adapt to the circumstances. For example, I had an armored vehicle. There were many kidnappings, but I kept a low profile, which was easier since I was a consultant and not a public figure. This was not a great period in Colombian history, and many bad things happened. But I would still say that Colombia during this period was not as bad as was portrayed in the media and in the movies in North America."

"The presidency of Alvaro Uribe was enormously important," he continued with as much animation as I ever detected in this understated man. "Crucial. He saved Colombia. Uribe will be seen in history as a great hero of the people of Colombia. He coined the phrase 'democratic security' in an attempt to capture the importance of the rule of law but the absolute necessity of reclaiming the role of the state in enforcing the rule of law. He captured the inner belief of most Colombians, which was that we must respect our democratic traditions, but we must fight back. Without Uribe, we would be a failed state today."

"I feel most rewarded by the work I did with the Colombian government. For example, McKinsey was retained to work with the city government of Bogota to develop a rapid transit system, which opened for business in 2000. As another example, McKinsey worked on the development of the 'Productive Transformation Strategy,' which promoted the growth of a Business Process Outsourcing industry in Colombia for the Spanish-speaking world."

"A third project was in telecommunications. McKinsey supported the design of a program called 'Live Digital' that made telecommunications accessible to underserved populations. This was yet another source of satisfaction to me because it went straight to the heart of my goal to relieve suffering among the poor and to help people to upgrade their skills and give them access to the means of improving their lives."

"In general, although I worked for many profit-making corporations in the course of my career with McKinsey, it was the government projects which improved the lives of the ordinary citizens of Colombia that were the most fulfilling. I like to solve difficult problems that contribute to the peace and prosperity of the country."

The Next Chapter: Public Service

McKinsey was hired by newly elected President Santos in 2010. This engagement gave Luis the opportunity to get to know the president and his inner circle of senior staff members. He mentioned to the president's chief of staff that he would be available and open to opportunities to serve the government full-time. Suddenly, the presidency of a new federal agency, the National Infrastructure Agency (ANI) became available and President Santos offered Luis the job. The mandate of ANI was – and still is – to develop infrastructure (mostly roads) for transportation through Public-Private Partnerships.

"Initially, I was reluctant to accept this offer," said Luis ruefully, "because it was a difficult, probably thankless job, the leader of which would be buffeted by many political winds. I understood that it would be a real challenge to be successful. But I reprimanded myself, remembering that this was just the kind of challenge I had long hoped to embrace. I realized that I could not decline this position just because it would be difficult and thankless. In fact, these were the reasons that I had to accept the offer. Plus, if I succeeded, it would make a big difference to the country and all its citizens."

Up until that time, ANI's predecessor agency had not been successful, and the consequences have been severe, especially for the areas outside the major metropolitan centers. "It was a painful experience for me to move into the public domain as a decision-maker as opposed to a consultant. It's a lot easier to make suggestions than to make decisions. I was subjected to criticism, impugned with lies, and otherwise distracted from the actual business of building infrastructure. I stopped a practice that had become generally accepted by awarding 'additions' to contractors without a bidding process, amounting to several times the value of the original contract. I also introduced changes in the new contracts with strict performance standards that contractors had to meet and real penalties that would be assessed if they failed to meet the performance standards. You can easily understand why I had enemies among the private contractors. Without a good reputation, your position is insecure. Even with a good reputation, my success is not guaranteed. I could be fired tomorrow. Politics are still important, and powerful interest groups could ask for my head on a platter."

"In an interesting way, this is another instance of adaptation. In this case, instead of adapting to the violence of guerillas, I must adapt to the vicissitudes of politics, all the time remembering not to compromise my principles or my vision of the long-term goal. My job is not to be universally loved, but to build the roads that will help Colombia and its citizens. I acknowledge and accept the fact that politicians have legitimate interests that must be accommodated. I am not a firebrand. I am a technician with his eye on an achievable goal. So, without compromise on matters of principle, but with flexibility as to tactics, I adapt. This means that I must accept risk, which I do willingly."

Andres Maldonado

I spoke to Andres Maldonado, a former colleague of Luis and a McKinsey Partner who left the firm three years ago to start his own company. Andres first met Luis about twenty years ago, when Luis was the Partner in charge of the McKinsey Bogota office, and the only McKinsey employee in Colombia. Andres joined the firm as employee #2 and worked with Luis for six years.

"Luis is a fun person, both intellectually and socially," he started. "Intellectually, he enjoys thinking big, and floating trial balloons that may seem outrageous. This kind of thinking stimulates others and forces them to think creatively. It also makes thinking enjoyable instead of laborious. He is an endlessly positive person. Socially, he always has time for a friend, whether it is entirely for enjoyment or when the friend needs help. He always brings good humor and a positive attitude to anything he does. Luis is also self-critical in a humorous, self-mocking way. It is surprising how effective he is as a leader with this humble personality."

Back to the National Infrastructure Agency

Searching for an objective evaluation of Luis' work as president of the Colombian National Infrastructure Agency, I turned to an article in "MoneyWeek," a British print and online financial magazine, entitled "If this man succeeds, he'll transform Colombia's economy." The title is a give-away but let me quote one section of the article that seems particularly relevant.

> *…if Andrade confounds the critics and pulls off this infrastructure programme, it will give a massive boost to the economy.*

"Infrastructure is mostly about finance, less so about engineering," said Luis. "My job is to organize money for long-term projects."

The Road Ahead

"What about your future?" I asked. "You are only 53, which is the prime of your life. You are young enough to have energy and wisdom enough to know how to use it productively."

"I really have no idea what I will do next," Luis replied, smiling. "What I enjoy doing is what I am doing now; engaged up to my armpits in policies and projects that make a difference in the country. But I am different now. Formerly, I would plan my life in some detail. Now I am trying to be more flexible and let destiny take control."

"Would you consider running for elective office?" was my next question, and I had a pretty good idea what his answer would be.

"Maybe," was his coy disclaimer. "In order to be elected, you need three things. First, you need to be well-known. My work with McKinsey helped me to meet leaders of industry and government, and now ANI helps put me in the spotlight with the public. Second, you must be recognized for something. If ANI is successful, I will be known for the success of a big project that changed the lives of millions of Colombians for the better. Third, you need a political party to back you. So, it is all quite complicated, but if I have the opportunity, I will do it, probably at the level of the city of Bogota."

Who Is Luis Fernando Andrade Moreno?

Andres Maldonado, already quoted above, summarized his feelings about this remarkable man: "Luis is a very spiritual person, although not in the traditional sense of attending Mass and following rituals. His spirituality is grounded in self-understanding and strong values that he lives in his interactions with others."

Although I have always had great admiration for Luis, I had not realized until I spoke with his friends and read about him in the business press what an audacious dreamer he is. Luis is a humble, gentle, soft-spoken person but he is also quite capable of flights of imagination, rooted in the reality of politics, finance, and accountability. This man has found his calling as a strong and selfless public servant. And in doing so, he has given up a lucrative career as a McKinsey Partner. In this way, Luis had chosen to help others, without benefit to himself, and in fact, at some cost to himself. He is the first, but not the last, individual I will profile who has been successful as a giver rather than a taker, in Adam Grant's terminology. I have learned a great deal about this commendable, but rare, personality type in the course of the research for this book. It is part of why I have such respect and affection for Luis.

Moving on to Jakarta

The air is thin and cool at Bogota's altitude of 8,675 feet above sea level. Our next destination is Jakarta, at (and sinking below) sea level, and the air is thick and hot. This journey is long – 12,323 miles, or almost exactly an antipode. This is not yet a heavily trafficked route, so we will need to stop along the way to change planes. I am curious to learn when commerce and common interests between Colombia and Indonesia will make it profitable to establish a direct air link.

Devoted to the Commonweal

Boediono

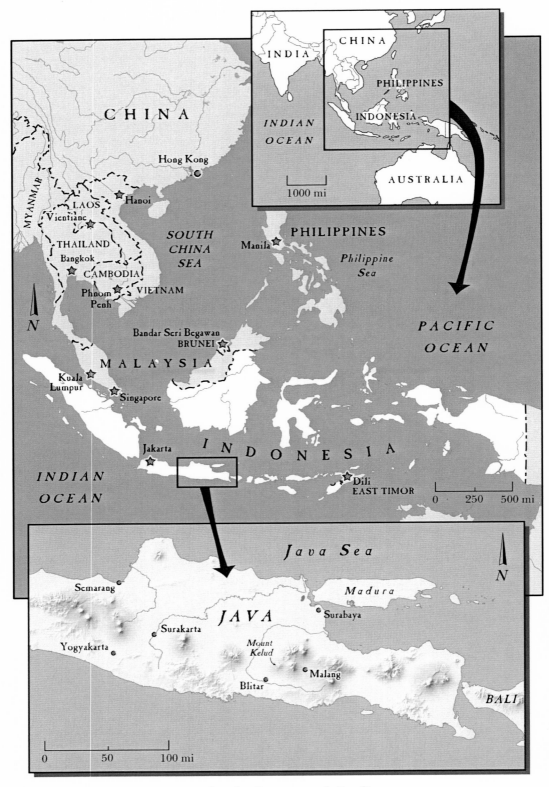

Devoted to the Commonweal: Boediono

First Impressions of Indonesia

M y first trip to Indonesia many years ago was a profusion of sights, sounds, and fragrances. It was August 17th, Independence Day. *Pancasila*, exemplified by the tens of thousands of citizens marching through the streets of Jakarta, opened my eyes to patriotism much younger than I had experienced in the United States, but no less enthusiastic. The sound of the Muezzin calling the faithful to prayer at the ubiquitous mosques echoed in my ears. The pungent aroma of clove cigarettes everywhere initiated my nostrils to an entirely new ambient fragrance, accompanied by a most intriguing crackling soundtrack. It was also my first meeting with Dr. Boediono. My informants all said that Boediono was a brilliant economist, with integrity and promise for the future.

I engaged a Blue Bird Taxi from the hotel (later I learned that for a slightly higher fare, the Silver Bird Taxi provided a more comfortable, more reliably air-conditioned ride) and headed off into the sunny, steamy morning. Much to my surprise, as soon as the driver turned out of the hotel driveway, he stopped and picked up a young man who quietly sat in the front seat. After pondering this behavior for a moment, I asked the driver who our guest was and where we were taking him.

The driver replied, "You must be an American." I acknowledged that he was correct and added to my list of questions, "How did you know?"

"You are obviously a Westerner," was my driver's reply (his name was Bagus, meaning "good" in Bahasa Indonesia). "If you were English," he continued, "you would not have said anything. If you were German, you would have told me to stop the car and remove the passenger. Only an American would ask why I picked him up."

"But to answer your question, he's a 'car jockey.' On the main road, Jalan Sudirman, cars must have a minimum of three people. This is an effort to reduce the number of vehicles and to limit congestion. When taxis have a single passenger, the driver picks up a car jockey. I pay him a small amount of money. After you reach your destination, he takes the bus back to the same spot and waits for another opportunity. An energetic car jockey can make a living doing this, although he will never get rich."

The Early Years

Boediono was born on February 25, 1943, in Blitar, a quiet and charming small town in East Java, despite its location not far from Mount Kelud, a temperamental volcano that blows its top periodically. He calls Blitar "digestible," a good place to be born and live as a child. It was a never-changing part of the far eastern reaches of Java, 466 driving miles from Jakarta. The dark side of this time was that his birth came at the mid-point of the Japanese occupation of Indonesia (1942-1945), following three centuries of colonization by the Dutch.

"I would say we were lower middle class," he began. "Not poor, but certainly not rich. My parents were small traders. Our home had a shop in the front where my parents sold batik. My mother eventually opened a small store in the traditional market in Blitar."

"I remember my father telling me stories with Hindu origins. The stories all had morals, and I learned to understand the difference between good and bad, and between truth and falsehood. My father had attended school only through the equivalent of the eighth grade. Indonesia was not a country when he grew up, and he learned Dutch as most people did when our country was a colony," he concluded, without a trace of bitterness or rancor.

Blitar had a native son who became a household name in Indonesia before Boediono. Soekarno was also born in Blitar and is buried there. His home still stands and serves as a museum and library. When Boediono was a child, Soekarno would visit his mother in Blitar, and local children including Boediono would follow him through the streets. I asked Boediono if Soekarno and his achievements were inspirational to him as a child. "Hero worship, perhaps, but not inspirational," he replied with his trademark wry smile.

Indonesia declared its independence on August 17, 1945, (eleven days after the United States dropped an atomic bomb on Hiroshima and two days after Emperor Hirohito announced Japan's surrender) and Soekarno became its first president the next day. Boediono was only two years old at the time of his country's start as an independent nation. This momentous event for Indonesians was hardly noticed in the rest of the world amid the excitement about the end of the Second World War.

Academic Inflection Points

There may be as many as 400 languages and dialects spoken in Indonesia, and most Indonesians speak their local language or dialect as their first language. Accordingly, Boediono's first language was Javanese. The national language, Bahasa Indonesia, is the first language of a small minority of the population. He learned Bahasa when he attended grade school and high school in Blitar. Boediono is a first-generation child of the Republic of Indonesia, whose knowledge of colonialism is derived from history books and not personal experience.

After graduation from high school, he was admitted to Gadjah Mada University. Today it is the largest and oldest state institution of higher education, located in Yogyakarta, about 187 driving miles from Blitar. But at the time Boediono entered its freshman class, Gadjah Mada was quite new, having been founded in 1949. He was in his second year at Gadjah Mada University when "out of the blue" he learned of an offer by the Australian government of scholarships for young Indonesians to study in Australia. This, he reflected, was the first Black Swan in his life, the moment briefly offered and seized with enthusiasm. Fifty-one years later, Boediono said that he thought that what happened to us in life was "40 to 50 per cent due to our efforts. The rest is fate."

He applied for the scholarship and much to his surprise was accepted. There followed eight years in Australia, first at the University of Western Australia in Perth, from which institution he earned a degree in economics in 1967; and then at Monash University in Melbourne, where he earned his master's degree. His friend and college classmate, Abdillah Toha, who later had a dual career as a successful book publisher and member of the Indonesian Legislature, recalls that Boediono was somewhat different as an undergraduate than how he was later perceived as a sober government official.

"When Boediono and I were university students together in Western Australia many years ago," Abdillah began, "we had a five-member band that played Calypso music. We especially admired Harry Belafonte, and even appeared on television. Boediono played the guitar and I played the bongo drums."

After completing his studies in Australia, Boediono returned to Indonesia. A job as an internal auditor at the Bank of America bored him; an application to Bank Indonesia (the country's central bank) was never acknowledged; an application to the Ministry of Finance met the same fate.

After landing a job at Gadjah Mada University in 1973, he met his next Black Swan when the Rockefeller Foundation announced a competition for young Indonesian academics to study for doctoral degrees in the United States. Boediono again seized this opportunity and won a scholarship. He applied to several universities and was admitted to the Wharton School of the University of Pennsylvania. His dean at Gadjah Mada urged him to go to a different university, since in his opinion the "chances of failure were too high at Wharton, which is an exceedingly demanding and rigorous program."

Boediono had heard about the work of Professor Lawrence Klein (who would be awarded a Nobel Prize in Economics in 1980) and was undeterred by the warnings of his dean. For the next three and one-half years, he studied in Philadelphia. He earned his Ph.D. degree in Management Science and Applied Economics in 1979. The subject of his thesis was economic development in Indonesia.

A Career in Public Service

Returning to Indonesia after graduation from Wharton, he entered public service. I asked Boediono about his choice of public service as a career. He replied in several ways, neither of which was particularly direct, but indirectly started to provide an answer. "Money has never motivated me," he observed. "Whatever you have in front of you, do it well," he continued.

Despite his challenge at explaining why he chose this field he tried his best to answer my question. "It was a matter of evolution. The accumulation of experiences. I knew that I should do what my heart felt was good. I felt public service was right for me." Boediono is a gentle man, humble and unassuming, although I would not call him diffident, with its connotation of a lack of confidence. One can easily miss the intellectual strength and confidence in this man, but it is there, hidden below the self-deprecation that is ever-present on the exterior. One cannot imagine a person less likely to gain prominence in politics. His early years in public service were spent under Suharto, who had become president in 1966 following the *coup d'état* that removed Soekarno.

When I first met Boediono, he was Deputy Chairman for Fiscal and Monetary Affairs of Badan Perencanaan Pembangunan Nasional, better known as "Bappenas," the Indonesian State Ministry for National Development Planning. His talents as a technocrat of unimpeachable integrity were recognized, and he received promotions regularly. He subsequently served as Deputy Governor of Bank Indonesia and as State Minister of National Planning and Development. These were complicated times for Indonesia, and he earned the title of "the nation's financial rudder" because of his steady, professional guidance during the Asian Financial Crisis of the late 1990s.

After Suharto's resignation in 1998, Abdurrahman Wahid was elected President. Wahid, colloquially known as Gus Dur, did not have a role for Boediono in his administration. Abdillah Toha, introduced above as his fellow Calypso enthusiast, recalls Boediono's hiatus from government during the administration of President Gus Dur. "One of the remarkable things about Boediono," observed Abdillah, "is that he never got any of the jobs he had in the government by requesting them or applying for them. He has been a reluctant recruit every time. When he left the government for two years during the administration of Gus Dur, he had no backward glances. He has no enjoyment in power for the sake of power. He enjoys power only for the sake of helping Indonesia and Indonesians. When he was dismissed by Gus Dur, he returned to Gadjah Mada University and resumed a career teaching and researching."

The next two presidents called him to service once again. He was appointed as Minister of Finance by President Megawati Sukarnoputri and served in this post from 2001 to 2004. In the first term of President Susilo Bambang Yudhoyono (colloquially known as "SBY") from 2005 to 2008, he served as Coordinating Minister for the Economy. He was next elected Governor of Bank Indonesia, an irony not lost on the man who had been ignored when he had applied for a job at the bank many years before. He served in this post from 2008 to May 16, 2009, when he was asked by President SBY to serve as his running mate in the national election for the presidency.

The Political Career

"When I was asked to run for Vice President, I really hesitated because I had never sought this role. I discussed this with my family, and my daughter was opposed at first. But in the end, I decided that if I could contribute a bit more to help the country, I had the duty to accept. So here I am," he concluded with a smile.

The election was held on July 8, 2009. The running mates of SBY and Boediono won in a landslide, with 61% of the votes, amounting to 73,874,562, or 4,417,665 more votes than were cast for the team of Barack Obama and Joe Biden in 2008. As far as I can tell, more votes were cast for SBY and Boediono in 2009 than for any other team in the history of free, direct presidential elections world-wide (until Joe Biden in 2020).

Yopie Hidayat, a former journalist who served the Vice President as a special adviser on communication and media relations, told me that Boediono had established his "mission statement" using a traditional three-word Javanese proverb, namely *"Sabar, Sareh, Seleh."* I asked the VP to explain this Javanese wisdom to me. He laughed and said that it was true he had chosen this proverb as his mission statement, but he warned me that Suharto had chosen the same three words to guide his administration.

"*Sabar* translates as 'patience,' but it is more complex than this single English word. It also tells us that we should not take action until the time is right. It connotes a respect for the rhythm of life outside yourself, or an understanding of your relationship to the external world. It advises us how we should deal with other people."

"*Sareh* also translates as 'patience', but again it is more complex than this single English word. This word is directed more towards your inner self and counsels you not to rush yourself. Make best efforts but conduct yourself properly. It advises us to be peaceful within ourselves, and act only when you are ready."

"*Seleh* does not have a single word in English to which it corresponds. If you are religious, it translates as 'leave it to God after you have done your best.' If you are more secular, it translates as 'leave it to the process after you have done your best.' In either case, you should not get too agitated if you fail, and you should not get too excited if you succeed. Work hard but be at peace with yourself."

While this philosophy sounds straightforward, if convoluted, to the Western mind, I am mindful of the difficulty that an outsider encounters when attempting to understand the Javanese. Indonesians tend to achieve their goals by indirection and with reliance on obscurity. There is no question in my mind that Boediono's success in public service has depended to a high degree on a tolerance for ambiguity, but at the same time, I am also convinced that he is a man with a glass front, if tinted with Javanese hues. He has adapted his cultural background to the rationality of his Western education, but he has never lost his genetic imprinting. This may in some ways have limited his effectiveness, since his openness, integrity, and unmovable principles were at times out of step with the environment in which he operated, particularly when he entered the fray of politics. I detect in Boediono's ethical framework an animist's interpretation of Peter Singer's conclusion that we are ultimately responsible for our ethics, and that there is a single ethical imperative, which is to accept that your personal interests must not take precedence over anyone else's interests. I believe that the history books will speak of Boediono in reverential terms. He is a great, if reluctant, hero.

Indonesia and the World

When I met on another occasion with Boediono in his office, I observed that he had recently given a speech to the opening of the 39th Al-Irsyad Al-Islamiyah Congress, a non-partisan organization established in 1914 to promote the education, health, and welfare of the Indonesian people. In his speech, he had commented on the difficulty of maintaining unity while also practicing tolerance toward other faiths. I asked him for his thoughts on this inherent contradiction between unity and tolerance. As usual, his response was indirect (not evasive.)

"How will the world evolve in the future? There are clearly some areas that our small planet will need to face that require more unity and less emphasis on sovereignty, such as global warming and the environment, public health and pandemics, global financial contagion, and others. But at the same time, the natural tendency of humans seems to be to look inward and to reinforce their core values and exclusivity when faced with threats, whether local or global. Leaders have a duty to behave in a way that reconciles impulses that might appear contradictory."

"Nation states, nationalism, and religiosity will persist, regardless of globalization. But this does not preclude the balancing of national self-identity, with its focus on control, and global identity, with its attendant relinquishing of control. This applies to a variety of areas, ranging from the environment to finance. Globalization is a funny thing. It makes possible growth and the broadening of both culture and prosperity, but it also has the unwanted side-effect of creating bigger crises in its wake. During crises, which are inevitable, national self-identity is critical as an anchor. In this sense, national self-identity is and will be more important than religious self-identity. It is clear to me that we humans have created an efficient but fragile world through our attempted mastery of nature. I fear we will pay a high price for not trying harder to be respectful of nature."

"Indonesia is an ancient civilization. It is also a unique civilization, with over 17,000 islands, only about a third of which are inhabited by humans. This civilization has drawn many visitors with its attractive climate and vast resources. The Dutch were only the more modern influence in a series that included the Hindu and Islamic civilizations. Like China, Indonesia absorbed all foreign influences and yet retained its unique character. They were all part of Indonesia's journey towards a society in which its people can live better and happier lives."

"Indonesia as a political entity was a new concept in the twentieth century. The Dutch really united us," he laughed. "In 1928, a youth congress declared that Bahasa was the national language of unity. This was a tremendous boost to the independence movement, since it gave us coherence as a nation for the first time. Of course, the Dutch opposed this decision because it threatened their ability to rule a divided population. Opposition to Dutch rule was an important factor in creating the idea of Indonesia."

"The end of Western influence is far away. Western culture and values will continue to influence Indonesia for many years to come. But we will not lose our Indonesian identity just because we absorb Western ways. In the same way that Indonesia absorbed Hindu, Islamic, and Dutch culture, we will stay the same, but with some slight modifications. It is a sign of the strength, not the weakness, of Indonesian culture and civilization."

The Legacy

Towards the end of his term as Vice President, I met with Boediono, this time in the Vice President's Official Residence (*Istana Wapres*), in downtown Jakarta. "Looking at your career in the Indonesian government, what would you say were the projects in which you were involved that did the most to help the people of Indonesia?" I asked.

The VP squirmed a little at this question, and finally said that he had some difficulty answering because he had not thought much about the scorecard. His personal philosophy was to move on to the next challenge rather than to gloat over a success or stew over a failure. *Sabar, Sareh, Seleh*. I did not press him to answer, although on separate occasions, I asked others the same question. Yopie Hidayat, introduced previously, was not so shy about describing Boediono's accomplishments as Vice President:

"His most important accomplishments have been in the strengthening of Indonesia as a modern democracy," stated Yopie. "He has laid the infrastructure for long-term stability and equity. For example, he chaired the Commission on National Poverty Eradication that created the first nation-wide Social Security System based on a well-organized and reliable database. He believes that one of the key characteristics of a durable democracy is true social security for those who cannot support themselves adequately. Boediono's goal was to establish a system that would be supported by data and that would be outside political manipulation, and he has been successful. This system not only helps the poor, but it also fights corruption from within by eliminating its sources."

"Boediono also chaired another committee that focused on the reform of regional bureaucracies, which had grown bloated and ineffective over the years. In a dramatic gesture, he ordered that all hiring in the government would stop for 18 months. And Boediono is the kind of guy who is very firm when he decides. He does not surrender to political or media pressure. Any hiring during this moratorium, and of course there were certain exceptions that had to be made, had to be approved by the VP personally. Following the work of this commission, the entire structure of the regional bureaucracy changed. The VP was responsible for instituting a new philosophy of organizing the state apparatus. Now there are job descriptions, responsibilities, accountability, transparency, and a host of improvements designed to reduce corruption and enforce performance."

"But he is doing all this quietly, without causing ripples. You do not read about this in the press and he doesn't get much credit for these major reforms. His approach is to do things patiently but relentlessly. It takes enormous self-confidence to accomplish these fundamental reforms. I remember on the first day we met, he told me, 'You don't need to sell me. As long as the programs work, that is enough. I do not need to be in the newspapers. Let's work together to make Indonesia secure for the next century.'"

The Challenges Ahead

"We are at a critical stage in the evolution of our nation," Boediono stated, "and the further development of democratic political institutions and systems is critical to our continued success. You know, we tried democracy once before, in the 1950s, but it did not deliver the benefits that it promised, and we reverted to authoritarianism for the next 32 years. Now we have a young democracy again and we cannot afford to fail the way we did in the 1950s. The next twenty years or so will be both important and dangerous. We must make the political transition to institution-building and political sustainability. And I do not mean the forms, which we have already. I mean the content and the conduct."

"This is why we need to reform our educational system. Recently, my colleagues in the Ministry of Education rolled out a nationwide, unified curriculum for primary through high school education. It is all taught in Bahasa, which will contribute to national unity. But the challenge now is to deliver high quality education to all the children of Indonesia. If we want unity as a nation, we must pay attention to all our inhabited islands, not just the big ones."

He waxed philosophical, "A country must settle on its collective moral compass. Therefore, we have embedded the transmission of values into the new nationwide school curriculum. We must make these values palatable to kids, but they must be given the right start to finding their moral compass. This is the only way to build a real participatory democracy, and it will take many years."

I later spoke with Farid Harianto, one of Boediono's informal but influential advisors. "The Vice President is focused on the long-term," Farid began, "and is constantly frustrated by the attention that is focused by the media on short-term goals such as quarterly GNP growth rates. The Vice President wants to use his term in office to help reinforce the values and to build the institutions that will support equity, prosperity, sustainability, and national unity for the next 100 years."

Towards the end of our conversation on February 14, 2014, I noted to Boediono that the Founding Fathers of the United States, in particular George Washington, took great pains to base their actions and decisions on a strong belief that whatever they did would create precedents for tens and possibly hundreds of years to come. This is one of the reasons that Washington declined to be appointed king. I asked Boediono if his decisions and actions as Vice President of the Republic of Indonesia during this youthful period of Indonesian democracy were inspired by the same motivation. His answer was notable because it was the only time in which he did not smile during our ninety minutes together. "The short answer," he said with utter seriousness, "is that this motivation was present in every single thing I did as Vice President."

Who Is Boediono?

And now, my chapter on Boediono is complete. As was the case with Luis Andrade, and as will be the case with the fifteen additional exemplary individuals yet to come, I could have written much more. And I am sure that extensive biographies will eventually be written on all seventeen. But my goal in this book is to tread lightly and move quickly, repeatedly asking if there are commonalities.

I hope that what I have written here communicates the deep respect and affection I have for Boediono. One particular advantage I have in writing about him is that I have known him as a personal friend for more than three decades, during which time I have met with him perhaps two dozen times in the many roles he served in the Indonesian government.

The strongest impression I take away from my long acquaintance with Boediono is his devotion to service to others, without a trace of personal ambition. There have been few individuals in history who have attained such distinction, position, and power while having such a complete absence of personal ambition. I cannot yield to him the likelihood that fate had something to do with it, although he could have declined any of the positions he did not solicit but had thrust upon him. But he certainly had his share of Black Swans, to all of which he responded robustly and courageously. Boediono could have made a lot of money in the private sector, but he chose a life of service to the people of Indonesia, with no benefit – and at considerable cost – to himself.

The second impression, and one which everyone notes when they meet him, is the man's humility. He is funny, he is confident, he is courageous; but he does it with the humblest demeanor. And it is not an act. He does not break into tyrannical rages; he does not boast or keep score.

The third impression is of the acute intellect that has fueled his rise to influence. He is just more likely to be correct in his analysis and policy prescriptions than most other people.

The fourth impression, and this one is made possible only because of my long acquaintance with him, is his stability. He has not changed, either as he gained power or as Indonesia has moved through successive stages of self-governance. And he is always the same person, with the rich, the powerful, the poor, or the weak.

Moving on to Phnom Penh

Our next journey is a very short hop, 1,221 miles from Soekarno-Hatta International Airport to Phnom Penh International Airport. The flight time is under three hours. We leave an enormous country, with the world's fourth largest population, and enter a much smaller country, ranking #71 in the world in terms of population. Metropolitan Jakarta has roughly double the population of the entire country of Cambodia. Since Phnom Penh is the same latitude north of the Equator that Jakarta is south, the weather is still hot and sticky. But we will encounter an entirely new culture and civilization, this time Buddhist rather than Islamic, the victim of French colonialism rather than Dutch, speaking mostly Khmer rather than Bahasa Indonesia, and organized as a constitutional monarchy with a parliamentary form of government and a prime minister rather than a constitutional republic headed by a president.

Devoted to the Commonweal

Chanthol Sun

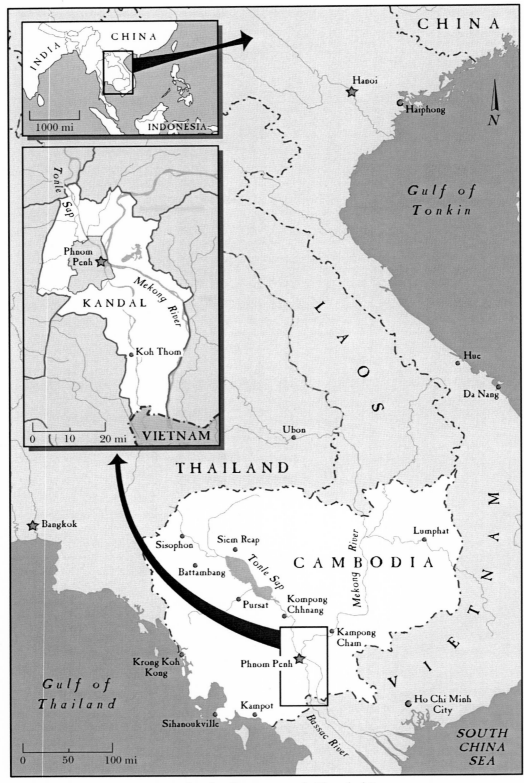

Devoted to the Commonweal: Chanthol Sun

Some Comparative History

The construction of Notre Dame Cathedral in Paris, France, began in 1163 and took over one hundred years to complete. The population of Paris at that time was approximately 200,000, with no elephants. The construction of Angkor Wat in Siem Reap, Cambodia, started at almost exactly the same time and took about thirty years to complete. Comprising over one thousand buildings, Angkor Wat was and is still the largest religious structure in the world. The population of Siem Reap at that time was about a million, with 50,000 elephants.

The Early Years

Seven hundred years later, in 1863, Cambodia became part of the French Colonial Empire. After 90 years as a "protectorate" of France, Cambodia became semi-independent on November 9, 1953. Chanthol Sun was born in Koh Thom, Kandal Province, Cambodia, in 1954 (coincidentally the same year as the French were defeated by the Vietnamese at Dien Bien Phu). Kandal Province surrounds but does not include Phnom Penh, Cambodia's capital. Koh Thom was and still is a farming village, 35 miles from Phnom Penh. But it might just as well have been 3,500 miles from the capital. In Chanthol's words, life in Koh Thom was "static, peaceful, and unchanging." A traditional, isolated community in a small, poor country, with no prospects for growth or change. Everyone's life was determined from birth, and relationships were fixed and stable. Everyone was a devout Buddhist. Chanthol's family consisted of his mother, his father, three sisters and five brothers (including Chanthol).

In 1957, when Chanthol was three, his parents moved to Phnom Penh, an unusual but not unknown event for families in Koh Thom. Chanthol stayed behind and lived with his grandparents until 1961, when at the age of seven he joined his parents in Phnom Penh. His father had by that time started a small business, renting and repairing cyclos, a three-wheeled, sometimes motorized vehicle, the primary form of hired transportation at the time. He also opened a small bookstore. From 1967 to 1973, Chanthol attended Sisowath High School in Phnom Penh, at the time considered to be the best high school in Cambodia. The language of instruction was Khmer, and he learned French as his first foreign language. After school, he worked for his father, selling books and newspapers as well as repairing cyclos.

This was a gruesome time in Cambodian history. Soon after his inauguration on January 20, 1969, President Richard M. Nixon, on the advice of Henry Kissinger, ordered the bombing of Cambodia. This secret war rained death and destruction on an innocent and helpless population for 14 months from March 1969 to April 1970 while Chanthol was in high school. No one knows how many Cambodians were sacrificed to the American god of imperialism, but some estimates of the death toll from the bombing are in the range of 250,000.

I was an active participant, at Columbia University where I was a student at the time, in massive protests against this illegal and immoral bombing campaign. I remember well that the university had to shut down in the spring of 1970 because of the protests, although our actions had no apparent effect on U.S. government policy. We were inspired by Robert F. Kennedy, who was murdered two years earlier, when he used words remarkably Buddhist when he confidently predicted that "Each time a man stands up for an ideal, or acts to improve the lot of others, or strikes out against injustice, he sends forth a tiny ripple of hope" that, added to millions of other ripples, "[will] build a current that can sweep down the mightiest walls of oppression and resistance."

In March 1970, the Cambodian Prime Minister Lon Nol led a *coup d'état*, instigated by the Nixon/Kissinger team, that ousted Prince Norodom Sihanouk. A month later, U.S. troops invaded Cambodia. One of the legacies of the invasion and subsequent military actions is the millions of land mines that still kill and cripple Cambodians two generations later.

The invasion, combined with the bombing and land mines, had driven rural people into the cities, causing the collapse of the nation's agricultural system, bringing chaos to the country, and contributing to the rise of the Khmer Rouge. A homegrown communist movement arose out of anger with the United States and the regimes of Prince Norodom Sihanouk and General Lon Nol, but later metastasized into a disease that would all but consume the country. I feel shame and remorse for this monster that my country helped to create in Cambodia, another proxy victim of the Cold War.

Chanthol's First Black Swan – United States of America

By 1973, the U.S. had abandoned its support for Lon Nol and within two years, the Khmer Rouge took full control over Cambodia. It is challenging for me, in retrospect, to imagine the despair that must have descended on the long-suffering people of Cambodia, caught between impossibly miserable alternatives. For some, including future Prime Minister Hun Sen, the choice was to join the Cambodian *maquis* and engage in guerilla warfare. For others, the choice was to seek a safe haven. Many years later, when I asked Chanthol why he did not become a guerilla fighter, he laughed without a trace of bitterness. "Can you imagine me with the Khmer Rouge? They would have killed me in a week."

In 1973, a chance encounter with an American backpacker inspired Chanthol's older brother to go to the United States. In August of that same year, Chanthol completed high school and applied for a visa to follow his brother. He knew that his future in Cambodia was bleak for the foreseeable future but had faith that someday he would be able to return to serve his country.

Chanthol sold his motorbike to purchase a one-way ticket to Washington. D.C. His grand-mother gave him US$50 and he left home with two suitcases (one filled with clothing and one filled with books). He arrived in Silver Spring, Maryland, intending to enroll at American University, to which he had been admitted. He needed a job to support himself, so he visited Georgetown. Nearby, he was offered a job as a dishwasher at a restaurant named "Jour et Nuit." He sent most of the money he made home to his parents in Phnom Penh.

The Khmer Rouge and General Electric

Meanwhile, back in Cambodia things got much worse. The Khmer Rouge, having defeated Lon Nol in 1975, initiated the political and humanitarian nightmare that became known as the "Killing Fields," and which resulted in the extermination of almost two million Cambodians, uprooted the entire nation, and plunged the country into four years of self-in-flicted terror. The regime asked all Cambodian students living abroad to return home and join the revolution. Every student who accepted this request was immediately murdered on arrival in Phnom Penh. Chanthol wisely stayed in the United States. Senator Ted Kennedy of Massachusetts sponsored legislation that granted "Green Cards" to all Cambodian students in the United States. Chanthol received his Green Card through this legislation.

He graduated from American University in 1978, was recruited by General Electric, and started work soon after graduation. In that same year, he applied for and was granted U.S. citizenship. For the entire four years of the Khmer Rouge reign of terror, he heard nothing from his family. But he was sustained by a strong belief, based on nothing but his innate optimism, that his family members were safe.

In 1979 the Khmer Rouge was defeated by the Vietnamese and driven out of the capital and into the Cambodian jungle. Slowly, the full story started to be told. Tens of thousands of Cambo-dians were living in refugee camps in Thailand. Finally, Chanthol located his family and learned that his father, two brothers and two sisters were safe, although suffering horribly in one of these refugee camps. His mother had died in a Khmer Rouge labor camp in 1979, and one brother was missing (Chanthol will only call him missing, although he never has been seen again after 40 years.)

In 1980, he petitioned the International Committee of the Red Cross to sponsor all his living relatives. He sent money to the survivors so that they would be able to come to the United States. Miraculously, everybody still living in 1980 escaped. Ten family members in all (including the husband and children of one of his sisters) left the refugee camps and arrived in the United States unannounced, utterly destitute but profoundly grateful for their lives and their freedom. They all arrived within one week of each other over the Labor Day holiday in 1980 and Chanthol suddenly had ten mouths to feed and ten sleeping bags on the floor of his small apartment as he went through the General Electric Training Program.

Sotha, Ratavy, Nyny, and Mony

During this time of exhilaration that most of his family had survived, but also of exhaustion from the workload of supporting ten people, he met his future wife, Sotha, in 1982. They married and started a family. Their eldest daughter, Ratavy, was born in Chicago, where Chanthol was assigned in 1986 when he joined GE Capital. Their middle daughter, Nyny, was born in Paris, where Chanthol was assigned in 1988 when he joined GE Medical Systems. Their youngest daughter, Mony, was born in Bangkok, in 2001. All three daughters would eventually enroll (sequentially) at the University of Pennsylvania and earn their undergraduate degrees. I have seen this family in operation, collectively and individually, in Cambodia and the United States. The Sun family is a happy family, full of love, support, mutual respect, and optimism for the future.

John Rice

By 1982, thriving in the GE meritocracy, Chanthol was invited to move to the GE Audit Staff, which would require long periods (4-6 weeks at a time) of travel away from home but which paid a higher salary. John Rice, in 2013 Vice Chairman of General Electric, joined GE at approximately the same time as Chanthol. John also was invited to join the Audit Staff, which he described as the "fast track" for those executives identified by GE as being "high potential" for advancement under the company's highly competitive, merit-based personnel system.

"Chanthol was a very special person, even then," John remembered. "He was both passionate and compassionate. In my more than thirty-two years of knowing Chanthol, I have never had the slightest doubt about his integrity or his passion. And this applies to Chanthol as a man, as a husband, as a father, as an executive, and as an advocate for Cambodia. He has always been the same person – positive, optimistic, and enthusiastic. He has always been a 'giver' without calculating what his reward would be."

"At GE, Chanthol was known for being relentless, but in a positive and infectious way. Everybody wanted to be on his team because any team that included Chanthol would always be high energy, high performance, and high morale," John added.

Chanthol's Next Black Swan: Cambodian Politics

Cambodia held a national election in 1993 with the assistance of the United Nations. Two candidates ran for the office of Prime Minister – Norodom Ranariddh, the second son of former King Norodom Sihanouk, and Hun Sen, the former Khmer Rouge soldier. The results of the election were ambiguous. FUNCINPEC (Ranariddh's party) won 45.5% of the vote and the Cambodian People's Party (Hun Sen's party) won 38.2% of the vote. A complicated dispute ensued, which was resolved with a typically Cambodian compromise. Two prime ministers were appointed. Prince Ranariddh was "First" Prime Minister and Hun Sen was "Second" Prime Minister. Ranariddh asked Chanthol to join the government as Minister of Energy and Mining. Chanthol, sensing that this compromise was destined to fail, declined the offer. But his care and concern for the Cambodian people were reignited by the prospect of joining the Cambodian government. Later that year, Ranariddh again asked Chanthol to join the government, this time as Minister of Tourism. He declined again.

In early 1994, Ranariddh asked Chanthol to join the government one more time, to head the Council for the Development of Cambodia, which would be the nation's engine for growth, the governmental agency responsible for promoting the direct foreign investment which Cambodia so desperately needed. Chanthol once again declined, for the third time.

By April 1994, Chanthol decided to respond to this Black Swan robustly, and accepted Ranariddh's request. He asked GE for a leave of absence and agreed to start the Council for the Development of Cambodia as Secretary General. His devotion to his homeland overcame his trepidations about working in such a complex political environment. Twenty-one years after his departure from Phnom Penh amid the chaos of war, he was back to do his part to rebuild his country.

According to John Rice, "Chanthol was doing well at GE and could have had a comfortable life. But he decided that his country needed him, and he left the corporate world to help the people of Cambodia. Chanthol is not content to leave the world as it is; he needs to help make the world what it can be." Once again, we encounter an individual who made a major commitment to help others, with no personal benefit, and at substantial cost to himself.

Three years later, in 1997, Chanthol was awarded a scholarship sponsored by the U.S. Agency for International Development and applied to the Wharton School's five-week Advanced Management Program. This was when he and I met for the first time. In one of those great ironic moments in life, on the day of his graduation from Wharton's AMP, Hun Sen seized power. Chanthol quit his job with the Council for the Development of Cambodia but returned to Bangkok (where his family was living). Ranariddh fled the country.

The next year (1998), Ranariddh was allowed by Hun Sen to return to Cambodia. In 2003, Ranariddh asked Chanthol to join his political party, FUNCINPEC, and run for public office. Chanthol agreed, campaigned for FUNCINPEC and successfully won a seat in the National Assembly, representing his home province of Kandal. You might call this the triumph of hope over experience, but Chanthol was hooked, and there was no going back to corporate life.

Hun Sen won the election with 47.3% of the vote but did not have enough seats in the National Assembly to form a government without forming a coalition. The result once again was political paralysis, and the new government was not formed until the next year

(2004). Chanthol was asked to take the post of Minister of Public Works and Transport, and he accepted.

Anvanith Gui, a childhood friend of Chanthol's wife, worked for Chanthol during this period as Chief of Staff. "When Chanthol was Minister of Public Works and Transport, he would frequently visit villages throughout Cambodia. His purposes were to see first-hand what condition the roads were in, and to build credibility with the villagers," remembered Anvanith.

"The villagers in the countryside were initially somewhat skeptical of Chanthol," continued Anvanith, "because he did not behave or look like either a villager or a government official. But the villagers were eventually won over by his energy, his down-to-earth demeanor, his commitment to the practical solution of basic problems, his sincerity, and his openness. People responded to the man and not to the office, which was new for Cambodia, where traditionally ministers do not care very much about their constituents but remained focused on power politics in Phnom Penh."

Reflections on Life and Politics

I met with Chanthol in his home in Phnom Penh to ask him about the people, forces, and ideas that shaped him. "Honest, hardworking parents and grandparents," he quickly and earnestly replied to my question. "They taught me to treat everyone with dignity. I was a Boy Scout in high school. I was a member of the swimming team. I am very competitive. I always want to win and to succeed. I always felt the duty to study and work hard. My purpose in going to the United States in 1973 was to study, learn, and someday to return to Cambodia to help my country and its people."

"All Cambodians are Buddhists, and so I am a Buddhist. I believe in the Law of Karma. What you do will come back to you. If I am wronged and I seek revenge, I gain nothing and in the next cycle of life I will suffer because of my selfishness. I also believe in the Principle of Detachment, which is a central belief of all Buddhists. We try not to worry too much about things. Too much attachment to power or material possessions is bad and delays our release from suffering. I believe it is important to detach from the need for power, money, recognition, possessions, even family."

"I will work hard and strive to succeed, but if I lose, I can detach. I am happy to go back to the farm in Koh Thom tomorrow, if necessary. I am not attached to material possessions or power and influence. It is a mistake to be greedy. I also need to be able to look Hun Sen or my youngest daughter in the eye and know that I acted honestly. Don't envy anyone, because if you have envy in your heart, you will never be happy."

Many of the leaders of Cambodia today, including Prime Minister Hun Sen, were Khmer Rouge who became disenchanted with Pol Pot. Some of the disenchanted escaped to

Vietnam and convinced the Vietnamese in 1978 to help them liberate Cambodia from the Khmer Rouge that they had once supported. "How can you work with former Khmer Rouge, knowing that one of them may have killed your mother?" I asked.

"We must be able to detach from our anger over what someone was or did and accept who they have become. The essence of Buddhism is to stop reacting to the human emotions which are unhelpful and cause us to suffer. I can work with them because they liberated Cambodia. In addition, they have changed. Hun Sen cares deeply about Cambodia. He changed. In addition, without his strength, Cambodian politics would be chaotic. There is no value at all in being old and angry. I cannot help the Cambodian people if I am alone and isolated."

"In General Electric, you work hard to increase shareholder value for thousands of anonymous investors. Working in the Cambodian government, my shareholders are all the Cambodian people. When I get discouraged or frustrated, I leave Phnom Penh and go visit the Cambodian people in the countryside. I am inspired and energized. The purpose of all my effort is to help the people of Cambodia."

Although he had joined the government at the invitation of Prince Ranariddh and in opposition to Prime Minister Hun Sen, Chanthol eventually switched parties and now is a member of the Prime Minister's party.

"This was a very hard decision for me because I am extremely loyal. But FUNCINPEC's ship sank and my larger loyalty is to the people of Cambodia, not to an individual. I determined that I would be able to bring about more positive change by working within Hun Sen's party than by being marginalized as an outsider who had no influence."

Chanthol continued, "Cambodia is full of a spirit that asks people like me to return home and to help. The spirit of the Cambodian people begged and pleaded with me. The Cambodian people have suffered so much and for so long. I could not refuse. I believe that you cannot bring about positive change by sitting outside and criticizing. You must be engaged and be part of the change you want to see happen."

Another Political Campaign

The year 2013 brought another national election in Cambodia. Chanthol was a candidate for the seat in the legislature that would represent the district in which his hometown of Koh Thom is located. "During my campaign, I ran from village to village to say hello to the people," he began. "I normally did around 10-12 kilometers each afternoon. I asked about 100 youths to ride motor bikes in front of me. They made noise to attract the people to come out and stay along the route to allow me to greet them."

"This campaigning style was good because the people along the route got a chance to see me and to touch me. They felt sorry for me for campaigning so hard. They had never seen a candidate run like this. Old folks cried and asked me to stop running. Some just wiped my sweat with their hands. It was a very moving experience for me. But I still lost the election in my district! Even though they liked me, some voted for the opposition because they promised to raise salaries, give free healthcare, reduce the price of gasoline, increase the price of crops, and so on. I refused to mislead them with false promises that I knew I could not deliver."

"I lost my district but the CPP (Hun Sen's party) won overall in the country, which allowed the CPP to form the government. Hun Sen asked me to serve as Minister of Commerce in addition to re-appointing me as a Senior Minister and Vice Chairman of the Council for the Development of Cambodia. I also serve the government as ASEAN Economic Minister for Cambodia. And finally, because of my past work with the Ministry of Public Works and Transport, I remain the liaison with the Chinese government, which supports construction of ports, roads, railroads, airports, and other infrastructure projects."

"On my first day as Minister of Commerce, I took two actions. First, I took the equivalent of US$10,000 in cash of my own money (no government funds!) and gave the equivalent of US$10 in cash to each of the top 1,000 staff in the ministry. I did this for two reasons. One was to tell them I appreciated their work. In addition, the day corresponded to the 'tomb-sweeping day' when Buddhists are expected to make offerings to their ancestors. I told everybody to use the money to 'make merit' with their ancestors. The other reason was to signal in a concrete way that in the future, promotion will be based on merit alone. My predecessor as Minister of Commerce had done a great job, and I was continuing the reform process that he had initiated."

"The second action I took concerned the procedure for doing business in Cambodia. I do not believe that Cambodians are dishonest people, but they are driven to be corrupt because of abject poverty. Previously, the system was set up to make it easier to demand bribes. For example, despite the fact that it was not legally or procedurally necessary, there were thousands of pieces of paper that needed to be signed, stamped or otherwise handled numerous times by ministry staff. I eliminated thousands of pieces of paper and their associated opportunities for corruption. For my next action, I plan to automate many of the processes that now are done by hand, including the registration of company names and the payment of fees. The next phase must involve finding ways to compensate staff appropriately so that they do not need to take bribes in order to pay for doctor's visits for their children. They are good people, hard-working, and eager to help. The government should not force them to do things they know are wrong. The minimum wage must be a living wage."

This is a good man, this Chanthol Sun. A happy man also, who is earning good karma. He has a glass front and a back built with high quality titanium. But he is not a revolutionary or an ideologue. There are those, not surprisingly, who advocate 'regime change' in Cambodia, but Chanthol has chosen to work with the existing political realities. As U.S. President Theodore Roosevelt wrote over a century ago when he was criticized by the investigative reporter Lincoln Steffens, who believed that radical measures were necessary to fix the American political and economic woes,

> *"You contend that [I am a good person] of limited vision who fight[s] against specific evils with no idea of fighting against the fundamental evil." After a quarter century in politics, Roosevelt observed, he had found that change was realized by "men who take the next step; not those who theorize about the 200th step..." Indeed, history suggested that those...who fought "the system in the abstract" accomplished "mighty little good."*

Chanthol Sun, with his indefatigable energy, unquenchable optimism, and unflinching integrity is a modern-day Cambodian version of TR.

Who Is Chanthol Sun?

I would evaluate my knowledge of Cambodia as better than the average American, but miserably inadequate to understand the country, its people, or its challenges. But Chanthol Sun is my friend, and I have undertaken to try to understand him, at least a little bit. I have also undertaken to place Chanthol in the context of this book.

It will not come as a surprise to the reader that I admire Chanthol Sun, nor will anyone be startled when I say that I have affection for him. He has come more than half-way. I do not speak a word of Khmer, and because of this simple but important fact, I have no way of knowing what part of Chanthol I will not understand.

Despite all these qualifiers, I feel confident in my judgement about Chanthol Sun. He is different in ethnicity, language, and history from Luis Andrade and Boediono, but I do not detect the slightest difference among these three men in terms of their inner selves. The fact that they all lived through difficult and frightening times in the history of their countries helps to illuminate their resilience. They all act with complete autonomy and freedom and are both fearless and harmless because every action they take is based on an understanding of their true, inner value systems. They also have chosen, at some cost to themselves, to benefit others with no benefit to themselves. I will always have challenges in understanding Cambodia, and I will certainly never be qualified to pass judgment on what has happened there, but I can say with conviction that Chanthol Sun is a once-in-a-lifetime person, and I feel lucky to have him as my friend for life.

Maybe Henry Kamm, towards the end of his 1998 book about Cambodia, prophetically put it best:

Cambodia needs not one man on horseback who will be the savior but an elite of aware men and women of goodwill and creative energy to whom the fate of fellow Cambodians matters.

Or, more poetically, it is quite possible that Chanthol took up Tennyson's challenge:

Rift the hills, and roll the waters, flash the lightnings, weigh the Sun.

Take your pick. Chanthol Sun gives me hope that someday we will achieve our goal of peaceful prosperity that is shared universally. Reaching this goal will require advanced skills in intercultural communication, and all of us would benefit from learning from him.

Moving on to Dakar

Our next journey takes us from Phnom Penh to Dakar, Senegal; but we will make a stop in Ann Arbor, Michigan, first, serviced through Detroit. A direct flight from Phnom Penh to Detroit is 8,695 miles, but we will require at least one connecting flight. After our stop in Ann Arbor, the flight to Dakar at 4,304 miles is only about half the distance from Phnom Penh to Detroit. We will need to stop twice, in Atlanta and then Paris. Flights to and from former French colonies in Africa almost always need to go through Paris. Even going from Dakar to Abidjan has until recently been likely to require a connection through Paris. It is another case of the colonial mindset.

Compassionate Capitalist

Dawn Hines

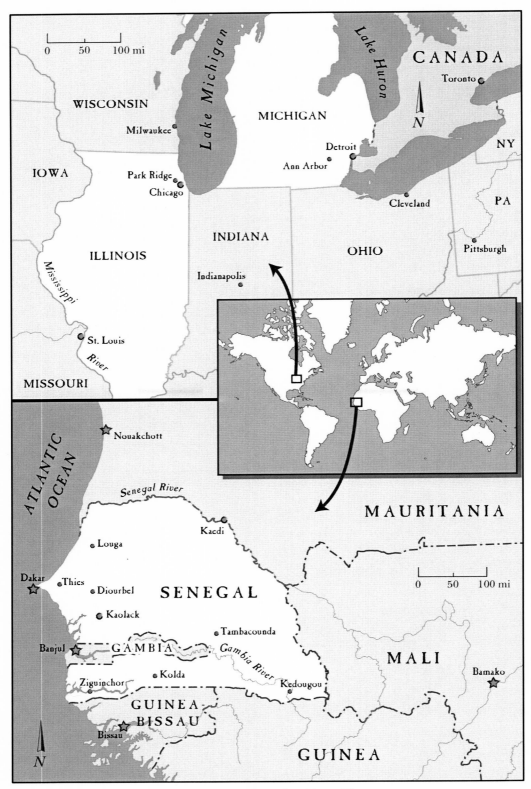

Compassionate Capitalist: Dawn Hines

1969

When I was much younger, I shared the spirit of change, movement, and adventure that my generation embraced. Genetic mutation DRD4-7r was obviously rampant among us. In addition to loving travel, we were concerned – in some cases angry – about injustice, poverty, racism, disenfranchisement, inequality, discrimination and the so-called "military-industrial complex" that seemed to us to drive governmental as well as corporate decision-making, all to the detriment of human and environmental values. Our responses took a variety of formats, and the year 1969 was in some ways a revealing microcosm in which to examine this variety.

At one extreme, my generation spawned the Weathermen, a small but disproportionately violent extremist group formed in 1969 with the avowed, if improbable, purposes of over-throwing the U.S. Government, destroying U.S. imperialism, and achieving a communist utopia. To my mind nothing, no matter how vile, could ever justify the violence perpetrated by the Weathermen. Anger feeds on anger. Violence begets violence. Evil does not eliminate evil.

The more widespread mainstream response of young adults in the late 1960s and early 1970s was the protest march. I remember in particular traveling to Washington, D.C. with a group of friends on November 15, 1969, to participate in what *The New York Times* called "the largest antiwar protest in United States history." Over a half-million Americans sent a strong message through their physical presence that we found the war in Vietnam to be in violation of American principles and did not advance American interests as we understood them. Nixon surrounded the White House with school buses parked head-to-tail and watched Saturday afternoon college football on television. I, among many others, was tear-gassed in Dupont Circle at midnight.

A third response of my generation, on the utterly frivolous end of the spectrum, was expressed in Woodstock, the absurd "Aquarian" festival that was held from August 15-18, 1969, in upstate New York on "Yasgur's farm," as Joni Mitchell's song reported. It also involved close to a half-million participants but was characterized more by the pervasive use of illicit drugs and endless rock 'n roll music than anything that might be called positive activism for social change, although budding capitalists made a lot of money selling tie-dye T-shirts, as well as drug paraphernalia and the recreational substances to fill them.

Some of us undertook activities that involved commitments of longer duration than a few days and that were grounded in reality. For me personally, this choice was to participate as a volunteer in an organization called Operation Crossroads Africa, which had been founded in 1958 by Reverend James H. Robinson (and coincidentally was credited by President John F. Kennedy for giving him the idea for the Peace Corps). The basic proposition of Operation Crossroads Africa was to send small groups of young Americans to African countries where they would spend the summer living and working with counterpart groups of young Africans. This was an early version of "cultural immersion" and it was designed to challenge our assumptions about each other. I spent the summer of 1966 helping to build a youth center in Bangui, the capital of the Central African Republic.

We were the Baby Boomers, the huge generation born in the optimism following the triumph of the Greatest Generation in World War II. We were determined to make the world a better place. We had the energy, the motivation, and the raw power of numbers, but – and this is an important "but" – we lacked the wisdom (maybe it was the perseverance or attention span) to turn our dreams into the peaceful utopia we aspired to create. In short, we achieved some successes, suffered some defeats, and defaulted to careers, families, mortgages and, eventually, retirement.

Luckily, a successor generation, fired with the same idealism and dreams of a society built on equity, fairness, opportunity, justice, and amity, is looking at the world's challenges differently. And to my surprise and relief, this new generation is taking an approach that reconciles two goals that my generation was convinced were irreconcilable, namely social and environmental goals, on the one hand, and free-market capitalist goals on the other hand. This approach even has a name that blends these opposites – "impact investing."

Of interest, but not by design, my choices of heroines and heroes included four people involved in this field of impact investing. In fact, they were all involved in the field before it was named (at a Rockefeller Foundation conference in 2007 in Bellagio on Lake Como). In retrospect, my choices are not at all surprising. I am instinctively drawn to those who try to make the world a better place, and to those who find a more successful way of changing the world for the better than did my generation. In this and the next three chapters I will introduce these four worthy inheritors of the unfulfilled dreams of my generation. Perhaps they will succeed where we did not.

Dawn Hines Is Introduced

I begin with a young girl growing up in Ann Arbor, Michigan, where the Weathermen established their violent organization. She has traveled a long and complicated (altogether peaceful) journey to arrive at her destination, but she has arrived as one of the leaders of a new and different form of change that is having a positive effect on the world and empowering an entire category of people who had been poor, powerless, and hopeless. I now introduce Dawn Hines, the first *Compassionate Capitalist*, with respect and affection.

I will begin by taking a short excursion into the history of Dawn's family. The Hines family was subject to four currents in the deep river of American history. The first current was their point of origin. Scots-Irish in extraction, the Hines family emigrated from Ireland (or Great

Britain) to the New World in the late seventeenth or early eighteenth century.

The second current into which they flowed took place in the late eighteenth century, when the British colonies in the New World headed inexorably towards independence and war. Many of the colonists were royalists and did not want either to join the fight against the British or to live in an independent United States of America. The option chosen by many royalists, the Hines family included, was to immigrate to Canada, in their case Nova Scotia. This was the same choice, coincidentally, as the family of my paternal grandmother.

The third current that carried the Hines family had two sources. First was the decline of the fishing trade in the Canadian Maritimes, which left the men without gainful employment. Second was the industrialization of the American heartland, which drew immigrants from around the world to stoke the fires and build the machines that powered national growth in the twentieth century. Dawn's paternal grandparents immigrated to the United States and her grandfather worked in a factory in Chicago.

The fourth current which swept the Hines family along the river to the present time dates back to the reason for the immigration of the first Hines in the late seventeenth or early eighteenth century, namely religion, and the profusion of religious beliefs that were propagated and flourished in a country born under the twin mandates of freedom of religion and separation of church and state.

Dawn's paternal grandparents were poor, having emigrated from Nova Scotia with few possessions other than their dreams of a better life in the United States. There was no time or money for school. Her grandfather did not receive a formal education but rose to the level of foreman at his company. Religion does not seem to have been discussed much by Dawn's paternal grandparents, although they were members of an evangelical Christian church.

Dawn's maternal grandparents, who enter the story at this point, were also evangelical Christians, but more fundamentalist than her paternal grandparents. They belonged to a church which prohibited its members from seeing doctors, believing that God would cure all through the ministrations of the leader of their church.

Dawn's father, Gordon Hines, was the fourth of six children, born in Chicago on the inauspicious date of October 30, 1929. He was, in Dawn's words, "a poor kid from South Chicago," and was the first in his family to earn a college degree. Although interested in social work, he majored in psychology because the Navy Pier branch of the University of Illinois did not offer a degree in that subject. Gordon had originally intended to devote his life to helping the needy and went to work at the YMCA after graduating from college. However, he quickly became disillusioned by the selfishness of the staff, who seemed more interested in helping themselves than in helping the children.

Gordon quit his job at the YMCA and took a job at a balancing company that made machinery for use in the automotive industry, which was booming due to both the unleashed consumerism of post-war America and the start of the Interstate Highway System in 1956. After trying unsuccessfully to convince the owner to make innovations which customers wanted, he left to form his own company which he called Hines Industries.

A Complex Religious Background

Dawn's religious background had a major influence on her, both for good and for ill. This is an important theme in her life and will reappear at every turn in the road she has taken. It is inextricably woven into the fabric of her life.

Both sets of Dawn's grandparents, as noted above, as well as her parents, were evangelical Christians, a faith that entails following a strict and unchanging path, including a literal interpretation of the Bible, an unquestioning adherence to the Bible's words, the need to be "born again," and an emphasis on "expressing and sharing the gospel" (a euphemism for proselytizing). The evangelicals did not "express and share" violently, but out of heartfelt sympathy. Motivated by a complete conviction of the validity of their views, they merely explained their faith to others so that they would not be ignorant and risk going to hell. It was permissible to discuss the minutiae of what the Bible said, but the evangelical never questioned that the Bible was the word of God, as factual as a newspaper article.

"While I was growing up," recalled Dawn, "my family's religion was not limiting to me or repressive. Much of it was quite positive – we celebrated nature with joy, and it was comforting to be surrounded by supportive and kind people." But as a thoughtful, independent, and free-thinking individual, Dawn eventually found herself at odds with this architecture of constraint. We will return to her crisis of faith later.

Dawn's Original and Continuing Hero

Dawn recalled that about the time her father became disillusioned with the social welfare system, he also became disillusioned with the church, which he criticized for not allowing free discussion and not meeting the real needs of its congregation. He did not lose his personal faith, however, and continued to read and study the Bible with informal groups of Christians and non-Christians alike.

Gordon was Dawn's original – and continuing – hero, a testament to the powerful influence that strong fathers can have on daughters. It was easy to see the source of Dawn's strength and personal value system. Her father is a towering figure in her life and contributed enormously to the compassionate and gentle person that Dawn is today.

"He was my hero because of the values he instilled in me," she stated. "He strongly believed that people deserved to be treated with respect – period. All people. No exceptions.

He was an independent thinker, a state of mind which ran contrary to the church, but not his beliefs. He made me fearless because he showed me personal courage."

Upon graduation from college, Dawn took a public finance investment banking job in New York City. Her parents visited her, and one evening they were walking in Times Square when they came upon a crowd standing in front of a theater, watching in paralyzed fascination as a man violently and repeatedly struck a women's head against a brick wall. Dawn's father instantly ran up to the crime's perpetrator (a good six inches taller and fifty pounds heavier than Gordon, in Dawn's memory), grabbed him by the shoulders, shook him forcefully, and stated firmly, "Don't you ever treat a woman like that!" This act of personal courage, which was purely instinctual and unpremeditated, still resonated with Dawn, thirty years after the incident.

Another reason for Dawn's reverence for her father was his commitment to social justice. According to Dawn, Gordon participated in the 1950s in the early stages of the Civil Rights Movement. She recalled that he had journeyed to the South to protest Jim Crow laws, including by sitting in the back of buses in the "colored" section as an act of civil disobedience.

"My mother was an elementary school teacher. She saw the world much differently from the way I see the world," Dawn began. "As an evangelical Christian, a mother, and a housewife, she accepted and never questioned the dogmas of her church or the norms and expectations of her society. She accepted the world as it was and did not think it could be – or should be – changed. She focused on meeting the expectations of her church and society, not question-ing them." Dawn, influenced more by her father than her mother, grew up thinking of the world as imperfect, but improvable. She would choose as her life's work the difficult but rewarding task of bringing about meaningful, positive change – impact. Dawn always had respect and love for her mother but could not accept what she saw as the straitjacket of evangelical Christianity.

Dawn's College Years

In college, for the first time Dawn was forced to confront the untenable contradiction between her rigid religious background (which stipulated that all non-Christian evangelicals would go to hell) and her inner, authentic self that respected all people and all beliefs in a non-judgmental way. Sorting out this contradiction was challenging but led straight to the autonomy and freedom that characterize her today.

Studying at the University of Pennsylvania with a major in economics, Dawn planned a career in government, devoted to working on the problems of inner-city poverty, to try to make a difference in the lives of others less fortunate than herself. Once again, it is not difficult to see the important influence of her father.

This was also the time when she was achieving some success in separating her personal beliefs from what she had been taught to believe as an evangelical Christian. Having met so many people from so many different faiths in college, she could no longer accept the notion that all non-Christian evangelicals (92% of the world) were going to hell. Her conclusion was that evangelical Christianity was based on negatives: be good or go to hell; you are sinful so you must ask for forgiveness; a bad thought is the equivalent of a bad action. She could not accept this negativity and eventually rejected and abandoned evangelical Christianity. She is a deeply spiritual person but she no longer adheres to organized religion and its dogmas.

After graduation from Penn in 1983, she took a job in public finance with Paine Webber, believing that this would provide her with the skills and knowledge she could take to a government role. She had been strongly inspired by Daniel Patrick Moynihan's book *Politics of a Guaranteed Income*. However, the government clients she met did not represent the dynamic, pioneering government culture she had imagined, so she surrendered her dream of a government career but retained the genetically acquired idealism of her father. She labored in this vineyard for four years but quit to spend a year (1988-1989) traveling and learning languages in Europe, Russia, and the Middle East. There is no question that she inherited the DRD4-7r gene.

Next, Dawn entered the Wharton School for the MBA program. She had considered law school but concluded that the legal profession was not right for her. Her reasoning provides another clue to understanding her personality. Dawn's preference is to solve a problem by finding the best solution, based on compassion and wisdom, regardless of its source, rather than using precedent to arrive at the course of action. This reasoning, interestingly, is quite consistent with her approach to religion and values.

Black Swans

With her MBA in hand, she surrendered to the demands of her DRD4-7r gene and wandered in Europe for five years. But like Odysseus, she was not yet home. To find her way home, she needed a Black Swan, and this came in the form of a decision to make a career change. She had a chance meeting with a classmate who worked in venture capital, and found the field to be intriguing. She eventually formed her first entrepreneurial venture, Aurora Venture Funding, a venture capital consulting company.

It was during this time of transition that another Wharton classmate, who had joined a non-profit organization in Senegal, invited her to go to Dakar for a vacation. She took this impactful step in December 2004. This was her first trip to Africa, and after ten days she was intrigued by what she saw, impressed by the people she met, and mesmerized by the Black

Swans she encountered. Looking for a reason to return to Dakar, she sourced a venture capital client in Senegal the next year (2005).

Senegal is a former French colony on Africa's Atlantic coast that became fully independent on August 20, 1960. In the words of Senegal's first president, Léopold Senghor, "Senegal is 90% Muslim, 5% Christian, and 100% animist." Senegal has a peaceful democratic history and is known for its religious and ethnic tolerance.

On her return to Senegal for business, she was disturbed, perplexed, and inspired by something she found. Despite the existence of many well-educated and entrepreneurial Senegalese, Africans had little to no access to early stage financing for business ventures. Close to 90% of the venture capital went to Europeans who created or expanded businesses that employed but did not offer equal opportunity or commensurate compensation to locally-based Senegalese. Dawn felt something was amiss here, but she also perceived an interesting discontinuity that might lead to an opportunity. She was distressed to learn that a major French-owned bank stated that it was in Senegal "to serve French companies" and had "no interest in providing loans to Africans." Nevertheless, she also saw an opportunity that was completely untapped because of the pool of Africans with business ideas that had not been developed because of a lack of money to get started.

"What can I bring to the agricultural value chain in Senegal to make it replicable and sustainable?" Dawn asked herself. The next inflection point was the answer to this question. In 2007 she decided to create a venture capital fund that would invest strategically to support and expand the agricultural value chain in Senegal. This was the start of Aventura Investment Partners. Dawn was finally home. Dawn had found her purpose in life. She realized this one day when she said to an early investor, spontaneously, "I am not doing this 'for fun.' This is serious for me. This is what I want to do for the rest of my life."

"It is interesting that agriculture is seen as one of the causes of endemic poverty in Africa, because I see it as one of the solutions to the problems of poverty," Dawn explained. "There are no big hits in this industry and in these companies. There are big risks and there is not yet broad management bandwidth. But long-term I think there is a payoff to supporting African agri-business and to providing the means to help it rise from subsistence to profitability."

Dawn's analysis of the challenge of developing the agricultural sector in Senegal was that no single investment could succeed in isolation. The problem started with the health of the farmers, who were frequently women, and in particular during and immediately after their pregnancies. Accordingly, Dawn's first investment was in a maternity clinic. Her strategic plan calls for investments in the full range of weak points in the farming business, including seeds, plowing, harvesting, refrigeration, marketing, and every other step needed to make Senegalese agriculture sustainable and profitable. The simple but elusive transition of farming from a barter- to a cash-based business holds the potential to change everything.

Dawn's next investment was in a company that provides machinery services to farmers to plow and harvest fields in northern Senegal. Charging the equivalent of US$60 per hectare, Dawn was warned that subsistence farmers would not have the cash to pay for the services her company would provide. Her experience is that farmers not only have the cash(which she requires to be paid in advance) but that she has a waiting list of farmers who have requested the service.

"What makes me passionate is that I truly believe that businesses can be the route to development, much more so than donations and more traditional forms of government-to-government assistance. There is power for good in business, and this is what my father represented. Business leaders with wealth and influence can be a powerful force for good. I think that the keys to success are to make management roles and ownership opportunities available to rural Senegalese. I want to offer opportunity to those to whom opportunity has been limited – especially to women in rural zones."

Dawn and Money

"I am confident that I will be well-off, but making money is not on my list of priorities. I believe that it is possible to make money and at the same time to have a positive impact on the lives of people in need. My top priority is to have a positive impact on people's lives. I will probably never be a wealthy philanthropist. Furthermore, I think that empowering people to rise above a subsistence living is a more valuable contribution to improving lives than making financial donations."

"Lots of things came together for me in Senegal," Dawn explained. "The realization that I had been enormously lucky to have been born where I was, when I was, and to have a father who gave me faith in myself and the courage to carry out my convictions. I felt a strong sense of gratitude for my luck, and a responsibility to try to empower those who had been less lucky than I. My life's mission is to offer economic opportunity to those, especially women, who were born into less favorable circumstances. The focus of the business is to make money but at the same time to give opportunities to people who never had opportunities. Aventura is a business solution to a problem that charity hasn't been able to solve after many years of trying, which is endemic poverty and underdevelopment in agricultural communities in Africa."

I spoke to one of Dawn's close friends, Ann Daverio, an accomplished woman whose professional journey has taken her to senior levels of both the treasury and finance tracks of General Motors and banking in Europe. Ann had an interesting comment on Dawn's personality. "Dawn is a true believer when she takes on a project. This is a great asset to her because she has no doubts about its value or ultimate success. She also has a unique ability to evaluate a person quickly, but non-judgmentally. She can quickly analyze how someone thinks and she has good judgment about potential business partners. This ability to size up people is one of the reasons that Dawn has been successful. She wants to have an impact on as many people as possible and she has no time to waste."

The Challenge of Charity

We talked about charity, government development assistance, and impact investing. "I think that charity has a role. For example, there is no possibility of making a profit from the operation of a home for battered women. This must be supported by philanthropy. Similarly, a school for disabled children cannot be run as a business and must be supported by philanthropy. But philanthropy can kill the entrepreneurial spirit in people. The NGO [*non-governmental organizations*] sector can be a threat to economic development. There are countries that are permanently disabled by development assistance. My goal is to help break this cycle of dependency by creating businesses, jobs, and self-sufficiency."

Malaria is endemic in Senegal. Everybody needs to sleep under a mosquito net. A Senegalese entrepreneur started a company that manufactured and sold mosquito nets. He created jobs, made money, and helped to combat a debilitating disease that puts all Senegalese at risk. "So what happens?" Dawn asked with a mixture of incredulity and exasperation. "The U.S. Agency for International Development donates a million mosquito nets to the government of Senegal, thinking that it was doing the country a big favor. The consequence was that the entrepreneur was forced out of business, people lost jobs, and a black market in stolen mosquito nets popped up overnight. No good came of this well-intentioned donation, and there were many negative consequences."

"Our tractor business is also at risk for the same reason," she continued. "If China decides to donate 1,000 cheap tractors, we will go out of business. And there will be a waterfall of secondary effects. Because the tractors will be donated as a one-off proposition, there will be no spare parts or maintenance facilities and when the tractors break they will be worthless. The farmers will revert to their subsistence businesses and the endless cycle of poverty and dependency will resume. This is one of the reasons I feel it is so important to develop my business. The Senegalese need jobs, rural value chain services, and access to capital, not handouts and misguided assistance."

Who Is Dawn Hines?

Dawn leaps out of bed every morning with a burst of energy. As far as I can tell, she has been leaping out of bed every morning since she was fourteen. I have such admiration and affection for this good-hearted but hard-headed woman. She went through a challenging intellectual, spiritual, and emotional journey, and discovered her own inner spirituality as well as her direction in life. While she has not studied Buddhism, I see in her the kind of person whom The Buddha hoped to inspire:

> ...he [The Buddha] would say that a person seeking enlightenment must be 'energetic, resolute and persevering' in pursuing these 'helpful,' 'wholesome,' or 'skillful' states that would promote spiritual health...instead of simply avoiding violence, an aspirant must behave gently and kindly to everything and everybody; [she] must cultivate thoughts of loving-kindness to counter any incipient feelings of ill will.

And, returning to the start of this chapter to bring it full circle, Dawn has fully embraced the idealism of my generation, but has taken the implementation of these ideals to an entirely different and more practical level. Instead of anger and protest, Dawn applies strong business skills (the very skills that we denigrated and excoriated in 1969!) and a commitment to impact, all softened with compassion and care for others. She is intensely ambitious, but not so much for herself as for the African farmers she is committed to empowering. The consequences are exciting to me, and I see opportunities for others to follow her leadership. She is contributing to the enhancement of human flourishing, a worthy goal if there ever was one.

Moving on to Abidjan

We now embark on one of the shortest journeys we will take in this book – 1,117 miles southeast from Dakar to Abidjan, formerly the capital of Côte d'Ivoire. In 1983, the capital was moved a three-hour drive north of Abidjan to Yamoussoukro, coincidentally the birthplace of then-President Félix Houphouët-Boigny. Senegal and Côte d'Ivoire share the heritage and burden of slavery and French colonialism, but not much else. Contrary to widely-held but ill-informed opinions, "Africa" really only applies to the geographic outline of a continent. Africa is endlessly diverse – historically, culturally, linguistically, and gastronomically.

Compassionate Capitalist

Eric Kacou

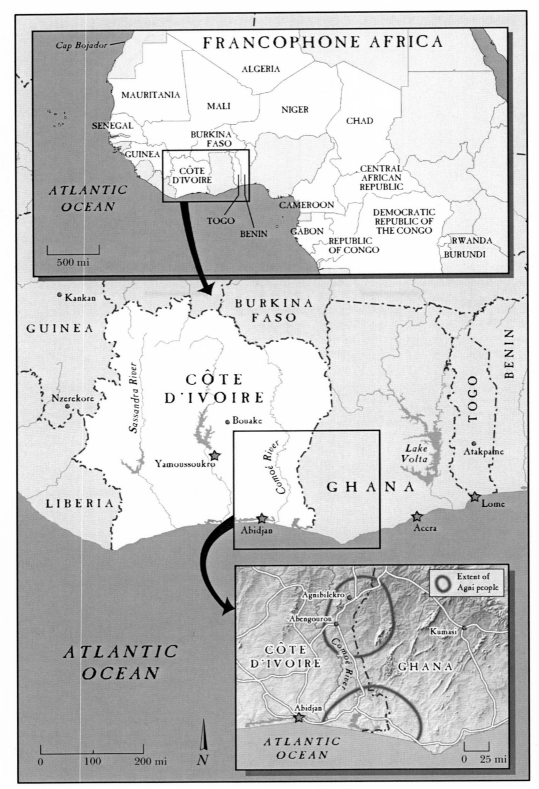

Compassionate Capitalist: Eric Kacou

The Akan People

There is something special about the Akan people of West Africa. Many of them were sold into slavery in the eighteenth and nineteenth centuries and ended up working on plantations in the New World, but they had an inner spirit and resilience that manifested itself repeatedly and could not be suppressed. Frederick Douglass, a great African American leader who was born into slavery, was Akan. W.E.B. Dubois, another great African American intellectual and leader, was Akan. Marcus Garvey, a Jamaican activist and proponent of Black empowerment, was Akan. Kofi Anan, the former Secretary General of the United Nations, is Akan. The hero of this chapter, Eric Kacou, is Akan.

According to oral tradition, the Akan people of West Africa originated in the northeastern part of the African continent, probably in the area now called Egypt. In the sixth century CE, the Akan migrated across the Sahara to present-day Ghana. Their society evolved and developed as, unknown to them, Europeans were timidly venturing down the western coast of Africa, still laboring under the illusion of knowledge that just past Cap Bojador, the world would come to an end and their ships would fall off. Finally, in 1434, one of Prince Henry the Navigator's captains, Gil Eannes, sailed his ship past the perceived point of no return, and returned safely to Sagres. More assertive voyages followed by the Portuguese and other Europeans in their quest for riches, empire, and bragging rights. In 1637, the French first made contact with the area now known as the Côte d'Ivoire.

Human civilization was highly developed in West Africa at this time, with hundreds of kingdoms flourishing and competing. Even in the twenty-first century, Africa is still the most linguistically diverse region in the world, reflecting the continent's genetic diversity, itself a consequence of being the geographical origin of the human race. By the end of the seventeenth century, the slave trade was one of the reasons that the economy was thriving along the "Gold Coast" (which later became Ghana), as some African tribes were profiting handsomely from their participation in the merchandising of humans. The Asanti of Ghana, for example, traded slaves for guns, which permitted them to expand their empire and acquire land, riches, and more slaves to perpetuate the cycle.

As a result of a feud over tribal succession, the Akan fled west from Ghana and the Asanti in the 1750s. Led by a strong and determined leader named Queen Pokou, the Akan understood that the alternative to flight was to be sold into slavery in the New World. According to legend and oral tradition, when the Akan reached the Comoé River, which marked the boundary of the Asanti Kingdom, with the Asanti warriors in hot pursuit, they were stopped by turbulent water which was impossible to cross. The high priest of the Akan conferred with the spirit of the waters and reported that the sacrifice of a human baby would be required for the tribe safely to cross the river. Queen Pokou stepped forward and immediately threw her infant son into the river. She cried "Ba-ou-li!" "The child is dead!"

There are several versions of what happened next. One version reports that a gigantic tree sprouted on the bank of the river and bent over to the opposing bank, allowing the Akan to walk across. A second version recorded that an enormous herd of hippopotamuses swam into the river and formed a mammalian bridge over which the Akan walked. A third version – possibly Moses-inspired – called for a parting of the waters and the dry-footed march of the Akan across the bed of the Comoé.

In any case, the Akan successfully crossed the river, which once again resumed its impassible nature as soon as the Asanti warriors arrived. The Akan, now free from the threat of enslavement, settled in what is today the Côte d'Ivoire, and were henceforth known as the "Baoule," commemorating their Queen's selfless act. All Akan people trace their lineage to Queen Pokou, revered for sacrificing her son for the good of the tribe.

By the early years of the nineteenth century, Great Britain had banned the slave trade from the Gold Coast, although by 1874 it had claimed the area as a British Crown Colony. The Emancipation Proclamation in 1863 took the United States out of the slave trade equation, and other European nations followed suit by banning the trade in humans from the areas in Africa that they controlled.

Although the slave trade dwindled, the so-called "scramble for colonies" hit fever pitch in the second half of the nineteenth century, more as a consequence of European power politics than economic necessity, despite what the Marxists say. In 1884, a conference was called in Berlin by Chancellor Otto von Bismarck to regulate trade and colonization on the African continent. The outcome was that literally thousands of African kingdoms were reconfigured into about 50 European colonies. No consideration was paid to the interests of the Africans, their cultures, languages, or political organization. Africa was literally divided up by rulers with rulers, resulting in geographical absurdities that persist to this day.

France was "awarded" a broad swath of West Africa by the Berlin Conference, and by 1893, the Côte d'Ivoire became a French colony. This colonization was contended by some of the inhabitants, including a tribe called the Agni, a member of the larger Akan community. The Agni resisted the efforts by the French to impose control, even after colonization. The Agni, vitally interested in self-determination, resorted to both sabotage and circumvention to express their independence. The French, for their part, seemingly did everything possible to alienate the population. The French ignored the traditional leadership structure and chose collaborators for their compliance. This meant that the French would dismiss leaders who had been selected locally, replacing them with others who were not perceived as bearing legitimate authority. The regrouping or consolidating of villages to rationalize authority according to French organizational theory further disrupted the existing social structure of the Agni.

For the next 67 years the Côte d'Ivoire proved challenging for the French to administer as a colony, and eventually it was one of the seventeen African countries to declare independence in 1960. Independence started optimistically in the Côte d'Ivoire. Endowed with abundant natural resources (cocoa, timber, coffee, pineapples, and palm oil), most of which matched rising world demand, the country was cited as the economic miracle of African decolonization. Nevertheless, this economic success based on raw materials masked an underlying challenge which would come back to haunt the country in future years. This challenge was the lack of home-grown entrepreneurs and the absence of local value-added products and services. Even the cocoa was exported in an unprocessed state for the next fifty years. Economic value was extracted from the people and products but not returned as investment.

Introducing Eric Kacou

We now, however, step backward a few paces from the macroeconomic to the personal in order to introduce the next hero of this book, Eric Kacou, the second *Compassionate Capitalist*. Eric was born in Abidjan on February 1, 1976, the sixteenth year after the Ivory Coast gained independence from France and at a time of prosperity, due to abundant natural resources and political stability under the paternal eye of President Félix Houphouët-Boigny.

At the time of Eric's birth, his mother, Chantal Yoboua Djedje, was a senior in college. His father, Germain Kacou, was a professor of industrial design at the Center for Technical Studies and worked for the national power company and other employers. They were both Akan and Agni, from the village of Agnibi Lekro, located in the eastern part of the country near the border with Ghana.

Unfortunately, the optimism and prosperity of the first years of Ivoirian independence did not last. A decline in world prices for commodities, an increase in the price of imports, towering foreign debt incurred to fuel the grandiose ambitions of an authoritarian leader, extensive corruption, and governmental belt-tightening that alienated the broader population, all contributed to a gradual decline in the country's fortunes.

The French attitude towards the Côte d'Ivoire was no different than its attitude toward Senegal, which we visited in the immediately preceding chapter. The colonial power captured the value of the nation's natural resources, excluded the country's citizens from all but menial participation in the economy, and progressively bled the country dry, leaving poverty, disease, underdevelopment, dependency, and despair as its legacy. I have always believed in the importance of applying the principle of contemporaneity to analyzing history, but from my twenty-first century perspective, the behavior of the French (and all colonialists) is simply inexcusable. I find this behavior difficult to forgive.

When Eric was 11 years old, in 1987, the nation's debt had become unmanageable, and the government unilaterally suspended payments to foreign creditors. President Houphouët-Boigny, having been in office for thirty years, was losing his ability to rally the country. He passed away when Eric was 17 years old and in his final year of high school.

Eric attended boarding school in the Côte d'Ivoire from the age of 9 through high school. He chose to leave his native land to pursue his university education and earned his under-graduate degree in 1997 from the *École des Hautes Études Commerciales* (HEC) in Montréal. Perhaps that was his DRD4-7r gene kicking in, or maybe he had a foreboding about Ivoirian politics.

In any case, the Ivoirian military took control through a *coup d'état* two years later. The First Civil War started in 2002 when Eric was 26. The Second Civil War started in 2010 when he was 34 years old. His mother's home in Abidjan was looted and his family urged him to stay away. This was a challenging period in the history of his country, and Eric was lucky to avoid the worst of the calamity, not that differently from Chanthol Sun, whom we met two chapters ago.

"These conflicts are really a single conflict, going back 20-25 years," Eric stated, "and the roots are in a power struggle between groups who are fighting for dominance. The underlying causes of the power struggle are the lack of an effective governance structure and the civil institutions that empower people. This is the sad story of underdevelopment and the vicious cycle that keeps a country poor and in conflict. Development is truly freedom. If you invest in education, then the necessary civil institutions develop. But you cannot invest in education if the society is disrupted by conflict. In fact, education is one of the first things to go."

"I do not subscribe to the theory that the conflict in the Ivory Coast is religious," stated Eric with conviction. "Religion is not the cause of the conflict, but a tool used by the leaders. The Ivory Coast is quite diverse in terms of religions, with Islam and Christianity the most prominent imports. The powerful may invoke religion because they feel this will motivate a large group of followers, but the people themselves are not primarily motivated by religious animosity."

An Akan Man of the Modern Era

Having learned something about the Akan and the Agni, I asked Eric about his ancestors and origins. He explained that the Agni today number about 600,000 individuals who share a common language, set of beliefs, and profession (cocoa farmers in the case of Eric's tribe). This tribe is governed by 3-4 kings, whose roles are now largely symbolic but who are responsible for maintaining tribal traditions. Eric's lineage is distinguished. Both grandfathers were part of royal families, although the system is matrilineal, presumably in homage to Queen Pokou. One of his grandmothers was the niece of the king. One of Eric's uncles is a current king. The process of choosing the next generation of leaders is complicated. Those chosen for future leadership roles are raised outside their family, in order to teach them humility.

Eric noted ironically (irony is as far as he will go; there is no cynicism in this good man) that the borders drawn by Europeans in 1884-5 during the Berlin Conference had little to do with the way tribes were organized or where they lived. In fact, the people of Eric's tribe in the eastern part of the Côte d'Ivoire are closely related to the people in the western part of Ghana. So, although the Côte d'Ivoire was "French" and Ghana was "English," the original linguistic, social, cultural and business boundaries were different from those superimposed on the West African landscape. A farmer, he laughed, might sleep in his home in the Côte d'Ivoire, but, unwittingly, tend his cocoa crop in Ghana, a short walk from his bedroom.

I asked Eric about the impact of colonization on the social organization of Ivoirian society. He responded that the disruption was subtle, but important. The French educated and installed in power those with whom they did business, not necessarily those who would have been chosen by the traditional methodology. The consequence was a profound disruption of traditional forms of indigenous leadership.

Eric's tribe has a traditional set of beliefs based on a reverence for nature and ancestors. There is not a single god, but a more pantheistic belief in the deity of all things, from the earth to the ocean. Monotheism was introduced to the region through Islam and Christianity, and interestingly, both took root. Today, according to Eric's estimate, about 40% of Ivoirians are Muslim, 40% are Christian, and 20% are a mixture of other religions, including Buddhism. Everyone is an animist. Eric grew up a Roman Catholic, by choice.

Eric is above all else a compassionate person, an altruist. "My compassion comes from my self-perception of having been lucky," he stated with conviction. He genuinely believes this. Fate determined that he would be successful, and he celebrates this luck by helping others, which is a uniquely self-determined path. In Eric's case, I perceive that his tendency to ascribe his path in life to fate is primarily out of humility; in his actions he is an exemplar of free will.

Eric's Black Swans

Eric attended secondary school at a boarding school located 250 kilometers north of his ancestral village. From the age of 9 to 16, he lived away from home, but modestly declines to attribute this to an intention to prepare him for a leadership role in his tribe. This was a formative experience for him because the school was a true meritocracy. Family or wealth did not matter. (The school was sponsored by the government and everybody had a scholarship.) Part of the formative experience was that he had frequent malaria infections, one of which was nearly fatal. Staggering to his mentor's home, he was by his estimation only hours from death when he was given care. This was Eric's first Black Swan. He emerged from this experience with a strong sense that he had survived for a reason, which was to help others and to live a life of service.

Another Black Swan occurred when he was in high school. As he recounted in an interview with the online magazine *Next Billion*, "The seminal event [*was*] a seminar in high school where we visited successful leaders across sectors in Côte d'Ivoire. The entrepreneurs clearly stood out in my opinion... They [*were the*] most interesting, innovative and passionate... [*they*] seemed to be the ones who were able to maintain the greatest control over their destiny."

Looking back, he feels that this seminar had been a turning point in terms of setting his direction, which was that he wanted to "make a difference in the lives of others," but that it took a number of years before it became clear how he would accomplish this goal.

Aimé Bwakira

By the late 1980s, when he was approaching high school age, the Ivoirian economic and political miracle was fraying at the edges. For college, as previously noted, he attended HEC Montréal. He wanted to study business and thought that North America would be the best place. In addition, he did not speak English yet. He attended the University of Montréal from 1994 to 1996, earning his undergraduate degree in two-and-one-half years. In Montreal he met and became lifelong friends with Aimé Bwakira. Aimé was born in Bujumbura, Burundi to a Burundian father and a Rwandan mother. Aimé is one of the most perfectly bi-lingual and bi-cultural individuals I have encountered, despite the fact that all his schooling (even in New York) was in the French system. This made him, to my way of thinking, a unique informant.

"Eric was the best man at my wedding. My mother 'adopted' him as another child in our family. I don't know if it is a coincidence, but his daughter's given name is the same as my mother's," he began. "Eric is a man of immense integrity who is transparent in his dealings with all and unwavering in his adherence to his principles. He is very positive. He wants to make the world a better place. Eric is a spiritual person whose generosity is heartfelt. Just a wonderful human being. What you see is what you get and that has been the case since we were 18-year olds together in Montréal."

Eric Enters the Working World

In Eric's senior year at HEC he had several offers, and accepted a job with Monitor Group, a strategy consulting firm. After three years with Monitor Group, in 2000 he took a job with *ontheFrontier*, a new firm founded by Michael Fairbanks with the mission to enhance competitiveness in emerging economies. He explained that *ontheFrontier* had been engaged by President Paul Kagame and the Government of Rwanda. Eric encountered his next Black Swan when he was assigned in 2001 as a junior member of the team to work with the Rwanda National Innovation and Competitiveness Program. "This engagement had an enormous impact on me. It was a massive transformation – a once-in-a-lifetime opportunity to be inspired. I learned that great things can be accomplished as a result of vision." I observed that President Kagame's press is mixed, and Eric did not argue with the ambivalence that people have about him. "But," he went on, "he is a real visionary. He cares for his country. And he has the ability to get things done." I reflected on how similar this perception was to Chanthol Sun's evaluation of Hun Sen. I find that the capacity to forgive that these two men (and others, as will be explained later) share is remarkable and unusual. I learned a great deal about the concept of forgiveness from Eric.

Eric wrote a book in 2010 which was published by Wharton School Publishing. In this volume, to which we will refer in more detail soon, he summarized his analysis of what was accomplished by President Kagame in Rwanda: "The nation's biggest innovation is its reframing of the discussion around wealth creation as opposed to poverty alleviation."

Nevertheless, Eric did not leap to the defense of President Kagame. "Rwanda has done pretty well. It is one of Africa's success stories. But you must remember that 14 years is a short period of time in the life of a country. And it is easier to fix infrastructure than it is to change people and their mindsets." I sensed a calm, reflective, and long-term thinker at work. He is clearly not sufficiently satisfied with Rwanda to pronounce it a success, but neither is he quick to condemn its slow and uneven progress.

After two years of challenging and meaningful work with *ontheFrontier*, he decided that he needed to upgrade his skills. Accordingly, he applied to and was admitted by the MBA program at the Wharton School. Upon graduation from Wharton in 2004, Eric had several options but decided to return to *ontheFrontier*, which had matured into OTF Group. For the next six years (2004 to 2010), he worked for OTF in Kigali and Johannesburg, first as a manager, next as Regional Director for Africa and finally as Global Managing Director. His engagements included work in Burundi, Angola, Southern Sudan, and Mali, in addition to Rwanda. In 2009, he was invited to advise the Presidential Commission on Competitiveness in Haiti. OTF was a crucible for Eric, where he forged his theory of "survival traps" and "mindsets" which would eventually find intellectual expression in his book and practical expression in the company he would form.

In 2010, sensing a personal sea change, Eric applied to the John F. Kennedy School for a one-year program as a Mason Fellow. I asked him why he did this. It seems there were four reasons. First, he had the entrepreneurial "itch," and wanted to start his own company. Second, he felt that the opportunities at OTF were not well-aligned with his personal goals. Third, he had a non-compete obligation to OTF and was not able to start his own company in the same business for a year. Fourth, he was working on the book that articulated his strategies for development. His year at the Kennedy School allowed him to accomplish all these goals, as well as to develop a business plan with Rob Henning, who would become his co-founder, for the company they called Entrepreneurial Solutions for Prosperity (ESP) Partners. "I decided that I should be a vehicle to give to others the good life that I had been given," Eric reflected, years later.

The Formation of ESPartners

"The reason we started ESPartners was," Rob explained, "that despite our obvious differences, Eric and I had common beliefs, values, and experiences. We also had the same goals. Over time, we built trust. We shared the conviction that we could make a difference in the lives of others."

ESPartners opened for business in January 2011 to provide "entrepreneurs and other leaders with the right mix of insights and capital needed for prosperity." The company's fundamental proposition is contained in the book Eric wrote and published in 2010. As he explained at the start of the book:

> Understanding the unique nature of BoP markets, especially Africa, enables us to identify and address the barriers to transformational change. The important component is to see opportunities where others see the need to fix problems.

He saw two big obstacles to success. First were "survival traps:"

> The Survival Trap is a vicious cycle that keeps individuals, businesses and leaders in the developing world pursuing the same strategies in the face of chronic problems. This habitual process robs them of the power to solve their problems and catalyze significant change... stakeholders stuck in The Survival Trap become overwhelmed by their operating reality and its difficulties. As a result, they develop reactive mindsets that fail to imagine solutions beyond their immediate challenges.

Second, and just as challenging, were "mindsets:"

> Focusing solely on 'operating reality' leads stakeholders to consider generic or massive solutions, to shift the locus of responsibility, and ultimately to reinforce feelings of powerlessness. Instead of confronting reality, one ends up shifting responsibility for the challenges one faces. Focusing on mindset, however, invites stakeholders to recognize the

central role individuals play in bringing change to massive systems. That realization is powerful because it makes substantial change possible.

ESPartners has worked in Côte d'Ivoire, Rwanda, Uganda, and Haiti. I asked Eric how things are going. He was – I am not sure if it was humble, diffident, or realistic – not willing to emote about its success. He said that business has been "O.K." I asked him how he defines success. "Three ways. First, you must have the right team. Second, you must have customers, especially repeat customers. And third, you must make sure there is impact – institutions created and flourishing, businesses started and successful."

I asked Eric if ESPartners was his life's work, or if something else was next. He said that it was a little too early to tell what his life's work would be (he is only 39 and became a father for the first time only in March 2015.) He said that if he were invited to run a big institution that would inject billions into Africa, he would consider it. Eric said, "I want to be involved in solutions; the bigger the scale, the better. And so I need to learn, adjust, twist and change as opportunities present themselves."

Who Is Eric Kacou?

Eric put a lot of himself into his book. I think that two sentences near the beginning of the book summarize well who he is:

> *In an era in which no one knows what is the most effective way to build political democracies in the developing world, freedom of choice in the market can be a place where dignity and the democratic exercise of free choice can be promoted. If we can democratize access to prosperity, we increase society's ability to build institutions and increase the potential impact of leaders...*

Eric dreams about a better world and takes action to make the world a better place. He is an impact-driven person. While he is a theorist and an intellectual, his primary goals in life are to bring about change and to alleviate suffering. He does not insist on purity or a lack of blemishes. He deals with the world on its own terms. Eric is an individual of impeccable integrity, but he does not insist that others match his level of integrity before he agrees to help them. He is a compromiser and a realist.

And Eric, please do not forget, is an Akan person. The Akan are fiercely independent, courageous, self-sacrificing for the good of the larger community, astutely intellectual, inspiring, and consensus-building. Eric is a worthy inheritor of this lineage, from Queen Pokou and Frederick Douglass, all the way through to Kofi Annan.

Eric is a large person, both as to his corporeal presence and the size of his heart. I have never seen him frown. Despite working on the frontlines of grief and misery, he is endlessly optimistic and yet perfectly stable. I am proud to call him my friend and feel the greatest respect and affection for this citizen of the world who has committed his life's work to having a positive impact on those less fortunate then himself.

Moving on to Lima

We next travel from Abidjan (5° north latitude), on the west coast of the African continent to Lima (12° south latitude), on the west coast of the South American continent, a journey almost due west of 5,156 miles, crossing the Atlantic Ocean, the Equator and the broad expanse of the Amazon Basin as well as the mighty Andes. We will leave behind the bitter aftertaste of French colonialism, only to encounter the equally rancid residue of Spanish colonialism. Six modern heroes and heroines so far, each attempting to overcome the inequities and frightful legacy of the racist arrogance of power.

Compassionate Capitalist

Rosanna Ramos Velita

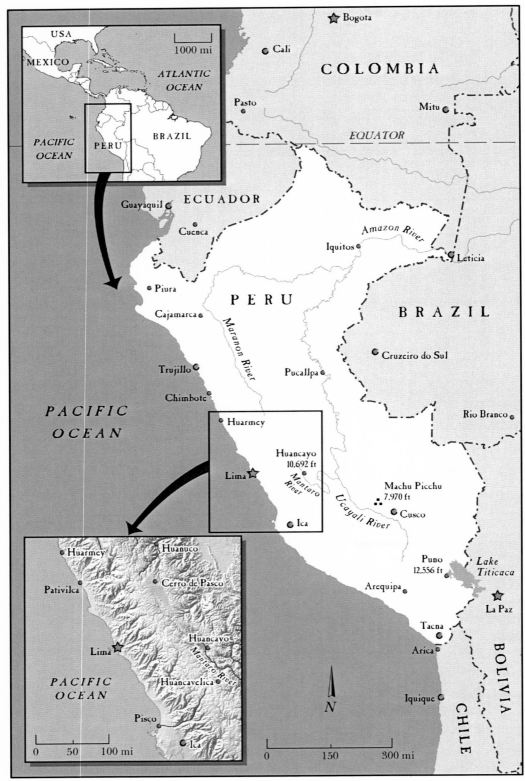

Compassionate Capitalist: Rosanna Ramos Velita

Rosanna's Roots

The story of Rosanna Ramos Velita starts in two Peruvian cities, one a small fishing village northwest of Lima and the other a mountain town due east of Lima. Not very different from three others who have recently been introduced – Boediono, Chanthol Sun, and Eric Kacou – Rosanna's origins are in small towns where life has been static for generations. Life was digestible, to be sure, but unchanging for most of the residents. Opportunity was limited and generally defined by what your forebears had done.

"The Spanish conquest came about 500 years ago," Rosanna began, dispassionately. "As a consequence, most Peruvians are of mixed blood. One interesting demographic is that the amount of Spanish blood in Peruvians is inversely proportional to the elevation at which the inhabitants lived, since the Spaniards did not go too far into the Andes. I do not have good genealogical information for the generations before my grandparents, but I must assume that my ancestors have been in Peru forever, although we undoubtedly have some Spanish blood in our line."

"My mother came from an Andean city called Huancayo, which is in the Peruvian central highlands at an elevation of close to 11,000 feet. It is about 200 miles east of Lima. Although the area was inhabited as early as 500 BCE, the city itself was 'founded' in 1572 by the Spanish, forty years after Francisco Pizarro defeated the Inca Emperor Atahuallpa in the northern Peruvian highland city of Cajamarca, itself at an elevation of over 9,000 feet."

"My maternal grandparents had four daughters. Although he had not attended a university, my grandfather was determined that his daughters would do so. Accordingly, my mother attended the Universidad San Marcos in Lima and studied pharmacy."

"My father was from a fishing village called Huarmey, located 175 miles up the coast to the northwest of Lima. 'Huarmey' translates as 'City of Women.' It was a tiny, very poor village. Even as late as the 1970s it had no electricity. He eventually studied medicine at the Universidad San Marcos in Lima and became a psychiatrist. My parents met at the university. My father joined the military after graduation and was sent to the city of Ica to work in the military hospital there."

"This is how I came to be born in Lima in 1962, but to move to Ica when I was a very small child. Ica is located about 160 miles southeast of Lima. It had been inhabited for centuries, but the Spanish conquistadors claimed to have 'founded' the city in 1563, nine years before they 'founded' my mother's hometown." Ica lies near the active boundary of the Nazca and South American tectonic plates and suffered severe damage and loss of life in an earthquake in 2007. It also lies on the border of the Atacama Desert and has one of the driest climates in the world.

"My mother and father worked very hard. They were devoted to their work. They never took vacations. I grew up in a culture that emphasized hard work. I never knew anything else."

"One of my mother's sisters eventually became the first from our family to go abroad. This came about when my grandfather gave her a trip to Europe as a graduation present. She returned to France to study for a Ph.D. in gynecology and fell in love with a Frenchman. This was a lightning strike for our family and would soon change everything, especially for me. This aunt, Cristina Velita Laboureix, is now the Peruvian Ambassador to France."

"My first personal inflection point was when I was 13 and my Aunt Cristina invited me to go to France for the summer of 1975. My parents did not think much of the idea, but I was determined to go, and I did. I returned home at the end of the summer, but everything had changed for me." Here it is again: whether it is caused by the DR4R-7r gene or something else, Rosanna is the sixth out of six (so far) of my heroes and heroines to have been driven by a sense of adventure, fueled by insatiable curiosity.

Early Influences

"My maternal grandfather and my father both believed in me and expected a lot. They had high expectations. I was deeply influenced by their support, which made no allowances for my being a girl. Most of my role models were male, but that had no negative influence. I never believed that there were barriers to me because of my gender."

The unconditional support that she received from her maternal grandfather and father, combined with their high expectations for her success, were unquestionably important sources of who Rosanna is today. This is a universal phenomenon. I know this to be true because I have observed the consequences across continents, cultures, religions, ethnicities, and languages. Every one of the women in this book had strong support from a father and/or a grandfather. Girls who, at an early age, get strong support from the important men in their lives grow up brave and harmless.

"I grew up in the Catholic religion, but I would not say that the theology or doctrine was that important to me. Our family was strict in its observances, but it was mostly to follow the normal church traditions rather than to impart values. We already had family values that did not require validation by a church hierarchy. I also attended schools that were run and taught by Spanish nuns. They were also strict, but I was an excellent student, so I had good relationships with the nuns. The nuns taught me social values, such as respect for others, the need to give back, and the importance of fairness. I felt very privileged to have had such a good education."

The College Years

"Inspired by the example of Aunt Cristina, I decided to go to the United States for college and to study engineering. At that time, we knew nothing about the educational system in the U.S.

The Peruvian model was for a student to pick a subject and then stick with it for life. I had no idea that people could keep reinventing themselves. This was a key finding for me and made me realize that I had the freedom to become who I am today. The transition from surrendering to fate to believing in free will was breathtaking."

"In any case, it was not easy getting information about colleges and universities in the U.S., or studying English, or even learning how to take the required standardized tests. But I studied English on the weekends in Lima, which was quite an excursion, since even today it takes more than four hours to get from Ica to Lima by bus."

"My first encounter with racism," she stated without bitterness, "was when I went to the Roosevelt School in Lima (founded in 1946 and still in existence today) to take the SAT and the TOEFL. This was the school attended by expatriate children and the blue-eyed Peruvians who were more Spanish than local."

"I also learned about the Fulbright Foreign Student Program administered by the Institute for International Education (IIE). I applied and was accepted by the University of North Dakota in Grand Forks! It might as well have been on the moon for all I knew about North Dakota. But I was determined to study in the U.S., and this is where the IIE had awarded my scholarship, so I went."

"There were so few foreign students in North Dakota that we were all assigned to host families. My host family was of German extraction, and the father was the head of the Presbyterian Church in the mid-West. It was a great introduction for me to the United States. I earned my undergraduate degree in electrical engineering in the spring of 1984 from the University of North Dakota."

Rosanna spoke movingly about her gratitude for the opportunities she had been given, especially since none of her classmates from Ica had been able to aspire to anything remotely resembling her new life outside Peru. She felt a need to "give back" but did not yet know how to do so. Putting this strong sense of obligation into action would take a few more years.

Rosanna's Working Career Begins

This was not an auspicious time in Latin America and especially in Peru. Starting in the early 1980s, Latin America experienced a debt crisis that precipitated what is now called the "lost decade" when economic activity encountered significant headwinds and inflation ravaged most of the countries in the region. The economic crisis also kindled the rage of certain parts of the population, and the Maoist guerilla group called the "Shining Path" in Peru was one of the most violent of the radical groups. Rosanna decided to look for work in the United States rather than to return to uncertainty and danger in Peru. There was also little opportunity for meaningful work in Peru.

"In my senior year in North Dakota, I was interviewed by a number of companies and accepted an offer from AT&T Microelectronics to work in Allentown, Pennsylvania designing microchips. I would receive what to me was a very large salary of $27,800, an unheard-of sum in Peru. AT&T also sponsored me to earn my master's degree (in electric engineering) at Lehigh University. My thesis advisor at Lehigh suggested that I consider Wharton for an MBA instead of the Ph.D. in engineering that I was thinking about at Stanford. I investigated and learned about Wharton and the Lauder Institute, where I was admitted into the French track. This was my second inflection point and represented a radical change in my career path."

"My best friend at Wharton was Dina Weitzman, my polar opposite, a Jewish girl from Bergen County, New Jersey. We became best friends as soon as we met, and shared a bond that made us inseparable," remembered Rosanna with a warm and affectionate smile.

Twenty-four years later, Dina would reflect, "I was admitted to the Lauder Institute, and spent two deliriously happy years at Penn from 1990 to 1992. This was in no small part because Rosanna was in my class. We met on the first day of class and immediately became best friends for life."

"When I graduated from Wharton in 1992," recalled Rosanna, "Latin American markets were starting to open again as the debt crisis was reaching a resolution. I took a job with Bankers Trust and worked on Mergers and Acquisitions in Latin America."

"Meanwhile, in 1994, I became a U.S. citizen. I took a new job at UBS and started to enter the upper levels of management as a Senior Vice President. But I knew in my heart that my real interests lay elsewhere. I loved working in Latin America, but I still felt a need to give back. I also was forming a strong conviction that the way to relieve poverty in Latin America was to bring capital to people who previously had no access to financial services. I enjoyed the compensation I was receiving at UBS, but I also realized that compensation was not my principal goal, but only the means to allow me to attain my more important goals of having an impact on others in need."

The First Compassionate Entrepreneurial Venture

"After we graduated from Lauder, our lives diverged for the next eight years or so, although we kept in touch," continued Dina. "I took a job with a bank and was sent to Spain. I loved this as well. But towards the end of the decade, several trends emerged that brought us back together."

Rosanna and Dina decided that this was a perfect time to start a business focusing on the Hispanic market in the United States. They wanted to educate the Hispanic community about financial services, which were underused. At the same time, they wanted to be involved in selling these financial products (checking accounts, home mortgages, business loans, etc.) to the Hispanic community. They felt it was a win-win situation for the Hispanic community and for the financial services industry. They called their business eLuminas Capital. The only flaw was that they unwittingly picked exactly the wrong time to start this company because the bursting of the Internet Bubble in 2000 made financing impossible.

"This was a painful but instructive experience," Rosanna continued, "and taught me much that I later applied to the concept of micro-loans. When Dina and I pitched our idea to banks and other sources of funding, they generally responded with stereotypes. 'If you are poor, you don't deserve credit because you will not repay the loan,' went the usual drill. Dina and I understood that our concept was impossible to launch by ourselves, but we could not convince banks that this was a potentially lucrative as well as socially responsible business."

Rosanna and Dina were ahead of the wave. Muhammad Yunus was just beginning to articulate his concept of micro-finance; C.K. Prahalad and Stuart L. Hart had not yet published their seminal article on "Bottom of the Pyramid" markets; and Antony Bugg-Levine was eight years away from coining the phrase "Impact Investing."

At the same time, Citi was making a major move into the consumer financing business in emerging markets and asked Rosanna to take a full-time job as Chief Financial Officer of Global Marketing for Consumer Business. After a lot of soul-searching, she accepted. A worthy experiment with bad timing, eLuminas Capital quietly folded.

Never Underestimate the Impact of a Taco Lady

Rosanna learned that, contrary to Citi's experience in other emerging markets, the small borrowers in Mexico did not use their loans for consumption. Instead, they used the financing to re-invest in their businesses. And their best clients were women. She decided to investigate.

"I went to visit one of Citi's micro-loan customers in Mexico City, a woman who started with a one-burner taco stand. When I told her I was from Citi and I wanted to thank her for her business, she literally leapt across her kiosk and gave me a warm and lengthy hug. She expressed heartfelt appreciation for giving her the opportunity to change her life so that she could 'feed my children, send them to school, and put a roof over their heads.' She had taken three loans from Citi and repaid them all, on time and in full. Her husband, who had worked as a taxi driver, quit his job to work for her. She opened a second and then a third taco kiosk. She was succeeding as an entrepreneur without even knowing the word. The light bulb went on. In an instant, I knew what I wanted to do. Everything came together with the hug from the taco lady. My future course was set."

Rosanna came back to New York City accompanied by her Mexican Black Swan and spoke with her boss, Marjorie Magner, who at the time was chairman and CEO of Citi Group Global Consumer Business. Marge was also the chairman of the Citi Group Foundation, which had made substantial donations to Muhammad Yunus' Grameen Foundation.

Marge detected a new spark in Rosanna and introduced her to both Professor Yunus and Alex Counts, who had established Grameen Foundation in Washington, D.C. to spread the concept of micro-credit world-wide.

"I came to understand that finance can be a positive tool for the poor," said Rosanna with conviction and vehemence. "Finance does not have to be predatory. But this new understanding at first was disorienting, because my observations in the field were at variance with what I had been taught at Wharton and with the way in which financial institutions operated. Mainstream finance was dismissive of poor people, but I could see that poor people could be responsible customers."

Once she understood her mission in life, good things started happening. Alex Counts asked her to join the board of the Grameen Foundation in Washington. She quickly became the volunteer treasurer of the foundation and formed (and agreed to chair) a Latin American board of the foundation. Then Muhammad Yunus won the Nobel Peace Prize (2006) and suddenly micro-credit was a global phenomenon.

The Second Compassionate Entrepreneurial Venture

In 2007, Rosanna and Alex Counts travelled to Peru together to study the conditions for micro-credit. Her indistinct thoughts took shape, and she started looking for an opportunity either to start or to buy a bank to launch her own micro-credit institution in her homeland. Rosanna resigned from her job at Citi Group and went to work full-time pursuing her dream.

A friend at the Peruvian counterpart to the U.S. Securities and Exchange Commission brought to her attention a small bank in the city of Puno, at an altitude of 12,556 feet on the shores of Lake Titicaca, in southeastern Peru. This bank, which was beset by mismanagement, capital inadequacy, a large portfolio of non-performing loans, and a host of other problems, had been told by the Peruvian SEC that it would have to be sold or taken over by the government. The owners resisted either solution for almost a year, but finally agreed to sell their interests to Rosanna.

"It is very different doing a deal when you are investing your own money as opposed to being a banker," Rosanna explained. "Finally, I was able to secure a capital infusion from a private equity firm in Seattle called Elevar Equity. Elevar had experience in investing in micro-credit financial institutions, so I was confident that they would be a 'patient capital' investor."

I spoke with Maya Chorengel, one of the three co-founders of Elevar Equity. Elevar was founded in 2008, largely as a result of serendipity. The three co-founders were all pursuing careers in the financial services industry. "But," Maya began, "something was missing in our lives." One introduction led to another and they decided to go out on their own with a fund that specialized in impact investing.

Elevar started with a fund of $24 million and raised $70 million in a second fund. When I spoke to Maya, they were fund-raising for a third fund, this one also targeted at $70 million. The founders are committed to supporting the social and environmental goals of the companies in which they invest, but they also expect to make a profit that will satisfy their investors.

I asked Maya what they look for in an entrepreneur. "First, we look for true passion and a commitment to the customer. Second, we demand a high degree of professionalism. Third, our entrepreneurs must have multinational capabilities that transcend borders. Fourth, high integrity is essential. Fifth, the entrepreneur needs a local network in the location where the business will operate."

Elevar posted a photo of Rosanna on the home page of its website, with the following commentary:

> [Rosanna's] vision is to create a leading microfinance institution of scale, and the preeminent provider of financial services in Peru's rural market... [through] a profitable, deposit-taking, regulated bank that caters to the needs of the rural community in the southeast Andean region of Peru. [Her plan is to be] positioned as a leading community bank with a recognizable, trustworthy brand, strong consumer focus, cost-efficient culture, and a unique credit model focused on high-quality, underserved rural customers.

The deal closed in November 2010, and Rosanna became Chairman of the Board of Caja Rural los Andes, in Puno, Peru, with the tagline, "Banca de Inclusión Social." Her life's dream and abiding passion were finally realized and she was launched on her career to bring financial services to the poor, marginalized, and until now hopeless subsistence farmers in her native country.

Rosanna's model, as correctly analyzed by Elevar, was entirely new. Her model was based on the needs of the rural, hard-working poor. Lending decisions would be based on a ground-level understanding of the seasonal rhythms of subsistence farming in the high-altitude Andes, and not on credit scores. Over 70% of her customers are illiterate. They speak either Quechva (an Incan language that has no written form) or Aymara (another non-European language that is spoken, but not written, in southern Peru). Most of her customers are women. The women who cannot read or understand Spanish bring a child or younger relative who has learned the language, and with their support, they agree to the terms of the contract with a fingerprint, because they cannot sign their names.

I also spoke to Johanna Posada, another of the three co-founders of Elevar Equity. Johanna immediately felt an affinity with Rosanna, stating, "It was clear we were both very much speaking the same language. It is true that we both grew up in Latin America and that our common first language was Spanish, but when I say, 'speaking the same language,' it had more to do with our attitudes and approaches to social change through investments."

"Rosanna had such a passion to give back to Peru, and although she had not lived there in a number of years, she had maintained her local knowledge and contacts. She had so many characteristics that we look for in our entrepreneurs: she is articulate, determined, serious, tenacious, passionate, caring, patient, and stubborn."

Johanna and Maya feel very excited about their support for Rosanna. They also both mentioned that most people who enter large corporations lose their willingness to take risk, but this is something that Elevar evaluates as essential to success. Well-meaning amateurs, without hard skills, will find it difficult to succeed. Elevar looks for successful professionals who are willing to put the big salaries behind them, fly in economy, and get their boots muddy on the ground. This combination is just what they found in Rosanna.

"In my way, I want to bring about change. I am fed up with how unfair things are," Rosanna stated with fire in her eyes. "The exploitation of the poor and the power of the rich in Peru are wrong. The purpose of the revolutionaries, such as the Shining Path, is good, but of course violence never improves anything. My father was very political, and he even wanted me to enter politics. But I am a capitalist and chose economic empowerment as my vehicle to deliver social change. The more I work in the field of micro-credit in Peru, the more I believe that the right to health care and education are basic human rights, just as much as justice and freedom. Government institutions in Peru are weak and corrupt. I hope that what I am doing will help bring about change. When people gain access to financial services and break the vicious cycle of disenfranchisement, then things can change. Bringing opportunities for women, who then invest in their businesses, build homes, educate their children, and have a stake in the future – these are my goals. I want to equalize the right to finance and banking for even the poorest women with the least education. I want to start a virtuous cycle that will have no end."

Who Is Rosanna Ramos Velita?

We are now at the end of the sixth of this book's biographies. The first three – *Devoted to the Commonweal* – involved individuals who were having a positive impact on large numbers of people. In the case of Boediono, the number of people was literally in the hundreds of millions. But in the cases of the *Compassionate Capitalists*, the number of people affected is several degrees of magnitude smaller. Dawn Hines helps farmers to plow their fields, Eric Kacou's co-founder expressed frustration that the scale of their business is too small to have impact commensurate with the value of the services provided. And now we have Rosanna, who poses proudly for a photograph with the woman to whom she has just made a loan to buy a second cow. What is the meaning of scale in my universe of estimable individuals?

In certain endeavors, scale seems to matter. Bill Gates found that eliminating polio was not a simple matter of inoculating everyone. The root cause of polio and all the other diseases that held back poor societies was much deeper and more difficult to eradicate. Clean water, sanitary disposal of human waste, personal hygiene habits, and the entire chain of basic assumptions that rich countries take for granted were missing in poor countries. Billions of people lack these necessary preconditions to change, growth, and prosperity. Even Bill Gates' billions cannot solve these problems. And this is why scale is necessary but not sufficient.

I have learned that scale is a proximate cause but not the ultimate prerequisite for meaningful change. Society will change only when good people – Rosanna among them – by example and by direct, positive action democratize the financial services industry, one cow and one taco stand at a time. The individual attitude – the 'mindset' to use Eric Kacou's term – must precede the scale. Without the proper mindset – creating opportunity and wealth rather than simply alleviating poverty – scale is not likely to be successful. If enough people like Rosanna take enough small actions, one day a person like Steven Pinker will be able to write a book that explains how financial services became democratized and how this made the world a wealthier place, with more equity and more prosperity among those who previously had no hope.

Rosanna is a warm, caring, hard-nosed, and effective human being. She is creating a replicable model for change that will result in improved lives for people who for generations had no path out of poverty. Starting on a very small scale, one cow at a time, she is burning with ambition, but not for personal gain or fame. This is the most estimable of pursuits, and I have deep admiration and warm affection for Rosanna.

Moving on to Dhaka

We have now made six voyages together, and we are accumulating many Frequent Flyer points. Our next journey, a long one from Puno to Dhaka, will add 11,288 miles to our account. We will depart from Inca Manco Capac International Airport in Puno. The airport is named in honor of the (possibly mythical) founder of the Inca civilization in Cusco. It is designated "international" as an aspiration, since its only destination currently is Lima. The distinguishing feature of this airport is that, at 12,552 feet of elevation, it is one of the world's top ten highest airports and requires an exceptionally long runway. After stopping in Lima to change planes, we will cross the Andes, the great Amazonian Basin, the Atlantic Ocean, much of Africa, the Arabian Peninsula, the Bay of Bengal, and the broad expanse of India before finally landing in Dhaka, Bangladesh at Hazrat Shahjalal International Airport, named in honor of a respected Sufi saint. Because the airport in Dhaka is located at an elevation of just 27 feet, we will add 2.37 miles to our journey because of the descent from the altitude of the airport in Puno, which is 12,525 feet higher.

Compassionate Capitalist

Durreen Shahnaz

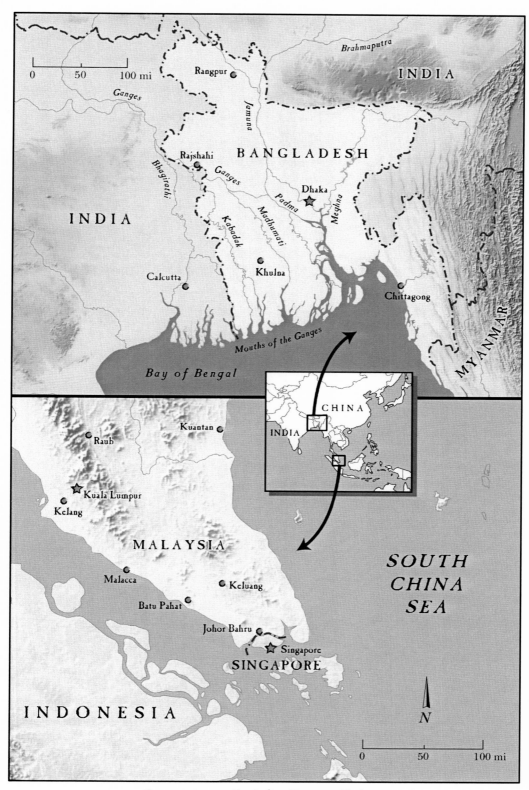

Compassionate Capitalist: Durreen Shahnaz

Every time I eat a tangerine, I think of Beirut in 1967, just before I had my innocence shattered forever by the Six-Day War in the Middle East, quickly followed by the horrors of 1968 – The Tet Offensive, the murder of Martin Luther King, Jr., the murder of Robert F. Kennedy, the siege of Columbia University and the arrest of 900 students in the early hours of a gentle spring morning. This was a sobering year, but it all started with a tangerine in the Beirut souk on a cold, damp afternoon in early 1967. A *mémoire involuntaire*, in Proustian terms.

I had graduated from high school in 1966, and, like so many young people at that time, I had been inspired by President John F. Kennedy. His exhortations to service were thrilling to me and corresponded perfectly to what I felt in my heart. The Peace Corps, in particular, was such an obviously persuasive concept that I immediately internalized its goals and methods. As Jack Vaughn, the second Director of the Peace Corps, so eloquently argued when presenting his budget request to the House Foreign Affairs Committee in 1968, "It costs less money to make peace than war."

I was determined, accordingly, to change the world for the better, and to work towards a future when the swords would be beaten into plowshares. My post-high school plan called first for a summer as a volunteer for an organization called Operation Crossroads Africa in Bangui, already noted above during the chapter on Dawn Hines. The second stage of the plan called for spending my freshman year in college at the American University of Beirut, preparing myself for a life of service as a citizen of the world. Then I would return to Columbia University to complete my college education. I had a vague idea about joining the U.S. Foreign Service after graduating, but eighteen-year-olds are famous for their short planning horizons, so I was not overly concerned about something that would happen in four more years.

Introducing Durreen Shahnaz

Meanwhile, unknown to me, a girl was about to be born in Dhaka, the largest city in the "East Wing" of Pakistan, which as a country was just one year older than I. In retrospect, what an unnerving coincidence that our paths, so utterly different and so many thousands of miles apart, would improbably cross and that we would find common ground, indeed a spiritual match of beliefs, values, and life goals. I, for one, can only marvel at the good fortune I had to meet Durreen Shahnaz and to learn so much from her about standards, resilience, optimism, tradition, and defiance. And so, I introduce my book's fourth *Compassionate Capitalist*, yet another *Homo sapiens* who inherited the DRD4-7r gene.

Durreen was born on April 24, 1968, twenty days after the assassination of Martin Luther King, Jr., and just as the protests at Columbia University were starting. Dhaka is one of the world's megacities, with a sprawling metropolitan population of over sixteen million inhabitants and growing at more than 4% annually, which is more than 1,700 boys and girls born every day of the year. Dhaka is also today the capital of a crowded country, with over 1,000 people living in every one of its 147,000 square kilometers (although not evenly distributed.)

Her ancestors on both sides were originally Persian and Muslim but had migrated to India by the time of her parents' births. Her grandfather had been sent to what was at that time eastern colonial India to manage government properties, which accounted for her birthplace. Her *de jure* nationality after partition and independence in 1947 was Pakistani.

Durreen was born female in a middle-class Muslim family with five children in a male-dominated society in one of the poorest societies in the world, during war and revolutionary ferment. This was not an auspicious beginning, but Durreen has succeeded to a degree that would have been unimaginable in 1968. She attributes much of her success in life to this ominous beginning, which she claims left her "defiant, optimistic, and self-sufficient."

I asked Durreen about the chronology of her family moving from Persia to India to East India/Pakistan. She explained that this happened "five generations ago" and mentioned that she had recently discovered a family genealogy that her father had written. She noted ruefully that the genealogy only followed the males in the family, and females were mentioned only as having borne males. But the genealogy did reveal her father's knowledge of the family tree, seven generations on her mother's side and six generations on her father's side.

Maternal Ancestry

According to this hand-written family history, on her maternal grandmother's side, the most distant ancestor, Lal Gazi Chowdhury, a local Muslim warlord, sided with Mir Kasem (the Nawab of Bengal from 1760 to 1763) who tried to eject the East India Company from Bengal. "Mir Kasem lost," noted the genealogy. "The British then instigated Maharaja (King) of Tripus to destroy the power and authority of the warlords who opposed them. The Maharaja defeated them, including Lal Gazi Chowdhury and took over their zamindari (feudal chiefs) under the authority of the British."

Her mother's great-grandfather married the daughter of a Kazi, who was himself the grand-son of a judge under the new judicial system introduced by the British. Her maternal grand-father was raised as an orphan because his father (Durreen's great-grandfather) had died of cholera. Durreen's maternal grandfather was a self-made man who went to law school in India and became a judge. He married his cousin, who was 11 years old at the time. Durreen's mother was the only child of this union, and she lived her early life in purdah, the practice of sex segregation in certain Islamic countries, which concealed women from men.

Paternal Ancestry

On her father's side, the family history begins in the mid-eighteenth century, with a jurist and theologian named Sharafuddin. The Nawab of Bengal appointed this ancestor as Kazi of Bedarabad Parganta, and in compensation was granted ownership of a sizable parcel of land to enjoy "La-Kheraz" (exempted from payment of land revenue tax.)

The grandson of Kazi Sharafuddin, Badinzzaman, inherited the title Kazi. "However," continued the hand-written document, "in about 1830, the British abolished the old judicial system of the Moguls and retained till then despite many years of British rule. New judges were appointed on cash salary for fixed terms. Consequently, halfway through his career, he lost his judgeship."

According to family lore, Durreen's paternal grandmother was to enter an arranged marriage at the age of 11 to a man whom she would meet for the first time on her wedding night. However, her great-grandfather caught the prospective groom smoking before the ceremony and peremptorily dismissed him. Since it was traditional that a girl must marry by sunset on the night of her betrothal or forever remain unmarried, her father asked a freeloader, who had crashed the wedding for the food, to marry her. He consented and their life together began before the sun set that day. The record reveals that they had eleven children, one of whom was Durreen's father.

Durreen's father was well-educated and attended Dhaka University after India's independence and simultaneous partition on August 15, 1947. He entered the London School of Economics, intending to earn a doctorate. However, his mother told him to return home and to take the Pakistani Civil Service Examination so that he would be able to earn a living and support his family. To his distress, but no doubt to his mother's satisfaction, he scored well enough to be first on the Civil Service list.

Durreen's father was, in her words, a "card-carrying communist at age 10." According to Durreen, he was unconcerned about money, just like his father, who would distribute family land to the poor. His sense of social justice carried over into the period of ferment in Eastern Pakistan during 1951-52 when the government proclaimed that Bengali must no longer be spoken or taught in schools, and that henceforward only Urdu would be allowed. This caused unrest and protest. Many lost their lives defending their right to use their mother tongue. Durreen's father was one of the leaders in this protest movement.

Her father's work as a civil servant assured the family would live in genteel poverty. Through dint of hard work, he rose in the ranks of the civil service (first of Pakistan and subsequently of Bangladesh) and became a Secretary in several ministries, including the ministries of education and energy.

Household Formation

Durreen's parents' marriage was also arranged. Her father's work as a civil servant required him frequently to be on assignment somewhere outside of Dhaka. The consequence of this lifestyle was that Durreen was raised mostly by her mother and maternal grandparents.

Durreen was raised in an intellectual environment, with what she describes as a theme of social justice that profoundly influenced her adult life. Certainly, the knowledge of her father's social activism, as a communist and as a Bangladeshi patriot, was of enormous importance to this impressionable and bright girl. She was also inspired by her father's commitment to service through his employment. She was raised in a family that felt an obligation to feed the poor, but in her words, it was always at "arm's length." This dissonance was something that she would actively seek to resolve in her professional career by shortening the distance between her heart and her deed.

The Bangladesh War of Independence

"Bangladesh is a language-based country," Durreen observed. "International Mother Language Day is February 21st, and this date was chosen because of the sacrifice of Bengali students on that day in 1952 at Dhaka University. The decision to secede from West Pakistan was taken in large part because of Pakistani suppression of the Bengali language. Language means everything to us and is a source of pride and national cohesion. In 1972, the teaching of English was stopped in schools in favor of providing all instruction in Bengali."

When Durreen was three years old, on March 25, 1971, East Pakistan seceded from its union with West Pakistan, and the war for Bangladesh's independence took place. The war lasted nine months and ended with the establishment of the People's Republic of Bangladesh. Pakistan resisted with extreme violence and gross human rights violations. Too many Bangladeshis died during this war.

The war was a Cold War proxy as well as a war for independence, and the United States will always bear some of the responsibility for its intensity and mayhem. At the time the war started, the United States was deeply involved in secret exchanges about opening up relations with the People's Republic of China. Henry Kissinger, at that point serving as National Security Advisor to President Richard M. Nixon, felt that both parties were on the verge of a breakthrough. Pakistan was serving as the mutually trusted intermediary in these discussions. According to Kissinger, "... to condemn these [human rights] violations would have destroyed the Pakistani channel." Since the Nixon administration considered the opening to China as essential to the national interests of the United States, Nixon and Kissinger ignored the frantic reports from American diplomats in Bangladesh and allowed Pakistan's genocide to go unchallenged. The U.S. went further, giving military assistance to Pakistan. In the last phase of the war, the US ordered a carrier battle group led by the USS Enterprise into the Bay of Bengal, in support of Pakistan. Many years later, Kissinger disingenuously asserted that ".. the results require no apology" and that "There was never the choice between the suffering in Bangladesh and the opening to China."

The Early Years

"My great-grandmothers were illiterate," Durreen began. "My grandmothers were able to sign their names. My mother was educated through the age of 19. All ten of my aunts and uncles were educated. The society changed over three generations such that my fourth generation had fewer impediments, although even educated women did not work outside the home. My mother lived a traditional life in purdah, but she had a rebellious streak. I am certain that I picked up on this rebelliousness as a small girl. Being defiant certainly helped."

"In addition," she continued, "after the war for independence there were fewer workers because so many of the men were killed. This made it imperative for women to come out of the home and out of purdah. War in this sense was an agent of social change. After the war, many foreigners came to Bangladesh under the auspices of non-governmental organizations (NGOs), and they also played a role in empowering women."

"Although my father was an atheist, the Muslim religion was a central part of my life from the moment of birth, even during the time when I went to college in the United States. I think of religion as a form of governance. It teaches values and it gives structure to your life. I learned Arabic before I learned Bengali so that I could read and memorize the Koran."

"Nevertheless, I always hated the restrictions that my religion placed on a woman. I had a friend at Wharton who was an Orthodox Jew. We became close friends when we discovered that we both hated the restrictions that our religions placed on women, which were virtually identical."

"As a child, I was not trained to be rational. My mother and grandmother threatened me with 'God's curse' if I misbehaved or did not practice my religion according to the precise instructions handed down to women through many generations of subjugation. As a child, I was taught that I should do good and help the poor because God would reward me. But it was an arm's length relationship and had nothing to do with my feelings of empathy or sympathy with the poor. My own personal code of ethics and my personal beliefs are now grounded in empathy and sympathy rather than expectation of divine reward or punishment."

Durreen's First Journey Begins

In 1982, when she was 14 years old, her father was appointed an Executive Director of the Asian Development Bank. He was posted to The Philippines and Durreen, speaking little English and with no experience with boys, went to 10th grade in the International (American) School in Manila, where the language of instruction was English and where boys and girls mixed freely. Initially startled and confounded by this overwhelming blend of new experiences and challenges, Durreen was driven to succeed. "I used Manila as my ticket out of a system that I didn't like," she stated.

When she was applying to colleges during her senior year in high school, she was drawn to Berkeley and Columbia because of their reputations for social activism, something to which I could attest through personal experience. Her parents opposed these schools as they were both coeducational and perceived as cesspools of liberalism, another point to which I could attest. Parents and daughter compromised on Smith College, a women's college in a semi-rural setting in Western Massachusetts. Ironically, I had grown up in the shadow of Smith College, at which my father was a professor from 1954 to 1968. Her college years, from 1985 to 1989, bracketed Durreen's self-described "feminist" period.

Durreen is a deeply spiritual person. "When I went to college at seventeen, religion at first gave me something to hold onto. I could recite a prayer when I was afraid, for example. But it also created confusion for me. I was never taught theology – I was simply required to memorize and to follow the rules. I never understood why the rules were established. I memorized most of the Koran, but I never understood its meaning. Questioning the rules was forbidden. But in college, I was taught to question everything. Smith was such a rational place that at first it created real confusion and internal conflict for me."

"Smith was remarkable because I started to question why things were the way they were. Coming from a restrictive society where I was always told what to think, the rational discourse at Smith was frightening but liberating. Other Bengali women became passive and accepted their lot in life as prescribed by centuries of tradition. I chose to fight."

"When I fell in love and decided to marry, the fact that my fiancé was a Christian was devastating to my family. They insisted that he convert to Islam, and that his conversion had to be heart-felt and not simply as an act of expediency to be permitted to marry me." He did convert – an act with which Durreen was not comfortable but to which she and her fiancé succumbed following a threat from her parents that, if he refused, she would never be allowed to come home.

"All traces of religion disappeared for me after the birth of my second daughter. My younger daughter was born with a congenital challenge, and my mother's reaction was to blame it on my defiance of God's will. She advised me to pray for my daughter's recovery, which struck me as ludicrously passive. God had nothing to do with a genetic mutation, and I was determined to find a medical solution to the challenge. Religion makes you blind to things so that you don't question why things are the way they are. I found my mother's religion to be stultifying, paternalistic, and simplistic."

Her sister Shabnam put her response to this challenge in perspective: "Whatever Durreen does has to be perfect. She disdains the acceptable. All her life is devoted to doing things better than they have to be. One of Durreen's daughters was born with ichthyosis. She has been relentless in her pursuit of a cure and has tried literally thousands of ways to help ease her child's suffering. In an effort to help other families with children who have this condition, she has kept a book that meticulously describes every attempt to alleviate the symptoms of the disease, both as regards the cream, lotion, or ointment, and also as regards to the result. She is the same way with her businesses. No detail is too small, and no effort is superfluous."

Durreen's Intellectual and Professional Journeys

"Growing up in a country that was highly dependent on foreign aid, I was made aware of two themes," she started with a steady gaze. "One was that, no matter how generous the aid from developed nations or NGOs, the need always exceeded the available funds by an enormous margin. The other was that the use of aid was most often dictated by the needs of the donors, whether they were countries or NGOs. And it was clear that the interests of the donors were largely unrelated to the needs of the country. There is a subculture of aid workers living extravagant lives in the developing world, spending vast sums on themselves and on projects that do little to help the poor of the countries that they purport to support. It was obvious to me that this was not working for the benefit of Bangladesh. I felt certain that there had to be a better way."

"When I went to college, I was a rebel, but I was also a realist. After graduating from Smith, I took a job on Wall Street with Morgan Stanley. I took this job because I wanted to go where the power was located and to learn how to use this power to help Bangladesh and the developing world more generally. For me," she said with a laugh, "Morgan Stanley was an anthropological field trip."

"After two years on Wall Street, I departed to work for Grameen Bank, which had been founded in 1983. At this time (1991-92), Professor Yunus and Grameen had not achieved the international recognition that was to come later, but they were already doing interesting things, and I spent these two years learning about micro-finance. I also had some ideas about how to empower people in the developing world by giving them better market access."

"At that point in time, I decided that I needed to go to graduate school and applied to the School of Advanced International Studies at Johns Hopkins University. While this program was interesting and inspiring, I quickly understood that if I wanted to have a real impact on development, this was not the place to get my education. The students at SAIS were mostly heading for 'development jobs' with USAID or any of a number of NGOs. I already realized that these people, while full of good intentions, were not going to have the kind of impact that I wanted to have. SAIS had a joint degree program with Wharton, so I applied for the MBA in my first semester. This was the better choice for me, since the credential I would earn from Wharton would give me access to the sources of power and finance."

"One morning in 1999," Durreen recounted with fire in her eyes, "I woke up and realized that I had to start my own business. This was a lightning strike, but it was the logical evolution of the ideas I had developed during my employment with Grameen Bank."

The First Entrepreneurial Venture

"I learned that although the Grameen program addressed women's credit needs, there was no system in place to advertise and sell their output in Western markets. I really thought it was a long shot that these women who couldn't read or write were supposed to work out distribution strategies for their handicrafts."

Durreen founded a company called OneNest in 1999, an online global wholesale marketplace for handmade goods from all over the world. As she put it later, "I was a social entrepreneur, running a social enterprise, without realizing it. These labels came later."

"OneNest was a cooperative venture that empowered women from many countries to sell their handicrafts by linking the artisans of the world directly to buyers. OneNest was a thrilling adventure for five years, but I decided to sell it for several reasons. First, I was depleted by my dealings with venture capitalists. I could not finance my business without them, but their interests were always focused on 'How do I exit my investment?' Second, I wanted to move back to Asia and be closer to Bangladesh, if not actually in Bangladesh. I moved to Singapore and did a lot of writing and teaching, focused on big questions: How can I make a big impact on people's lives? How can I bring finance and development together to make a difference? I had a rudimentary idea that kept developing and kept intriguing me." This in turn led her to identify her true passion and life's work, which was to help identify investors for profit-making companies with social and environmental missions.

The Second Entrepreneurial Venture

"Somebody must have noticed what I was writing about because I was invited by the Rockefeller Foundation to attend a conference they were running in Bellagio on development and finance. Ironically, this is the conference at which the term 'impact investing' was coined, by a Rockefeller Foundation Managing Director named Antony Bugg-Levine. Antony offered to support my ideas through the foundation, and this was my Black Swan. As soon as I returned to Singapore, I started writing the business plan for Impact Investment Exchange (Asia). This was a new concept and it took some bold moves, but IIX was launched in 2009. I had found my calling in life."

By this time, Durreen had identified two groups that would eventually form the core of her mission in life. First were the entrepreneurs running social enterprises but who lacked access to capital. Second were the impact investors, with the capital and the interest in what she calls the "triple bottom line" of economic, social, and financial goals. What was lacking was the platform to bring these two groups together. The solution to this challenge was quickly forming in Durreen's mind. The solution was the Impact Investment Exchange (Asia) Pte. Ltd. (IIX), a company "deeply rooted in the belief that capital markets can create social good for the world."

Judith Rodin, former President of the Rockefeller Foundation, defines this type of investment strategy as follows:

> … *impact investments are intended to deliver both financial returns and social and environmental benefits… a new way of deploying capital that can combine the demand for profitability with a desire to solve social and environmental problems… [Impact investing] offers a middle way between philanthropy and pure financial investment.*

As conceptualized by Durreen, IIX would address the needs of developing companies in Asia that are designed to be profitable, earning a fair return on investment, while at the same time serving the long-term social and environmental best interests of the people and the countries where they operate. In effect, Durreen was looking to help companies escape the "survival trap" so clearly and persuasively described by Eric Kacou, whom we met two chapters ago.

"How do you put together the needs of the social enterprises and the investors with trillions of dollars to spend? Stock exchanges have existed for centuries and today are capitalized world-wide at over 65 trillion U.S. dollars. But not a single cent of this amount went to economic development. I thought, why not create a stock exchange that would explicitly issue stocks and bonds that were oriented towards social and environmental returns, while at the same time achieving satisfactory financial returns? This was the concept behind Impact Investment Exchange (Asia)."

"I met Durreen in Singapore in 2009," said her friend Sue Suh, "when she was conceptualizing what is now Impact Investment Exchange Asia. We had great chemistry and I really enjoyed brainstorming with her about this idea. She eventually invited me to join Asia IIX as its first volunteer. I worked with her on the 'nuts and bolts' of the exchange in its formative stage. Now I serve on the Operational Advisory Council."

I asked Sue what role money played in Durreen's vision for IIX. Her response was not at all surprising. "Durreen is not particularly motivated by money but does not demonize it either. Professionally, she has a clear and strategic understanding of what capital markets can potentially unlock for social enterprises and the greater good. I believe that her work towards linking social enterprises with capital markets elevates and empowers the social impact field."

IIX seeks to "address the various stages of capital raising that a Social Enterprise may encounter throughout its lifecycle." IIX also helps companies access capital in private transactions. It allows larger social enterprises to access public capital markets through the listing and trading of securities. IIX increases awareness, provides opportunities for companies to raise their visibility, provides technical assistance, builds investment platforms, connects social enterprises with impact investors, and facilitates meetings with potential investors. The idea is flourishing. Four examples will give a flavor of the type of enterprise she seeks to support:

– Sun-eee Pte. Ltd., a Cambodian company whose mission is to provide affordable electricity from sustainable sources to rural customers.
– East Bali Cashews, an Indonesian company that uses sustainable, eco-friendly business practices to process unshelled cashews, and to package and sell them to the domestic and international markets.
– iFarmer, a Bangladeshi company that bridges the gap between smallholder farmers and investors through digital applications.
– Sheba Platform Limited, another Bangladeshi company that operates an ecosystem of interconnected mobile apps to track receivables, keep records, and monitor credit scoring for microentrepreneurs.

Who is Durreen Shahnaz?

I have the greatest admiration and affection for this strong, kind, and loyal woman who is equally modern and traditional. I especially respect her deep spirituality, forged in the crucibles of both Islam and Christianity, but in its mature version, unrelated to any of the world's established religions.

Her sister Shabnam reflects on Durreen's respect for tradition, wrapped in an international package. "She is deeply respectful of her tradition, and the roots of her existence. She is a proud Bengali woman who teaches her daughters to read, write, speak, and understand their mother's mother tongue. She follows the tradition of addressing her older sisters using appropriate words (to demonstrate respect) that we have in Bengali, and not by their given names. She always wears a sari for important public events and meetings. But she is a most modern woman in the sense of having emotionally and intellectually overcome the inhibitions of the cultural value system she inherited."

I believe that Durreen, along with the other three Compassionate Capitalists, Dawn Hines, Eric Kacou, and Rosanna Ramos Velita, are in the forefront of bringing about profound change in the world. As noted above, the amount of money available to assist the so-called "developing world" through charity and government assistance is a small fraction of the corresponding pool of assets held by the world's investors. If a convincing case can be made that impact investing can harmonize both investment strategies and societal/ environmental goals, the result can have far-reaching consequences.

When I was a student, my cohort was enraged by the inequities in the world. Our solution was to get angry, misbehave, and try in all the most unlikely ways to force adults to change their behavior. We had good hearts and brave intentions, but our methodology was impractical and usually doomed to failure. Today's generation is just as enraged as my generation was, but the big difference is that defiant optimists such as Durreen are taking more constructive and quite possibly successful approaches.

Moving on to New Delhi

Next stop: New Delhi. We will board a plane in Hazrat Shahjala International Airport in Dhaka for the short flight of 887 miles to Indira Gandhi International Airport. Geographically (at least according to Mercator), we are still in "South Asia," but many of the superficial characteristics of the two civilizations will be different. For one example, we will move from a spirituality almost exclusively (over 90%) based on Islam to one more diverse, based primarily (80%) on Hinduism, but with a sizeable percentage (15%) based on Islam, and a smaller percentage based on independent religions such as Sikhism (2%) and Jainism (< 1%).

Steward, Not the Owner of His Wealth

Shiv Vikram Khemka

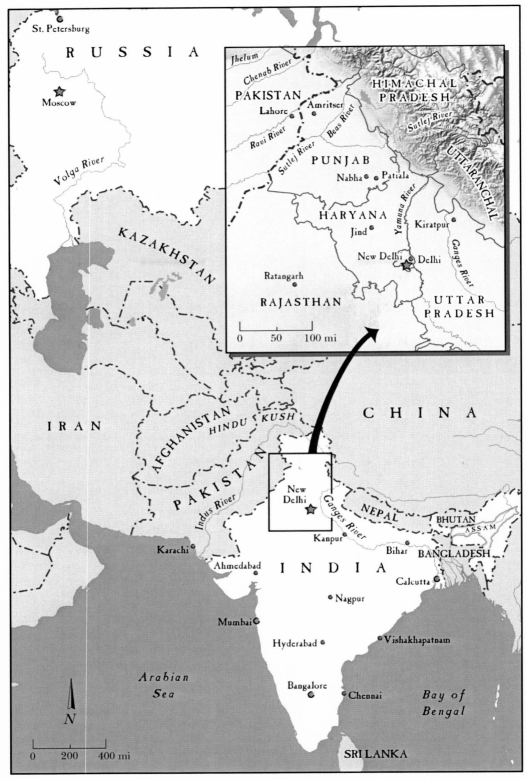

Steward, Not the Owner of His Wealth: Shiv Vikram Khemka

W e now turn to the first *Steward, Not the Owner of His Wealth*, Shiv Vikram Khemka. Shiv is a complicated person who carries in his gene pool long histories of two quite distinct, but equally strong, cultures and sets of traditions. In order to understand him, we must go back in history twice before we have a fully informed view.

The Sikhs

In what is now the northwestern part of India, on the border with Pakistan, there is an area called Punjab, a Farsi word meaning "land of the five rivers." Because of its location, Punjab was a gateway between India and the civilizations of Europe and the Middle East. Originally Hindu in culture and faith, Punjab was by the sixteenth century CE under Muslim political and military domination. There was considerable conflict between Hindus and Muslims. In fact, it was an astonishingly brutal and sadistic period when measured against twenty-first century norms.

Around 1500, there lived in Punjab a Hindu holy man by the name of Guru Nanak, who had from his birth been expected to serve an important function. One day, as legend has it, Guru Nanak disappeared while bathing in a river. When he returned three days later, he brought with him a revelation. Some say that this revelation was a synthesis of Hinduism and Islam and reconciled their doctrinal conflicts. Those who were drawn to Nanak's revelation said that the revelation was from God, and although conciliatory in its philosophy, lacked political goals of reconciliation.

In any case, Guru Nanak's revelation, which evolved into a set of religious beliefs known as Sikhism, attracted millions of Punjabis with its message of peace and harmony. Nine more gurus would follow Nanak before the human line of Gurus was disbanded in favor of textual guidance. The population of Sikhs worldwide has risen to more than 20 million, most of whom still reside in Punjab.

> *What drew people to the Sikh faith was the idea of equality; of respect for people's worth and not their birth; of human beings as God's creations, not as a species to be manipulated and graded by self-appointed arbiters of the upper castes.*

Sikhs reject the notion of castes because they believe in the equality of all people (including gender equality). They also believe in the importance of charity and volunteering to help others. They abjure superstition and images as aids to worship. Sikhs also mandate simple, truthful living, and accept the doctrine of human reincarnation. Like the Hindu, the Sikh understands that he is free to choose any course of action, but that there is a consequence in one's next life to any action taken in the current life.

As for "God," the Sikhs believed in a new form, that would:

> *... serve a strife-torn society, erase divisions and despair, and help people overcome their prejudices and mindless preoccupations.... Not a God with a physical form but an amalgam of truth, integrity, courage and enlightened thinking. An inner God present in every person. Not the property of a few purveyors of priestly wisdom but of all living things.*

In the seventeenth century, an all-out effort to exterminate anyone who refused to embrace Islam led the Sikhs to develop a fierce, combative side, and they eventually became known for their warrior spirit and courage in self-defense. Nevertheless, from a theological perspective, Sikhism is based on conciliation and Sikhs in the modern era retain a deep commitment to peacefulness and the acceptance of all.

Shiv's Maternal Lineage

"Maharaja" is the Sanskrit word for "emperor," translated literally as "great king." India had for centuries prior to colonization by the British been ruled by a series of kingdoms headed by maharajas. They were hereditary titles, generally passed to the eldest son of the preceding maharaja. Shiv's maternal great-grandfather, a Sikh, was the Maharaja of Nabha, one of three regions that covered most of Punjab. The other two regions were ruled by his cousins. Family records have been maintained so meticulously that his mother can with certainty trace her lineage, including by name, back at least one thousand years.

Shiv's family was touched personally by the seventh Sikh Guru, as explained in the following manner:

> *Guru Har Raj succeeded his grandfather as the seventh Guru. Born at Kiratpur on 16 January 1630, he was a saintly man...His kindly interest in a poor young lad, Phul, led the boy eventually to found the families that later ruled the princely states of Patiala, Nabha and Jind.*

Phul had six sons, and Shiv's mother is descended from one of them. His royal line is, accordingly, called "Phulkian." Shiv's maternal great-grandfather (a Phulkian), was Sir Maharaja Hira Singh of Nabha (December 18, 1843 to December 24, 1911). According to the online *Sikh Encyclopedia*, he was "one of the ablest of Nabha rulers, wise, liberal and pious." He was also legendary for his fairness and generosity. Upon the death of Hira, he was succeeded by his son, Shiv's maternal grandfather, whose name was Maharaja Ripudaman Singh (March 4, 1883 to December 13, 1942).

Ripudaman was studying law in the United Kingdom when his father died in 1911. When he returned home to take his place as the next Maharaja of Nabha, he had his first dispute with the British concerning his coronation ceremony. The source of the disagreement was his insistence that the coronation be carried out in the traditional manner, which the British felt was insufficiently subservient to George V.

Shiv proudly stated that Ripudaman was at that time the only maharaja openly to support the independence movement in India, and not surprisingly, he was considered dangerous by the British. To mitigate his risk to the Empire, the British removed him and sent him into exile in India's deep south in 1926. In 1931, he was forced by the British to abdicate his throne, and his kingdom was given to his son by his second wife, presumably a young man more obedient to the British colonialists. Shiv's mother Jeet was, ignominiously, born in exile in 1934.

By the late 1930s and early 1940s, the Indian independence movement was gaining traction. In 1939, Shiv's grandmother and her children (including the five year-old Jeet), returned to Nabha, but were interned in dungeons in the family's own palace. According to Shiv, the rise of the independence movement put his grandfather at grave risk, and on December 13, 1942, Ripudaman suddenly "died." Suspiciously, within two weeks of the death of Ripudaman, all of his bankers, financial advisers, and closest staff also "died." The circumstances of all these deaths were explainable singly, but collectively they were held by the family to be deliberate acts of the British to stifle dissent and extinguish a spark of support for the independence movement. Following Ripudaman's death in 1942, and continuing until 1947, his widow and children lived in extreme poverty, all traces of the family's wealth and ownership of property having been erased through the deaths of those with knowledge and documentation of the assets. With independence in 1947, India recognized Ripudaman as a freedom fighter, and created a "privy purse" to compensate his family for their losses under the British. Jeet, only 13 years old at the time of Indian independence, then went to school.

We will now leave Jeet for a moment in order to take our second historical journey to visit Shiv's other gene pool, in Rajasthan.

The Marwaris

To the south of Punjab there stretches the largest state in India, now called Rajasthan. Rajasthan encompasses a vast and inhospitable desert, although in its westernmost part it parallels the Indus River, the cradle of one of the world's oldest human civilizations. Shiv's paternal family traces its ancestry to the Indian ethnic group called the Marwaris of Rajasthan. An understanding of the role that the Marwari community has played in the evolution of business in India is useful in understanding the Khemka family and, hence, Shiv.

Forbes India devoted its March 21, 2014, cover and theme to "Marwari Power." As explained by R Jagannathan, the Editor-in-Chief, "The Marwaris are, arguably, among the three or four most influential business communities in India… [and] have largely excelled in trading and commodity-based businesses."

The Marwaris were a relatively small (some say "tiny") community that originated in the desert sands of Rajasthan, and who migrated in the eighteenth and nineteenth centuries to thousands of towns in all corners of India. They had strong traditions, perhaps genetically derived, or more probably accumulated from thousands of years of practice. Whether or not you believe in Lamarck's theory of the heritability of acquired characteristics, the Marwaris certainly act as if it were true.

First, the Marwaris had a tradition of entrepreneurship and risk-taking. This may have come from the strong aversion in the community to working for others. The tradition may also have emerged out of necessity. The desert from which the Marwaris originated was arid and inhospitable to agriculture. In any case, the value held by the Marwari was that it was preferable to own one's small business rather than to work for another person's large business. Many small Marwari businesses flourished following this philosophy, often nurtured by risks taken by the founding entrepreneur.

Second, the Marwaris had a joint family support system that ranged from the *basa* (a kind of hostel maintained by Marwaris where new-coming Marwaris were welcome to stay at no charge when they arrived in unfamiliar towns) to the *parta* (a cash-based accounting system that reconciled profit and loss on a daily basis). Marwaris took care of each other, starting with the family, which has always been of paramount importance.

This social conservatism contributed to their success in business, but also led to a certain degree of social ostracism, and there is an extensive literature that focuses satirically on *kanjoos* (loosely, "stingy") Marwaris. The Marwaris, not surprisingly, explain their behavior differently:

> *"Money will come in the long term, but integrity and credibility cannot be wasted on short-term financial goals," says Gulab [Kothari, chairman and editor-in-chief of the newspaper Rajasthan Patrika]. "Beyond a point, all the extra money you earn is merely adding to your bank balance. Respect is the biggest asset you can gather in this lifetime. And that is the most important thing for us Marwaris."*

Third, perhaps due to their diaspora all over India, they developed an ability to adapt to new environments. Or perhaps their innate ability to adapt made it easier for them to succeed in the towns to which they migrated.

... the Marwaris will find opportunity even in the most seemingly unreachable places... What has helped has been the ease with which the traders have integrated with the locals, taking up their language, customs and names.

Fourth, the Marwaris developed a tradition of philanthropy, which exists to the present day. This value has always been closely linked with the Marwaris' penchant for frugal and austere living. One of the most famous Marwaris, GD Birla, who founded what is today one of India's largest conglomerates, wrote a letter to his grandson, who at the time was attending the Massachusetts Institute of Technology in the United States. This letter became legendary and, published in many formats, has come to summarize the ethic of the Marwari merchant. In part, he wrote:

... eat only vegetarian food, never drink alcoholic beverages or smoke, keep early hours, marry young, switch off lights when leaving the room, cultivate regular habits, go for a walk every day, keep in touch with the family, and above all, don't be extravagant.

Shiv's Paternal Lineage

The Khemka family had, by the early 1930s, migrated from Rajasthan to Bihar, in the northeastern part of India. Gandhi, in his autobiography, referred to the Bihari as being noted for their "humility, simplicity, goodness, and extraordinary faith," a set of characteristics that was no doubt congenial for the Khemkas. In Bihar, this Marwari family owned and traded in grain, timber, iron ore, and other commodities. Shiv's father Nand was born on the banks of the Ganges River, two days after a massive earthquake in 1934 (the same year that Jeet was born in exile in southern India). India felt the effects of the Great Depression, and the Khemka family business was, accordingly, severely impacted.

Nand grew up a deeply spiritual person but shunned the rituals of religion. The youngest of seven brothers, Nand attended Xavier's in Calcutta and studied economics. Later, he attended the Columbia Business School in New York, which was unusual for a young Indian in the early 1950s. In 1955, Nand was sent by his father to Tokyo to develop a market for the export of iron ore, which he assumed would be required for the steel production needed to rebuild Japan after the devastation of the Second World War.

Next the Khemka family encountered a Black Swan that would change everything. In 1957, Prime Minister Nehru, influenced by the Soviet example, nationalized the iron ore industry, wiping out the Khemka family business. Undeterred, the family repositioned its business in Moscow with the objective of trading in mining equipment to sell to the Indian government to use in the iron ore mines that had been previously owned by the Khemkas.

Our Next Hero Is Introduced

Nand met Jeet through mutual friends, and they were married in 1961. The marriage was unusual in that Nand and Jeet came from two distinctly different communities, as the preceding pages will have made clear. Intermarriage of this sort was discouraged in mid-twentieth century India and was therefore rare. But Nand and Jeet are unusual people, and spent their lives doing unusual things. A son, Shiv, was born to Nand and Jeet on August 19, 1962. And so we introduce the next hero of this book, the first *Steward, Not the Owner of His Wealth*, who would spend his life respecting as well as being driven by these two unique cultures, namely the Sikh and the Marwari.

Nand and Jeet raised their children to understand and respect all religious traditions. They believed that people who are secure in their beliefs and who are faithful to their values will not be threatened by other beliefs. Nor should a person confident in his relationship to the external world feel a need to proselytize on behalf of any single faith. To Nand and Jeet, the essence of spirituality was the simple practice of tolerance, kindness, compassion, generosity, and forgiveness, which they felt were more important than formal worship in a building designed and constructed for that purpose alone.

Shiv attended St. Columba's School in New Delhi until the age of eleven, which was in 1973. Because of severe asthma, which was exacerbated by the climate in New Delhi, his parents decided to send him to Europe for school. Accordingly, Shiv was sent to school in France for a year and then to Eton in the U.K. for four years. After graduating from Eton, not ready for college, he took a "gap year." It was a wild and wooly year in Shiv's terms, which although not anti-social or rebellious, was quite spirited.

"I grew out my hair and had it permed," he laughed. "It was a gigantic Indian Afro. I spent four months in Paris studying Afro-Brazilian dance. I played the Sarod (a lute-like stringed instrument) in the Metro. I engaged in wine-tasting, took a sculpture course, and wrote poetry. I published a volume of poems. Later I spent a month in Mexico and another month at a Buddhist monastery."

"On my return, I went to Brown University as an undergraduate because I wanted the freedom to take courses in many departments. I had been admitted to Oxford, but I would not have had the opportunity to take courses outside of a very narrow range of options. At Brown, I pushed the academic envelope, taking courses in 14 different departments. I started a company, was involved in student government, threw many parties, and still managed to get good grades."

At Brown, he met and became lifelong friends with a Norwegian, Yngvar Berg. Yngvar recalls, "Shiv was wild in college, but when I say 'wild,' I mean in the sense of being exuberant. He was never malicious in any way. He was always a very open guy who made friends easily.

Shiv was adept at understanding and evaluating people. He drew people out of their shells by his charm, good humor, and guileless personality. It was hard to resist Shiv. People naturally opened up to Shiv because he was open with them. But at the same time, Shiv had very high standards that he embraced and insisted that others embrace as well."

Yngvar warmed to the memories of his time as an undergraduate at Brown with Shiv. "He is a study in contrasts," Yngvar averred. "He was and is the most modern person and embraces change with enthusiasm. But at the same time, I knew Shiv to be most respectful of tradition. I watched him kneel to touch the feet of his elder relatives. And he performs these traditional rites unselfconsciously and without cynicism."

The Latin American Interlude

After graduation from Brown in 1985, Nand sent Shiv to Venezuela and Brazil. Shiv explained this seeming anomaly as a logical decision by his father to encourage an ability independently to develop and run a business in a part of the world where the family had no contacts or knowledge. Shiv threw himself into the project with enthusiasm, selling steel and petrochemicals from producers in Latin America to customers in Asia. He made his first U.S. dollar million by the age of 25. When it was time for graduate school, he applied to the Lauder Institute at the University of Pennsylvania, again choosing a program that gave him the greatest latitude to study a variety of subjects. Required to select a language for study, he chose the Portuguese track, planning to return to Brazil.

Russia

Half-way through his MBA, Shiv watched from the tranquility of Philadelphia as the Soviet Union began to collapse, one of modern history's great Black Swans. The Khemka family business in Moscow, which had been founded more than thirty years earlier, was confronted with both opportunity and risk. The Soviet government of Mikhail Gorbachev had initiated a program of reform that centered on privatization, and yet the Khemka business had relied on trading with the previous government and state-owned enterprises. Sensing a once-in-a-lifetime inflection point (we here visit Taleb's *Extremistan*), Nand took Shiv to Moscow in the summer of 1990 to explore business opportunities. They elected to conduct due diligence on the possibility of making direct investments in the new Russian economy.

By mid-1991, the new Russian Government, concerned about the widespread and harmful effects on the population of excessive vodka consumption, was encouraging beer consumption as a "soft drink." The Khemka family, vegetarian and teetotalers, made the decision to invest in the beer brewing business (their second choice was chocolates). In Shiv's words, "The industry presented a massive consolidation and growth opportunity," due to a lack of quality and a highly fragmented market.

By 1992, the family had established a subsidiary called Sun Brewing, and started visiting potential acquisition targets. Shiv personally visited eighty breweries. The Sun Brewing team visited a total of one hundred forty. That summer they made the first purchase, which was quickly followed by four more. Sun Brewing combined consolidation with good business practices, and growth followed. Shiv eventually elected to exit the business through the sale of the Khemka family shares to the newly formed InBev (created through the merger of two large brewing companies, Interbrew and AmBev) for cash and stock. Shiv had built the business from a standing start to a $4 billion conglomerate, and with this well-timed exit realized a significant profit for the family business.

What had begun as a detour from his intended return to Brazil transformed into a major life project for Shiv. He lived in Russia for twenty years, and along the way learned enough Russian language and culture to engage comfortably and enthusiastically with his host nation and its citizens. He returned to New Delhi in 2009, and with the proceeds of the sale of its stake in Russian beer, the family diversified into investments in oil and gas in Nigeria, gold mining in Kazakhstan and Russia, and real estate (and other investments) in India.

The Global Education and Leadership Foundation

Deep in his heart, Shiv understood – through both nature and nurture – that he was the steward and not the owner of substantial wealth. As he approached the age of 50, Shiv started thinking about his duties and plans for the time when he would step back from business and devote himself to philanthropy and working exclusively for the betterment of others. Shiv's personal interest is in education, and he has created a vehicle to implement his ideas about value-based leadership. "The Global Education & Leadership Foundation" (tGELF) was born in 2006.

"I wanted to build a social enterprise business that involved leadership training," he began. He gets very animated when he talks about tGELF, and his enthusiasm is infectious. Everyone he encounters succumbs. "One truly great leader can change everything. Look at Gandhi. Now imagine a world with 500 Gandhi's. How can we identify them, nurture them and empower them? I am convinced that they exist, but they are not being encouraged to grow in the right direction. Our educational system does not allow them to grow into great leaders. I want to identify and 'curate' 500 Gandhi's. This is the purpose and goal of tGELF."

"The curriculum we have developed is a 'selection engine,' designed to identify and then shape these future leaders. What makes 'great' different from 'good'? We believe that the differentiating factors are a.) Ethics, b.) Altruism, c.) A bias for action, and d.) Expressed leadership. Please note that I did not say the smartest, although sometimes they are also very smart. We look for students in the age range of 13 to 18 who score high on these four characteristics. Then we mentor, train, and support them. So far, we have trained 2,500 teachers to integrate the tGELF curriculum into their schools. It cannot work as an 'add-on;' it must be mainstream. These 2,500 teachers have trained more than 500,000 students in twelve countries. We selected one hundred boys and girls out of these 500,000 as the potential 'Olympians.' Sixty of these students are now in Ivy League schools in the United States and forty are in the top Indian universities. We actively mentor them through an annual conference, cohorting, service projects, and other methods. The real measure of success in any human is spiritual balance," he concluded with a broad smile.

While Shiv describes the foundation with passion and conviction, I will turn here to Mrs. Gowri Ishwaran, the founding Chief Executive Officer of tGELF. "Shiv and I share a common vision," said Mrs. Ishwaran, "about the need for value-based education for future leaders. Shiv so impressed me with his long-term vision. He had a 10- to 15-year plan, and it made perfect sense to me. We both felt that the educational system had lost sight of spirituality, which involves knowing yourself, being yourself, and anchoring yourself in firm values that you will abide by. Indian education used to include this kind of training, but it somehow got lost along the way."

Mrs. Ishwaran laughed in a knowing way. She is a happy, positive, person who smiles as often as Shiv, which is always. "His dream is quite different from other philanthropists. He doesn't need his name attached to a building or a school; he simply wants to make a difference in the lives of as many children as possible. His reward will be in the multiplier effect of children with strong inner cores and with spirituality, growing into adults who make informed, ethical, and value-oriented decisions as leaders of society."

Forgiveness

In this book, I keep returning to the question of forgiveness. I have no choice. As you have read in this and the past seven chapters, every one of the brave and harmless people drawn from my card file has suffered at the hands of colonialism, imperialism, racism, or the residue of slavery. And yet, none of them expresses bitterness, anger, or a desire for revenge. The source of this equanimity is of tremendous interest to me, and of great importance to the hypothesis of this book.

I asked Shiv how he was able to forgive the British for killing his grandfather and jailing his grandmother, after having dismembered his grandparents' household and expropriated the patrimony for sympathizing with the Indian independence movement. Shiv, in much the same manner as Chanthol Sun, really has no anger in his heart although his family was abused in violent and heinous ways. His compassion is not feigned.

"I guess that I do not think about forgiving because anger and resentment are not in my heart. But if you need me to go back to the reasons I lack feelings of anger, I suppose there are two, one of which is Western and one of which is Indian. Philip Zimbardo, a professor at Stanford University, wrote a book called *The Lucifer Effect*. This book looked at how good people can do bad things, and how systems, and the situations created by systems, can have overwhelmingly negative effects on even the most moral individuals. This book helped me to understand the sources of evil and to learn how to forgive."

The other source, Shiv explained, is based on Hindu, Sikh, and Buddhist beliefs. He noted that there is no word for "evil" in Hindi, which is explained simply as an "absence of light." Religion, he feels, is only packaging, which gets corrupted because of ignorance and insecurity. Anger and revenge, to Shiv, are not solutions to suffering. On the contrary, they perpetuate suffering. The best way to overcome suffering is to forgive by detachment from the acts that caused us pain. If we can train ourselves to stop reacting with what are normal – but dysfunctional – emotions, we can cease to suffer. Rather than punish those who wound us, our best strategy is to calm ourselves and not require anger or vengeance. The consequence is forgiveness on the part of the person hurt, for the person who caused the pain. For Shiv, it has nothing to do with qualifying for Heaven, Nirvana, or other putative resting place. It is merely a prescription for a happy, healthy, and harmonious life. These are difficult concepts for the Western mind to comprehend, much less to put into practice, but they are tantalizing.

Who Is Shiv Khemka?

To answer this question, we have traveled back in time to Punjab at the birth of Sikhism, and to Rajasthan at the time of the migration of the Marwaris out of the desert, and quite logically from India to France, the U.K., the U.S.A., Venezuela, Brazil, Russia, Nigeria, China, and back to India. I think that much of Shiv can be understood by examining the origins of Sikhism and the diaspora of the Marwaris. He is a most intriguing combination of these two disparate cultures and traditions. But regardless of the reasons for his psychological profile, Shiv is a good man. He has a warm and compassionate heart, matched not incongruously with a brilliant and indefatigable business sense. He has followed his Marwari roots through Brazil and Moscow but is also coming back to follow his Sikh roots with the founding of tGELF. Shiv made a lot of money in beer (and other investments) but he is giving back a significant portion of his wealth to help "curate 500 Gandhi's." His goal is to achieve the maximum amount of good he can do with his money, regardless of what percentage of his fortune he needs to spend. He is truly the steward of his wealth and does not claim ownership of the millions he has accumulated. And like all the others who have ever met Shiv, I have a deep and abiding affection for this gentle and guileless man. Shiv is a charming and irresistible force of nature who exemplifies all the moral dispositions that permeate the women and men in this book.

Moving on to Stockholm

Our next journey is from New Delhi to Stockholm. We will depart from Indira Gandhi International Airport and fly some 3,460 miles north and west over many countries, including Afghanistan, Uzbekistan, Kazakhstan, Belarus, Russia, and Latvia, before crossing the Baltic Sea and arriving in Arlanda International Airport. Sweden is a small country of ten million, which has had an involvement in the world greater than might have been expected, largely because of its international outlook. India is an enormous country of 1.4 billion, whose involvement in the world was held back because of its colonial past but which is moving forward with increasing velocity. Looking at how far we have come, it may be instructive to note that the first eight countries we encountered (Colombia, Indonesia, Cambodia, Senegal, Côte d'Ivoire, Peru, Bangladesh, and India) have all suffered the indignities of colonialism, imperialism, and racism. Sweden will be the first country in our mix which was never colonized and made some efforts to be a colonizer herself.

Steward, Not the Owner of His Wealth

Jacob Wallenberg

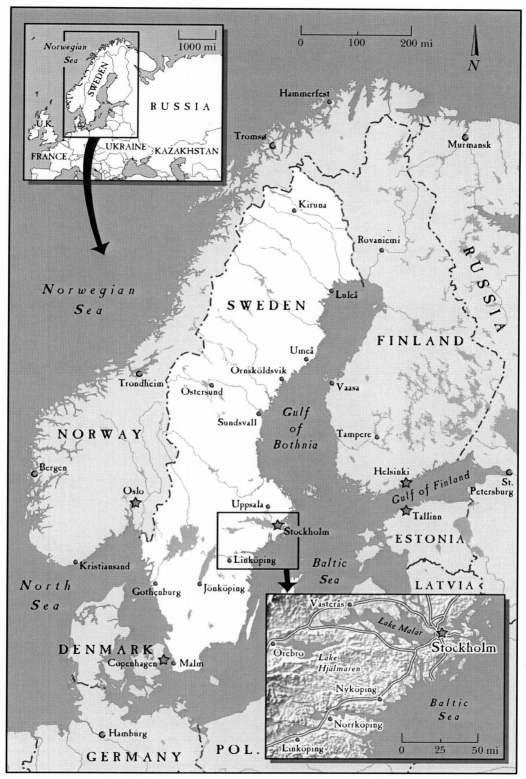

Steward, Not the Owner of His Wealth: Jacob Wallenberg

Sweden and Colonization

Some say that the Swedes voluntarily surrendered the option of exploration and ocean-based colonization in favor of commerce. Others contend that the root cause was the impoverished condition of the country and an authoritarian monarch. I am inclined to believe that, at least in part, this decision was inevitable, given their geography and weather.

Let us consider for a moment the obstacles to launching voyages of discovery and conquest in the great era of exploration by Europeans that took place from the fifteenth to the seventeenth centuries. The Swedes took twelve such voyages to the New World, the first of which was launched in 1637. Departing from Stockholm, there is the difficulty factor of hundreds of small islands clogging the water route into the Baltic Sea. Once clear of these obstacles, the intrepid captain must travel south and then west and then north again, through a narrow channel that separates Denmark (the Danes took advantage of this geographical coincidence to tax ships that passed by) from Sweden, and thence into the North Sea, only to suffer the challenges of rounding the northernmost reaches of the British Isles or navigating the English Channel before reaching the Atlantic Ocean.

By then, the mariners would need to head south, passing France, Spain and Portugal before they would catch up with the fresh team composed of the descendants of Prince Henry the Navigator's sailors, just heading out from Sagres. And the Swedes' difficult journey is raised to an even more complicated level in winter, with little sunlight and an ice-bound harbor. Suffice it to say that for the Swedes, there were adequate reasons to surrender to geographical and meteorological determinism and to leave the exploration and subjugation to those countries with easier access to the Atlantic Ocean.

Nevertheless, in Philadelphia, Pennsylvania the American Swedish Historical Museum, "Old Swedes' Church" (opened in 1700), "Catherine" Street, and "Queen" Village preserve the memory of Sweden's brief colonial foray into the New World. The museum displays a fresco on the ceiling of its rotunda that commemorates the "establishment of civilization" in the Delaware Valley in March of 1638, complete with Swedes in feathered hats and armor arriving in what is now Wilmington, Delaware, flanked by Native Americans kneeling at their feet. The fresco was painted in 1928, when Franz Boas was 70 years old. Margaret Mead was 27 and had published *Coming of Age in Samoa* the same year. Apparently their ideas about cultural relativism had not yet arrived in Philadelphia. The microaggression lives on.

Enter the Wallenbergs

Around the time of the Swedish efforts to become a colonial power, most of Sweden's population was engaged in farming. The better educated and more ambitious men would aspire to enter the Lutheran ministry, and through industry and diligence might rise to leadership positions. Marcus Wallenberg was born in 1774 in Linkoping, a small city located 122 miles to the southwest of Stockholm. Better educated and more ambitious than many of his peers, Marcus became a Lutheran minister and in due course was appointed the bishop of Linkoping, living a righteous life until he passed away at the age of 59 in 1833. Marcus had a son whom he named Andre Oscar, born in 1816 when Marcus was 42. "A.O.," as he is often called by his descendants, was the first of this clan of Wallenbergs to enter the business world. Little could he have imagined the wealth that he started to accumulate would be preserved and so significantly augmented by the next four generations of his descendants.

A.O. was an admirer of the United States and traveled there to study the banking industry. On his return home in 1856, he founded a bank, Stockholms Enskilda Bank (SEB), which still exists today. A.O. passed away at the age of 70 in 1886. Led by his eldest son Knut, born in 1853, the family business prospered in the third generation. Knut and his wife Alice had no children, and decided to donate their fortune, which was considerable, to establish an eponymous foundation in 1917. Knut donated his wealth in the form of shares in many Swedish companies to the foundation that he and his wife created, with the provision that it make grants to support scientific research of benefit to the citizens of Sweden.

Jacob's Journey Begins

With Biblical repetition, Wallenberg sons (descendants of Knut's siblings) named Marcus, Peter, Jacob, Gustav, or Raoul were born and entered each generation of the family business. As Sweden grew and prospered, the foundation's assets also grew. A fifth generation Wallenberg, unsurprisingly named Jacob, was born on Friday, January 13, 1956, in Stockholm. And so the second and final *Steward, Not the Owner of His Wealth* of this book is introduced.

Jacob is the eldest child of Peter Wallenberg, who also fathered a younger sister and a younger brother with Jacob's mother. Jacob's parents divorced when he was four years old. His father lived abroad until he was fourteen, and consequently Jacob lived with his mother, who re-married to a silversmith who had a small business.

I asked Jacob if he had any choice about his profession. "Surprisingly, yes," he replied. "I actually contemplated two other careers. The first was in the armed services. I spent three years in the navy after high school, and I enjoyed this type of life. The armed services to me had a good combination of education and on-the-job execution. There was both study and implementation. It was very practical, and this appealed to me."

"I contemplated medicine as well. I have great respect for doctors. However," he said with a rueful laugh, "in Sweden we are a very strict meritocracy, and my grades were not good enough." Jacob is a humble man, very open about his deficiencies. He does not lack confidence, and his humility is disarming, coming as it does from a man so distinguished by lineage and so accomplished in his professional life. "This meritocratic system is quite good, because it means only the best of the best become doctors, lawyers, and so on, but it also has a downside, which is that Sweden does not nurture and celebrate the wild, crazy, and creative entrepreneurs who bring about change."

Beatrice Bondy, a straight-talking and self-assured Swiss woman, has worked for Jacob since 1994 as, in her words, "the classical advisor." She is his sounding board, and they speak every day. Knowing Jacob in this different capacity, Beatrice was a useful source of frank information about him. After speaking with her, I cannot imagine that Beatrice would sugar-coat any opinion she had or coddle any idea he had that she felt was mistaken.

I asked her about Jacob as a young man. "It was not clear when he was young that he was up to the task," she began. "Luckily, you don't have to prove yourself when you are in your thirties." I observed that Jacob had not been pushed by his father to enter the family business and had considered several other professions before doing so. Beatrice concurred, noting that "It was very clever of his father to leave his career choice up to him. Peter never pushed him. But now that he is in his fifties, he has matured into an important leader of his generation. Like a good Bordeaux, he has improved with age."

Jacob's Educational Choices

"After studying the options, and getting lots of advice, I applied to the Wharton School of the University of Pennsylvania, and was admitted for entry in January of 1978," he recounted. "I never had a 'master plan' for my life. I chose Wharton because I thought it would be interesting to study some practical applications of what I learned. It was not really because of my family, and I never really felt pressure from the four previous generations to go into the family business."

After his graduation from Wharton, he joined SEB, the bank which A.O. had founded in 1856, with the understanding that it was a meritocracy, just the same as everything in Sweden. Promotion would be based on performance, and not on his family name. He described his marginal value to SEB being relatively high for several reasons. First, he worked harder than anybody else. "I was the first one to arrive at the office in the morning and the last one to leave at night," he stated proudly. Second, he said that at the time, the late 1980s, the work ethic he brought back from the United States was refreshing and invigorating. He described the lunch habits of the Americans in London – a quick sandwich at your desk – as contrasting sharply with the Europeans, who would go out for a long lunch with wine and return to the office with correspondingly diminished productivity in the afternoon. Third, his education at Wharton proved useful. He really did learn practical skills that he was able to use in his work at SEB.

Ruminations on Life and Career

I asked Jacob what he found most satisfying in his career. "Performing properly," was his first answer. "Having responsibility and doing a good job," was his second answer. Although he did not use this word, I also sensed that he placed great value on being generous – unselfish. This theme will reappear later, as part of his personal value system as well as the general ethos of Swedes. 'Merit' and 'unselfishness' are clearly important parts of the ethical framework of Swedish society. As with so many of the men and women profiled in this book, Jacob brings to mind Peter Singer and his definition of ethical behavior as "the impartial rationality of the principle of equal consideration of interests."

I asked Jacob what or who was inspirational to him as a child. "How did you get to be the person you are today?" was how I asked the question. To my surprise (at first, but not later), he shrugged his shoulders and declined to name any individual, although he did, on reflection, concede that he was proud of his forefathers' beliefs and achievements. "I was inspired to follow in the family tradition," he concluded. "I was never a rebel who distanced himself from the family or its work."

I asked him about religion. He said, with a laugh, that many people think that the Wallenbergs are Jewish because of the "berg" in their name. But, he said, "berg" in Swedish means "rock" or "mountain." The Wallenbergs were Lutherans (remember that one of his pre-business ancestors was a clergyman who became a bishop), but after the switch to business, nobody was very religious. In fact, he said, "I am not at all religious. Religion is not important in this society." He noted that the values of the society, such as respect for others, knowing right from wrong, basing decisions on merit, and unselfishness, may have originated in religion, but mutated into cultural values rather than religious laws with threats of punishment from an omnipotent being if they were transgressed.

I asked him about Raoul, perhaps the most well-known Wallenberg internationally. It was Raoul Wallenberg who successfully rescued as many as 100,000 Jews from certain death in Nazi-occupied Hungary in 1944. Jacob expressed great admiration for Raoul, who was his father's second cousin. "Of course I was inspired by his example," he said. "That Raoul could have done so much, while putting himself at such risk, must create enormous respect." It was one of the few times in my conversations with Jacob that I felt awe in his voice. He is humbled by the work and sacrifice of this uncle who elected to apply his definition of ethics as "the equal consideration of interests" of the Jews threatened with extermination by the Nazis.

A Unique Financial Institution

We discussed the Knut and Alice Wallenberg Foundation, and this is when I started to learn about Jacob and his role in life. In the current (5th) generation, Jacob, his brother Peter, Jr., and their cousin Marcus all share an office – "a Partners Room." Marcus is the Chairman of the family bank, SEB; Peter, Jr. is Chairman of the Knut and Alice Wallenberg Foundation (KAW Foundation); and Jacob is Chairman of Investor AB.

Investor AB is a publicly listed investment management company, with over US$30 billion under management. Jacob is the non-executive Chairman of this company. Investor is the lead shareholder in dozens of prominent Swedish companies, most of which are Wallenberg-controlled, including ABB, Ericsson, SEB, Electrolux, Atlas Copco, Astra Zeneca, Saab Defence, and many others. The KAW Foundation is a not-for-profit organization under Swedish law and the lead shareholder in Investor AB, which is the source of the income spent by the foundation. None of the members of the Wallenberg family have personal ownership of any shares that were originally owned by Knut. While the family is powerful in the sense of controlling tens of billions of kronor of assets, their control is limited to a charitable purpose, namely the Knut and Alice Wallenberg Foundation.

I do not think that it would be an exaggeration to say that the Wallenbergs abhor ostentatiousness, and they certainly do not feel the need to make a big deal about who they are or what they have. The family motto is *esse, non videri*, which is Latin for "to be, not to seem."

For the first 85-90 years of the existence of the KAW Foundation, grants were targeted at building auditoriums at universities, purchasing microscopes for university biology courses, and making it possible for universities to acquire other tangibles that were lacking in the Swedish academic system. This was an era when the physical infrastructure of Swedish universities was relatively underdeveloped. According to Jacob, there have been two significant changes in the foundation in the last 10-15 years.

First, grants are now targeted at long-term research projects rather than infrastructure. The goal is to give the best academic researchers the freedom to take on difficult projects that may not show concrete results for years to come. The foundation's current philanthropic philosophy is that the physical infrastructure is largely in place and that its renewal is now the responsibility of each university. Göran Sandberg, Executive Director of the KAW Foundation, described one of the results of this new grant-making policy:

> Our influence can also be demonstrated through the programmes we support: The Human Proteome Project, for example, received a grant of approximately 9 million euros to describe the human proteome over the next ten years. They have thus far produced antibodies for 50 per cent of all the human proteomes, and they are distributing this information free, worldwide.

Second, the family has concluded that it needs to be more forthcoming in its promotion of the work of the foundation. This decision came about reluctantly, since the family has always held modesty as a cardinal virtue and has never sought either publicity or credit for its good works. However, the family now feels that their efforts to be low-key have resulted in the creation of some misunderstandings, suspicion, and envy. They have always been transparent, but they feel that their reticence to claim credit has been counterproductive. Jacob, as a result, is giving more interviews. It was clear to me that he neither promotes his availability nor relishes the interaction with the press but undertakes this is as an obligation of leadership.

"I have always believed in the importance of doing well whatever job I am given. I have never felt the need to show-off. As a society, we are quite low-key. Perhaps this is a bit Lutheran," he said with a smile. Today the assets of the Knut and Alice Wallenberg Foundation amount to approximately 128 billion Swedish kronor, or about US$14.8 billion at the current (2021) rate of exchange, almost triple the size of the Rockefeller Foundation and roughly equal in size to the Ford Foundation, although only one-third the size of the Bill & Melinda Gates Foundation. The KAW Foundation has awarded nearly $4 billion in the course of its existence and awards approximately $250 million annually in grants in recent years.

Personal Wealth

I asked Jacob about the personal wealth of the Wallenberg family, a matter of some mystery and confusion to the world at large. "All the assets of the Wallenberg family were donated by Knut and Alice Wallenberg to the foundation almost one hundred years ago. None of us has personally inherited any shares in the companies founded by Knut. I am compensated with a salary, not dividends, and my salary is a matter of public record. I cannot sell shares for my personal benefit. In any case, wealth only gives you freedom. It must not be an end in itself," he replied with a finality that indicated there was nothing else to say about money.

Not getting much insight from Jacob himself, I asked Beatrice Bondy about Jacob's relationship with money. "The Wallenbergs are in the news every day. They play an outsized role in Sweden. I don't know of any other country where a single family so dominates industry." She said that there seems to be an obsession with the Wallenbergs that is quite unusual. She speculated that the role of the family was unique in the world because of their great wealth, combined with the fact that they do not in any way benefit financially from the billions that have accumulated from the legacy of Knut and Alice.

"Jacob could have become rich," Beatrice observed. "But he didn't. There were many opportunities for him to take advantage of his position and knowledge, but he always acted from a sense of responsibility. On the scale of 'Wealth in Sweden,' Jacob is nowhere. He isn't poor, but he isn't rich. It is ironic: the Wallenbergs are the 'royalty of wealth' but they are at the bottom of the wealth list."

"It is not that he lacks the talent. Jacob works very hard to create wealth for the foundations,"

Beatrice continued, "and he has been very successful. The companies in Investor's portfolio are extremely well-managed and this generation of executives is highly competent."

Business Philosophy

Swedes do a good job of shielding patriotism from nationalism by an intense international focus. Sweden is a paragon of how a country can synchronize with the world without losing its cultural identity. At another time and place, Jacob provided an interesting counterpoint to this theme:

> *The small size of the Swedish internal market means that our economy is largely export dependent... This gives us a world view which is no doubt somewhat different than if we were in the US, the population of which is thirty-three times that of Sweden.*

"I am impressed at the tenacity with which Investor AB holds on to Swedish businesses in its portfolio. How nationalistic are you about Swedish business?" I asked.

"For any small country, and of course Sweden is a relatively small country, it is fundamentally important that you have some clusters of excellence," he replied. "You cannot do everything, so you must concentrate on a few things. If you do not have the head offices of your companies in your country, you will lose this excellence. The people, the culture, the common vision, will all deteriorate." In Jacob's view, the "home office" drives the demand for excellence. It is paramount – fundamental – to the success of the company. This is not nationalistic, in his opinion, but simply commercial. Is this another instance of an anachronistic approach to a world that has changed? Perhaps, and if so, I suspect that the implementation of the Swedish philosophy will change. Swedes are above all pragmatists.

At the same time, he holds what might be considered a contradictory view, which is that he always strives to do what is best for the success of the company, Investor, and the KAW Foundation. He did not support the sale of AstraZeneca to Pfizer, for example, but only because the offer price was insufficient. He observed that at some price, his fiduciary responsibility to the shareholders would have required a decision to sell. "You cannot hide behind emotional arguments," he said. "Your position must be supported by facts, and if the fact is that the company will unlock shareholder value through a merger or acquisition, then I must make my decision based on the long-term interests of the lead shareholder, which in my case is the KAW Foundation."

The Wallenbergs and China

Jacob has served as a member of the Advisory Council to the Mayor of Shanghai, including a two-year term as Chairman. "Well, this was very easy for me," he started. "China is hugely important to Sweden and Swedish industry. Since we are a small country, we understand very well that we must export and be international in our thinking in order to succeed. In fact, we have known this for 150 years, since Andre Oscar Wallenberg spurned the Lutheran ministry to become a banker. Every day, we build on our international dimensions. Sweden has always been an early entrant into other countries."

"I first went to China in 1984, and my father had been there well before that time. We always understood the importance to the Chinese of building long-term relationships. The Chinese were particularly interested in our industrial (including high-tech) companies, such as ABB and Ericson, and we have received many Chinese visitors in Stockholm. My father knew Jiang Zemin when he was Mayor of Shanghai. He also knew Zhu Rongji. And these relationships were extremely important to us. We are acquainted with Hu Jintao and Wen Jiabao. We have met Xi Jinping and Li Keqiang."

"Wallenberg businesses have invested in China for the long-term. I think that they respected this long-term commitment and even more importantly respected the fact that we were coming to them as a business with five generations of continuity and therefore credibility."

I have already quoted Jacob's speech to the Wharton Global Forum in San Francisco. During that speech, he had some interesting comments about China and the so-called developing world:

> ... Shanghai has harnessed the forces of globalisation with laser focused policy and ambition. It is no longer reacting to the West but is instead setting the agenda...
> I am very much looking forward to what this new world may look like. There is so much we can all learn and share to create the next era of growth and opportunity...

Who Is Jacob Wallenberg?

"How do you want to be remembered in 100 years?"

"As a significant part of a chain of individuals that fulfilled their responsibilities to the Knut and Alice Wallenberg Foundation by managing the asset base in a responsible fashion." I asked Beatrice if there was anything that she knew that others might not know. She said that there were two things, both little-known because "Jacob is a very humble guy."

"First, Jacob has a lot of compartments in his life. He is quite knowledgeable about modern art and French wine, for two examples. He has a lot of interests, but he doesn't make a fuss about them. Second, he is very loyal. He will always try to help a friend. Jacob is such a good person! He is absolutely unselfish, generous, and other-oriented."

Henrik "Sputte" Baltscheffsky, who is one year younger than Jacob, has been his close friend since they were teenagers. I asked Sputte, "What kind of a person is Jacob?"

"Jacob is a joyful person," responded Sputte immediately. "He has a world-class ability to defuse a serious issue with laughter. This does not mean he is not serious or responsible, but it does mean that he feels positivity and optimism are key attributes of successful problem-solving."

As I think about Jacob, I am reminded of some wise words written by Steven Pinker in his book on the decline of violence over the centuries:

> *Mutual unselfishness is the only way we can simultaneously pursue our interests....*
> *Morality, then, is not a set of arbitrary regulations dictated by a vengeful deity or written*
> *down in a book; nor is it the custom of a particular culture or tribe. It is the consequence*
> *of the interchangeability of perspectives and the opportunity the world provides for*
> *positive-sum games.*

Jacob was born into a family of great wealth, but he does not have access to this wealth for his personal use. He earns a salary and his single hero is a man who gave his life to save others. He is a steward of great wealth, handed down through the vision of his distant ancestor more than one hundred years ago and nurtured with responsibility and diligence by four subsequent generations. As Beatrice Bondy told me, "Jacob could have become rich." But he did not; instead he chose a life devoted to benefiting others, with no benefit – and with considerable cost – to himself.

There is a growing anger in the contemporary world about the poison of income inequality and the "1%" that control such a vast portion of the world's resources. If ever there were an effective antidote for this poison, the Wallenberg family would be its leading example. Jacob, as a leader of the fifth generation of this remarkable family, is living proof. It is proof by exception, of course, because there are still far too many of the "1%" who are selfish hoarders of unconscionable wealth, supported by corrupt and immoral politicians who condone and protect them.

I think he is a man of unflinching ethics as defined by Pinker and a hero, too, as defined by Zimbardo. Jacob is also a sunny personality who exudes enthusiasm, and a person for whom I have the greatest respect and warm affection.

Moving on to Cape Town

As I write this paragraph it is winter in Stockholm, and there is daylight for only 6 hours, 4 minutes, and 44 seconds, with the sun setting at 2:48 in the afternoon. Our next journey will take us to the other end of the earth, Cape Town, South Africa, where it is summer and there is daylight for 14 hours, 24 minutes, and 4 seconds. Stockholm is separated from Cape Town by 6,451 miles, and once again we will pass over many countries during our flight, including seven in Europe and six in Africa. Stockholm is located at 59° north latitude; Cape Town at 34° south latitude. Most of the dry landmass of the Earth is located north of the Equator. At 59° south latitude, the only dry landmass is a microchip called Bristol Island, located in the South Sandwich Islands.

The Long Legacy of Echo

Anthony Hamilton Russell

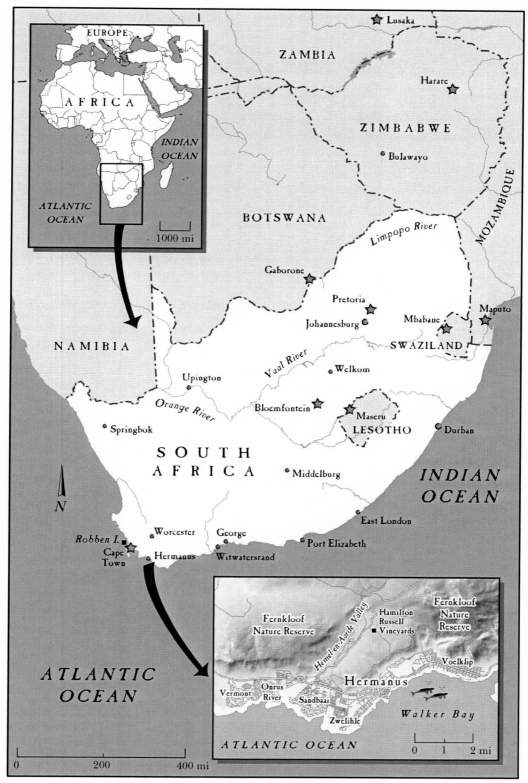

The Long Legacy of Echo: Anthony Hamilton Russell

A Kick in the Head

I found the research on my next subject, Anthony Hamilton Russell, to be complex and surprising, but ultimately understandable and rewarding. After learning about his family, spanning five generations, I am convinced that we need to know something about several of his progenitors before we can understand who he is and why he is that way.

I am struck by how fortuitously it all began – with a kick in the head on a rugby pitch in Oxford in 1927. If ever there were a Black Swan, this kick in the head was it. Let us begin at the beginning, with Anthony's paternal grandfather.

James Hamilton Russell

James Hamilton Russell was born in 1904 in Woodstock, a suburb of the South African city of Cape Town, tucked in between the docks to its immediate north and the foothills of Table Mountain to its immediate south.

The Russells (only later did they become the 'Hamilton Russells,' alphabetized under H) were Anglophiles, and James in due course enrolled in Oxford as a Rhodes Scholar, where he was a sportsman, playing cricket, lacrosse, and rugby. His first Black Swan took place in 1927, as just noted, when he was kicked in the head during a trial rugby match, suffering a concussion. The master of his college (University College), Sir Michael Sadler, offered to accommodate him during his recuperation.

As luck would have it, Sir Michael was visited during James's convalescence by a distinguished South African, General Jan Smuts. His pedigree was unusual. General Smuts had served as Prime Minister of South Africa from 1919 to 1924 and would serve again in the same office from 1939 to 1948. Smuts was to be the only person to sign the treaties that ended both the First and Second World Wars. He was also the only person to sign the charters of both the League of Nations and the United Nations.

In Sir Michael's residence, James had the good fortune to dine with General Smuts, who took an interest in the young man's future ambitions. James expressed an interest in entering South African politics, and Smuts encouraged James to contact him to discuss his plans when he returned to South Africa. He also advised the young man to endeavor to attain financial independence before running for office, noting that if he could make himself financially secure before going into politics, he would be free to bring independence of judgment to bear on all political questions.

This advice would prove to be crucial in James's political career, since his thinking was quite out of step with the views of a majority of his contemporaries on matters concerning race relations, even including Smuts himself, who supported racial segregation. James's family was unalterably opposed to the precursor policies to apartheid and eventually to apartheid when it was formalized into law. He disliked the Afrikaans community and pitted himself against them and their policies.

James returned to South Africa following the completion of his studies at Oxford and entered the advertising business in Johannesburg. Having been financially successful over the following decade, James felt that the time had come to pursue his dream of a career in politics. Sixteen years after his kick in the head, in July 1943, James was elected, with the support of by then and once again Prime Minister Smuts, as a member of the South Africa Parliament by the voters of Woodstock. At some point he was either given or adopted the nickname "Hamo."

In retrospect, it is complex to understand the challenges he faced and the courage that was required (despite his financial independence) to fight for principles that had so few supporters and against such a powerful enemy. James actively agitated for the voting rights of Coloreds. History records that he was unsuccessful during his lifetime but was eventually vindicated in 1994. He also fought against such policies as the reclassification of the races of family members when such reclassifications broke up families. These were risky principles to advocate. As Nelson Mandela later wrote: "The state had grown stronger. The police had become more powerful, their methods more ruthless, their techniques more sophisticated. The South African Defense Force was expanding. The economy was stable, the white electorate untroubled. The South African government had powerful allies in Great Britain and the United States who were content to maintain the status quo."

Despite his liberal views, Hamo was no firebrand. The truth was quite the contrary. Neville Rubin, an anti-apartheid South African who was active in the African Resistance Movement during the early and mid-1960s, knew the Hamilton Russell family quite well. Years later, Rubin recalled that, "Hamo was very much a part of the 'clubbable' English-speaking Cape Town establishment. I well remember not even being surprised when visiting him at his home – 'Cecilia Ridge' in Constantia – to see him in 'plus fours,' presumably on his return from the golf course."

Five years after Hamo's entry into electoral politics, in the 1948 election, a watershed moment in the history of South Africa, the United Party of Jan Smuts was defeated by the Afrikaans National Party, which had publicly sympathized with Nazi Germany. To Hamo's dismay but not surprise, the National Party proceeded to implement a legal system that separated the races politically and socially. This new system was called apartheid, and its purpose was to give the white Afrikaans total economic and political control of South Africa, despite the fact that they constituted a small minority of the population. Hamo felt he could accomplish more within the system than by being an isolated dissident and remained a member of parliament.

In 1963, however, the National Party instituted the so-called "detention without trial" laws. This was the final indignity for Hamo, and a matter of principle. He resigned his seat in Parliament in protest. Thereafter, he was not re-elected to Parliament, but was an active member of the Progressive Party which had been founded in 1959 to oppose apartheid and to champion the rule of law. He passed away in 1981 at the age of 77, having lived a good life and having fought the good fight.

The Children of James Hamilton Russell

The apples did not fall far from the tree in Hamo's case, and although they pursued widely differing professions, his six children followed their father's example and led lives of purpose and in service to others, in several cases having world-wide impact. At least four of the six led lives of relevance to the present study, and their journeys will be described briefly here to provide some clues to understanding the life of their son and nephew, Anthony.

The eldest of Hamo's children was Michael, born in Cape Town in 1932. Mike's chosen profession was medicine. His specialty was psychiatry and his sub-specialty was cigarette smoking. A pioneer in the understanding of why people smoked cigarettes, what addicted them to the product, what killed them in the end, how passive smoking harmed bystanders, and how smokers could be helped to stop their habit, Mike's research formed the basis of much of today's governmental policies on smoking worldwide. Mike and his wife lived most of their lives in the United Kingdom because of their deeply-felt disagreement with the political situation in South Africa.

The fourth and fifth of Hamo's children were twins, Diana and David, born in Cape Town in 1938. Diana graduated from the University of Cape Town, and, following her older siblings, went to the United Kingdom for higher education. She was drawn back to South Africa because of her outrage at the moral bankruptcy of apartheid, matched with her feeling of personal responsibility to work for its eventual demise. Originally committed to peaceful protests, she was by the early 1960s convinced that non-violence was futile against the brutal and implacable forces of the South African apartheid government. In 1968, Diana moved into voluntary exile in the United States and pursued a career as a prolific academic in the emerging field of women's studies. Her focus was sexual violence against women and girls, and her work was both pioneering and impactful.

Diana's twin, David, also attended Cape Town University, and dutifully trotted off to the U.K. for his next degree, taking an M.A. at Oxford. However, his career diverged from his siblings when he entered the ministry of the Anglican Church and was ordained in 1965. He eventually was appointed the 12th Bishop of Grahamstown, a city some 300 miles due east of Cape Town. David, probably more than any of his siblings, took to heart the imperative inherited from their father to demonstrate his total rejection of the policies of the South African apartheid government. And he did this, despite great personal risk, outside the confines of the parliamentary cocoon that had shielded Hamo. David was a lifelong activist against apartheid, as well as a fervent advocate of human rights.

Hamo's second child, born in 1934, was Timothy Patrick Hamilton Russell. Tim, as he was known to all, was the only one of Hamo's children who showed a penchant for business. Accordingly, after the obligatory educational journey from the University of Cape Town to Oxford and then back home, Tim inherited the family advertising business. While possessing a social conscience, Tim was not an activist in the sense that Diana and David were, nor did he choose to enter a profession, as did Mike, that changed the lives of millions for the better. His special role in this story is his passion for the cultivation of grapes and their subsequent fermentation into wine.

In due course, Tim met Athene Wendy Bindon, a young woman of German/Scottish/Irish stock, whose family had lived in South Africa since 1878, when her grandfather arrived to fight in the Zulu War. They had four children, two girls and two boys. Their second child was a son whom they named Anthony Hamilton Russell, and who was born in Cape Town on May 14, 1962. Accordingly, the next card drawn from my card file, and the first *Long Legacy of Echo*, is introduced. Hereinafter, the stories of Tim and Anthony are intermingled, and we will follow them in tandem as far as they go, before Anthony strikes out on his own.

Anthony's Godfather, Robert Watson

Anthony started life with powerful, positive family influences in the form of his aunt and uncles. Interestingly, Tim chose an unusual and remarkable person, Robert Watson, to be Anthony's godfather. Watson was a shadowy figure who might just as easily have been a fictional character in a James Bond novel. Anthony's mother suspects that Robert may have been involved in "a little more than regular" army work. Indirect evidence suggests that he was actively involved in the anti-apartheid movement.

Neville Rubin, already quoted in this chapter, also knew Watson. His understanding of Watson's origins adds to that of Anthony's mother, which confirmed the air of mystery and intrigue. Quoting Rubin again from his email to the author dated October 25, 2014:

> *To start with, though, he was not a South African. He was British, emerged at Cape Town University in 1961, saying he had been in Malaya as a commissioned officer in the British Army, at the time battling a communist insurgency there… He wanted to make contact with non-communist, anti-government activists and said he was in a position to offer training in the use of explosives. I therefore introduced him to those*

on the National Committee for Liberation (later renamed the African Resistance Movement), an underground organisation of which I was a member, and he did indeed provide training for some of us in the use of explosives...

Rubin's conclusion, many years later, was that Watson had been "in fact (and had always been) in the UK secret service and had in fact been planted on us in Cape Town in that capacity."

It is not for me to judge or to try to interpret these varying reports and differing histories of events and personalities engaged in a profound and titanic struggle over fifty years ago. However, I do think that they add depth and texture to the story of Anthony Hamilton Russell.

Anthony's Educational Years

In the same year (1975) that Anthony started high school, Tim purchased undeveloped land in Hermanus, seventy-five miles southeast of Cape Town at 34° South latitude, very close to the actual southernmost point of Africa. The purchase price was Rand 58,000, "The same price as a Range Rover with a few miles on it," Anthony observed. On this land, Tim founded an eponymous vineyard.

Tim developed the vineyard as a hobby and a passion, but he did not expect to make a living at it. Although it was never a source of profit for him, Tim's hobby was a great success in terms of what he set out to achieve. In an obituary published in the trade publication, *Wine Spectator*, shortly after his death in 2013, the author writes, "While highly successful in advertising, Hamilton Russell had a passion for growing and making wine and was the first to see the Hemel-en-Aarde Valley's potential for producing quality wines."

Later in the same article, the author notes, "In 1989, Tim Hamilton Russell and four other Cape winemakers formed the Cape Winelands Commitment, which rejected apartheid and outlined improved farm employment practices. A London newspaper quoted Hamilton Russell that year describing many of the South African wine industry's labor practices at that time as 'morally indefensible.'"

Anthony enrolled at the University of Witwatersrand in Johannesburg. Known as "Wits," it was founded in 1896, the same year in which Shanghai Jiao Tong University was founded in China. Nelson Mandela, who enrolled at Wits for his LL.B. in 1943, wrote that "The English-speaking universities of South Africa were great incubators of liberal values. It was a tribute to these institutions that they allowed black students. For the Afrikaans universities, such a thing was unthinkable."

The high school and college years were complicated for Anthony, a sensitive lad who grew up surrounded by contradictions. "South Africa in the mid-1970s was seductively wealthy," he explained. "It was difficult to resist the beautiful life. The norm was apartheid, so it was accepted. Society was fully stratified, so there was very little mixing of races or languages. I knew that apartheid was wrong so I protested, but my protests took small and invisible forms. For example, I refused to sing the National Anthem, which was in Afrikaans. I felt like a hypocrite because my protest was meaningless. As a teenager at the time, I was a little unhappy that my father did not take a more active role in opposing apartheid."

Anthony hated and feared the Afrikaans police who were cruel, relentless, and unforgiving. Wits was a hot bed of radicalism and large student protests, some of which he attended, were beginning to gather momentum. However, the government was brutally effective in suppressing student dissent. Upon graduation in 1984, he continued, "I left the country to avoid national service in the army. When I arrived in London, I sent my South African passport to Pretoria and renounced my citizenship. At the Irish consulate in London, I applied for citizenship, which was granted."

It was not until 1989, when he was 55 years old, that Tim moved back to Cape Town, having retired from the advertising business. His father's return to the vineyard in 1989 coincided with the sprouting of a seed in Anthony's fertile imagination. He had entered the Wharton School in the fall of 1988 with the intention of learning how he might contribute to the growth of Hamilton Russell Vineyards through the professionalization of its management; in other words, by turning his father's hobby into a larger and more profitable business.

At Wharton, Anthony met several individuals who would become life-long friends. Curtis Brashaw stands out among them. An American whose grandfather was a notable Presbyterian fundamentalist minister, Curtis has for 25 years been restoring the hotels that had in the early twentieth century made Cape May, New Jersey, a popular tourist attraction. "Anthony is the kind of person you would like to have speak at your funeral. He is so articulate and so warm," Curtis told me.

Graduating in 1990 with his MBA degree, Anthony took a job with Bain & Company in London, but this was clearly not destined to be his life's work. Simultaneously, one of the world's great tectonic plates shifted, when on February 11, 1990, Nelson Mandela was released from prison. This was also Anthony's Black Swan, and in due course he seized the opportunity. He decided to return to South Africa and begin work on the farm (it is more than a vineyard, encompassing the commercial production of both honey and olives in addition to grapes and wine). He moved quickly after completing his responsibilities at Bain, understanding deep in his heart that he would never be happy in London.

Anthony served as "Managing Director" of Hamilton Russell Vineyards from 1991 until 1994, when he bought the property from his father, then age sixty. This moment marked the start of formalizing the passion for which he had been preparing, haltingly but unceasingly, for his first thirty-two years.

Anthony's Life's Work Begins

To understand Anthony, one must recognize that he is fiercely attached to South Africa, and especially to the land. When I asked him what books he read as a child that had influenced him most profoundly, he said, without any hesitation, "*To A God Unknown*, by John Steinbeck." In an instant, I understood that Anthony Hamilton Russell is a South African Joseph Wayne. "If you own land," he stated in a subsequent conversation, "you develop an inexplicable spiritual relationship with it. You cannot think of a farm only as an asset. I will stay involved with my property until I die, just like Joseph Wayne. In this book I really understood Joseph's direct line to nature and his relationship with the land."

"At the age of 9, as I was walking through the garden," Anthony reflected, "I decided that there could be no such thing as 'God.' I have felt uncomfortable with organized religion since that walk in the garden and have been an atheist for much of my life. If you have your own sense of right and wrong, and a moral compass, then there is really no need to be lectured on a weekly basis. Despite my atheism and annoyance with organized religion, I have always been superstitious. I fully acknowledge that there are some things that cannot be rationalized. I do not believe that this acknowledgement needs to be formalized or set to liturgy. Being a farmer makes one an animist. I get enormous spiritual income from the farm."

Curtis Brashaw took note of his friend's non-traditional spirituality. "I have always been impressed by Anthony's artistry and sense of wonder," said Curtis, "although he is an atheist. Anthony is one of the most philosophically deep and intellectually rich people I know."

Now, noted Anthony, he is starting to think how best to provide for the next generation, and how to plan for the succession of ownership to one or another of his four daughters, the great-great-grandchildren of Hamo's father, who emigrated to South Africa. He is intent on keeping the farm in the family. His perfect life, he laughs, "would be for my wife and me to be global brand ambassadors for Hamilton Russell Vineyards while a daughter owns and runs the business."

One cannot talk about Anthony without talking about Olive, his wife, soulmate, constant companion, muse, and love of his life. They come as a unit; one does not see Anthony without Olive. They both have strong and independent personalities but complement each other in the best possible way. After spending time with both of them in Hermanus, Cape Town, Johannesburg, Santiago de Chile, and Philadelphia, I know how important she is to him.

I asked Curtis to help me understand Anthony's stated intent to pass the ownership of Hamilton Russell Vineyards to one (and only one) of his four daughters. Curtis laughed and observed that Anthony was simply following matrilineal primogenitor. He has no sons, but he understands that splitting up the inheritance will mean that it will eventually dissipate. The only way to ensure that his legacy is intact is to insist that a single progeny take full responsibility for the land and for passing the land on to another single progeny in the next generation. "For somebody who doesn't believe in God, Anthony feels that his legacy will be for Hamilton Russell Vineyards to live on as a whole," observed Curtis. "He sees the land and the vineyard as the custodian for something bigger than a single individual."

As far as Anthony is concerned, Hamilton Russell Vineyards is inviolable as to the land, the brand, and the vines. He and his wife own it 100% and would not allow any non-family member to own even the smallest share in it. Nevertheless, he has created second and third wine properties, one of which is at a more "accessible" price (he does use a considerable number of marketing clichés, but I forgive him for this minor indiscretion). One of these brands is called 'Southern Right' after the whales of the same name that can be seen spouting in Walker Bay, which the property overlooks at the geographical meeting point of the South Atlantic and Indian Oceans.

Long Legacy of Echo

"Anthony, you strike me as a classic traditionalist," I said, reflecting my emerging sense of his place in the taxonomy of my book. "Tell me about this aspect of your personality."

He started by asking what I meant by "traditionalist" because he thought I meant "antiquated" or "backwards." I explained that what I meant was that he was modern but retained a strong interest in and great respect for his roots. With that clarification, he was comfortable with being called a traditionalist. "I certainly draw inspiration from the past, and I find that many of today's 'innovations' are merely a return to past practices. For example, everything used to be 'organic,' but we lost touch with the natural ways of doing things. Wine is a link to nature, which is vitally important to me. I am not that interested in the financial aspect of wine and sell it in order to finance my lifestyle. What I find nurturing is the land, the rain, the harvest, the production of the wine, and especially the growing of the grapes. Wine is a form of expressing the land. I also believe in creating new traditions and in respecting traditions. Keeping HRV in the family is perhaps the strongest of the traditions I intend to keep."

"Although I am not religious and have already told you that I resent being lectured on Sunday mornings, I have constructed a family chapel on the grounds of Hamilton Russell Vineyards. Maybe my daughters will get married in it. I also planted a long line of Yellow Wood trees, a slow-growing, indigenous variety that I will not live to see at their maturity. This does not bother me at all if my daughters and my grandchildren do so. I am frightened of rootlessness. I feel that moving a home is risky. I want to give the family roots. I want to leave my mark on the farm for centuries to come."

"Anthony is very focused on his legacy," Curtis Brashaw later confirmed. "Perhaps this is because he is an atheist and sincerely believes that there is no afterlife. Did you know that he keeps a diary? Every day, he pastes something from that day – maybe a movie ticket stub or a wine label – and writes notes around it. He has volumes and volumes of these materials – the physical record of his existence. Anthony also collects things. Somehow, they all tie into the focus on his legacy. He wants to leave behind as much as possible about himself because he does not expect an eternal life in heaven."

"Man evolved in a happy state because of his co-existence with nature," continued Anthony. "With the development of agriculture and the permanent societies that grew up around it, this happy state was interrupted. Modern society, I think, is uncomfortable with this interruption of our hard-wired state. The result is dysfunctional behavior. Having a relationship with nature is essential for everything from spirituality to physical well-being."

"At Hamilton Russell Vineyards we are investigating the concept of 'biodynamics,' which is a spiritual-ethical-ecological approach to agriculture, food production, and nutrition. It is not new – it was first introduced almost a century ago. Biodynamic farmers try to create a diversified, balanced farm ecosystem that generates health and fertility as much as possible from within the farm itself. It is innovative in the twenty-first century but draws on ideas that have existed since the 1920s. Biodynamics is beyond simply organic. It encompasses the entire cycle of the environment. It strives to be spiritually in tune with the ecology of the farm. This is what I mean by humans being 'hard-wired.' We lost touch with our hard-wiring and biodynamics is a path back as well as forward."

"A biodynamic approach considers the whole ecology of a property and looks to keep all components in a virtuous balance. From my point of view, sustainability, balance, and biodiversity make me a happier farmer! Our whole team simply feels better about our wines knowing that they are made virtuously with respect to our surroundings and our place in nature. I concur with the view that excessive specialization can cause one to lose understanding of the 'whole.'"

Anthony has some eccentricities which puzzle casual acquaintances, but they all make sense in terms of who he is. For example, he collects Stone-Age implements and tools. I doubt that he will use them to farm his land, but they are perfectly consistent with his interest in bio-dynamics. He also collects wine corks and has thousands. He would never consider bottling his wine with a screw-top or a plastic cork. He carries a lethal-looking six-inch folding knife (incongruously for such a gentle man) which he uses at every meal. He likes the continuity of eating his food with the same implement. He mentioned that he was bringing home some acorns from Curtis Brashaw's farm in Cape May, New Jersey, to plant an oak grove on HRV.

Anthony is full of contradictions, which only contribute to his attractiveness as an interlocuter. He is a classic extrovert, and loves being around people. But he also lives with his wife and four dogs in a huge house on a gigantic farm with no near-by neighbors. When I asked him about this, he had a ready but surprising answer.

"Outsiders have a better sense of human nature. If you are not part of the mainstream, you have a higher 'E.Q.' because you need to read people more accurately to survive. Insiders are comfortable, and you stop thinking and feeling when you are comfortable. I am instinctively scared of those who are insiders. I am suspicious of any tightly formed group which is intolerant of outsiders. This behavior creates closed minds and a false sense of comfort. I am afraid of mobs which feel entitled to inflict their views on everyone. Self-righteous indignation bothers me a great deal."

Who Is Anthony Hamilton Russell?

Anthony is first and foremost a good man. As I think about Anthony, I cannot help but believe that his genes – of his grandfather, who took such principled stands as a South African politician against apartheid and of his Uncle David and Aunt Diana, who enlisted in a clandestine organization, membership in which brought with it the gravest personal danger – animate much of his thought and actions. I also cannot help but believe that in choosing as his godfather a man who probably worked undercover against the apartheid regime, Anthony's father was sending his son a message that would reverberate in strange and wonderful ways.

Anthony is also a modern-day Joseph Wayne. Hewn from the same rock as the character in Steinbeck's *To A God Unknown*, Anthony is a *bhumiputra*, Sanskrit for "son of the soil." In this sense, he is so solidly grounded that he carries a comforting feeling of permanence, based on respect for bedrock values with which nobody can disagree. One never wonders if Anthony Hamilton Russell will be true to his word or his principles.

Anthony did not stay and fight apartheid when he graduated from college in 1984. He eschewed the violence that Robert Watson had promoted. He saw, perhaps, as futile the parliamentary route taken by his grandfather. He rejected his father's passive stance. He ran away and took Irish citizenship in impotent protest. But he had bigger things in mind. I think he recognized that apartheid would not last forever, and that the time would come when he could return to the country he loved and engage in the work that was embedded in his genome. In this way, he resembles others in this book, people who all declined confrontation, violence, or destruction in favor of peaceful reconciliation and construction. By now I hope you will have perceived that the author feels enormous respect and affection for this type of individual.

Moving on to Tokyo

As I sit on a rock at the Cape of Good Hope (not exactly the southernmost tip of Africa, but close enough for my purposes), I reflect on the journeys taken so far in this book. We have come a long way and discovered many truths that were not apparent to the unaided eye. Now, once again, we take to the air, this time travelling 9,175 miles north and west from Cape Town to Tokyo, mostly over the Indian Ocean, crossing the Equator once again before making landfall over Thailand. Laos and Vietnam are next, followed by a long passage over China. Finally we cross the East China Sea, make our second landfall over southern Japan, and land at Narita International Airport, incongruously and conspicuously perched amid rice fields 37 miles from Tokyo's Imperial Palace. Narita was opened in 1978 despite the strenuous objections of rice farmers who would lose their land through its construction. Some of the farmers refused to move and thirty years later the most hardline ones are still there, sandwiched in between runways. It is an uncomfortable sight for the passenger landing at Narita to see the aged farmers frozen in time amid the high velocity and ever-changing industry of modern aviation.

The Long Legacy of Echo

Keisuke Muratsu

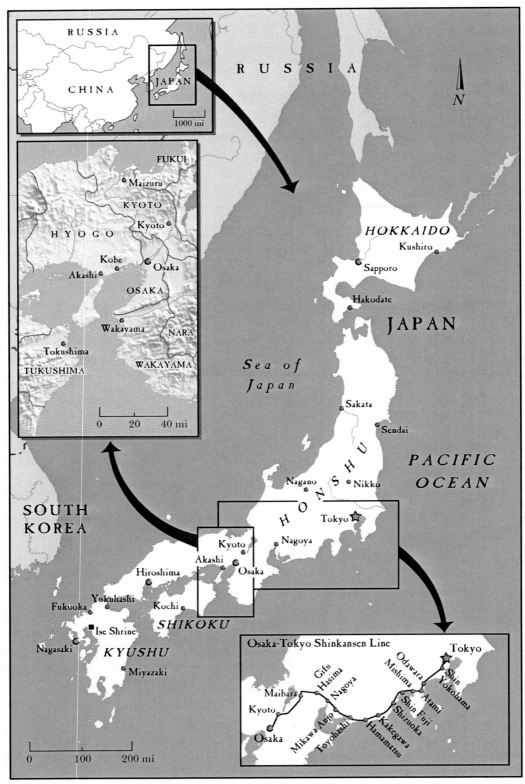

The Long Legacy of Echo: Keisuke Muratsu

Latitudes of Time

February 3rd dawned cold in Tokyo, with the brilliant sunshine of a crystal-clear winter morning. Visibility was endless. Not a single cloud obstructed the bright blue sky as I looked out over the Imperial Palace from the balcony on the 19th floor of The Palace Hotel Tokyo, whose chairman, Takashi Kobayashi, has been my good friend for many years.

I was soon to be accorded a rare privilege for a Westerner, namely, to attend a performance of Katoubushi, a relatively obscure style of Japanese singing. In the words of one twenty-first century Japanese admirer of this genre, "Kato-bushi is an area about which the general public knows little." What made this day special was that my friend of thirty years, Keisuke Muratsu, would be performing the lead role in a Katoubushi play entitled "Yuya." The play was about a master and a mistress, and Kei would play the part of the mistress. I knew about Takarazuka, another Japanese theatrical genre in which women played all the roles, including the male roles, but a man playing a woman was new to me.

How complex for my Western mind to grasp and understand. I obviously had much more to learn about my friend and about Japan, despite the fact that I had been visiting Japan since 1980 and had made well over 100 trips to visit most of the largest cities and dozens of historical sites in the country. My earnest attempts to learn the language had been largely unsuccessful, if somewhat amusing to my Japanese friends.

Noh, created in the 14th century, is the oldest form of Japanese musical drama. The actors wear masks and show emotion by very slow dancing and singing. This dramatic form was most popular with the noble and samurai classes. Kabuki started later, around the time of Shakespeare. The actors wore make-up instead of masks and spoke directly to the audience in a colloquial style. Kabuki was popular with merchants, craftsmen, and ordinary civilians.

Katoubushi was created as an art form in 1717. This was well before the United States of America was founded, less than 60 years after the Peace of Westphalia and only one hundred years after Macbeth and King Lear were first performed. While these comparisons may seem incongruous, my point is that Katoubushi is a traditional art form that dates back into what we would call antiquity. It survives unchanged three centuries later, with the meticulous attention to detail, precision, and continuity that is needed for a performance art to survive.

Another interesting feature of Katoubushi is that Japan was closed to the outside world for over two hundred years, from the Seclusion Laws of the 1630s promulgated by the Tokugawa Shogunate to Commander Perry's Black Ships anchoring in Tokyo Bay in 1854. During this period, Christianity was outlawed, foreign influence was abolished, and foreign trade was limited to a single Dutch company that was confined to a small island in Nagasaki Harbor, itself located on the southern shore of Kyushu, Japan's southern-most island, as far removed from Tokyo as was geographically possible. Katoubushi is a completely Japanese art form, not influenced by other cultures.

My friend had been trained by an elderly woman who passed on her love for the tradition that means so much to Japan and the Japanese people. Indeed, this type of training is essential because Katoubushi is not written with the Western form of musical notation as used by Mozart. The "sheet music" consists of highly-stylized Chinese characters that serve as guidelines, but the way the words are sung can only be taught by someone who knows how to sing them. There is no musical score in Katoubushi. If the human chain is broken, it can never be revived. Without someone training the next generation, there would be no more living Katoubushi, and it would become extinct as an art form.

Keisuke Muratsu Is Introduced

Keisuke Muratsu, the second *Long Legacy of Echo*, was born on March 30, 1949, in Akashi City in Hyogo Prefecture, an hour's drive almost due west of Osaka, 232 years after the establishment of Katoubushi. His father was descended from the Tatsuno family, which had made soy sauce for many generations. To the Japanese, soy sauce is more than a condiment. In fact, its taste, called umami, is considered a fifth taste (after sweet, sour, bitter, and salty). The Tatsuno family's "Higashi Maru" brand of soy sauce is still well known and prized by many as the best of all the hundreds of varieties of soy sauce made in Japan.

Kei's paternal grandfather had diversified the family business into both textiles and fertilizer. Then came the cataclysmic and catastrophic Kanto Earthquake of September 1923. Since the family depended on transporting their products to the Kanto region, including Yokohama and Tokyo, and the earthquake having destroyed all transportation links along this route, their businesses were also destroyed. At this time, Ryoukichi (Kei's father) was 5 years old. Kei's mother's aristocratic ancestors were famous as naval warriors.

There were very few jobs in Japan in the years immediately following the end of the Second World War. Faced with this uncertainty, Ryoukichi decided to start a business in 1946. Previously, glass ampules for medical uses were hand-crafted, and it was his innovation to develop a manufacturing process for these products. "My father," wrote Kei, "started manufacturing ampules in 1946 as an individual person and incorporated into a 'limited company' in 1951." The company celebrated its 70th anniversary on November 5, 2021.

Kei was born three-and-a-half years after the end of the war and has few memories of Japan in the early 1950s. He does not recall feeling poor, although he remembers how little the family had to eat. His strong memory was of a father who supported his son, who valued the father-son relationship, and who looked forward and not backward.

Japan is a Confucian country, and Kei is a Confucian without having to say so.

Confucianism has cohabited quite peacefully with Buddhism in Japan (as well as in China). The Muratsu Family is also Zen Buddhist. I asked Kei what values he learned from Zen Buddhism. His first thought was "love for family and others." I asked him about fatalism, and he acknowledged that this was certainly one component of Zen philosophy. He states that he "believes in God," and meditates, not in the Zen manner or in the Christian manner but following his own beliefs. Kei feels that his values are syncretic, coming from both Zen Buddhism and Catholicism. When I asked him to describe how he fits Confucianism into his personal philosophy, his response was interesting. "I have no idea of 'Confucianism.' I have never studied it nor been educated under its influence," Kei wrote to me. "My father was a Buddhist and my mother was Christian (Catholic). During four years' stay in the Middle East, I learned some about Islam. I cannot tell if I am a Confucian. You decide from your observation."

As we discussed life philosophies, we spoke about free will and fate. This seemed to touch his deeper set of values. Kei expressed the belief that life's misfortunes are the consequences of the misbehavior or misdeeds of one's ancestors (whether emperors or mosquitos). This led him to the conviction that he has an obligation to behave well in his lifetime to protect the future inheritors of his soul. Nevertheless, there is no question in my mind that Kei believes he has the ability to make choices and to respond to evolving and unexpected circumstances in ways that change the future for himself and others. The many Black Swans he would encounter and to which he responded robustly provide strong evidence to support my conclusion.

Wanting to learn about his character from another person, I spoke to Hur Kwangsoo, a Korean who is a close friend of Kei. Kwangsoo is the second-generation owner of a group of companies in Seoul, but his passion is golf, and it was through golf that he met Kei. They are both members of the Asia Pacific Golf Confederation.

"I have observed," Kwangsoo began, "that during meetings of the APGC, of which Kei is now a vice president, he is quite effective in helping the group to reach a consensus. I think this is because he is open, straightforward, and consistent. With members from 37 countries, there are inevitably conflicting views and needs that must be reconciled. The other members know that he will be fair and not compromise on matters of principle. He is also effective because he is humble. He makes his point openly but not in a threatening way."

The First Black Swan

In 1967, soon to graduate from high school, Kei was invited to go to Tokyo with a friend to visit the city and the University of Tokyo. This was the first of several life-changing experiences that would profoundly affect this young man's direction in life. He decided to apply to the University of Tokyo, which changed his world from the static environment of his youth to the dynamics of change.

The year 1968 was confusing, disquieting and disillusioning for those of us who were college students at the time. Some of us were even enraged. In the United States, the response to the Tet Offensive in Vietnam (started on January 30th), the My Lai Massacre (March 16th), the murders of Martin Luther King (April 4th) and Robert Kennedy (June 6th), and a host of other painful incisions in the fabric of society, was a wave of student rebellions from Berkeley to Columbia. Paris followed for different but related reasons, and Tokyo was no exception.

The origins of the unrest in Japanese universities are as complex and as contested as the uprisings in the United States, but surprisingly similar in their trajectories. At that time, Japanese universities were managed as paternalistic, authoritarian regimes. Because of the recovery from the war and rapid economic development, students were unfamiliar with the hardship of the preceding decades, and impatient with the pace of reform. There was deep discontent about the U.S.-Japan Mutual Cooperation and Security Treaty, which was up for renewal. Japanese students were well aware of the student-led rebellions around the world, and no doubt the mood was contagious. Some of the discontent, such as opposition to the American war in Vietnam, was universal among students. The response of the authorities to student protests was dismissive, insensitive, and eventually brutal, which further motivated the students to misbehave. What had started as campus-based disputes evolved into anger about broader political and social issues. The University of Tokyo was so deeply affected that it closed for eleven months between 1968 and 1969.

One of Kei's closest friends at the University of Tokyo was Kozo Yamamoto, who was born in Yukuhashi, Fukuoka, also in Kyushu, as previously noted the southernmost of Japan's islands. He worked for the Ministry of Finance after college, earned an MBA from Cornell, and in 1993 was elected to the House of Representatives of the National Diet.

"I would say," Yamamoto-san started, "that Kei and I were both 'neutral.' We were not conservatives. But we were also not radicals; we did not participate in the vandalism or fighting, and we were never arrested. However, we understood the radicals and had sympathy for the matters about which they were protesting. We disapproved of their tactics but supported their goals. It was difficult to know how to participate in bringing about change but also to work within the system."

There are many echoes of Confucianism in Kei's life, despite his disavowal of any knowledge of this philosophy. This moment, as described by his college classmate, is an example. The Confucian feels a need to remonstrate against a ruler who has strayed from the path of benevolence and righteousness. But at the same time, the Confucian is not a rebel, and is committed to working within the system to correct any imbalance.

"Kei and I both chose a seminar taught by Professor Ryutaro Komiya," Yamamoto-san continued, "who at the time was both a famous professor and an intimidating presence. But it was a difficult time for Professor Komiya. Because of the respect everyone had for him, the president of the university asked him to serve as a 'special advisor' for the purpose of negotiating with the radical students who were occupying the campus. The negotiations were unsuccessful, and the police were eventually called to end the campus occupation. There was fighting, resulting in injuries and many arrests. This must have caused Professor Komiya deep pain to have failed in his mission. He would have a strong influence on Kei's and my thinking."

The Second Black Swan

We next find Kei at loose ends in 1968 due to the closure of his university after the completion of his first year as a student. He never considered sloth and indolence as options. What would a young Japanese student, already imbued with tradition, and full of ideals and ambition, accomplish during this interlude? Kei packed up his fears, his limited English, and his innate curiosity, and set off for California, then Michigan (Ann Arbor), then Pennsylvania (Philadelphia) and finally Washington, D.C., always through fortuitous connections. He spent a month in the United States, and although initially concerned about hostility, found only friendliness and welcoming people everywhere. When he asked how he could repay their kindness, he reports that he always received the same answer – please be kind, welcoming, and open to others.

By the time of his graduation from the University of Tokyo in 1971, he was already dating his future wife, Masumi. Masumi (known to all as "Mami") is descended from an aristocratic family. Her grandfather was Chairman of the Moustache Society of Japan, and his sculptured bust (with a prominent moustache) adorns the lobby of the apartment building they own and in which they live in Minami Azabu. Mami also attended a Catholic school, called Sacred Heart and went to "finishing school" in Geneva and Lausanne. Her family owns a country inn, now managed by Kei, in Nikko, a town of under 100,000 inhabitants that is a popular tourist destination, a two-hour drive due north of Tokyo.

The Third Black Swan

After graduation, Kei started work at Marubeni, one of the large Japanese trading companies, with a corporate history dating back to 1858. He was assigned to the power plant export unit with specific responsibility for negotiations with Meralco, the Filipino electric company. He described to me his next inflection point, which occurred when he was involved as the most junior member of a ten-man Japanese negotiating team that was matched with a two-man Filipino negotiating team. Although the Japanese side had quite senior negotiators and handily outnumbered their Filipino counterparts, he observed that the team from Meralco constantly outmaneuvered the Marubeni side. Consisting of two America-trained MBA graduates, the Filipino team made a profound impression on Kei and influenced his next big decision, which was to go to the United States for his MBA.

He applied to the Wharton School in 1973 and started his MBA in January of 1974. His daughter, Midori, was born in Japan and accompanied Kei and Mami to Philadelphia at the tender age of 5 months. At first, he was disoriented and confused. He discovered that his English language abilities were insufficient for the rigor of the course load and he floundered. Kei told me about his distress following his first class at Wharton, taught by Marshall Blume, a distinguished professor of finance. He recalled that he had returned home after the class and instructed Mami to pack their belongings as he would have to return to Japan, having understood not a single word of the first lecture. Mami encouraged him to give it another try, which he did.

Upon graduation from Wharton, Kei was hired by First National City Bank (now "Citi") and sent to Beirut for training. He brought Mami, Midori (still not yet 2 years old), and his mother-in-law. Much to his consternation, he and his young family were soon caught up in the Civil War in Lebanon, which commenced in 1975. After taking cover in a hotel for a few days, Kei and his family were evacuated to Athens by a plane chartered by FNCB, where he resumed his training program. After nine months of training, he was dispatched to Riyadh (he had requested an assignment anywhere as long as it was on an ocean), where he stayed for four years.

He returned to Tokyo in 1980 as "international staff," which meant he was on a higher pay scale and had a better housing allowance than "local hires." He worked hard, and achieved important milestones for Citibank, including the development of a branch network, and the installation of an ATM system.

The Fourth Black Swan

In 1985, his next turning point arrived courtesy of an offer from Citibank to send him to New York. This happened at roughly the same time that his father suffered a stroke. Although his father recovered from the stroke, he asked Kei not to go to New York and to take on more responsibilities at the family company. This was the first time in his life that Kei's father had denied him his wish to follow his instincts. Kei had no choice but to stay in Tokyo, where he resigned from Citibank and formed a personal company that he called "Activity International." He engaged in advisory work for clients with excess liquidity, an increasingly prevalent phenomenon as Japan entered its "bubble" period, while at the same time getting immersed in the family business. He had four distinct personalities, distinguished by the way he identified himself: "sacho" to his employees, "papa" to his children, "Muratsu-san" to his Japanese friends, and "Kei" to his Western friends.

Necessity is often the mother of invention (and entrepreneurship), and as previously noted, Ryoukichi Muratsu had founded a company soon after the Second World War ended. Through hard work, and with the tailwind of an expanding market, he built the company, called "Naigai," into the largest supplier of one-use glass ampules to the Japanese medical community. A quirk of the industrial and distribution systems in Japan cost him profits. All the glass tubing that Naigai used to make the ampules was supplied by a domestic company called Nippon Electric Glass (NEG) that held a monopoly on this business segment, and distributed by another domestic company called Nissho, which also had a monopoly. This would have been acceptable except for the fact that these Japanese companies charged 30% to 40% more than non-Japanese companies charged for the same product and service. Ryoukichi accepted this premium as a condition built into Japanese business culture and for forty years he earned less but lived at peace with his supplier and distributor.

By 1991, Ryoukichi's health had deteriorated to the point where he could no longer run the company. Accordingly, and with dignity, he retired. Kei succeeded him as president and chief executive officer. One of Kei's first actions was to set in motion the sourcing of glass tubing from suppliers in Germany and South Korea. This action, which violated an unspoken Japanese code, was alarming to NEG and Nissho. If Naigai got away with this behavior, what would prevent all the other companies in this industry from doing the same? NEG and Nissho saw a threat to their monopolies.

This action also reflected two wellsprings in Kei's character. The first was his global sensibility, honed through his education at Wharton and his years with FNCB in Riyadh. It just seemed illogical to him to pay extra because of a tradition that penalized one side of the transaction, and for which there was no domestic remedy because the power was held by a monopoly. The second was his ethical belief – the system was wrong, and the system needed fixing. A monopoly was a contradiction in terms in a "free market."

Because a percentage of Naigai's customers specified NEG glass and would not accept ampules made with foreign glass, NEG still had some leverage over Naigai. When NEG learned that Naigai planned to diversify its sources of tubing, it retaliated by charging a premium to Naigai, discounting the price to Naigai's competitors and doing everything possible to retain its monopoly. Muratsu-san filed a lawsuit alleging "unfair trade practice" and "unreasonable restraint of trade." A long (24 years and counting) and costly legal battle ensued.

According to Kozo Yamamoto, "This anti-trust case was a test of his character as a man, as well as his patience. The process dragged out for a long time, and he was at one point at risk of corporate and personal bankruptcy. He had severe difficulties, but he showed great resilience in the face of overwhelming odds. Kei is a man of principles, and he refused to give up. I admire him for his strength of character, regardless of what he may or may not accomplish."

Green Shoots

On May 25th, I had the good fortune to drive from Tokyo to Narita Airport, as noted in the concluding paragraph of the previous chapter, set in a rice-growing region some 37 miles northeast of Tokyo. As my bus neared the airport, I noticed green shoots of rice plants growing in the paddies that bracketed the highway. I estimated that they are not more than four inches above the water. Orderly row upon orderly row, as they have been on every May 25th since humans changed from hunting and gathering to agriculture.

In these years of personal growth and professional development, Kei's life flowered with his deep involvement in two very traditional activities, one an import from Scotland and the other an indigenous art form.

The first was golf. While he was always a devoted golfer, his interest in the rules and traditions of the sport led to his participation in the Japan Golf Association, as a volunteer at matches and eventually as Chairman for Rules. This passion and respect for the traditions of the game animate Kei in everything he does. He is a stickler for playing the game according to the rules, and insists that there are no "winter rules," "mulligans," or "gimmies," although he does allow a free drop in the event of landing in "GUR."

He finds strength and comfort in the rules of golf. This is an echo of Kei's deep roots as a Confucian, although he would deny any knowledge of this root. It is also an echo of an important characteristic of the Japanese people, which is the respect and consideration which everyone pays to all others. I can see clear parallels and similarities between the Japanese form of respect and Peter Singer's philosophy. A Japanese believes and acts on the belief that his or her interests are no more important than the interests of any other person, simply because they are his or her interests. Playing by the rules shows respect to your fellow golfers. In this way, I feel that Japan, more than any other country I have visited, lives this principle on a day-to-day basis, and not just for special occasions. This is part of what makes me feel so comfortable in Japan, despite its many superficial differences from America. Kei's respect for the rules and formality of golf is an interesting and completely understandable merging of Japanese values with a sport invented in Scotland.

The second traditional activity in which he participates is a form of singing that has been in existence for more than three centuries, as noted at the beginning of this chapter. As we relaxed over a dinner of sushi in Tokyo on February 2nd, I asked Kei to help me understand his relationship with this art and why he practiced it.

"It is called Katoubushi, and it was originated by Masumi Katou, a major wholesaler in the largest fish market during the middle of the Edo Era in 1717," he started. "Katou-san loved Kabuki and wanted to revitalize this art form by introducing some Noh stories. Noh was enjoyed in a restricted way by a limited number of people, as it is now. So Katou developed Katoubushi as an alternative form of music, which combined elements of Noh with elements of Kabuki, but without movement or dance. Katoubushi is unique because it was created in Edo (now Tokyo) while other artistic traditions including Noh were created in either Kyoto or Osaka."

"The title of the drama in which I will sing tomorrow is 'Yuya,' and it is identical to the Yuya of Noh. I sing the part of Yuya, a mistress, and a well-known geisha from Shimbashi named Kiyoha sings the part of Munemori, a master."

"A long time ago, when I returned to Japan from four years in Saudi Arabia, I felt in my heart a need to return to Japanese culture and to immerse myself in what it meant to be Japanese. I started learning Kabuki, but eventually a friend urged me to try Katoubushi, which he felt would suit me better. He was correct, and I have been studying and performing Katoubushi for more than twenty years."

"There are some young women who are learning the *shamisen*," he smiled ruefully, "but there are very few young people who are willing to make the commitment to learn the singing, which is quite difficult and takes many years to perfect."

"I know this may sound strange," he laughed, "but the gender of the person who sings a particular part is not important. It is more a question of which part is more important. In the case of the song I will perform, the part of Yuya, the mistress, is the most important, so I sing it. The part of the master is just a supporting role. As you will notice tomorrow, there is not really any gender in the singing, which is expressed as human emotion, rather than male or female emotion."

"The story is really quite simple, although fraught with emotion," Kei explained. "Yuya is the mistress of a master named Munemori. She learns that her mother is ill and begging her daughter to return home before she dies. Yuya asks permission from Munemori to go to her mother, but he denies her permission because of a most selfish reason, namely that it is springtime in Japan, and he wants her to entertain him as he and his friends watch the cherry blossoms. While entertaining her master, she recites a poem about her love for her mother which moves even the hardest of hearts. Munemori finally relents and gives her permission to go to her mother."

We return now to the cold, clear morning of my first encounter with Katoubushi, with which this chapter began. The performance took place on the 8th floor of a nondescript Tokyo office building. Upon entrance into the performance hall, I was greeted by several ladies in kimono, who appeared startled to see a Westerner, but quickly reverted to kindness and smiles. I estimated that at 64 years of age, I was probably the youngest person in the room. There was a performance underway in the auditorium directly off the foyer. I was very politely asked to wait a little. *Shosho o-match, kudasai.* My first Japanese cultural tutor, a delectable mountain named Takubo Kohei, told me that this expression was so polite, you would even be able to ask the Emperor himself to wait if you used these words.

The auditorium, which had about 500 seats, was at first sparsely populated, again with a geriatric crowd, some of whom appeared to be sleeping. The others were enjoying the outing, and various members of the audience seemed well acquainted with one another. The first act I watched consisted of two female singers and two female musicians playing the *shamisen*. I learned later that the lead *shamisen* player, a lady I estimated to be in her seventies, was a "national treasure." The singing and playing were new to me and bore no resemblance to Western music. Where Western music is mathematical in its rhythms, Katoubushi seemed to be more dependent on the rhythms of human breathing. Everything was controlled and perfectly disciplined. The singers sat on their knees utterly motionless and expressionless, while expressing strong emotions through the sounds of their voices.

The musicians were equally disciplined. While their fingers, wrists, and forearms moved with blinding and unerring speed, nothing else moved. Their expressions were as impassive as those of the singers, and no other body parts ever moved. In the Western world, we often equate creativity with a lack of discipline, wildness, and personal expression. In Katoubushi, by contrast, iron-willed discipline and perfect control were the sources of the creativity and self-expression. The audience was appreciative of the performance, which lasted about ten minutes.

Finally, the curtain came up on my friend. The tableau consisted of five performers. Three were female instrumentalists, all playing the *shamisen*. One of them was the national treasure mentioned above. Paired with Kiyoha playing the master, Kei dutifully performed the role of the mistress. It was stunning for its completely unexpected delivery. Neither performer looked at the other. There was no gender-bending. Neither performer had any mannerisms that would be called masculine or feminine. Kei did not sing in falsetto, although the voice he used was unrelated to his normal speaking voice.

Kei's performance was controlled, rigid, and expressionless, but at the same time full of emotion. The methodology, mannerisms, voices, and staging were all outside of anything I had ever encountered before. I have always felt that it is important to attempt to understand other people by trying to see things from their perspective, rather than expecting them to conform to my own conceptions. I came away moved by my new appreciation for a non-Western style of creative expression that was so different from how Westerners feel about creativity and creative expression.

Who Is Keisuke Muratsu?

What is the inner spark in this extraordinary, exemplary man? In his words, "Things you do not foresee or cannot control can change your life, but you need to be ready and willing to act on these inflection points. Otherwise, you will have no break-out moments."

Fate, it seems, trumps planning to this Zen Buddhist. Or maybe not; maybe it is a willingness to change and a corresponding detachment from what might seem to be a predetermined path. In a sense, this is a contradiction – allowing a lightning strike to divert you from the path that was set for you. I think that Kei's health, happiness, and harmony are based on his ability and flexibility to seize these moments without hesitation. Kei's life was changed by at least four such inflection points, always guided by respect for tradition and a duty to lead a life that would not damage the chances of the next incarnation of his soul.

The population of Japan is shrinking and aging; they have been beset with tragedy from political miscalculation, technological hubris, and natural disaster; and their economy has fallen from the pinnacle of material success and power to the abyss of the "lost decade." And yet, something sustains this homogenous, proud country. I see no signs of collapse, ennui, or malaise when I visit Japan (and I have visited Japan three to four times every year since my first trip in 1980). In trying to understand why and how they endure, I always return to two themes: respect and tradition. The Japanese respect each other. Despite the fact that it is a severely hierarchical society, the hierarchy is carefully defined to give dignity to all, regardless of their position in society. Everyone is genuinely considerate of all others. The Japanese also have a deeply engrained love and respect for tradition. Whether it is in the eternal rebuilding of the Ise Shrine that started in the fifth century or the generational renewal of Katoubushi that was begun 300 years ago, the spirit of Japan, defined by tradition, cannot be extinguished. Henry Kissinger reached a similar conclusion when he wrote that Japan has a "...resilience sustained by an indomitable national spirit based on a distinctive national culture." Kei Muratsu represents all that is wise, humble, principled, and enduring about this great culture, and I have the greatest respect and affection for this complicated but jovial Citizen of the World.

Moving on to Valladolid

We will now travel mostly westward but also somewhat south, from Tokyo to Valladolid, in northwestern Spain, a long journey of 6,647 miles. We will assume that our flight (at least from Tokyo to Madrid) is non-stop, which will allow us to take the Great Circle Route. We head due north from Narita, crossing Siberia, nearly nipping Nova Zemla, then heading south over the Scandinavian countries and Western Europe before landing in Spain after a flight of almost sixteen hours. It is tiring, but thoughts of the almost two years it took the Dutch to travel for the first time from Rotterdam to that small island in Nagasaki Harbor at the end of the sixteenth century will shame us into quietly enduring any discomfort caused by our choice of entrée not being available for dinner on the flight.

The Long Legacy of Echo

Arantxa Ochoa

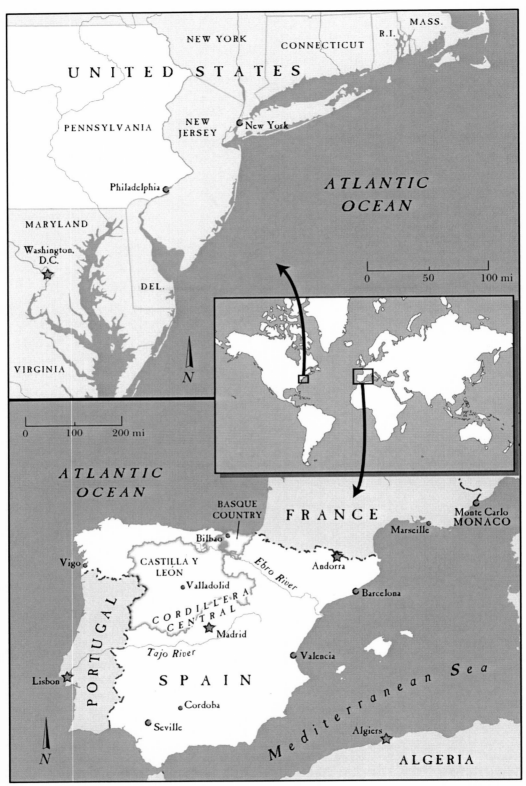

The Long Legacy of Echo: Arantxa Ochoa

Setting the Stage, Valladolid, Spain, Circa 1550 CE

With the discovery by Christopher Columbus in 1492 of what he hoped, and mistakenly thought, was a western route to India, an assortment of opportunities as well as challenges opened for Europeans. The encounter with existing populations who were neither Asians nor monsters meant that the fortune hunters, conquistadors, and colonizers were confronted with a dilemma. How were they to categorize these new beings? The "Indians" were easily subdued by the Europeans' "guns, germs, and steel," and were quickly killed or enslaved. But at the same time, a variety of Christian theologians (there were many theologians, but they tended to be quiet) and human rights activists (there were few human rights activists, but they tended to be noisy) insisted that the mistreatment of the Indians was immoral because the local population consisted of humans who were equal to Europeans in the sight of God. Under the circumstances, what was a Pope to do? Pope Paul III (who also commissioned Michelangelo to supervise construction of St. Peter's Basilica) issued a bull in 1537 confirming that all men are capable of "receiving the doctrines of the faith." The Catholic faith to be sure; many of different faiths (Jews, Protestants, and Muslims) had been tortured and killed during the Spanish Inquisition.

When the practice of killing and enslaving the Indians continued unabated, King Charles V of Spain, no doubt conflicted over the peril and promise inherent in this debate, elected a different approach. On April 16, 1550, he "ordered that conquests in the New World be suspended and not be resumed until his theologians had agreed on a just way of proceeding." Accordingly, the king summoned a fourteen-member council of learned councilors to consider the question of the humanity of the First Americans.

This council met during the summer of 1550, in Valladolid, which with an average midsummer temperature in the low 70s was a delightful location for a conclave. Ferdinand and Isabella, who had bankrolled the 1492 voyage of Columbus, were married in Valladolid in 1469, and had established that city as the capital of their kingdom. Miguel de Cervantes, the great Spanish poet, novelist, and playwright, lived and worked in Valladolid, which was a cultural center during the Spanish renaissance. The city is steeped in tradition and the Spanish "soul" is present everywhere.

Having received testimony (with passionate views expressed on both sides of the question), the members of Charles' council dispersed to consider the evidence at their leisure. Reconvening in January of the following year, they were expected to vote on the question, but found themselves unable to reach any decisions. In practical terms, the convenience and impunity with which the conquistadors did as they pleased with the Indians meant that they would continue their practices in the New World. In addition, the gold and silver that existed in such immense quantities in the New World proved irresistible to the mercantilist Spanish. But the effort made by the church to argue for the humanity of the Indians would forever change the terms of the debate. No longer would enslavement be undertaken without questions, and "Not merely the Spanish but European peoples on all continents would be haunted for centuries by the question debated at Valladolid."

Introducing Arantxa Ochoa

Nearly half a millenium later a girl was born in Valladolid, destined to become a world famous ballerina and an inspiring teacher. Her name is Arantxa Ochoa, and she is imbued with the Spanish soul she acquired both genetically and through osmosis. She has benefited from tradition and carried on tradition so respectfully that she is a third perfect embodiment of *The Long Legacy of Echo*. An understanding of this remarkable woman must begin with this look at the history of Valladolid, since she still carries with her the culture, the grandeur, the strength, the lust for adventure, the curiosity, the forces in conflict, the strong moral code, and all the ambiguities of her heritage.

It is well-documented that Arantxa was a vivacious, mesmerizing, and legendary performer. Her long and distinguished career as the principal dancer at Pennsylvania Ballet was recognized by the critics, the audiences, and the community of professional dancers. She was respected and beloved by all, whether she performed as Aurora in *Sleeping Beauty*, Giselle, Odile/Odette in *Swan Lake*, or Sugarplum in *The Nutcracker*.

Janet Anderson, in her review of a world premier presented by Pennsylvania Ballet, wrote, "Arantxa Ochoa is the unifying figure; she is the priestess and guide, leading, interacting and occasionally disappearing.... Ochoa is marvelous."

Jim Rutter, in his review of Balanchine's *Agon*, presented again by Pennsylvania Ballet, wrote, "... Arantxa Ochoa... blended gymnastics, contortionism and the execution of seemingly impossible poses. ... With each slight, painfully executed movement, the gasps of the audience increased in both frequency and intensity... I've rarely seen such displays of tensile strength. To see it coupled with *Agon*'s required grace and charm, well, the words 'respect' and 'admiration' fail to convey my regard for an athlete like Ochoa."

Lee Deddens, the father of two girls who were students at the School of Pennsylvania Ballet, recounted an interesting anecdote about Arantxa. He had taken his daughters to the Philadelphia Zoo expecting to see elephants, tigers, and chimpanzees, but ended up being most fascinated by the pond where the swans were swimming placidly. The reason for his fascination was that he recognized Arantxa, sitting quietly by the side of the water, intently watching the swans. He checked and was not surprised to find that Tchaikovsky's *Swan Lake* would be premiering at Pennsylvania Ballet the next week and that Arantxa was scheduled to perform. Not content with the traditional interpretation of how a swan would move, she went straight to the source for inspiration.

I had seen Arantxa perform at least 25 times, and each time (as I learned more about dance from my younger daughter and her experiences as a student of ballet) my esteem for her had increased. But the performer is not necessarily the same as the person, and I was eager to learn whether my instinct about Arantxa was correct.

One of the first and most important impressions I had of Arantxa as a person is that she completely confounded my deeply held misunderstanding about the personality of ballerinas. Before I met Arantxa, I assumed that her stage personality – intense, uninhibited, and dramatic – was the same as her real-life personality. The reality is quite the contrary. Arantxa the person is surprisingly reserved, and while not in any way insecure, she is profoundly humble in her demeanor. I was initially startled by this apparent discrepancy between the stage presence and the private presence, but I quickly understood that this dichotomy was merely testimony to her great gifts as a performer. Arantxa can project a character of any sort through the force of her fearless determination but revert to a charming and altogether normal person after the show.

I have always been confused about the concept of the "Spanish soul," and asked Arantxa to explain it for me. "It is so hard to describe. But it is something that comes from here," she responded, cupping her hands – more over her stomach than over her heart. "It is deeply emotional and permanent. Anyone who is born in Valladolid will feel it and carry it with her forever. In the old days, this was the city where the King of Spain lived. We still take great pride in our history. The Spanish soul animates everything we do and gives us passion. When I dance, I am expressing the Spanish soul, with all its joy, anguish, strength, weakness, conflict, conviction, ambivalence, and other emotions."

I later met Arantxa's parents, Emilia G. Ayala and Jose Ignacio Ochoa, in Philadelphia when they visited their daughter, son-in-law, and grandson. I asked them about the "Spanish soul." Jose Ignacio replied, "The Spanish are very passionate. We think with our hearts instead of our heads. Especially the Basques. The Catalans are a bit more cerebral, but not much." Emilia looked at it a bit more domestically: "We come from a Mediterranean culture. We live outdoors and have many relationships in the street."

Like Arantxa, both her mother and father are soft-spoken to an extreme. They were not shy or retiring. In fact, they were very open and forthcoming. They are just gentle people. Arantxa's father had a firm, but not overpowering, handshake. I could tell that he worked with his hands during his career. He also gave me the impression of being a man of integrity and principles. I trusted this man, immediately.

How could one have predicted that the daughter of a Basque mechanic in a Spanish automobile factory and an office worker from Valladolid would become a world class ballerina half a world away, marry a Russian, and become a beloved teacher? It was a series of opportunities – a few unfortunate, but mostly good. None of it was predictable. The outcomes were the result of conscious choices made in response to unplanned events and total support –

no, beyond total support – from her parents. This happened repeatedly to Arantxa. You might say she lived a charmed life, but I (and now you) know better. She encountered Black Swans, responded quickly and robustly, made many courageous choices, bounced back from misfortune, worked hard, and never gave up. There is no magic in all this, except to 99.99% of the world, but that is what makes this heroine so special.

Arantxa's Life Work Begins at the Age of Six

For most of this book's subjects, their life's work begins somewhat later in life. You have already read about the long and arduous (sometimes dangerous) journeys that preceded the attainment of their goals. Few have known from a young age exactly where they were headed. Arantxa has known where she was headed longer than any of the other sixteen individuals profiled in the book.

"The elementary school I attended in Valladolid offered rhythmic gymnastics, and I was drawn to it," Arantxa began. "I was lucky because my teacher was the coach of the Spanish National Rhythmic Gymnastics Team, and she felt I had some talent that was worth encouraging. Of course, I was only six years old at the time, so there were many girls with 'promise' whom she encouraged. I learned under her guidance for several years."

"When I was around eight years old, my coach suggested that I enroll for ballet classes, as a way of helping me to improve my rhythmic gymnastics. I fell in love with ballet, and at a young age I was torn between these two beautiful endeavors. By the age of nine, I had decided that I wanted to be a ballerina and dropped rhythmic gymnastics. I bet my coach was sorry she introduced me to ballet," she concluded with a grin.

When she was eleven years old, Arantxa went to Madrid for summer intensive ballet and studied under Victor Ullate, one of the legendary Spanish dancers and teachers. Again showing promise, Arantxa was asked by Ullate to stay enrolled, which would involve commuting home on weekends. This was a difficult and frightening experience for a pre-teen. Arantxa told me how meaningful these commutes had been to her father and her. She said they forged an inseparable and permanent bond through this joint sacrifice. "My father would touch my ankle gently," she recalled, "and ask me if I was O.K. That was enough to keep me going."

Her next big break was being accepted at the American Ballet Theater in New York City for summer intensive, followed by admission to the Princess Grace Academy in Monaco. This was quickly followed by an offer to attend summer intensive at the School of American Ballet (also in New York City) and her first professional contract (at the age of 19) at the Hartford Ballet. After an ill-fated detour in Los Angeles, she had the good fortune to be recruited by Pennsylvania Ballet, where she would spend the remainder of her professional career as a dancer.

How Others See Arantxa

The Academy of Music is the home stage for Pennsylvania Ballet. It is maligned by snobbish critics for its poor acoustics, but I have always found it the most congenial place in the world for the appreciation of music and dance. The Library is a small, windowless room, one floor above stage level, deep inside the Academy. It is cramped in an academic way, and stuffed to the brim with all the scores, books, and other memorabilia of the one hundred fifty plus year history of the academy (it opened in 1857). I imagine that Mozart or Tchaikovsky would have felt right at home in this environment. It is so steeped in the tradition of music that I felt uplifted just being there.

Beatrice Affron is the Music Director of Pennsylvania Ballet, a position she has held since 1997. She is also a close friend of Arantxa. I spoke to her in this library on a warm spring day. "My relationship with Arantxa is different from the hundreds of other relationships I have had with Pennsylvania Ballet dancers over the course of 21 years," Beatrice began. "Arantxa has a special way of listening to and hearing music. She truly followed Balanchine's guidance to 'see the music; hear the dance.' She understood at a visceral level that 'dancing is music made visible,' another comment attributed to Balanchine."

The Principals at Pennsylvania Ballet are assisted by dressers who make sure that their costumes are in perfect order (including "steam and press") and fit well, and that they are onstage and ready to perform on time. For as long as Arantxa was a Principal at Pennsylvania Ballet, she was dressed by Rosemary Ogle.

"Arantxa is so professional. She is never late. She never complains. She is always in a good mood. She is such a joy. She literally lights up a room when she enters it," Rosemary said with a smile and a sigh. "We were very close. We shared a lot of things in her dressing room, but none of them ever left the room. But don't get me wrong. She was always very kind. She never ran anybody down. She always had nice things to say about everybody."

Not surprisingly, the feeling was mutual. Arantxa said of Rosemary, "She really was some-body special to me. She was not only my dresser but the person that made me feel safe, like a mother figure in the theater. She didn't say much but she didn't need to, with just a look or a hand on my shoulder, I knew that I was ready to go onstage."

Thoughts on Life

I asked Arantxa how she became the woman she is today. "What happened in those early years? Who influenced you?" I inquired.

"My father, of course. He is so strong. He inspired me and gave me 100% support. Also my mother, because of her independence, her focus, and her work ethic. Both of my parents worked very hard and instilled in me a commitment to succeed, even in the face of challenges."

"What was the role of religion?' I asked.

"Well, of course I was raised a Catholic. Everybody in Spain is Catholic. And of course, I believe in God, or at least some 'spiritual something' up there," she said, looking up at the ceiling. "But my family did not go to church, except for my grandmother, who would take me with her. Really the first time I went to church by myself was when I was in Monte Carlo. It was the first time that I was away from home for so long, and I was lonely. I think I needed God as a friend."

"I was also inspired in Monte Carlo by Marika Besobrasova, for whom the school had been created by Princess Grace and Prince Rainier. She was my first mentor. She told me that I had something special that cannot be taught. This was both inspiring and frightening, but it gave me motivation because I felt that I needed to make good use of this special gift, for the benefit of others. I learned a lot about life from Marika, who was quite old and very wise at the time."

"Beauty of soul reflected mysteriously in the beauty of body," was how Marika expressed her aspirations for young dancers. This exhortation certainly had the desired effect on young Arantxa.

"What is your relationship with the concepts of free will and fate?" I asked.

"We make our own fortunes. We are in charge of our own lives," Arantxa replied with a level gaze. I began to see another dimension of the titanium back of this woman with a glass front. "But I was always willing – eager – to seize opportunities that crossed my path. Some of them were detours or false doors but most of them opened new vistas and opportunities for me."

So many times, the women and men of my book have said this to me. They all had an iron-clad determination to take responsibility for their own lives, but to be ever-vigilant for the once-in-a-lifetime Black Swan that is both terrifying and life-changing. This is certainly one of the characteristics that is common to these women and men across cultures, languages, histories, and ethnicities.

"Balanchine always said, 'Don't think – dance,' and I agree with this. Thinking is distracting. To me, there is something spiritual about dancing without thinking. When it comes from your heart and your soul – I don't know – it is almost an 'out-of-body experience.' You become one with the music. Of course, this doesn't happen every time, but it is as close to perfection as I have come when it does happen. If you try to recapture this feeling, then you are thinking too much and you will probably fail. It is the same when you make a mistake. When you make a mistake, you are tempted to start thinking about the mistake and the risk of future mistakes. You can only achieve your goal if you forget about your fears, allow for the possibility of failure, and permit your heart to take over."

"I lived alone, away from my family, from a young age. This was very painful for me because family is so important to me. But it made me emotionally and mentally strong. I had to be strong to survive. Maybe if I did not miss my family so much, I would not have toughened myself. Maybe if it had been easy, I would not have developed a strong back."

"How can you be both open and strong at the same time?" I pondered.

"A ballerina must be open and vulnerable. It is only this way that she can make the audience feel and be moved by the ballet. We want the audience to forget their lives for an hour-and-a-half and to enter our world. But we cannot create this illusion without extreme self-discipline, control, and strength. These three qualities may seem incompatible, but they are perfectly complimentary." 'Self-discipline, control, and strength' – quite similar to the characteristics required by a Katoubushi singer.

We talked about money and what it meant to her.

"I have always been an artist, and money never meant anything to me. I am Spanish, and I was born into a society that moved at a slower pace, a society that valued family, discussion, enjoying life, much more than the frantic pace and focus needed to make money." Tim Kasser wrote about the sources of motivation: "Materialism derives from a motivational system focused on rewards and praise; autonomy and self-expression derive from a motivational system concerned with expression of interest, enjoyment, and challenge, and of doing things for their own sake." I cannot imagine an individual who represents Kasser's ideal of autonomy and self-expression better than Arantxa, although she does not mind the applause after a performance.

"But now," she laughed (Arantxa laughs easily and often), "my husband and I work night and day to make enough money to provide a good education for our son. I guess our perspective changes when we become parents. So now I work differently but I enjoy every minute of it."

We Take Risks to Heighten the Drama

In one conversation after another, across cultures, languages, religions, and nationalities, I have heard so many times the easy commitment that my subjects make to do things better than they need to be done, even when others will not know about this commitment. I asked Arantxa about this human characteristic, and whether it applied to her as a performer.

"Absolutely not!" was her surprising response. "A performance can never be good enough. There is nothing hidden in a performance, and the audience can see everything you do. This is why ballerinas have such a problem with perfectionism. We can never be satisfied with our performance because it can never be perfect. Even if you have done Sugarplum for seventeen years, it still must be better. It can never be good enough."

"The standard of a professional dancer is so high; it is impossible to be better than necessary. As a dancer, you are always working to be better. There is always something you can improve, even if it is a small thing to the audience. For example, in the *pas de deux* in *Nutcracker*, when Sugarplum twice in succession jumps onto the cavalier's shoulder, there is an infinite number of ways that a dancer can do this. The inexperienced Sugarplum will start close to the cavalier, take many small steps and jump only when she is very near to him. As we get more experienced and comfortable with the part, we step back farther, run more confidently with longer strides, and take a longer leap when we are farther away from his shoulder. The cavalier always starts by using two hands to catch and balance Sugarplum on his shoulder. The experienced cavalier can do it with one hand. We take risks to heighten the drama of the moment. Not everybody in the audience can see this, but it is meaningful to the dancer. We are always trying new things, even in familiar roles. To add something exciting, such as one or two extra seconds to a pose. The better you know a part, the more risks you are inclined to take."

"I always rehearsed roles much more than was technically necessary," she admitted. "Some people said I over-rehearsed, but the only way I could be confident in a role was to rehearse it so many times that I did not have to think at all about what my feet or arms were doing. If I over-rehearsed, it was so I could go on stage and not worry or think. The part must come from instinct in order to have no doubts. Only then could I unleash my spiritual interpretation of the part. The worst thing for me was to be under-rehearsed. I would come into the studio on Sundays and holidays to rehearse again and again." She smiled pensively, remembering her days as a performer.

Better than it must be. Arantxa could only achieve her goal of manufacturing risk by being over-prepared. She was never better than it must be in her terms, but this was only because she was always better than it had to be in everybody else's terms.

"If you think that it is good enough, or even better than it has to be, you have to stop dancing," she continued, adamantly. "But in my opinion, you always deserve more, and your audience deserves more. The improvements never end, especially because each performance is live. Recorded ballet is a shadow of live ballet. Each performance is a creation, and a creation can never be perfect. Because it is live, there is always risk. We make people feel when we dance. You know that you are creating something new each time. One of the interesting features of a performance is that because of the lighting, you cannot see your audience (except maybe the first row and the last few seats on the side of the balcony), so you must literally feel the audience and in turn, they must feel you."

Arantxa the Teacher

Arantxa retired after the 8:00 PM performance of Giselle on Saturday, October 27, 2012, (I know this precisely because I was in attendance). A thousand flowers descended on the stage during the standing ovation that would not stop. The next morning, she assumed the position of Principal Teacher at the newly reopened School of Pennsylvania Ballet.

"Many people have asked me how I could just stop performing. It was easy. I felt that one chapter in my life was complete, and I was ready for the new chapter. And I so love teaching, although it is completely different from performing. Now I want to guide and inspire the young people to be the best dancers they can be. I know from my own experience that there are sacrifices that you must make, that you must have a glass front and a titanium back, that you must love what you do more than anything, and that you must never believe that your effort is better than it has to be. So I need to be tough on the kids because I want them to be ready for the challenges. But I do not want them to fear me. It is a delicate balance that I need to find between pushing and nurturing. But I love it. This is the next chapter of my life. I have no regrets and I do not wish that I was back on the stage."

Arantxa was asked to assume the responsibility of Director of the School of Pennsylvania Ballet in addition to her role as Principal Teacher. With characteristic vigor and enthusiasm, she threw herself into the new role, with outstanding results. One of the initiatives for which she was responsible in her new role as School Director was an end-of-year performance in which every single one of the 160 students participated.

The day after the first such show on June 6, 2015, with tears in her eyes she said to me: "I performed for over 20 years, and I had the most wonderful experiences onstage, but nothing can compare with the feelings I felt yesterday watching these children perform. I was emotional all day long, I felt so proud of them and so happy."

Who Is Arantxa Ochoa?

"How would you like to be remembered?" I asked, as a way of concluding our conversation.

"I would like to be remembered as somebody that made a difference for the better in people's lives. If they came to see me perform, I hope I made them feel something special when they saw me dance. I hope I brought a little bit of happiness in their hearts. If I taught them, I hope they remember me as somebody that made them be the best they can be."

It was clear to me by this time that the ballet dancer can make the world a better place by touching the souls of the members of the audience. Ricardo Muti felt the same way:

> ...By opening yourselves to art and to other new ideas, you can make the world
> a better place. Because just as the artist's most important function is to touch our souls,
> it is in the way we receive that touch... that the quality of life is really to be found.

This is a different type of impact than that of the Vice President of a country of nearly three hundred million people, and equally different than that of a banker helping a poor woman to purchase a second cow, but all three are equally valuable.

The reader will recall the start of this chapter and its discussion of the challenge to the King of Spain to decide whether the Indians in the New World were human or not. The mid-sixteenth century was a fecund time, and there is often a great deal of nuance and ambiguity as well as originality in such an era. This was also during the Great Age of Exploration when so much "knowledge" was discovered to have been illusion. Cervantes certainly reflected in original ways and at length on the human condition. On the dark side, the most intense period of the Spanish Inquisition had only recently ended (in 1530). The discovery of the New World by Europeans opened up virtually limitless opportunities, often fraught with ambiguities. Arantxa's choice of classical ballet, I believe, is a good medium to showcase the Spanish soul of Valladolid. Classical ballet frequently involves tales of conflict, moral quandary, and even despair, as well as the positive emotions of joy, hope, passion, forgiveness, and compassion. Through her interpretations of these ballets, Arantxa has drawn on the wellsprings of her Spanish soul and has given new insights into the variety of emotions that make us all human. In this way, she has uniquely achieved her goal of causing her audiences and students to reflect more deeply on who they are and what values they hold dear. She is a completely modern person who at the same time is deeply immersed in and respectful of the traditions of her native Spain, and the classical ballet that she interpreted as a dancer and now inspires as a teacher.

Beatrice Affron, the Music Director of the Pennsylvania Ballet, summed up well the value of being close to this brave and harmless woman. "I wish I could adequately describe the feeling of working with Arantxa and being her friend. We 'feel' each other. This is unusual. The very best relationships are collaborative and the relationship we have is more than collaborative. It is symbiotic. She made me a better conductor. I hope I made her a better dancer. Everything we did together was upgraded."

You will not be surprised, after reading this chapter, to learn that I have the utmost respect and deep love for Arantxa as a dancer and as a teacher, and above all, as a wonderful human being who cares for others and who wants to have an impact on the world.

Moving on to Taipei

The next journey will require us to travel 6,686 miles, east and south from Valladolid to Taipei, traversing Europe and Asia, but staying in the Northern Hemisphere. We will fly almost the precise reverse of our flight from Tokyo to Valladolid. In this case, we will be aided by the jet stream, which is a narrow, fast-flowing, meandering air current in the tropopause, conveniently located at the cruising altitude of modern aircraft. There are multiple jet streams that travel around the world and most of them flow from west to east. This makes the trip between two cities briefer (but not shorter) when flying east and longer when flying west. Taipei is farther from Madrid than is Tokyo, but with the help of the jet stream the two journeys take about the same number of hours.

The Seventeen
Heroes and Heroines

Devoted to the Commonweal

Luis Andrade sailing on Tomine Reservoir, created in 1967 to provide drinking water for Bogota (37 miles to the south) and to enable more predictable water flow to hydroelectric plants.

Vice President **Boediono** on February 13, 2013, at the home of former President B.J. Habibie on the 1,000th day commemoration of the death of former First Lady Hasri Ainun Habibie binti Mohamed Besari.

Chanthol Sun, indefatigable, forgiving, resilient, running a marathon in Singapore on December 4, 2012.

Compassionate Capitalists

Dawn Hines (center, with pink hair ornament) dancing at the wedding of friends at 4:00 am at Kronenschlösschen Villa, Rhine River, near Frankfurt, Germany. Dawn is a joyous person, as well as a compassionate capitalist.

Eric Kacou, a man who combines the cerebral thoughtfulness of an intellectual with the dynamic practical focus of an entrepreneur. A passionate activist wrapped in a professorial demeanor.

Rosanna Ramos-Velita (second from left) with one of her micro-credit customers in Puno, Peru. The woman with the hat owned a cow and sold cheese. With a small loan from Rosanna's bank, she is expanding her business with the purchase of a second cow.

Durreen Shahnaz (center, in orange sari) with micro-finance borrowers in Tamil Naidu, India, in 2008.

Stewards, Not the Owners of Their Wealth

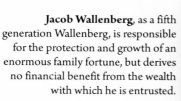

Shiv Khemka serenading his wife, Urvashi, who wrote, "Shiv is a music lover and plays the Sarod, an Indian classical instrument. It's something he is passionate about, also a side of him that very few people know about. This is him playing a tune that he had composed for me just after we got married."

Jacob Wallenberg, as a fifth generation Wallenberg, is responsible for the protection and growth of an enormous family fortune, but derives no financial benefit from the wealth with which he is entrusted.

The Long Legacy of Echo

Anthony and Olive Hamilton Russell at home in Hermanus, South Africa. Their farm consists of biodynamically-raised grape vines, olive trees, and honeybees. They sell the wine they ferment to support their brave and harmless lifestyle.

Keisuke Muratsu at home in Tokyo on March 19, 2014, rehearsing for a performance of Katoubushi, a Japanese singing style that was created in the eighteenth century.

Arantxa Ochoa performing the 'Dark Angel' in Serenade, a ballet by George Balanchine, set to the music of Tchaikovsky.

Breaking with Tradition

Leslie Koo in the Dr. Cecelia Koo Botanic Conservation Center in Pingtung County, Taiwan. The Center is named in honor of Leslie's mother.

The Sidorov Family: Victoria, Veronika, Vassily, and Eva, at their *dacha* on the outskirts of Moscow in August 2021.

Ebullient Survivors

Roberto Canessa, pictured with his book, *I Had to Survive*. Inspired, but in no way changed by an unspeakable tragedy, he never gives up on anyone, no matter how dire their circumstances.

James Kim Joo Jin survived a brutal colonial occupation, a world war, and a civil war, and takes a long-term view of health, happiness, and harmony.

Michael Yu Minhong, who failed his university admissions examination twice, is now the teacher of tens of millions of students and inspires them with the admonition, "You can!"

Breaking with Tradition

Leslie Koo Cheng Yun

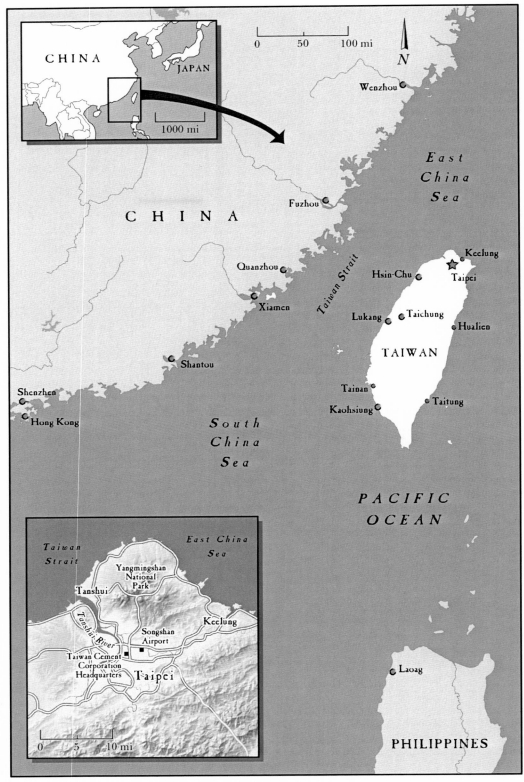

Breaking with Tradition: Leslie Koo Cheng Yun

160

Ancestry

We will now encounter several more Black Swans, confront additional ambiguities, explore the nature of accountability, question the limits to forgiveness, and witness the successful breaking of tradition. In order to introduce the next exemplary individual drawn from my card files, I need to go back more than a century to the time of his grandfather and then to the time of his father.

The Sino-Japanese War of 1894-95 was "nasty, brutish, and short," and Japan decisively defeated China in eight months, two weeks, and two days. Corrupt and mismanaged, the Qing Empire was no match for the Meiji Empire, which had recently modernized its military. The Treaty of Shimonoseki, which ended the hostilities, entered into force on May 8, 1895. The terms of the treaty combined straight-faced farce with overwhelming force. Under the first (farce) article of the treaty, China "recognized the full and complete independence and autonomy of Korea," a euphemism for Japan taking control of Korea as its colony. Under the second (force) article, China ceded "in perpetual and full sovereignty" the island of Formosa (today's Taiwan) to Japan.

While the Kwang-su Emperor, the 10th Emperor of the Qing Dynasty, had little choice in the matter, the people who lived on Formosa were unwilling to accept Imperial Japan as their master, and resisted the terms of the treaty. The Republic of Formosa was, accordingly, declared on May 25, 1895, seventeen days after the signing of the treaty. Hostilities ensued when Japanese troops arrived and resistance was, at least initially, stiff. However, as the Qing troops had evacuated the island, the situation was hopeless. In the city of Taipei, civil unrest turned into lawlessness and chaos. A group of business leaders decided that accommodation was preferable to extermination and decided to engage in discussion with the invaders, with the goal of requesting their assistance in restoring order and preventing further loss of life. This would mean surrendering the sovereignty so recently asserted.

One member of this group, Koo Hsien-jung, individually reached an agreement with the Japanese, whose ships were anchored in the near-by Port of Keelung. Koo then opened the gates to the city, allowing the troops to enter and take the city without bloodshed. Full pacification of the island quickly followed. In appreciation of his cooperation, Koo Hsien-jung was awarded monopolies of the salt and sugar trades. The Koo family became wealthy, and during the ensuing fifty years of Japanese occupation, continued to cooperate with the colonial power. Some excoriated Koo Hsien-jung as a traitor. Others, like him, felt that since resistance was futile, the preferred course of action was to make the best of a bad situation and hope that it would not last forever. Some have never forgiven the Koo Family for what they consider to have been the betrayal of Koo Hsien-jung.

Koo Hsien-jung had many concubines and even more children. His fifth son, Koo Chen-fu, was born on January 6, 1917, in the Taiwanese city of Lukang, 114.5 miles to the southwest of Taipei. Although Taiwan was ruled by Japan from 1895 until 1945, Koo Chen-fu was trained from birth to respect and to practice Confucian principles. Part of this was because his father trained him to be trilingual (Chinese, English, and Japanese) and taught him Confucian values at home while he was going to school to be indoctrinated into the Japanese way of life.

When his father passed away at the age of 71 in 1937, Koo Chen-fu was 20 years old. These were difficult times. As far as the Chinese were concerned, World War II started in 1937. It is difficult to argue with the contention that the Rape of Nanjing, which started on December 13th of that year, was an act of war. In any case, the war in Europe began two years later when Hitler invaded Poland. During the war, Japan used Taiwan as a staging ground for its forces, built and maintained dozens of air force bases located there, conscripted Taiwanese "volunteers" to fight for Japan, and located notorious Prisoner of War camps on the island.

The war ended in the Pacific on August 14, 1945, with the Japanese surrender. The civil war with the Chinese Communists, which had been put on hold during World War II in order to focus on the defeat of Japan, resumed in earnest. Koo Chen-fu's children remember their father showing them a letter from Generalissimo Chiang Kai-shek (known as "CKS") to their grandfather, requesting his help in dissuading the Japanese from supporting the Chinese Communists.

The four years after the end of the Second World War were eventful times in world politics. Indonesia declared its independence on August 17, 1945, as we discussed earlier in the chapter on Boediono. India and Pakistan were founded on August 14-15, 1947. The State of Israel was declared on May 14, 1948. And in China, the People's Republic was founded on October 1, 1949, following the ignominious retreat of Chiang Kai-shek and the army of the Kuomintang to Taiwan, where they established the Republic of China (in temporary exile, they insisted). There was another momentous event in 1949, when Cecilia Yen, born in Fujian, married Koo Chen-fu. The next generation of Taiwanese Koo family men soon made their appearance. Their first son, Chester, was born in 1952 and was given Chinese names that signify "taking initiative" or "opening up new doors."

Leslie Makes His Appearance

Their second son, Leslie, was born in Taipei on November 28, 1954. Accordingly, the next card drawn from my card file is introduced as the first *Breaking with Tradition*. His parents gave him the Chinese given names "Cheng Yun," which signify "following" or "succeeding." These names (and those of his brother) were Confucian in spirit and represented their parents' hopes and expectations regarding their sons' accomplishments in life and respect for age, hierarchy, and loyalty.

Henceforward, the lives of Koo Chen-fu and his sons would be closely interrelated. Chester, one of the kindest and most generous human beings ever to live on the planet, tragically passed away from cancer on December 24, 2001, much too young, at the age of 49. Leslie, as we will learn in the pages ahead, resolutely and loyally carried on the family name and traditions.

Shaping the Future That Leslie Would Inhabit

In the early 1950s, the government of Taiwan (headed by Chiang Kai-shek) decided to privatize many of its basic industries, while at the same time they inaugurated a plan of land reform. This dual strategy had two objectives. First, they were capitalists, not communists. The government was convinced that more people needed to be landowners, and that this was the best way to assure prosperity as well as political stability. Second, there needed to be a method of compensating the landholders for the land they would lose to the (soon-to-be) former peasants. This compensation took the form of shares in the newly privatized companies, which included cement. The Koo family was, accordingly, compensated with control of Taiwan Cement Corporation in return for surrendering their landholdings. A subsidiary benefit of this policy of land reform and privatization was that it confirmed the capitalistic nature of the economy in Taiwan, and inspired a generation of entrepreneurs, many of whose descendants today control vast commercial empires. The result was that Taiwan became one of the first of the Asian "Tiger" economies.

It soon became desirable to provide a secondary market for the shares in the newly privatized companies and to give others an opportunity to participate in the growing prosperity of the Taiwanese economy. The Taiwan Stock Exchange (TSE) was duly founded in 1961. Koo Chen-fu was one of the founders of the TSE. The establishment of the exchange further stimulated the entrepreneurial spirit in Taiwan, and many companies were founded in the following years. Meanwhile, the Koo family accumulated assets and influence, while at the same time earning respect. The ghost of Koo Hsien-jung, while never fully dissipating, became less distinct.

After the United States withdrew diplomatic recognition of the Republic of China in favor of the People's Republic of China on January 1, 1979, Koo Chen-fu took on the stature of a business-statesman and represented Taiwan in an unofficial capacity at gatherings where it would have been politically awkward to have an official representative of the "Republic of China." Photographs record his fascinating position, totally unofficial, standing shoulder-to-shoulder with heads of state at APEC forum meetings.

In due course, he was asked by his government to engage in so-called "cross-straits conversations" with Wang Dao Han, a former Mayor of Shanghai and senior Communist

Party Official. While the "Wang-Koo Talks" showed promise in 1992-1993, they were scuttled by the seemingly endless round of provocations and counter-provocations in which the People's Republic of China and the Republic of China engaged in the 1990s.

I had the privilege of meeting Koo Chen-fu on a number of occasions. What struck me more than anything else about this great man were his humility, humanity, and stability. He never spoke at any volume above a whisper, and it was difficult to hear what he said. Nevertheless, those to whom he spoke leaned forward and listened attentively, hoping to catch every word. Dr. Koo was a man of wisdom, compassion, and integrity, and I often think of him when I am confronted with moral dilemmas.

Education and Early Career

Leslie was educated through high school in Taiwan. An accident with a shattered eye glass lens left him exempt from military duty. "I was not a good student, and I failed the Taiwan university entrance examinations," he stated with a rueful smile. Since he was still in need of treatment for the injury to his right eye, and an uncle was a doctor at the University of Washington Medical School, he decided to go to college in Seattle. He worked hard in his first two years, intending to prove to his Confucian father that he was not lazy. But lethargy set in by his junior year, and his GPA plunged. He graduated in 1977 with a serviceable but not distinguished record, having majored in economics and computer science.

"During my college years, I was an avid scuba diver," he related. "One weekend, a friend and I went diving to catch fish for a dinner party we were planning. There was a problem with my tank regulator and I completely ran out of air at a depth of around 80 feet. After signaling to my buddy that I needed assistance, we started sharing his regulator. Suddenly, he panicked and headed for the surface, leaving me behind with no air whatsoever. I remained calm and decided that I was not willing to die for the silliest of reasons, which was that I had promised fish and crabs to my friends for dinner. If I died, I would break my promise. So, I started to ascend. My mind eventually went completely blank and I instinctively tried to avoid breathing water, which of course would have proved fatal. I eventually made it to the surface safely. After resting for a while, I went back down, speared some fish, and caught some crabs. I prepared a feast for my friends that night and never mentioned the harrowing experience. But I never went scuba diving with that friend again."

After graduation, he returned home to work as an accountant for Arthur Andersen in Taiwan. This lasted for three and one-half years, at which time he applied to the MBA programs at Harvard, Stanford, and Wharton. "Wharton was the only MBA program that admitted me," he said with his disarming, transparent grin. In 1981, he returned home to work for the family business, which by that time was widely diversified into financial services and other sectors of the economy. He was not interested in finance or banking, so he and Chester agreed to divide the family businesses into "with a chimney" and "without a chimney." Leslie got the chimneys, which meant cement. He started as a junior staff member in the computer department, and earned promotions to General Manager of Corporate Planning, Vice President and Chief Financial Officer, President, and (in 2003) Chairman.

Regardless of where they are born or what passport they hold, most ethnic Chinese pledge their first loyalty to a civilization and not a political entity. Leslie is no exception. His current affiliation is to Taiwan and the Republic of China, since this political entity allows him the political and economic freedom that are so important to him. He is agnostic about the People's Republic of China and said that if that political entity became a democratic nation that respected the rule of law and allowed individual freedom of expression, he would have no problem with the two countries merging into one. I asked how long this might take to be realized and to resolve the philosophical differences. His ambiguous answer was "20 to 50 years." But he feels strongly that Taiwan needs an independent identity until the political differences have been resolved.

"My parents were the greatest influences on me," he observed without hesitation in response to my question. "They taught me to be humble, to be honest, and to have faith in the goodness of human nature. My father was a classic Confucian gentleman who had humility, a sense of mission to society, respect for hierarchy, a belief in the need for harmonious relations, and a tremendous feeling of duty to all Taiwanese. Everyone understood that he was interested in the welfare of all the people, and they respected him for this. He was living proof of the Confucian belief that moral force was stronger than physical force. Of course, I am not like my father, and I never modeled myself to be like him. But I think that, deep down inside, I have the same values."

Leadership of Taiwan Cement Corporation

"I was eventually appointed Chairman of Taiwan Cement Corporation (TCC) in 2003 when my father was no longer able to take an active role in the company. He passed away two years later, in 2005, at the age of 88. When I assumed responsibility for TCC, I learned that there were many problems that had been neglected for too long. Many of the problems had not been solved but had been glossed over by my father's reputation and age. No one could challenge him. In addition, the entire organization was both conservative and complacent. No one took initiative. No one was accountable. There was enormous internal resistance to change. I could see quickly what would happen when my father retired. The organization would still be unable to change, but no one would protect the organization from shareholders, customers, and competitors."

"The staff was characterized by what I call the 'rationalization of failure.' Nobody solved any problems, but everybody had an excellent excuse, prepared in advance, for their failure. Rationalized failure was acceptable in the culture of TCC. I was worried about taking over this organization and considered quitting. Two things convinced me to stay. First, the market for cement in Mainland China was booming. I saw a business opportunity. But second, and even more importantly, I knew that if I declined this challenge, the company would no longer be a great company and might even cease to exist. As a responsible person, I could not let this happen. I had a duty to my father, to my family, to the employees, to the shareholders, and to society to save the company from the disaster towards which it was heading. I sensed a great urgency to change just about everything."

"The Board of Directors elected me as Chairman in 2003 because my father asked them to do so, and of course they could not refuse. But as soon as my father was out of the picture, I became a target and was immediately challenged by the board, by senior management, and even by some shareholders. My plan to overhaul the management of the company radically was a tremendous threat to many people, and I was under fire all the time. There were quite a few unpleasant situations that threatened not only my job but the existence of the company."

"But now, after ten years, Taiwan Cement's revenue has grown four times, market capitalization has also grown four times, capacity has grown six times, and share price has risen 3.5 times. Taiwan Cement is probably the only major company in the country to have undergone this transformation, and the results have been largely positive," Leslie concluded with his trademark grin.

"I have what I call a 'parallel system' of communication. Let's say that the head of manufacturing and the head of sales are having a dispute. I require them to include me in their email communication. This way I know when the infighting becomes dysfunctional. Even junior people can include me in the communications loop if they feel it is important enough. I do not allow 'finger-pointing.' If somebody is blaming another, or making excuses for poor performance, I assemble everybody involved in my office to discuss it openly. No more email. The goal is to solve the problem openly and make sure everybody is accepting their responsibility."

"I believe that the bedrock of Confucianism is accountability. If there is no accountability, then you cannot have harmony, humility, and respect. The true Confucian is first accountable. This was a big problem at TCC when I became chairman. I made accountability #1 at Taiwan Cement so that we could have a harmonious environment where people were humble and respected each other."

"I observed that when senior people came to meetings, they always brought a subordinate whose job was to provide facts, statistics and other vital information. I stopped this practice and stipulated that all senior staff were required to know everything without needing an assistant to provide the facts. It was no longer the case that senior executives would be spoon-fed data from junior executives. The senior person – and this included me– had to have the knowledge to analyze and solve the problem. The new senior management team deserted the 'executive floor' of TCC so that they would be close to their staff and understand what was happening at all times."

Thrust and Parry

As Leslie had risen through the ranks at Taiwan Cement, he earned a reputation as that of a well-meaning and polite young man without the courage or the strength to become the CEO. "I love it when people underestimate me," was Leslie's response. "It gives me added incentive, but it also gives me an advantage because my enemies let their guard down and feel overconfident. I started by firing or removing many people, including very senior staff. They were outraged, of course, and some of them conspired with board members to get rid of me. They spread rumors in the financial community to undercut my ability to secure financing. It was a bitter struggle. And since by that time the Koo family owned only 5% of the shares of TCC, I did not have enough financial leverage to protect myself. The dissidents started planning a *coup d'état* at the Annual General Meeting in 2006 when my appointment had to be renewed. I decided to develop a defensive strategy."

"At the time I became chairman in 2003, the financial performance of TCC was terrible. The stock price was depressed. The dividend was an embarrassment. The future was bleak. Interestingly, less than 5% of the shares were held by so-called QFII investors. As investors, QFIIs are not emotional. They are interested only in financial performance. I decided I needed to get more of the company in the hands of QFIIs and at the same time to improve the company's financial performance. To accomplish these two objectives, I went on a roadshow to meet with institutional investors around the world. I asked each one, 'Why don't you invest more in TCC?' The answers were all the same. First, they said the company was too diversified and lacked focus. As a result, they felt they could not accurately predict our performance. Second, they said our dividend policy was not clear, meaning they could not predict their income stream. And third, they said the company's bonus policy was too generous and ate into profits that should have been distributed to shareholders. It was also clear to me that for a number of years, TCC had not communicated at all with investors and investment analysts."

"When I returned home from the roadshow, I divested all of TCC's non-core assets. I took the proceeds from this divestiture and invested them in our cement strategy in Mainland China. I clarified the company's dividend policy. I changed the bonus scheme from after-tax to pre-tax. I started going to investor conferences to explain TCC's new strategy. I sent monthly business reviews to analysts. I targeted pension funds and sovereign funds. By the time of the

AGM in 2006, everything had turned around. The percentage of shares held by QFIIs had risen from 5% to 43%, and most importantly, these investors were satisfied with TCC's strategy. The share price had risen from NT$12 to more than NT$30. The dividend had increased, and the financial performance was quite satisfactory. I won re-election in a landslide," he concluded with another smile, but not in any way gloating.

The Mainland Strategy

"Because of my father's role in the so-called 'cross-straits conversation' with Wang Dao Han, it was complicated for our group to go against the ROC government's policy of 'go slow' on investing in the Mainland. It was considered unpatriotic to do so, and no company associated with Koo Chen-fu could afford to appear unpatriotic, certainly not the flagship company of which he was the chairman. This meant that we were ten to fifteen years behind our competitors in investing on the Mainland. Nevertheless, by 2003 when I succeeded my father as chairman, it seemed like a good time to take the plunge. The environment had changed, and the ROC government was more open to investments in the Mainland. This was also a key part of my strategy to reposition assets after divestment from non-core assets."

"I decided that the only way to succeed would be to take an unorthodox strategy. Cement is a capital-intensive industry, and a traditional industry, which means that it is risk averse. The traditional strategy is to build a plant, bring it up to speed, determine that it will be successful, and then start the whole cycle all over again. I rejected this strategy because we were so far behind that we would never catch up if we built plants one-by-one. My strategy was to build six plants at the same time, thereby entering the market as a major player and announcing our arrival on Mainland China. Not surprisingly, the existing staff at TCC told me this would not work. The staff I sent to Mainland China to work on this strategy plotted to assure failure. I fired these staff and replaced them with young people who were not paralyzed by the rationalization of failure."

"I also made the decision that we would source our equipment locally. This decision was criticized because the quality of the locally-sourced equipment was poor. But the costs were less than one-third of the equivalent imported machinery, so we could afford to retrofit as needed and still be ahead financially. An additional benefit was that the government of China was excited that we were buying so much heavy equipment locally. We also created jobs, which made the local government happy. The consequences of these decisions were that we had economies of scale, low costs, and a friendly environment in which to operate. We were profitable in three years and exceeded all our growth targets."

"I find it very satisfying that today our position as a company is exactly where I hoped it would be, and greatly exceeds the limited expectations of the staff who predicted failure when

I announced our Mainland strategy in 2003. If I had not overruled the prevailing attitude in 2003, and had I not broken with tradition, none of this would have happened and we would probably have gone bankrupt."

The Surprising Environmentalist

"Cement is an essential part of modern life," Leslie stated, "but it is a dirty business. We extract non-renewable natural resources from the earth, we issue toxic wastes into the sky, and we create pollution as a by-product of our manufacturing. We make an awful mess and create a huge amount of CO_2. We could have had a 'corporate social responsibility' policy through which we tried to clean up after ourselves by adding scrubbers and sent the children of our workers to school. But my belief has always been that this is not enough. We must do much more than pay lip service to CSR."

"I asked myself why we couldn't break with tradition and do something that was positive for society and the environment. Something that was beneficial and not just responsible," he reflected. "My plan, which we have started to implement, is to develop an integrated business strategy fully to recycle our wastes, to limit our extractions, and to make a profit by doing so."

"For example, we generate a lot of sludge and mud from our cement production. Instead of draining this away and polluting the environment, we dry and compact it, and then burn it to generate heat and, through co-generation, generate electricity also. The ashes left over are high in heavy metals, which are particularly bad for the environment. But the manufacturing of cement uses these same heavy metals, so we recycle them. By recycling the heavy metals, we also reduce the amount of natural resources we must extract from the environment. In this way we never waste anything and have a net positive impact on the environment."

"So now we have an almost seamless loop of recycling. The only thing left is carbon. We generate huge amounts of carbon dioxide, and it is impossible to reduce the amount of CO_2 we generate. In fact, the more successful our business, the more CO_2 we generate. We needed to find a creative way to reduce its impact by keeping it out of the environment. Our plan starts with sequestration of carbon dioxide by pumping it underground into empty mines and caverns. This greatly reduces the amount of CO_2 that we release into the environment."

"Next, we use this captured carbon dioxide in two ways that will be revenue-generating in addition to being environmentally responsible. The first thing we do is feed purified CO_2 to a certain kind of algae that produces beta-carotene, which is rich in antioxidants and has beneficial effects on the health of humans. The second thing we do is to use the purified CO_2 we have sequestered to feed another kind of algae that is high in lipids and can be used for biofuels. We close the CO_2 loop, mitigate our waste creation, help the environment, create useful products, and – I think in about three years – we will make a profit."

"Another thing that I did was to create a botanical conservation center in the southern part of Taiwan. We have assembled a collection of over 25,000 live specimens of tropical and sub-tropical species. We believe this is the largest collection of its type in the world. It is open and available to researchers at no charge. My feeling is that climate change is so drastic, and deforestation is so widespread, that overall the biodiversity of the planet is threatened. My goal is to preserve species of flora so that we do not lose their genetic codes and so they can be re-introduced into the wild whenever and wherever possible. It is not so expensive to maintain this center, but neither is it profitable. This is simple philanthropy on our part. Someday this center may have a far-reaching impact on the diversity of the natural world. In a way, it is a long-term insurance policy against the possibility of ecological disaster."

Leslie and Money

Leslie is rich and makes no apologies for his wealth. However, he does not live to make money; he makes money to live. "It's impossible for me to work only for money," he began. "I have to work for something larger than myself; for something of higher value. We should be good at what we do and try to make money but accumulating assets will never be my goal or my motivation."

"I am not going to be a philanthropist. I think that philanthropy is ego driven. I have real doubts about how much philanthropy and government aid can accomplish. I believe that encouraging, mentoring, and funding entrepreneurs is a much better use of my personal fortune. I have already started doing this, but when I retire in ten or fifteen years, I will devote full time to compassionate capitalism, both through my expertise and with my money. I will start an 'angel fund' and teach entrepreneurial skills to young people. I am convinced that heavy taxation and forced redistribution of wealth are not the answers to poverty. The answer is to create more wealth by empowering the natural drive and entrepreneurial skills of the young."

Maybe future editions of this book will see Leslie moved to the *Compassionate Capitalists*, but for now I will keep him *Breaking with Tradition*.

Who Is Leslie Koo?

"Being willing to admit mistakes and to learn from them is central to my personal as well as my business philosophy. And I have made many mistakes," he smiled. "Mistakes are just part of life's journey. I always feel the consequences of my mistakes, and I refuse to accept failure as an outcome. I accept mistakes but I never accept failure."

"I want to be remembered as a survivor. I always prepare for the worst, but I always believe it will be sunny soon. I always push myself to do my best. And I will survive. I am sure of this. I felt that way when I was eighty feet under water with no air. I felt that way when I was under attack in 2003 after I became chairman of TCC. I also have varied interests and I never stick to a single thing. I am always ready to move on to the next thing. And I have a warm heart," he concluded with yet another big smile.

I have known Leslie for a long time; we met first in 1988. For years, he labored quietly and patiently in the long shadows of his father, his charismatic but doomed brother, his cousin (who was chronologically in his father's generation) and his two nephews (both of whom are chronologically in his generation). He had a reputation for being relatively meek, compared to this group of hard charging personalities, and not terribly promising as a leader of his generation or of a business. The consensus in the business community was that he would not last long as Chairman of Taiwan Cement. The expectation of his friends (and he always had many friends) and foes alike was that he was not destined for greatness.

Every prediction was wrong, every expectation was erroneous, and Leslie has succeeded on his own terms. He knew what the popular perception was, and he believed he was misjudged. Leslie is not aggressive or over-confident, but he is not timid or overly cautious. He is a man who knows himself and understands his relationship to the external world, takes measured risks as appropriate, feels comfortable with others, takes command with quiet confidence, and demands a high standard of excellence of himself and others. He has the courage of his convictions, even when others doubt him. He is fully transparent and acknowledges his faults and weaknesses.

Leslie is a warm and caring person who has succeeded to a degree that few would have predicted. And along the way, he has carefully and deliberately created wealth and value. He also has had an impact on the various communities in whose name he has stewarded the great wealth he inherited, restored, and created. Leslie is a man who, in breaking with so many outdated and counterproductive traditions, has enabled even more traditions of value to prosper. I have come to know this man well and to understand the principles for which he stands, as well as the genetic imprinting that contributed so much to the person. I find in Leslie a man whom I can admire and respect, and for whom I feel genuine affection.

Moving on to Moscow

The journey from Taipei to Moscow is 3,978 miles, a moderate flight in terms of the journeys taken so far in this book. We will fly northwest across the entire breadth of China and Kazakhstan before entering Russian airspace. What an exciting moment for me, who grew up assuming that I would never have the opportunity to visit Russia because of the fact that it was subsumed under the Union of Soviet Socialist Republics. The journey will take about eleven hours, non-stop, plenty of time to reflect on the absurdity of the Cold War, which consigned Americans to a seemingly endless downward spiral of vituperation with the Soviets.

Breaking with Tradition

Vassily Vassilievich Sidorov

Breaking with Tradition: Vassily Vassilevich Sidorov

Setting the Stage

The twentieth century was a difficult time for Russia. Not that Napoleon's invasion in 1812 had made the nineteenth century a picnic. It is just that the twentieth century was particularly gruesome. About three million Russians died in the First World War. The Romanov Dynasty, which had endured for 300 years, ended with the abdication in 1917, and then the murder in 1918, of Tsar Nicholas II. The country lurched from a monarchy to a communist state by fighting a civil war that cost around 8 million lives, mostly due to starvation and disease. The Red Terror from 1918-22 probably accounted for another two million lives lost violently. Stalin killed tens of millions of Russians. The Second World War took the lives of around twenty million more Russians. The Cold War immediately followed the close of the Second World War, and in its own way brought about great misery for uncounted Russians as the insanity of "mutually assured destruction" caused the Soviet state to divert an increasing percentage of the nation's wealth away from human needs to build weapons to threaten the United States of America.

One cannot help but appreciate the effect of all this murder, mayhem, misery, and fear on the collective consciousness known as the Russian "soul." Russia was mightily abused by outsiders and by its own leaders. This is not to say that Russia itself was just an innocent bystander, but we should not forget that the average Russian – 99% of the population – was the one who suffered, never having any choice in why.

Contrast this situation with that of the United States of America in the twentieth century. While we had our share of problems, there were simply no parallel catastrophes. It is challenging for Americans to grasp the world view of a country whose citizens carry the emotional, spiritual, and psychological baggage of Russia. Perhaps this is another instance of the incommensurability of perceptions that made it so difficult for Copernicus to convince others of the validity of his heliocentric discovery, or that made the Opium Wars between China and Britain inevitable.

It is a paradox of history that there was a moment in time when some Americans thought they understood Russia and the Russians. This occurred during that particular phase in the history of Russian-American relations, namely the decade of the 1930s, when a group of American intellectuals, writers, artists, and scientists flirted, some briefly and some for a bit longer, with the communist utopian concept.

It is possible to see, at least in retrospect, how thoughtful, compassionate, and intelligent people could have been "fellow travelers" or even embraced communism in the 1930s. The world was starting to feel dangerous to the thoughtful individual who believed in social justice and equality. The Soviet Union, on the other hand, was experimenting (at least in theory) with a new form of social organization, namely communism, which to a portion of the American intelligentsia appeared to advocate humane goals of equality, social justice, and the redistribution of wealth that had been accumulated through unrestrained corruption, greed, and unfair manipulation. The Soviet Union also shared the goals of Republican Spain and stood united against the fascists in Germany (except from 1939 to 1941) and Italy. The consequences of Stalin's policies were not yet well-publicized or understood in the West. Every American hated Hitler, Mussolini, and Franco, and some of them found the communist vision of the future to be intriguing.

At the same time, the Great Depression that took place in the decade of the 1930s left many in the United States destitute. Migrant farm workers, longshoremen, and all non-white people were treated so badly that the compassionate could easily be moved to anger at the political and economic systems that allowed this to happen, and to be attracted to the ideas of a political system that seemed to offer the promise of a more equitable society. They tended to support FDR and the New Deal but were not convinced of the ability of its social programs to withstand the budgetary assault of the war towards which the world was headed. John Steinbeck's novel, *The Grapes of Wrath*, which focused on the plight of some of those who suffered, was the best-selling American novel of 1939.

Not surprisingly, the Soviet-Nazi non-aggression pact of August 23, 1939, caused many left-leaning Americans dyspepsia, and hindsight is a stern judge of actions and beliefs. Nevertheless, I wonder how many of us would have been tempted by these ideas that sounded so humane, at least in theory. The more I read about this period, the more understanding (not necessarily sympathy) I have for all Americans, on both extremes of the political spectrum. There were plenty of illusions of knowledge to go around and much fear that needed to be cauterized.

For most of the Second World War, the USSR was, theoretically, an ally of the USA. But as the war ended, Americans started to perceive the Soviet Union as a threat. Joseph McCarthy, one of the most reprehensible and immoral demagogues in U.S. political history, stirred up what became known as the "red scare." There was a moment in time – soon lost – at the end of the war when the United States had an opportunity to change the momentum towards the Cold War. Yes, the Americans had a monopoly on nuclear weapons, but some (including Robert Oppenheimer and Albert Einstein) argued that an international body should be created to supervise the use of all atomic power. At the same time, the Soviet Union was weak – absolutely devasted by the war. Stalin, convinced that the rhetoric about the collapse of capitalism was no longer convincing, signaled his interest in working out a modus vivendi with the United States. Truman elected to try to take advantage of the huge military and economic imbalances to dominate the world. The 1946 Baruch Plan was a non-starter for the Soviets, who believed that it would merely allow the Americans to maintain the monopoly on nuclear weapons. The USSR perceived the Marshall Plan as an economic version of the Baruch Plan. Hostility set in; backed into a corner, the Soviets proceeded to build their "Iron Curtain," and the script was set for the next two generations.

For the first forty-one years of my life, I was taught that the Soviet Union was the enemy of the United States. I remember vividly crouching under a desk in my fifth-grade classroom in 1959 in what was ludicrously labelled a "civil defense" drill, in preparation for the possibility of an atomic bomb being dropped by the Soviet Union on the semi-rural hamlet of Northampton, Massachusetts. We were fighting something called the "Cold War," a phrase which I thought unduly softened the public perception of what was official insanity. We – and they – wasted trillions of dollars in the development and deployment of immoral weaponry which, if unleashed, would have murdered hundreds of millions of people, rendering Stalin's madness a rounding error. We – and they – waged proxy wars around the world for these forty-one years, killing countless innocents and causing physical damage and political mayhem, the effects of which are still felt several generations later. It all turned out to be meaningless, wasted, and poisonous. Each side was equally at fault. As I write these words, I fear that the United States is falling into the same unnecessary trap in its relations with the People's Republic of China.

The first time I stood in Red Square, presumably the bull's eye target for many of my country's thermonuclear weapons, was on a snowy day in late March 2003. I visited Lenin (3% flesh; 97% wax!) and saw Peter the Great's clothing in a museum (he really was a large person!). I felt a strong sense of betrayal and disgust; the Cold War never should have happened. I felt an overwhelming need to do something – no matter how small – to help avert a similar chain of events from ever happening again.

Vassily Sergeyevich Sidorov and Larissa Vassilievna Ivkina

Vassily Sergeyevich Sidorov was born in Moscow on January 2, 1945. His father, of "lower middle class" Russian ancestry, was a driver in the Soviet Diplomatic Service and had served his country in the United States and Norway. Vassily was born at a grim time. The Second World War was still raging, although the tide was turning. Three weeks later, Soviet troops would liberate the concentration camp at Auschwitz-Birkenau. Also in January of that year, the Battle of the Bulge would come to an end with unbearable devastation on both sides, but with victory for the Allies. Raoul Wallenberg would disappear on January 17th during the Siege of Budapest. Germany would surrender when young Vassily was just over four months old. The devastation in Russia was incomprehensible; but as always, the long-suffering but resilient people of Russia endured and resolved to rebuild their society. Freeman Dyson, trying to understand the emotional trauma of the Russians, put it this way:

> All alike carry deep in their consciousness a collective memory of suffering and irreparable loss. This is the central fact conditioning the Soviet view of war. Russians, when they think about war, think of themselves not as warriors but as victims.

Vassily Sergeyevich was educated at the Moscow State Institute of International Relations (MGIMO), which was and still is one of the finest institutions of higher education in Russia. He met and married a young woman named Larissa Vassilievna Ivkina, who was also a student at MGIMO. On her mother's side, Larissa came from a family of Kiev-based Ukrainian intelligentsia. Her grandfather had been shot during Stalin's time for organizing local cultural events that were labelled "Ukrainian nationalism." Her mother, Tatiana Feofilovna Prigoda-Movchan gave birth to Larissa at the age of 17 in Kiev. Tatiana, who died of cancer at the age of 54, was a true friend to not only her two daughters but to all her grandchildren, who would later recall that she served as their prime example of kindness and self-sacrifice.

Larissa's Russian father, Vassily Fedorovich Ivkin, was a veteran of the Second World War, who had enlisted at the age of 16 (by adding a few years to his age during the enlistment process) and, having fought all the way through 1945, returned home with various medals and nearly as many wounds. He later worked at the Ukrainian (later Soviet) Ministry of Foreign Affairs. He received a stipend (called "the Stalin's stipend") to take courses at Columbia University in New York. His career went downhill when somebody wrote an "*anonymyka*" (an anonymous report) on him alleging some fabricated wrongdoing.

Vassily Sergeyevich completed his studies at MGIMO in 1967 and entered the Ministry of Foreign Affairs when Leonid Brezhnev was General Secretary of the Central Committee of the Communist Party of the Soviet Union. As a professional diplomat representing the Soviet Union and, after December 25, 1991, the Russian Federation, he had a distinguished career, eventually serving as a Deputy Minister of Foreign Affairs. He retired from the Ministry in 2001 after serving as Permanent Representative of the Russian Federation to the United Nations Office in Geneva. His cousin was a senior government official during the Brezhnev era, serving as Head of the Soviet Information Department and later the State Information Agency.

Vassily Vassilievich Sidorov Is Introduced

Early in his career, Vassily Sergeyevich was assigned to the Soviet Embassy in Athens. There, on February 2, 1971, Larissa gave birth to their second son, who was named for his father. And so, we introduce the next protagonist of this book, Vassily Vassilievich Sidorov – the second *Breaking with Tradition*. Years later, Larissa explained to me that she had altered her son's birth certificate to show Moscow as the city of his birth. "In those days, you never knew what would happen," she laughed, "and I did not want to risk my son's future by giving him an 'unusual' birthplace." The family lived in Greece for several years before being rotated back to Moscow and then to New York City, where they lived from 1976 to 1981.

By 1981, he was back in Moscow and attending elementary school. An important inflection point in his life, his first Black Swan, took place during his high school years. "One of my most important mentors and influences growing up was the principal of my high school," stated Vassily. "His name was Leonid Milgram."

Leonid Isidorovich Milgram

Leonid Milgram was born in Moscow on February 25, 1921. His father, Isidore Wolfovich Milgram, was a Polish Jew who became one of the Soviet Union's first intelligence officers. "My father had eight names and eight passports in different countries," recalled Leonid in an interview conducted on his 90th birthday. During the "great terror" of 1936-38, Isidore was arrested and shot. In Leonid's high school class, 25% of the students lost parents to the Gulag.

In 1960, he became principal of an educational institution that was poetically named School #45. By all accounts, he was an inspiring teacher and principal, who had what in retrospect could only be called a subversive mission. In Vassily's words, "The school ended up being at the forefront of many new trends: the first (Mac) desktop computers, the first swimming pool, the first exchange program with a school in the U.S., but more importantly a very informal and intellectually challenging culture, with a significant hint of dissent from the official ideology." Vassily would reflect that Milgram was one of the "semi-dissident" educators who were somehow allowed to teach in their own way based on their level of professionalism and contacts.

"I wanted the kids to become not just intellectuals," reflected Teacher Milgram, "but intellectuals with other qualities at the bottom of their hearts – decency, kindness, knowing how to live not just for themselves, but for society." One of his former students wrote, on the occasion of his 90th birthday, "The most important thing was that it was a school of humanism and that we were brought up to be free." This educator instilled values in his students that were at variance with the post-Stalin Soviet conservative and deeply indoctrinated educational philosophy.

Vassily thrived under Principal Milgram, who helped and encouraged this intelligent and sensitive student. "I was born into the mainstream of society," observed Vassily. "At School #45, I was chosen as the secretary of the school's Komsomol. I became a member of the Moscow City Komsomol Committee, whose members engaged in a variety of public service projects. It was not at all ideological in nature and conformed to Principal Milgram's philosophy of service to others. In fact, one of our main projects was helping in the restoration of Moscow churches."

University Life and Times

Vassily entered the Moscow State Institute of International Relations of the Ministry of Foreign Affairs in 1988, following in the tradition of both his mother and father, with the intention of joining the diplomatic service.

I spoke to one of Vassily's close friends and a classmate from university days, Irackly Mtibe-lishvily, a Managing Director of Citi, and the Chairman of Corporate and Investment Banking for Russia and CIS at ZAO Citigroup Global Markets. Irackly is Georgian and was born and raised in what he called the "deep periphery" of the Soviet Union. "For a communist country, the USSR was very elitist," said Irackly. "The proclaimed values were different from the real values." The alternative to university was the army, so for young men there was substantial incentive to aspire to higher education. I observed that this was the identical situation for young men in the United States in the 1960s.

Starting on September 1, 1988, they spent the next three years together as classmates. Irackly described his university years as a Faustian Bargain. For Vassily, who was "born into the main-stream" of Soviet society, it was less compromising. Nevertheless, they were both members of the Young Communist League. Although nobody believed in the rhetoric, they mouthed the words because they were the keys to advancement and, in effect, a graduation requirement. "The system was corrupt to the core," stated Irackly. He and Vassily became good friends despite the differences in their backgrounds. They had mutual sympathy and shared values.

According to Vassily, "This was an intellectually fertile time. There was openness and debate. Professors were reconsidering how and what to teach. There was not exactly turmoil, but things were starting to open up. The Gorbachev Era had started in 1985. I was caught up in the hopeful euphoria of that moment." I can only imagine how confusing and destabilizing it must have been when the Soviet Union collapsed on December 26, 1991, in the middle of Vassily's college years.

By his third year at MGIMO – 1991, Vassily felt he needed more. He denies that his wanderlust was political in nature; he just was ready for an adventure. Perhaps his DRD4-7r gene was activated. He started applying to universities in the United States. He was admitted to all ten universities to which he applied and decided to attend the Wharton School of the University of Pennsylvania because he wanted focus, and business seemed to be more focused than the liberal arts. By 1993, he had earned degrees from both the Moscow State Institute and Wharton, the first individual ever to have earned degrees simultaneously from these two institutions.

"What I respect the most about Vassily," stated Irackly, "is his ability to grow, mature, and change. I have witnessed these changes, starting from the dissolution of the Soviet Union. Vassily is also at peace with himself. His proclaimed values and real values are the same. He has a great sense of humor. He is ambitious. Smart. Capable of compromise. I wish that people like him were running the country."

Vassily's Career Begins

In 1993, following graduation from Wharton and MGIMO, there existed an apparently endless stream of opportunities in the new Russia, and Vassily entered the job market in both the public and private sectors, with high hopes and expectations. I observed that he seemed to have broken with many traditions in his career, starting with the family tradition of government service with the Ministry of Foreign Affairs.

"Yes, I have broken with tradition. But I have not rejected all traditions," he smiled. "I have the greatest admiration for Pushkin, Chekhov, Dostoyevsky, Tchaikovsky, and other giants of our culture. But when you look at my career, you can detect that I have been committed to a break with tradition. For example, when I was at Svyazinvest, I worked to convert a bloated and inefficient Soviet-style monopoly into a modern company that met or exceeded international standards. It was clearly essential to break with tradition, but I chose to make this break within the system, not from the outside or in opposition to the system. I am not a rebel; I am a reformer. Revolution can degenerate into negativity, which is counter-productive to positive change. So yes, I have a social conscience."

He spent three years as First Vice President with Sistema Telecom, from 2000 to 2003, which was when I first met Vassily. He then served as President and Chief Executive Officer of MobileTeleSystems (NYSE: MBT) from 2003-2006, after which time he turned to entrepreneurship.

"My income now comes primarily from private equity and venture investments, advisory mandates, as well as remuneration for board memberships. I am also involved in various pursuits that involve public service," he added, brightening. "I am a member of the Expert Council to the Government of the Russian Federation. I also serve on the boards of directors of Russian Railways, Aeroflot (the Russian airline), and Transtelecom (the telecommunications subsidiary of Russian railways), but these memberships are a combination of business and public service."

The Expert Council to the Government of the Russian Federation

When Dmitri Medvedev was president from 2008 to 2012, there was a political thaw in Russia, especially in the last year of his presidency. This thaw coincided with growing social activity on the part of the emerging middle class. Members of this middle class sensed that things were changing. Times were good and the economy was booming. But people were upset that politically they had gone backwards. They felt betrayed by the fact that elections were once again rigged, which left them out of the political process. Medvedev invited "experts" to advise him informally, in an unofficial capacity. This gave the people a sense of involvement and held out the hope of change for the better. He created what he called an "Expert Council" to capture the momentum of this initiative and Vassily was invited to join as a member. "This was not an exclusive membership," he laughed. "There were between 400 and 500 members."

"Basically, the Expert Council was viewed by many as a fig leaf over an otherwise non-transparent decision-making process," said Vassily, "but the trend inevitably created additional lifts for people like myself to get involved in certain important government initiatives, as well as to create their own initiatives. For example, Medvedev understood that corporate governance was a problem and that he had limited ability to reform state-owned or state-controlled enterprises. But by reference to the Expert Council, he was able to use our collective recommendations to bring about some reform in corporate governance."

Although the cynic will say that this was a sham, I am not convinced. I also believe, like Chanthol Sun, that civil society is built slowly, one small step at a time, even under the most harrowing conditions. Cynics do not create positive change; optimists are the ones who change the world for the better.

Vassily and I continued our conversation on a snowy evening in early April in Moscow. "We were directly able to bring about change in the Russian Railways system in ways that saved billions of dollars. The basic recommendations we made are not complicated – accountability, transparency, cost savings, rationalization of staffing, and the like. But the recommendations were rather new to state-owned and state-controlled enterprises. Medvedev understood that the bureaucracy was not capable of reforming itself. He needed spoilers to force the reform. This was exciting work and a good experience for me. I maintained my independence but was able to bring about positive change."

Dmitry Razumov

When I asked Vassily to suggest the most important of his friends with whom I should speak, he said without any hesitation, "Dmitry Razumov." Dmitry's mother and Vassily's mother are sisters. Both Dmitry and Vassily described each other "more as a brother than a cousin." They grew up together and have remained close. Dmitry probably knows Vassily as well as anybody. Dmitry is Chief Executive Officer of Onexim Group, which is the holding company of Mikhail Prokhorov, a Russian oligarch who is one of the richest men in Russia.

"Vassily is smart and ambitious," Dmitry began. "He is a good example for everybody. You never catch him hanging out. He is always working. As a student, he always got good grades. Vassily is an excellent role model. He really has everything you could ask for in a personality, including the ability to change and evolve. He adapted well to the collapse of the Soviet Union. We have helped each other in our careers, in good times and bad times. He is my brother."

"Vassily is patriotic in the sense of wanting Russia to be strong but not nationalistic at the cost of hurting others. He and I both share the conviction that isolationism has no value. We share the values of the civilized world. But there is a long tradition in Russia of aspiring to abstract goals at the expense of the well-being of the Russian people. This has been the case for centuries. Vassily and I believe that this unenviable track record can be broken."

"Starting in 1989, everything changed so quickly that there wasn't much time for introspection. But I feel that we must keep asking ourselves if we are growing as individuals. In the case of Vassily, I can truly say that he is growing as a person. And his principles are now very clear. He acts on these principles. Vassily is an honest man, and above all else, a reliable man. Another interesting facet to his personality is that, despite being self-assured, Vassily is at heart a sensitive person, an emotional person. He cannot be cold and heartless. He recognizes the human consequences of actions and decisions."

Reflections on Life, Liberty and the Pursuit of Happiness

Vassily is a philosopher and an historian even more than he is a businessman and a civil servant. He takes the long view of everything, from patient capital to the politics of Russia.

"I am not a revolutionary," he said again. "I fear instability, so I choose to work within the system. The rebels who work outside the system may be purer, but they are oftentimes ineffective. They do not bring about change faster while fighting the system. They inspire the government to dig in its heels and resist change, often arbitrarily and sometimes violently, which of course incites the revolutionary to engage in even more provocative behavior. I want to create a better world, not destroy the old world. The country needs many leaders in the private sector who create jobs, make prosperity more inclusive, and show the consequences of positive actions. Russia is at a critical juncture. If the freedom lovers leave, this will dishearten the entire society. This is part of the reason I stay – to help build the new Russia, brick by brick."

"There is still injustice and oppression in Russia," Vassily averred. "Here the state is the supreme entity that has authority over everybody. Your freedom and your assets can be taken away arbitrarily. This is the Russian way, and it has been true for centuries. Our democracy is a very young one. If one counts its history from 1991, then it has only been around for a very short time. But looked at historically, the limitations on our freedoms today are insignificant compared to earlier eras. Things used to be much worse. Russians have endured intolerable injustices and suffering at the hands of despots. The limitations on our freedoms now are very easy to tolerate if we remember where we came from."

Vassily was born into a family of civil servants and has never lost that genetic imprinting. He would like to do something meaningful for Russia. He explained that the level of corruption, hierarchy, and red tape is much worse than under the USSR. "Communist ideology was ridiculous," he said with a guffaw, "but at least it provided a framework. Now there is no framework to control the avarice, greed, and rapaciousness."

"I enjoy bringing about change and creating economic value. I also enjoy deal making. I find satisfaction in helping people come together to make good things happen. And I value my freedom. I also am still intrigued by the big picture. I would not call it my dream job, but I would not decline if I was asked to serve my country if the level was one that offered real opportunities to effect change on a sufficiently large scale. This must be the influence of Principal Milgram, who always told us to live for more than ourselves and that we had duties to others. And not in the sense of being a communist, but in being a thinking person, with freedom of choice to do good in the world."

Who Is Vassily Sidorov?

"I cannot say that I am perfectly ethical as defined by politicians or theologians, but I think this is irrelevant. I have bribed policemen to avoid speeding tickets," he confessed with a laugh. "I am not nationalistic in the sense of supporting megalomaniacal geopolitical ambitions. But I have never betrayed anyone, and I never will. Over time, I have acquired a good sense of what I can accept and what I cannot accept. There are fewer shades of grey for me now. Above all else, I value my freedom. I am not willing to belong to anyone. I cannot sacrifice my freedom or principles for financial gain or power. And having gone through this process of introspection and self-discovery, I cannot tell myself not to think critically. Once you begin thinking critically, you cannot stop. It becomes self-perpetuating and you cannot stop without compromising your inner self. I also cannot predict where this reasoning process will lead, but only that I must follow it. So, I cannot do something that is immoral, unethical, or will hurt another person, at least as defined by my principles."

Freeman Dyson, in his 1984 book *Weapons and Hope*, already quoted in this chapter, reported a conversation he had with George Kennan, perhaps the most widely respected American Sovietologist of his era and both an architect and advocate of the policy of containment that helped to precipitate and then characterized the Cold War. Kennan, Dyson recounted, made note of how surprised Americans were that the demise of the Russian monarchy in 1917 could lead to a form of government that they found even more distasteful. Kennan worried that although the fall of the Soviet state would be welcomed by Americans, such an event might result in a successor government even worse than the communists. He cited "recent evidence" of "social decay," including "a loss of sense of purpose among the children of the elite." Vassily Sidorov, 13 years old at the time, was certainly a member of the cohort to which Kennan was referring. With the benefit of a full generation of hindsight, I can assuredly pronounce Kennan mistaken in the case of this child of the elite. One wonders what "recent evidence" he drew upon to confirm the "loss of sense of purpose" among young Russians in Vassily's generation. Vassily is a man of purpose and principles, as are Irackly and

Dmitry. How many others lurk in the shadows, waiting for their chance to break with tradition?

As with so many of the others in this book, I have the benefit of time in evaluating Vassily. I have known him for almost twenty years and have had the opportunity to watch his behavior and judgment in many different circumstances, ranging from his interactions with the President of Russia to a family vacation that included our wives and children. He has visited my home and I have visited his home. I found Vassily consistently to be a man of great charm, wisdom, and integrity. I am lucky to be able to count him as my friend. I have the greatest admiration and affection for this individual who is leading a purposeful, spiritual life with the goal of having a positive impact on others. Although it is no longer surprising, I think it is important to note once again that despite the fact that Vassily's mother tongue, national history, culinary preferences, cultural traditions, and other superficial characteristics are unique, his character, moral dispositions, and world view are all a perfect match with the others profiled in this book. When he meets the others, he will have no trouble communicating across all the differences because fundamentally they are all the same person. There are no foreign lands.

Moving on to Montevideo

Our next journey is mostly south but also west, 8,302 miles and six time zones away. We will depart from snowy Moscow, crossing Ukraine, the tip of the boot of Italy, the Mediterranean, Algeria, Mali, the Equator, the South Atlantic, and catching a glimpse of Rio de Janeiro outside the starboard windows of our aircraft before arriving in the capital of Uruguay, "deep" in the southern hemisphere. As always when I cross the Equator, I ponder how much of human history may have been determined by the decisions of early cartographers on how to create a two-dimensional representation of the earth – a minor planet in the immensity of the universe, with no inherent "north" or "south." In the same way that the birthday of an important figure in one of the world's religions has determined the dating system used by most of the world's peoples, the Northern Hemisphere has been "on top" since the advent of cartography. Would history have turned out differently if Mercator had placed "south" at the "north" of his map?

Ebullient Survivor

Roberto Canessa

Ebullient Survivor: Roberto Canessa

Whirling Dervishes

Iam a romantic, but I am a scientist and I only believe in what can be established or proven empirically. I am skeptical about the existence of either God or gods, but I find all spiritual traditions to have relevant moral imperatives, except those that involve huckstering as an excuse for trying to convince others to accept how they implement their imagined realities. I am not superstitious, even when I am alone. I walk under ladders, love black cats, sit comfortably in the 13th row of an airplane and find Feng Shui to be mildly amusing, especially when I am teasing friends who really believe in it.

But there are a few phenomena involving humans that I cannot explain. For example, Whirling Dervishes. These are Turkish dancers who spin around in a tight circle to the beat of music, seemingly for as long as they wish. In Istanbul, I have watched this dance for as long as 15 minutes, which is about as long as tourists can pay attention without getting bored, but I am told that there is really no limit to how long they can whirl.

Their dance is an act of devotion on the part of practitioners of Muslim Sufism, and they believe that it brings them closer to God. Men and women participate, and they wear floor-length white gowns and tall, cylindrical hats. There are three steps, as far as I can tell, that are repeated. The left foot makes a 90° turn to the left, the right foot swings around over the left foot and the left foot snaps around to the original position. Each complete turn takes about a second. The billowing gowns create quite a dramatic spectacle, which is why visitors to Turkey enjoy watching the whirling dervishes. But this is not a performing art or an athletic event; it is a religious ritual, and one is not expected to clap or cheer at the end of the dance.

What makes this inexplicable? At the end of the dance, and a fifteen-minute version might involve 900 turns of 360^0, the dancers simply stop. They are not breathing hard, which I attribute to good conditioning. But also, they are not dizzy. They simply stop, and after a few moments, walk off-stage without the slightest sign of having spun around to the point where others would have been unable to stand up. I know how ballet dancers avoid getting dizzy, which is to spin their heads around so that they are looking at the same spot for 98% of the turn. But the dervishes do not use this technique. They simply turn. And they never get dizzy. This is inexplicable to my rational mind.

Introducing Roberto Canessa

Roberto Canessa is another inexplicable phenomenon. As I introduce Roberto, I must begin with the inexplicable, because his existence on earth today is utterly so. By all logic, he should have perished in 1972.

Roberto was a member of an Uruguayan rugby team whose chartered Fairchild aircraft crashed in deep snow in the remote Chilean Andes in October 1972. Everyone but their mothers and girlfriends gave them up for dead, and all searching was called off after some fruitless efforts by land and air to find them. It was irrational to expect that anyone could have survived the plane crash. If anyone had miraculously survived, then that person or persons would have perished within a day or two because of the snow, wind, cold, and exposure to the elements with no shelter. And if anyone had miraculously survived for more than a few days, they would have starved to death since there were only snacks on the plane for a few hours' flight. The rational mind was unable to accept that anyone was still alive.

Seventy-two days later sixteen of the crash survivors were rescued alive and brought back to civilization. All sixteen are still alive as I write these words. Their story has been told and retold in many books (including Roberto's own, to which we will soon refer), at least two movies, countless interviews and, in the case of several of them (Roberto included) motivational speeches about resilience and enthusiasm to academic, corporate, medical, and other audiences. Roberto played a central role in the survival of the sixteen as he and another of the survivors of the crash hiked over a mountain, defying the insurmountable odds of snow, wind, cold, starvation, exhaustion, and altitude sickness, to inform an uncomprehending world that sixteen of them were still alive. It is one of the most inspiring stories of endurance that I have ever encountered, and I had admired Roberto from afar ever since I read about this story. After his return from the Andes just before Christmas that year, Roberto resumed his study of medicine, specializing in pediatric cardiology, a profession he practices today.

I had heard Roberto Canessa speak to large audiences several times (in Santiago de Chile and Madrid, Spain) and I had concluded instinctively that he would be one of the heroes of my book. My admiration for his fortitude in 1972 was immense, but it was his life after his safe return from the mountains – the wisdom and compassion he showers on all he meets – that intrigued me even more than the physical heroism of his youth. I needed more information, so I contacted him through a mutual acquaintance, a Chilean sea bass named Claudio Engel. Roberto invited me to visit him in Montevideo.

In preparation for my visit, I read the book written by Piers Paul Read, entitled *Alive*, which recounted the story of the sixteen survivors and the seventy-two days. Finishing this book on a cold and blustery February night in Philadelphia, I reflected on the inexplicable, because this book involved so many experiences and circumstances that by any logical explanation never could have happened. I also read the book written by Nando Parrado, one of Roberto's fellow survivors. While the weather had cleared in Philadelphia when I finished Nando's book, the deep chill in my heart did not diminish. Utterly impossible. Have could anybody have survived?

Arrival in Montevideo

Uruguay is the second smallest country in Latin America and has a population that totals less than half the population of Hong Kong. It is a European country in all but geography, with influences coming from Spain, Portugal, Britain, and Italy.

March 2nd was a typical fall day in Montevideo. As my plane landed, it was pouring rain – in buckets. By the time I walked out of the airport, the sun was shining, and the sky was a brilliant blue. With no mountains to the east or west to block the passage of clouds, weather comes and goes quickly. The weather varies little from season to season. March 2nd was a balmy 75 degrees Fahrenheit, and comfortable.

Thirty minutes later, Roberto picked me up at my hotel, and took me to his home, a sprawling, rambling, one-story, living museum of his life, family, and personal philosophy. Dressed in jeans, driving a car of uncertain vintage, surrounded by the artifacts of a life well-lived, he exuded neither charm nor guile. What you see with Roberto is what you get. I felt immediately that here was a person from whom you would always get a straight answer. It turned out that his glass front was matched by a titanium back.

When I arrived at his home, Roberto introduced his daughter, Laura (26), her friend, his wife Laura, a visiting doctoral student from Argentina who was writing his thesis on leadership and had interviewed Roberto the day before, a marketing professor from the local business school, and two others. Later, his elder son, Hilario, Hilario's wife, and their very small baby boy arrived.

Laura

I must begin by introducing Roberto's wife, Laura. She is a strong, intelligent, devoted, and supportive woman. Laura was his girlfriend when the plane crashed in the Andes. She never gave up. Never. Not for a tenth of a second. She obviously has enormous respect and admiration for Roberto, and her unconditional love surrounds him, her home, her guests, and even a stranger who stops by on a Saturday afternoon. Roberto needs her, probably even more than he realizes. She is the glue that keeps him stuck together.

Roberto is a "people person," and apparently is always surrounded by many of them; some sycophants but predominantly a free-wheeling assortment of friends, relatives, neighbors, and those seeking to learn from him. Our conversation was unusual in that it took place in the presence of others. I never felt inhibited in asking questions, nor did Roberto ever show discomfort in responding or reluctance in revealing anything. Several days later, when Laura (his wife) asked me if I wanted to meet privately with him, I asked her if he would reveal a different side. She replied, "No, you will get the same answers. Roberto is never different. He is always Roberto." I declined the opportunity to meet with him privately. There was no need.

Ancestry

One hundred sixty-three years ago, the Canessa family emigrated to Uruguay from Rapallo, a coastal municipality in the Province of Genoa, in Liguria, itself in northern Italy. Roberto was born on January 17, 1953, in Montevideo, and grew up in the Carrasco District, which is a comfortable, middle-class residential area close to the airport but somewhat outside the business district. He bought the land and built the home in which he lives today.

The men in his family have generally followed one of two professions. Some have served the state. One great-grandfather was a Senator. His grandfather, born in 1901, was active in politics. Some were healers. Another great-grandfather was a doctor. His father was a cardiologist. Roberto chose to be a doctor (more on this later), but he also once ran for president of Uruguay (more on this later as well).

Our first conversation took place over a three-hour timespan in the large, busy, but comfortable environment of the "great room" in his home, surrounded by a rotating entourage of friends and relations. I counted a total of 22 humans and 4 dogs who were introduced to me in what was a seemingly typical Saturday afternoon for the Canessa family. I was able to ask many of the questions I had posed to previous interviewees, but it was clear right from the beginning that this was an unusual person, even by my standards, which categorically excluded the ordinary.

"I work at home in the mornings," he said as we walked past a 1929 Ford that was undergoing restoration in a garage near his home. "And then I go to the clinic in the afternoons. Weekends are usually, but not always, more relaxed."

I noticed that there were several individuals working on the car. One was a young boy and one was an elderly man. I did not attach much significance to this fact until later, when I spoke with one of Roberto's closest friends, Juan Berchesi. "Roberto employs a number of people at his home, working at odd jobs such as restoring an old car," Juan informed me. "You may have noticed them working in the yard. He has such a tremendous feeling for other human beings. Nothing can stop him. There is nothing he believes he cannot do. Roberto is the most positive person you will ever meet. This is part of Roberto's spirituality."

"Tell me about your concept of fate and free will," I asked Roberto, wanting to avoid making this yet another interview about the plane crash, but at the same time desiring to understand the inner person and what long-term effects the plane crash and its aftermath had on him.

"Fifty-fifty," he replied quickly, apparently having reflected on this question before. "But life is a game with constantly-changing rules. If you accept that the rules change, then you cannot be too upset with life. We can influence fate, of course. If you smoke, you tempt fate. If you sky dive, then the odds change, and the ratio is closer to 90-10. If you are eating dinner at home, the ratio changes to 10-90. If your plane has crashed in the Andes, the ratio changes to 99-1."

Like almost all the men and women in my book, Roberto carries some genetic and cultural baggage about "fate," but also like the others, he never acts on the basis of a belief in this imagined reality. He acts strictly from the perspective of a Sartrean hero.

Roberto's (Very Short) Political Career

"Why did you run for president?" I asked, referring to his one entry into politics that came in 1994 when he founded the "Partido Azul" (Blue Party). He laughed, and when he laughs, you know he is amused, happy. He laughs often and smiles almost always. He is a happy person, comfortable in his own skin.

"My political platform was suicidal. I got very few votes. First, I said that I would cut the parliament in half. We have too many politicians, too many staff, too many chauffeurs, too many hangers-on. This scared the politicians and their entourages. But I felt that the government was too big and unwieldy to govern effectively. This alienated me from all the legislators who feared losing power and influence."

"Next, I said I would close ministries that were dysfunctional. This, of course, cost me the votes of thousands of bureaucrats who feared losing their jobs."

"Then, I proposed putting the army to work on fixing roads, dams, ports, and other public works projects. Uruguay was at peace and had no enemies that justified maintaining an army that practiced shooting at people and things. I felt that 'national service' would be better served by putting these young men to work in ways that would improve the country. This part of my platform alienated the armed forces, quite naturally."

"Then I proposed paying teachers more and insisting on higher standards of instruction. While the idea of higher pay was appealing to the teachers, the threat of accountability was more than enough to offset the advantages, so I lost the votes of the teachers as well."

"The result was that I won a microscopic percentage of the votes and gave up my political career without ever getting started. I spent the equivalent of US$30,000 and 10,000 people voted for me. It was fun, but I will never do it again," he concluded. Similar to Chanthol Sun, his honesty and integrity did not translate into electoral success.

Career, Spirituality and Influences

I was curious about his choice of careers, and why he entered pediatric cardiology. In his book he wrote, "I was fascinated by surgery, because I saw the job as repairing broken parts or anomalies, and I'd always considered myself a Mr. Fixit."

When I asked him in person, his answer was different, but not inconsistent. "Pediatric cardiology was a new field in Uruguay in the early 1980s, and I was excited about the opportunities for helping children who might otherwise have died, either immediately or in mid-life. We did our first pediatric cardiac transplant in 1981, and since that time there have been many advances in pediatric cardiology. One of the most exciting is echocardiography, which allows non-interventional diagnosis. It is also exciting that we can detect and fix heart problems in children that would not have appeared until they were young adults, but which would have been fatal if not fixed in early childhood."

"But still," he said ruefully, "when a kid is dying, I ask God for His help."

"This is another important topic that I want to discuss with you," I said next. "Tell me about your relationship with God."

"When you are young," he responded, "God takes care of you. He provides support and is your protector during a time of great vulnerability. This is why we teach our children about God right from the beginning. Even the lullabies we sing to babies refer to the protective capabilities of God. But when you get older, you need God less because you are less vulnerable. In the Andes, God was neither my protector nor my salvation. He was my friend. After the avalanche, I became fragile and weak, so I needed God more. I promised God that I would do many things if I survived. All of my promises were highly commendable."

"Unfortunately," he laughed, but without a trace of embarrassment or regret, "most of the resolutions I made to myself were contaminated soon after I returned from the mountains. So, my sworn promises to live a better life went unfulfilled. The weaker you are, the more you need God. Sometimes life is very challenging, and it is nice to have a friend to whom you can turn. I did not expect God to save me in the Andes, but at least he was a constant companion as I tried to figure out what to do."

"I was considered to be very smart when I was a baby," he laughed (again). "But by the time I reached school age, I was a little bit unruly. In fact, I was a disciplinary problem, and I was sent to the office to meet with the principal on many occasions. I was eventually sent to a psychiatrist who diagnosed me as pre-criminal."

"Despite my disciplinary problems, I was always motivated by pride, the desire to compete, and the will to succeed. I also thought that if you are a little malicious," he said with a wink, "then girls would find you more attractive."

"I went to a school run by Christian Brothers who came from Ireland. They were very strict and held the students to a high moral code. They taught us that honesty was even more important than success. They were exemplary human beings and showed me that personal example is not just the best but the only way of teaching values."

"My mother was different from most mothers," he said, surprisingly. "She did not 'mother' me, but she supported me more than 100%. If I had told her that I wanted to fly to the moon, she would have asked me how many suitcases I needed. She took my most outlandish dreams and assured me that they were completely within the realm of possibility."

In his book, Roberto wrote that his mother told him, "Don't be afraid, Roberto. Fear is a fantasy. Rise above it and watch as it disappears." Several months later I asked another of Roberto's closest friends, Alberto Gari, a veterinarian, to tell me something that others may not know about Roberto. "I know that he misses his mother a lot," said Alberto.

Sunday Lunch *Chez* Canessa

The next day I was invited to Sunday lunch. I had a preformed image of a rather formal event, with white linen and candlesticks and perhaps butlers with white gloves. I could not have been more mistaken. Sunday lunch at the Canessa home is a jolly, completely informal, boisterous affair, more like a Chinese meal than a British meal. The lunch I attended included (by my count, which may have understated the number) eighteen people ranging in age from six months to eighty-seven years of age. Over a roaring fire, Roberto personally cooked gaucho-style steak, blood sausage, cheese and a variety of other foods guaranteed to make a cardiologist shudder. Everyone ate too much, laughed just enough, and sang songs until it was time to go.

One of the attendees was Sergio Abreu, a former Uruguayan Foreign Minister and at that time a candidate for President. Sergio is one of Roberto's three "spiritual advisors." The second of his spiritual advisors is the local veterinarian, Alberto Gari (already quoted above), who stopped by during lunch but did not stay. His third spiritual advisor is Juan Berchesi (also already quoted above), a former head of the Uruguayan Social Security System, the Uruguayan National Railroad, and a major private pension fund. As Juan explained, "Uruguay is a small country. It is difficult to specialize. You must be willing to diversify yourself."

I asked Juan what it meant to be one of Roberto's spiritual advisors. Juan laughed. "Roberto has many advisers, but he never follows anybody's advice. He reaches his own conclusions and acts accordingly."

Later, I asked Alberto the same question. He had the same answer. "Serving as Roberto's spiritual adviser involves listening to him and exchanging ideas. Roberto never takes any advice. He asks plenty of people and then he does whatever he thinks is best."

At the Sunday lunch, I spoke for some time with Juan's wife, Maria Isabel Varela, the co-founder of St. George's School in Montevideo. She was in attendance in her capacity as the first cousin or sister of Roberto's wife Laura. She told me the story of one of Roberto's many dogs, which as a puppy had been hit by a car. Everyone told Roberto to put the dog to sleep because it was badly mangled. But Roberto refused, and with his good friend and spiritual adviser, Alberto (the veterinarian), he nursed the dog back to health. The dog, now mature, hobbles on two normal legs and two horribly misshapen legs but seems to be in no pain and shows affection to everyone.

"Roberto fixes everything. It doesn't matter if it is a chair, a dog, a baby's heart, or anything else. He won't give up on anything or anyone," stated Maria Isabel with complete conviction and obvious admiration.

The Clinic

After lunch Roberto said, "Let's go to my clinic." As we drove downtown from Carrasco to the center of Montevideo, Roberto explained that he had been called to examine a one-day old boy who was born in need of a hernia operation.

I understood that the operation must take place immediately, which meant Monday morning, March 4th. But there were some complications. The boy (and his mother) had Marfan Syndrome, a congenital disorder that affected the connective tissue of the body. It manifested itself in long, slender fingers, which is how the neonatologist had diagnosed the condition. One of the possible ways in which this syndrome can threaten a newborn is through defects in the heart valves or the aorta. The hernia surgeon and the anesthesiologist were reluctant to operate since the child might die. Roberto was brought in to determine if the child's cardiovascular system was strong enough to tolerate the operation.

Roberto wheeled his echocardiography machine to the far wall of the neonatal unit and started to set up next to the bed of a young man not yet 24 hours old. He was sleeping peacefully. When all was ready, Roberto instructed me and the nurses to stand behind him. He squeezed some lubricant on the probe and touched it gently to the baby's chest. Then the most marvelous thing happened. The echocardiograph popped up on the screen, and in shadowy but discernible detail, revealed the baby's heart. Two valves, pumping rhythmically, sending blood out, bringing it back into the heart. Roberto pressed a key on the machine, and the echocardiogram responded with a full-color version of this miracle. He took some readings and a nurse transcribed them. Ten minutes later, he disconnected the machine, wrote his report, and said simply, "He is perfect. The operation can take place tomorrow."

As we retraced our drive back to Roberto's home to pick up Laura for dinner, he reflected on his many patients, their parents, and the tremendous obligation he felt to help these sick babies. "It is rewarding to me that these kids now get well and live normal lives, with one exception, which is that they have 'survivor mentality.' To use your metaphor, they have glass fronts and titanium backs," he observed.

There was no question in my mind of the perfect, seamless continuity in Roberto's mind between the courageous acts that he performed during the crash in the Andes and the devotion to the babies placed in his care as a pediatric cardiologist. He has always had, and will always have, a deeply emotional feeling of obligation, originally to his fellow airplane crash survivors in the Andes and now to new-born children with cardiac challenges. I was witnessing, once again, a person with the desire to leave the world a better place than he found it.

Juan also later recounted, "Roberto helps anyone and everyone in need. I remember one day when we were traveling by car and came upon a very serious accident. Roberto immediately stopped, attended to the injured, and transported three people to a nearby hospital. One of the injured later died. They were from Argentina. Roberto visited the families of the victims. You see, nothing stops Roberto's solidarity with people. Rich or poor. Black or white. He also has a strong inclination to help people who have committed crimes, especially young people. He has a farm where he employs some of these kids who were drug addicts and criminals. He always believes in his heart that they are not bad kids and that he can help them to reclaim their lives. This is what 'spirituality' means to Roberto."

The Burden of Fame

Roberto told me the story of a grateful parent of a patient. The father was employed as a porter at the airport. He said that once, after arriving at the airport and using this porter, he had tried to pay him. The man's reaction was swift and unambiguous. "I would rather cut off my hand than take money from you, Dr. Canessa," threatened the porter.

Roberto said that he has difficulty going anywhere in Montevideo without being identified. His intact shock of white hair makes him instantly recognizable. He cannot be anonymous. I sensed that he both loves and hates the notoriety, in a humble way.

He told me the story of another parent, the mother of a child critically ill because of a cardiologic problem. She came up to him as he left the room of a different patient in his clinic, and asked plaintively, "Dr. Canessa, I know you are busy. But may I have one minute of your time? I will walk along the corridor with you so that I do not waste any of your precious time." He said that he still gets tears in his eyes when he remembers that moment.

After leaving the clinic, we picked up Laura and went for dinner at an Uruguayan fast-food restaurant. Roberto and Laura knew most of the people in the restaurant. After dinner, the waiter brought the check, the total of which was "0." There ensued a spirited argument between Roberto and the waiter. It seems that the waiter's wife and newborn son had been patients of Roberto. The waiter refused payment and Roberto objected. The waiter was both adamant and animated, and after a lot of friendly arguing, we eventually left the restaurant without paying.

Farewell, Montevideo

"I am not content," he mused. "I never feel I do enough. But I have a deep sense of obligation to help. I just wish I could help more." In his book, he wrote that "I just can't simply ignore it when a problem falls into my path…What I see is not an elderly homeless person, or an invalid, or a drug addict, or a baby with hypoplastic left heart. Instead, that person desperate for help – is me."

I had the strong feeling, again, that he equates the Andes survivors with his pediatric patients. He felt responsibility in the Andes to save lives and he feels responsibility now to save kids. He has never been satisfied with his performance because too many died in the Andes and too many babies die. No matter how many lives he saves, he always feels he has not done enough. The world thinks he is a hero. He thinks he is – not a failure, but – not living up to his personal expectations of himself. Yet another case of someone with a deeply held conviction that he must be better than he has to be. By now I was no longer surprised to find more evidence that the Andes did not change Roberto. The crash gave him an opportunity to put his instincts to work in saving the lives of others. Maybe it even gave him some tools that he would use later as a pediatric cardiologist. But this innate compulsion to serve others was something imprinted in his DNA from birth, reinforced and inspired by a loving mother. He had no choice but to climb over the mountain to save his friends. He had no choice but to become a hero to countless parents of babies at risk. To Roberto, helping others is not even the altruistic action that others perceive; helping others is, for him at least, self-preservation.

Who Is Roberto Canessa?

After my visit to Montevideo, during which I spent sixteen hours with the man, his wife, his children, his spiritual advisors, his dogs, his friends, his fellow survivors, a 20-hour old baby, the grateful parents of his patients, and those who made pilgrimages to his door to learn from him, I formed some opinions about this remarkable human being.

Roberto is a wonderful person. He is a man of indefatigable energy. Like Henry James' description of Theodore Roosevelt, Roberto is a man of "pure act." This does not mean he only acts, but rather that "his thought and his action are fused together" in such a way that everything this deeply introspective and thoughtful man does seems spontaneous, impulsive, and incongruously wild. But in my opinion, the truth is quite to the contrary.

He also epitomizes perseverance and resilience. He never gives up. Roberto is an open, affectionate, and demonstrative man who cares deeply about others. He constantly worries that he is not doing enough to help others. He felt this way in the Andes. He feels this way with babies who have serious illnesses involving heart defects or disease. Roberto is a reluctant hero who never hesitates to autograph a napkin thrust in his path in the middle of the Montevideo airport. Roberto is a genuine person – what you see, hear, and feel is the real, inner man. He holds nothing back. Roberto is my brother, my best friend, and my inspiration. He is also Tennyson's Ulysses:

...I will drink
Life to the lees: all times I have enjoyed
Greatly, have suffered greatly, both with those
Who loved me and alone...
How dull it is to pause, to make an end,
To rest unburnished, not to shine in use.
...that which we are, we are;
One equal temper of heroic hearts,
Made weak by time and fate, but strong in will
To strive, to seek, to find, and not to yield.

Moving on to Seoul

The next journey, looked at from the perspective of the Eurocentric Mercator projection, is counterintuitive. Our illusion of knowledge is that our flight will head northeast from Montevideo, over the Atlantic Ocean, Africa, the Straits of Hormuz, India, and China before landing in Seoul. But in reality the Great Circle Route takes us due north from Montevideo, crossing Mexico City, Seattle, Juneau, and the Bering Strait before heading south over Kamchatka Peninsula, Vladivostok, circumventing the Democratic People's Republic of Korea before landing in Incheon International Airport, 12,175 miles from Uruguay. This is our second near-antipodal flight (the first was Bogota to Jakarta). If our plane can make it non-stop, then the same plane can fly from any point on earth to any other point on earth without refueling.

Ebullient Survivor

James Kim Joo-Jin

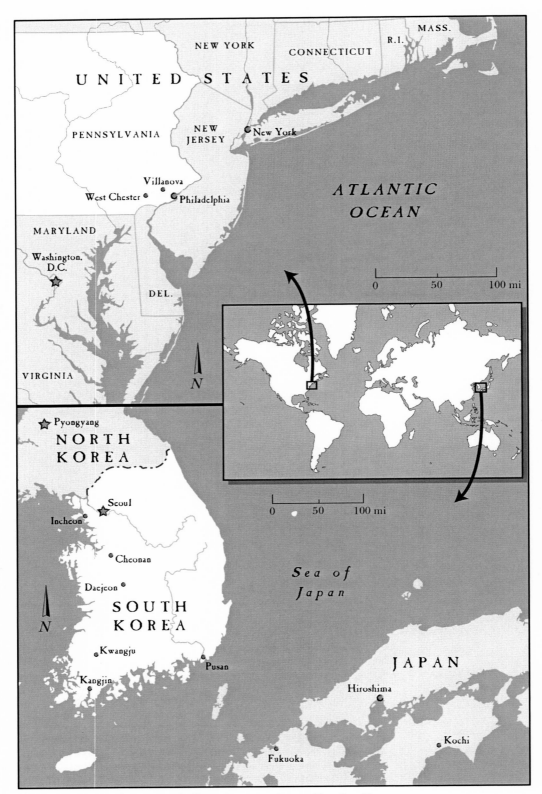

Ebullient Survivor: James Kim Joo-Jin

The Challenge of Translation

By the time I started writing this book, I thought I was reasonably conversant in intercultural communication. However, well into the task I had the good fortune to be reminded once again how little I knew about one of the central topics of my research, which was the comparison of cultures that were expressed in different languages. Among the seventeen individuals whose lives form the core of this book, only two speak English as their mother tongue. The remaining fifteen speak English fluently, but in all cases this is not their first language. In some cases English is their third language. Through the ease of communication with these wonderfully bi- and sometimes tri-lingual people, I gradually came to appreciate the complexity of understanding the roots of their personalities and value systems originally formed through the use of different languages, using a variety of alphabets and non-alphabetic characters. This question was brought to my attention early in my first interview with James Kim Joo-Jin, the second *Ebullient Survivor*.

I had prepared a list of questions I planned to ask him, and he had prepared answers for all of them. But as we started talking, we both ignored the agenda and the conversation took on its own character. The first topic that came up was language. Jim referred to an academic study he had read in which questions were asked of bi-lingual people. When a question was asked in one language, the respondent gave a certain answer. When the same question was asked in his other language of fluency, his response was different. The conclusion of the research was that language has an impact on how we view the world and how we explain our individual perceptions to others. Jim noted that we were speaking in English about many things that took place exclusively in the Korean language. He could not say for certain if his answers to my questions asked in English would be different from what they would be if they were asked in Korean. This is an interesting but ultimately unsolvable question for me, since I do not speak Korean (other than to say, "No more soju, thank you.")

After our conversation, I decided to investigate this conundrum, which was somewhat destabilizing to my smug assumption about my intercultural abilities. I learned that this is a hotly debated topic among linguists. This discovery opened an entirely new field of interest to me, which involves research and thought on the interaction of language and culture. Does the language spoken by a people influence their culture? Or does the culture influence their language? These questions suddenly bore relevance to everything in my book. This in turn led me to further reading about the work and conclusions of the anthropologist Franz Boas (whom we have already met in the Introduction to this book), his student Edward Sapir, and one of Sapir's students Benjamin Lee Whorf. Next, I picked up a book by a Columbia University professor named John McWhorter.

The Sapir-Whorf Hypothesis of Linguistic Relatively holds that the way people speak (their languages) affects how they think (their cultures) and ultimately has an impact on their world view. The consequence, according to this hypothesis, is that language ultimately affects behavior, making intercultural understanding (including translation) complicated and subject to misunderstandings.

Professor McWhorter's analysis questions the Sapir-Whorf Hypothesis. According to McWhorter, language does not influence culture and culture does not influence language, except in very minor ways. Language (all languages) is created randomly and incrementally. I found McWhorter to be convincing. His conclusion also supported my conclusion that since we are all humans and derive from roughly the same gene pool, our fundamental cognitive processes and moral dispositions must be, on average, universal. I ended up being reconciled to (even grateful for) the belief ("fact" would be pushing the envelope a bit) that language did not determine culture, since my book's hypothesis ultimately would have been challenged if this had been true. The triumph of McWhorter over Whorf helped to validate the Sheehan Hypothesis. I hasten to note that my analysis of this issue is superficial, based on limited reading. Further research would certainly reveal more complexity and ambiguity. In any case, it is an intriguing question to consider when conducting an inquiry into intercultural communication.

Seventy-Two Generations of Ancestry

Jim's father, Kim Hyang-soo, wrote an autobiography. In this tome, he states with conviction, "My ancestry goes back seventy-two generations of the Kim clan of the Kimhae region." I wondered if this was documented, or mythological? Jim explained that the seventy-two generations are not perfectly documented, but neither are they entirely mythological. There are many Kim families in Korea, and each one has a separate history. In the case of his branch of the Kim family, he believes that his distant ancestor was a king, who married a woman from India. They have some evidence of the early years from tombs of their ancestors in Pusan. It is part of their family tradition, regardless of how technically accurate it is.

I found several clues to Jim's personality and value system lurking in this recounting of his family history. Standards, resilience, forgiveness, tradition, adventure, and above all else personal responsibility as a consequence of free will are all integral to Jim's worldview and self-image. Each one of these words will re-appear in the subsequent pages of this chapter and will be reminiscent of the characteristics of all the other individuals with whom we have been engaged across superficially incommensurable global cultures.

A Child of Conflict

The first seventeen years of Jim Kim's life were subject to violence and were repeatedly disrupted, for three different reasons. The first was that he was born (January 8, 1936) during the Japanese annexation of Korea, a brutal colonization that lasted from August 22, 1910, until September 2, 1945. The second was that the end to this period of annexation was brought about only through the even greater brutalities of the Second World War, during which hundreds of thousands of Korean men were conscripted into the Japanese army and labor force, and countless Korean women were forced into sexual servitude as "comfort women." And third, no sooner had liberation come to Korea after forty years under the yoke of colonization and world war than the Korean civil war started, bringing with it by far the cruelest depredations and most gruesome hardships for Jim and his family. Survival required equal measures of resilience and positivity.

The Korean Civil War started on June 25, 1950, and was a terrible time for all Koreans. The Kim family evacuated from Seoul on the night of December 24, 1950, when the Chinese and North Korean armies invaded the city. Jim's father stayed behind to try to protect his business. Jim was still fifteen days shy of his fifteenth birthday, but he was the oldest male among the fifteen family members who set out by foot for Pusan, 243 miles to the southeast. The roads had been commandeered by the military, including UN troops, who were retreating as the Chinese and North Korean troops took over Seoul. There were trucks, tanks, and soldiers on the roads, and no room for civilians. As a result, the civilian refugees, including the Kim family, walked along the railroad tracks.

Late December in Korea is bitterly cold, and they had little food or protection from the weather. As the family leader, Jim brought the smaller children and the women together, but the night was so dark, and the conditions were so bad, that they lost contact with each other. Jim remembers that he eventually reached Cheonan (a city located about 52 miles south of Seoul) with his mother, who was carrying a new-born baby, and one additional family member. The other eleven family members were missing. Jim left his mother and infant brother in the Cheonan train station and walked back up the train tracks to find the others. By a miracle, he met his father, who had followed the fifteen family members. Farther up the tracks, Jim found the other eleven family members, holding hands to stay together, and shivering in the cold. All fifteen Kim family members survived that Christmas Eve and Christmas morning. Jim remembers all this very clearly, although he said that he has forgotten much about the war. I detected no anger or sadness, just recollection and inner peacefulness. Jim has gone beyond forgiveness and has accepted the events of his youth with equanimity. I felt great admiration and respect for him as we spoke about the events that took place during the winter of 1950-1951 in Korea.

Jim acknowledged that the relief agencies were "pretty good." They provided the refugees with rice. It was not much, but it kept them alive. They each received a ball of frozen rice which, "If you put it in your pocket, it would thaw out and you could eat it. You did not think about bacteria or dirt." They were also scavengers, and they appropriated anything they could find that was useful. Reunited, the members of the Kim family walked across frozen rice paddies with the goal of reaching Pusan. At one point, Jim's father, a bicycle manufacturer, made a cart from scavenged materials so that the small children could ride.

Jim said that they walked for thirty days, but he qualified his memory by noting that it is difficult to be certain because one day tended to merge into the next. They never made it to Pusan, but the family did reach Kwangju, which was not far from his father's birthplace, Kangjin. Eventually the family reached Kim Hyang-Soo's hometown, and stayed there for the rest of the war. Jim's father established a business importing bicycle tires and gears from Japan. This was unimaginably difficult under the conditions and circumstances. Jim helped by selling rice. In 1950, Jim was 14 years old and a freshman at Kyunggi Middle School in Seoul. From the start of the war until 1953, his education was, at best, intermittent. Jim laughed when he said that he did not learn much from books during the war. Survival, not surprisingly, was more pressing than studying.

The First Inflection Point

I told Jim that I was interested in those few moments, sometimes planned but more often unexpected, in a person's life when everything changes. He said that in his case there were two such moments. These two choices set his path in life, and this path has not changed. It was in this conversation that I learned something about Jim which is fundamental to his personality. At every moment in our conversations when he described a hardship, setback, decision, turning point, or catastrophe, he firmly and unequivocally stated that he took responsibility for what happened, what decisions he made, and what consequences ensued. Sounding like a combination of Ralph Waldo Emerson and Jean Paul Sartre, Jim is a champion of free will. He never blamed fate, others, or random chance. Nor does he ever evince regret, bitterness, or anger.

According to Jim, the first inflection point in his life was when he left Korea with the intention of enrolling in an American educational institution for college. Jim graduated from high school in 1955. In August of that year, he traveled to Hawaii, and then to Los Angeles, where he first felt the sting of racial discrimination, probably based on the mistaken assumption that he was Japanese. Jim spent the summer of 1955 in Philadelphia. He decided to accept an offer of admission to the Wharton School of the University of Pennsylvania because he was interested in economics. Jim wanted to help Korea, and it seemed to him that economics was an important discipline for Korea in its efforts to rebuild the country.

The Second Inflection Point

Jim's aspiration to be an economist was contrary to his father's wishes; but after graduation from Wharton in the spring of 1959, he secured a teaching job at Villanova University. He eventually decided to leave the academic profession because he concluded that he was not sufficiently brilliant to be a Nobel Prize-caliber professor. If he had been, he reflected, he probably would have stayed in the field. He really enjoyed teaching. Teaching was very important, he thought, in forming his character. But opportunity arrived in the form of his father's invitation to join him in starting a business in the semiconductor industry. His father's idea was to avoid the high cost of building a "fab" for the manufacture of wafers, and to focus on packaging and testing services.

Jim and his brother were skeptical because the family knew nothing about semiconductors. His father was a man with a mission, however, noting that knowledgeable people were then predicting that semiconductors would become as important to modern economies as were rice or oil. From the perspective of nearly a half-century later, he was correct. Kim Hyang-Soo named his business "Anam."

Around this time, Jim's ambivalence about his academic career was clarifying. He had been denied tenure at Villanova and had disputes with the dean over various matters. The next year (1970) brought bad news for his father's new enterprise, which was floundering. These were dark days for Anam. As Kim Hyang-soon wrote so poignantly in his autobiography,

> Forever confident in my powers of perseverance... I felt like a flame ready to flicker off because there's no oil left in the lamp... I turned to my son Joo-Jin for help... Joo-Jin said, "Father... You always said that the righteous path was the hardest to follow, that there was always a way no matter how bad things got..." My son gave me hope and encouragement with these words...

The confluence of his father's desperation, combined with his disenchantment with the academic profession, caused him to decide to resign from Villanova in May 1970 to help his father.

The Birth of Amkor

The biggest challenge for Anam was a lack of customers, so Jim set about to find a market in the United States for the packaging and testing services that his father had developed. In the summer of 1970, Jim established Amkor Electronics in the garage of his home in Devon, Pennsylvania (in the suburbs of Philadelphia), and hired an expert to teach him about semiconductors. The plan was to use Amkor as the U.S.-based sales and marketing division of

Anam. Jim would get a contract from a wafer-manufacturer in the U.S., and then send it to Korea, where Anam would perform the services. At that time, packaging and testing was labor-intensive, and Jim later established a joint venture in the Philippines, where labor costs were lower. The business gained traction and started to grow.

Several important developments occurred in the late 1970s. In 1977, Jim founded Electronics Boutique with a single store in the King of Prussia Mall, also in the suburbs of Philadelphia. The new company originally sold calculators and digital watches, both of which were novelty items at the time. It turned out to be a good business. By the early 1980s, Electronics Boutique had grown significantly and had stores in 25 shopping malls, with annual revenues of US$13 million.

Around this time, the semiconductor business started to automate, especially in the testing and packaging aspects, which had a direct impact on Amkor. By 1990, Amkor had grown to US$100 million in annual sales. The company needed long-term financing to grow, but Korean banks were allergic to any maturity longer than 90 days. The only way that Jim was able to get bank financing was to guarantee the loans personally. Amkor's guarantee was insufficient, although it was a going concern with excellent growth prospects. Jim's personal guarantees of Amkor's debt are a continuing theme in the history of the company, and although Jim does not show the slightest resentment or exasperation at this reality, he does keep coming back to it as a unique feature in the growth of his company.

Amkor really took off in the early and mid-1990s, with an annual compound growth rate of nearly 40%, although Jim noted it was still only the sales and marketing division of Anam and depended exclusively on Anam for business. It had no other customers. His father officially retired from Anam in January 1992 and handed over the helm to Jim. I first met Jim two weeks after he became Chairman of Anam.

Financial Crises and Recoveries

The 1997 Asian Financial Crisis hit Korea very hard, and Anam was a victim, through no fault of its own. The country was bankrupt, the banks were bankrupt, and all loans were immediately called in, resulting in all the companies being bankrupt. Even the Korean "whales" Samsung, Daewoo, Hyundai, and LG were at risk of insolvency. Anam, a "shrimp" in comparison, was in a perilous condition.

Jim had already (in 1996) begun to explore alternatives to the slow strangulation method of financing Amkor. On May 1, 1998, Amkor Electronics successfully "went IPO" at US$11 per share, selling US$650 million in new shares and convertible bonds. Amkor Electronics ended the day as Amkor Technologies, a listed company on the NASDAQ. Anam was still an independent company and still Amkor's only customer. In July of the same year (1998),

Electronics Boutique had its IPO as well.

Jim's next challenge came in the form of the "dot-com bubble," which burst in early 2000. In April of 2001, the *Philadelphia Inquirer* published an article on Jim that reflected the ambivalence of the era:

> *Jim Kim has lost $3 billion in the stock market during the last year, but he is still one of the wealthiest men in the Philadelphia Region. Amkor has 21,000 employees and 15 factories, mostly in Asia, producing computer-chip packages for cell phones, personal computers, digital cameras and air bags.*

I spoke to Louis Siani, Jim's tax accountant for half a century, about the kind of person he was in 1968 as compared to the kind of person he was when he became a billionaire. "Jim is consistent in his behavior and values," Louis stated. "He didn't change after his businesses were successful. He still has a small home. He still turns out the lights when he leaves a room. He won't buy a new car, so his daughter has to buy one for him."

Amkor and Anam weathered the Asian Financial Crisis and the dot-com bubble and, at the time of my interviews with Jim, enjoyed annual sales of $4 billion and employed over 30,000 staff.

Jim has photographs of his mother and father in his office at home. He often sits in his office and has "conversations" with his parents. He usually thanks them. "You left a lot of debt and problems," he says to his father's photo, "but I thank you because you gave me an opportunity to solve a variety of crises. Without the first crisis, Amkor would not have been created. Each subsequent crisis allowed me to take the business to a higher level. All these problems were opportunities for growth, renewal, and change."

I had originally struggled to understand Jim's feelings of gratitude and privilege, but I now comprehend that at a much deeper level, it all makes sense. Jim's feelings of being privileged and not downtrodden during the war, and his feeling of gratitude to his father for creating so many problems, are not anomalies at all; they are merely expressions of the inner peace and strength of this remarkable man. He truly feels this way; there is no dissimulation in Jim Kim. What you see and hear through his glass front is the real and only person. His effervescence, kind heart, courage, generosity, and ability to forgive come easily to him because they are intrinsic.

Spiritual Influences

Buddhism, Confucianism, and Christianity have all had roles to play in the development of Jim's spirituality, and the result is that Jim is a spiritual syncretist who has invented his own humanistic way of expressing his innermost self. He had some thoughts on the contrasting philosophies of Buddhism and Confucianism. "The Buddhist looks at understanding as a glass of water," reflected Jim. "If it is full, you cannot add anything. If you want to learn more, you need to empty the glass. This is the role of meditation, to empty your mind so that you can attain higher levels of understanding without the clutter of life's accumulated pettiness. Of course, Buddhists cannot run the country with this kind of philosophy. This is why Confucianism caught on, with its attention to service and meticulous attention to the requirements of social order. But it is the Buddhist in me that feels that I can only understand and appreciate brightness because I have experienced darkness."

Jim recounted the story of his relationship with a Buddhist monk, formerly from Korea but who now resides in France. In the early 1990s, this monk had told Jim that his life was set and what he did would influence many lives through his actions. He told Jim that he was unique and that he would have an impact on others. At the time, Jim found this prediction to be interesting but far-fetched. Today he wonders how the monk knew so well what would happen to him.

Jim had a problem with an employee of Anam in Korea who embezzled large sums of money from the company. Jim was conflicted about how to handle the matter, and he consulted the same monk. The monk advised him to forget about the matter and to move on, urging him to avoid reacting to this insult. He advised Jim that he would only hurt himself if he confronted the criminal. The monk counseled Jim that although in the short-term he might seem to lose by taking this position, in the long-term, he would win. Jim took this advice and avoided the issue, although the lawyers and prosecutors in Korea pursued the matter. This monk was a wise man who understood how to encourage Jim to choose the path of detachment, itself one of the central pillars of Buddhism. Forgiveness, regardless of the form it takes, benefits the one who forgives. The one forgiven still suffers, but it is because of his own actions.

The monk had warned Jim that if he got involved in business in Korea, it would hurt him. Jim has a soft heart, and the monk knew this. Korean business is rough-and-tumble, and people with soft hearts are disadvantaged in this system. Jim explained that he believes in both balance and in humility. He is willing to give up things in order to maintain balance. Jim feels that it is unwise to aspire to have everything because if we have too much, we break the balance in life and risk losing humility. When things are going too well, this is the time to be most careful. "Humility is of the utmost importance to me," said Jim.

I think also that Jim is an example of a true Confucian leader. Confucius taught that the most effective leadership was by living a righteous life of duty, humility, and concern for others, and not by conflict, threat, and punishment.

The Philanthropy of Jim Kim

When the $11 IPO price of Amkor quickly went to $60 and he became a paper billionaire, Jim gave a lot of thought to his responsibilities to society. He also realized that he needed to teach his children about the responsibilities of the wealthy to society. During this period in which he was a paper billionaire, he also made money in the stock market. He acknowledged that he was lucky to have sold his investments at a high point, allowing him to establish the James and Agnes Kim Foundation, which today has $40-50 million in assets, although he does not keep track.

"Part of me is a Marxist. After all, I was an economics professor," he laughed. But he clearly felt a need to strike a balance between the man with new-found wealth and the fourteen-year-old boy who left Seoul on foot as a refugee in the winter of 1950. The Buddhist monk understood this man, and by this point I was starting to understand him as well. The experiences of the Korean War (much more so than the Japanese annexation of Korea) still motivate and animate his gentle heart in ways that are virtually invisible to most of the recipients of his philanthropy. He feels gratitude, and therefore humility, for the little he was given during those years, and which somehow combined to help him not only survive but also to succeed far beyond the wildest dreams of his mother and father.

Jim decided that since he lived in Philadelphia, he needed to support local charities. He has also quietly supported the Gesu School in Philadelphia, a charter school that was formerly a Roman Catholic school. It is an inner-city school, and most of its students are African-American. A large proportion of the kids come from single-parent homes. This is a very successful school, and Jim feels his philanthropy is making a real difference in the lives of these children. He neither asks for nor wants any publicity. His charity is truly from the heart.

Jim and his wife Agnes feel a need to help Korean immigrants and refugees in the Philadelphia region. His preference has been to give money to a priest who works with immigrants and let him decide how to allocate the funds. Jim noted that this priest had given one of his kidneys to one of his parishioners. "I respect this man and trust him, so I gave him a large sum of money to help people. But I asked him to treat the gift anonymously. I told him he did not need to report to me on how he spent the money." This is philanthropy in the sense described by Peter Singer as the most moral and ethical.

He said ruefully that it is much more complicated than he thought to give away money responsibly. Jim asked rhetorically, "How do I respond to unlimited need?" He wonders if he should put all his money in the James and Agnes Kim Foundation. He ponders if his daughter is correct that he should give it all away during his lifetime? Or should he endow the foundation in perpetuity? He also worries about his children and grandchildren. They have had so much and suffered so little. How can they be taught humility, gratitude, and a sense of responsibility to the societies in which they live? As the monk advised him almost three decades ago, his decisions will have an impact on many others, and he feels a duty to make the right decisions.

Who Is James Kim Joo-Jin?

Jim concluded by expressing what to me was an easy concept to understand intellectually, but difficult to understand emotionally. He told me that he was privileged, in a relative sense, during the Japanese annexation, World War II, and the Korean War, and consequently felt humbled by all he had, then and now. As a child of peace, who never was threatened (except in an abstract sense by nuclear weapons), I am hard-pressed to see the privilege in the misery, deprivation, hardship, and danger that Jim endured. But this is, of course, part of what makes him a special person, and admirable.

Louis Siani, whose thoughts have appeared before in this chapter, had a comment on Jim, and it bore a striking resemblance to the way in which the others in my book have described their spirituality. "Jim has a good understanding of himself, what is going on around him, and his relationship to the external environment," Louis told me. Louis did not define it as spirituality, but the thoughts expressed are identical. Jim Kim is a deeply spiritual man, and despite a lack of interest in organized religion, he carries in his heart the beliefs, and more importantly the commitment to taking action, inherent in many of the world's spiritual traditions.

Jim Kim exhibits all of the moral dispositions and personal characteristics of the other sixteen individuals in my book so well that he is not difficult for me to understand. Still, it was not always so. I had known Jim for more than twenty years without really knowing much about him. Learning so much about him in our discussions allowed me to put my new knowledge together to create a picture of this remarkable man for whom I have the deepest respect and the warmest affection.

Moving on to Jiangyin

We will now move southwest from Seoul, traveling to the county-level city of Jiangyin on the southern bank of the Yangtze River, administered by the city of Wuxi, which is in Jiangsu Province in the People's Republic of China. Technically, it would be possible to make this trip by car, but this would be much farther and would involve what is currently (but probably not permanently) impossible, namely driving through the Democratic People's Republic of Korea. By air, this will be – at 594 miles – the shortest journey of the book. There is only one hour of time difference between Seoul and Jiangyin, and it exists because of a political decision, not because of distance. We can be thankful that there will be no jet lag. The climate, terrain, flora, and fauna will be similar; the cuisine, language, and culture will be, as has been the case in every one of the preceding journeys, quite different. Propinquity has resulted in certain commonalities, including Confucianism and the use of Chinese characters, but do not be lulled into a false sense of familiarity. These two countries are proudly and resolutely different, but only at a superficial level, as we have learned 16 times already.

Ebullient Survivor

Michael Yu Minhong

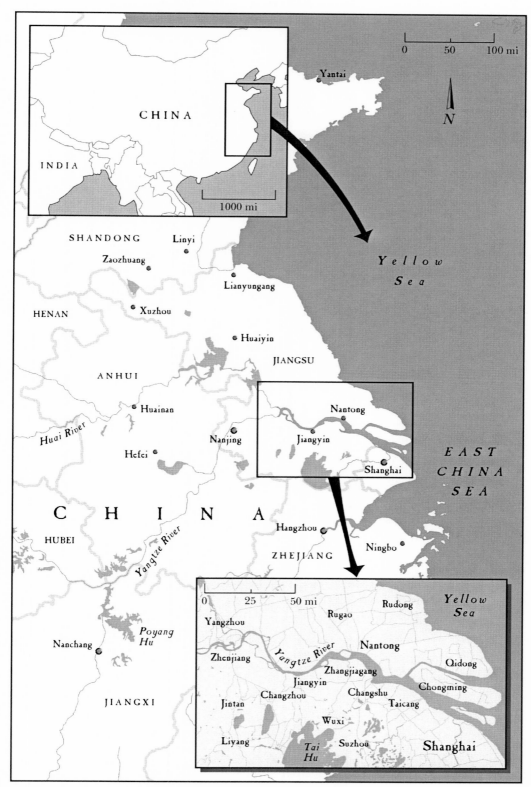

Ebullient Survivor: Michael Yu Minhong

The Great Leap Forward

Yang Jisheng, a journalist and member of the Chinese Communist Party, wrote a book that drew on previously unpublished data to document the human consequences of Mao Tse Tung's Great Leap Forward, which started in 1958. His tabulated information, arranged by province, lists two kinds of deaths. The first is "unnatural deaths," namely the number of deaths that exceeded statistical probabilities, and second, "shortfall in births," namely the number of children who were not born because of parental choice or infertility, again derived from statistical probabilities. He calculated the total number of unnatural deaths from 1958 to 1962 was 20.98 million. The total number of children improbably not born during the same period was calculated at 32.2 million. Yang concludes, therefore, that the national population loss during the great famine, which included deaths from and related to starvation, beatings, executions, and suicide, totaled 53.18 million. "I was born just after the Great Leap Forward," Yu Minhong stated matter-of-factly.

The Early Years

Yu Minhong was born on October 15, 1962, in Jiangyin, which at that time was a small, isolated farming village located on the southern side of a bend in the Yangtze River, 99 miles northwest of Shanghai. I noted that Jiangyin is now a medium-sized Chinese city with over a million inhabitants. Michael (his Western name) laughed, "In 1962, Jiangyin was a very small village. There were no roads connecting it to other villages. Just cart paths. We lived five kilometers from the nearest town. For us, an adventure would consist of a walk along a cart path to the town, followed by gawking in the 'big city' for a few hours before we returned home. Jiangyin has only grown in the last twenty years. Before that, for centuries it was a part of the countryside."

"My family was a countryside family and had always been so." Michael's description of his early years reminded me of Chanthol Sun's description of his early years, with the only (but significant) difference that China's farms were collectivized in 1962 whereas Cambodia's were privately-owned. In any case, each was born into an existence that was tied to the land and held little promise for change for each succeeding generation. The future for the youth of Jiangyin was even more circumscribed than that of the youth of Kohthom in Cambodia because in China all citizens were restricted by the *hukou* system of household registration, which regulated where a person was permitted to live. Nobody was permitted to leave Jiangyin without government authorization, which was never given. As a means of social control, it worked well; as an impediment to upward mobility, it was equally efficient.

When Michael was four, man-made disaster struck again, this time in the form of the Chinese Cultural Revolution, another political firestorm precipitated by Chairman Mao. For ten years, from 1966 to 1976, the country was seized with the demand for violent class struggle, to purge the members of society who were supposedly trying to reintroduce capitalism into China. The singular focus was on Mao's cult of personality and the need to eliminate all who opposed him.

To the eyes of Michael, as a child of four when the Cultural Revolution began, it was a frightening and confusing time. "My first memory is of my mother being arrested and put in jail because she was denounced by my cousin as anti-revolutionary and accused of being a spy for the Kuomintang. I went to jail with her because there was nobody else to take care of me. But my cousin's accusation had nothing to do with politics, and everything to do with jealousy and envy. In my limited experience, the Cultural Revolution was just a means for evil people to commit vile acts against innocent people. My mother and I were in jail for two months, until we were released when other villagers found her not guilty of the accusations of my cousin. My cousin and I are still in communication to this day and I bear no grudge. I am friendly to him and help him financially."

"Millions were jailed, tortured, and killed. Children even denounced their parents. Can you believe it? I never had any good feeling about the Cultural Revolution." Michael is disarmingly frank about absolutely everything, not so different from Roberto Canessa. It is unsettling at first, but after friendship ripens, it is a cherished characteristic.

Education

"I went to school at the age of six (1968) because Chairman Mao wanted to reduce peasant illiteracy. My mother encouraged me to learn, to become a teacher, and maybe even to leave the countryside. My parents were illiterate and bewildered by the Cultural Revolution, but they knew enough to want a better life for me and my sister. My mother had almost no money, but with what little she had, she would buy books for me before she would buy toys for me. She would even buy me books before she bought me food."

"I became a leader in school, not so much for my academic achievements, but because my parents were nice to other people to the extent that their limited means allowed. They were generous and good to others despite the hardship of their lives. I inherited this feeling of friendliness and responsibility to other people."

"I joined the Communist Youth League in 1974 at the age of 12 while the Cultural Revolution was still in progress. This was the first stage in joining the Chinese Communist Party. I was a good middle school student and well-behaved, so I became a leader in the Communist Youth League."

Michael laughs easily and often. He always has a smile on his face, even when describing the most painful memories and the most horrible injustices. He has inner peacefulness and bears no malice. His lack of anger reminds me of many of the other heroes and heroines of this book, who suffered horrible indignities and bear no scars. He is resilient and he forgives, although when I write this I realize that I am expressing my Western bias. To the Buddhist (and all Chinese are Buddhists, whether they self-identify or not), the goal is not to react to human emotions, but to address every situation from the perspective of compassion and find a way to reduce the suffering of all concerned.

The next roadblock for Michael occurred at the time he reached high school age. This was 1976, and the government had decreed that only one child per family was permitted to attend high school. His older sister had already attended high school, so he was disqualified. There were consequences to this disqualification beyond ending his education with middle school, one of which was that he was not permitted to join the Chinese Communist Party because only high school students could join.

Mao died in September 1976, and a month later, the so-called "Gang of 4" was crushed by Hua Guo Feng, who instituted modest reforms. By 1978, Deng Xiao Ping had forced Hua into early retirement and initiated the more ambitious reforms that led China out of Maoism and into the modern era. In 1979, Deng Xiao Ping reopened the universities and instituted a new policy whereby students admitted to universities outside their *hukou* would be permitted to change their residency in order to attend the university to which they had been admitted. This single act unleashed a tidal wave of merit-based advancement in China.

In March of 1977, Michael was admitted to high school when his mother requested an exception so that he might fill the seat that had been left empty when another student had dropped out. Michael eagerly joined the high school but suffered from poor grades. Deng Xiao Ping decreed that university entrance would be allocated by nationwide testing. Michael knew that he could not succeed but took the examination in 1978 regardless. His pessimistic certainty was validated by his score (33%), and he was not admitted to any university.

Returning once again to the farm, Michael was resolute. He committed himself to the "relentless pursuit of success," which ironically was to become the title of a book he wrote and published in 2007, soon after the initial public offering of his company instantly made him a U.S. dollar millionaire many times over.

"I was not very good in math, so I took the English-language entrance examination, which did not have a quantitative section. I did not speak English, but the examination was entirely written, so I focused on memorizing words and grammar rules." Students were permitted to re-take the university entrance again as many times as they wished, but only once a year. Huddled under the hissing light of a kerosene lamp every night for the next year, Michael persevered. He re-took the examination again in 1979, and failed again, although with an improvement to 55%.

The First Inflection Point

"I asked myself if I was destined to be a farmer," he mused. But then something unexpected happened that changed his life forever. The Education Bureau for the county in which Jiangyin is located started a school for the children who had failed the university examination. The thinking was that the students in this county were underprivileged by reason of both poverty and substandard schooling, and that if they might find some way to help a percentage of them to succeed, it would bring prestige and prominence to the county.

"This was my turning point. I entered this school, which was a boarding school. I lived in a room with thirty other kids, but the conditions were quite O.K. compared to how I lived on the farm. I became a leader of the group. I was greatly inspired by being chosen as a leader. I studied hard and went from being the worst in the class to being the best in the class in five months. Having learned from my parents about generosity, I helped others whenever I could. It was easy for me to make friends because I genuinely like other people and enjoy helping others. Being generous made me feel better and motivated me. I didn't lose by helping others. I gained."

After another year passed, Michael took the nationwide university entrance examination for the third time and scored 92.5%, placing him near the top and earning a seat in Peking University, the best university in the country.

"After I graduated from Peking University, I stayed on as a teaching assistant. Later I was promoted to a slightly higher grade, but still lower than a professor. I helped teach English to Peking University students. Along the way, starting in 1989, I applied to graduate schools in the United States, in political science or international relations. I was admitted to several programs, but I never received a scholarship. At the time, I still did not have any money, so I could not accept any of the offers of admission."

New Oriental Education & Technology Group

"By 1993, I gave up on going to graduate school, quit my job, and started my own business, which I called New Oriental Education & Technology Group, with the goal of training young people to succeed in the TOEFL, SAT, and GRE tests. It was just me to start, and I did not have many students, but I never gave up because I felt sure I would be successful. The growth of New Oriental was due to five factors. First, in 1993, the interest of Chinese students in going to the United States was expanding rapidly. Second, many Chinese families were accumulating enough wealth to make it possible for them to pay the tuition. Third, my teaching style attracted students because I combined enthusiasm and humor to make the classes interesting. Fourth, I developed a new methodology for teaching students how to succeed in the TOEFL, SAT, GRE, and other standardized tests. Fifth, I was good at helping students to succeed, so they told their friends about me."

"The training of teachers was very important, because I knew that New Oriental would succeed only if the students who took the classes were successful. This was not theoretical training. It was completely practical. So, as the number of students grew beyond what I could handle by myself, I personally recruited and trained teachers to teach with the same style. I had and still have three criteria for teachers at New Oriental. First, they must have a good knowledge of English and a comprehensive knowledge about the tests they were teaching. Second, they must be motivational as teachers. These tests are inherently boring, so you need a motivational teacher to hold their attention. And third, the teachers must have a good sense of humor and a consistently positive attitude. Without enthusiasm, the teachers would not be successful."

"By 2000, I realized that New Oriental needed to grow outside Beijing, so I established a branch in Shanghai. One thing led to another, and today New Oriental operates in 65 cities in China, through 700 learning centers. I employ 20,000 teachers and an additional 15,000 office staff, so I am a pretty big employer. I am now the most famous teacher in China," he concluded with a self-deprecating laugh.

On September 7, 2006, New Oriental Education & Technology Group was listed on the New York Stock Exchange. Today Michael is a U.S. dollar billionaire and New Oriental has trained more than ten million students, with two million more currently enrolled in classes nation-wide. Michael is widely known throughout China as the inspiration to students and the teacher who helps young men and women to realize their dreams. His company tagline is "Yes, You Can!" and he means it.

Zhou Chenggang

Zhou Chenggang is a Board Member and Senior Vice President of New Oriental Education & Technology Group. Concurrently, he serves as President of Vision Overseas Consulting Co., Ltd., which provides counseling to students and families about overseas education. Chenggang met Michael in 1979 in the "losers" school for students who had failed the university entrance examination. He reported that Michael, through the force of his personality, was chosen to be the "monitor," which was similar to the "head prefect" at an English boarding school. They both succeeded in this school and formed a close friendship.

"Michael is the same person today that he was in 1979," said Chenggang. "He has not changed at all. He was charismatic back then, just as he is today. He lost his magic for a while at Peking University. I think he suffered a lot during his university days. He missed a year because of illness. But even more importantly, he lost his way because everybody was so much more sophisticated and looked down on him as a kid from the countryside. But his humble origins kept him hungry."

The Dreams of Yu Minhong

"You started life as the poorest person in my book," I said to Michael on a cold and windy December evening in Philadelphia, "and now you are the richest. But your personality seems to me to be unchanged. If I am right and you have not changed, then I suspect that you will not use all your money to buy expensive things and to show off how much money you have. What will you do with all this money?" His reprimand of my assertion was gentle but firm.

"First of all," he replied with his trademark grin, "I was never poor, even when I had no money. When I was a child, I didn't have 'nothing.' I had wonderful parents who loved me and taught me that we need to help one another. I learned from my parents to be kind and generous. I had unspoiled nature – blue skies, sunshine, hills, valleys, rivers, streams, birds, fish, and other wildlife. Most of this is gone now and everything is polluted. You don't need to have money to be rich. Richness in life isn't about making money. There are more important things in life than money."

"I never thought I would become financially successful," he laughed. "But now that I have lots of money, I am still trying to make more money because money can be useful in helping others. This is what I will do with my money – help others. I have no need for this money because all my material needs are satisfied. But there are thousands – millions – of people who need help."

"I will leave some money for my children, so that they can get started in life, but I do not want to burden and cripple them with too much money to start. I have other dreams to make use of my money," he continued. "First, I am currently helping students with scholarships to attend universities. When I was a student, the government paid for everything, including my food. But now the universities charge tuition, and this is a challenge to the students from the countryside. I want to help students who are in the same position as I was more than thirty years ago, namely children of farmers who do not participate in the money economy and therefore have no money at all. I donate several million RMB every year and that money supports the tuition for about 2,000 scholarships. The tuition at Chinese universities is much less than the equivalent at American universities, but the gap between costs and the income of farmers is even greater than the same gap between U.S. education costs and the income of average Americans in percentage terms."

"I also donate RMB 2 million every year to help employees of New Oriental who have medical emergencies or other kinds of problems that they cannot handle financially."

"Long-term, I want to establish a private university that would rival the best public universities in China and match international standards. Recently I decided to work with another person who shares my dream, Wang Xiao Wen. Ms. Wang donated RMB 500 million in 2005 to start a college called Geng Dan Institute of Beijing University of Technology. We are working now to establish a private, non-profit foundation, similar to the endowment at American universities, to receive money to support this college. Once the foundation is established, I will donate a lot of my money to this college. Others will also be able to donate to the foundation, and I will use my connections to the China Entrepreneur Club and other organizations for the purpose of requesting additional financial support from other wealthy individuals."

Wang Xiao Wen

"My mother attended Peking University and majored in architecture," Wang Xiao Wen began. "My father attended Beijing Normal and majored in history. They both joined the army to fight the Japanese in the 1940s. My father served Chairman Mao as his secretary for a time. Later, he was denounced as a 'rightist' and sent to the countryside for 22 years. I was born in 1954, and during the Cultural Revolution, I cared for my elder brother, who had a mental illness and committed suicide. My mother also had a mental illness and committed suicide at the age of 44. I was sent to the countryside at the age of 15 (1969) and stayed there for three years." Ms. Wang recounted this tale of horror without the slightest trace of bitterness. I thought of Chanthol, Durreen, Shiv, and Jim. So many people with many reasons to be angry, but with no anger in their hearts.

"In 1984, I decided to set up my own businesses and become an entrepreneur. Some of these businesses succeeded and some of them failed, but I made enough money that I could carry out my dream, which was to start a university. I believe that education, medical care, and libraries should all be free. These are human rights and should not be available only to the wealthy. I bought a bankrupt factory and some land in 2003, and in 2005, I established Geng Dan."

"I met Yu Minhong and we shared the same goals. I invited him to join the Board of Directors of Geng Dan, and he agreed last year. Now he has agreed to take over my job as Chairman of the Board. It is fate that we met at this time. Our goals are identical, and I trust him to carry out exactly what I had in mind. I am completely convinced that Yu Minhong doesn't want to accumulate money for its own sake. His real idea is to build the best private university in China, which is my goal too. We will only put money into Geng Dan; we will take no money out. This will be strictly a non-profit university, but private in the sense of not being run by the government. It is funny that this is a new concept in China; previously we had only state-owned universities, then we had for-profit schools like Yu Minhong's, and now we are starting an entirely new educational concept in China."

Yu Minhong's Future Plans

"New Oriental is 21 years old, and demand increases every year," noted Michael. "I cannot predict how long there will be a demand for this type of education, but I feel confident in predicting that for the next half-century at least, New Oriental will continue to have good business. Chinese kids like to study abroad, and their parents support this interest. There still is not enough trust in the Chinese university system. This is part of why I am involved with Geng Dan. I want to put myself out of business by helping to create a new generation of world-class private universities in China."

"I will continue to support Geng Dan University, but I don't think I will give all my money to this institution. I still want to build it into a first-tier university, but I have some other ideas of how to spend my money. I came up with the idea of creating an 'angel fund' so that I could invest in innovative ideas that young people had to start businesses that help others, and even more importantly, so that I could receive more direct feedback from the smartest and most creative minds in China. When I have an idea, I like to act quickly. On November 26th, I had an opening of The Angel Plus Fund. Many people attended the opening and it attracted a lot of attention in the media."

"The fund also attracted a lot of interest among investors, and it already has about RMB 200 million, 10 percent of which is from my personal funds. My friends invested the rest. Within the first 10 days of its launch, I had received over one hundred business plans, and about 10 are fundable. I will invest anywhere from RMB 1-3 million in each one. I am convinced that this fund will grow to be one of the largest angel funds in China and that it will be successful in identifying excellent new ideas for businesses that help people."

"I recently had another idea, which is to start a foundation that will award prizes like the MacArthur 'Genius Grants' to people who are working on ideas that will make other people's lives happier. The winners can be artists, philosophers, scientists, poets, or innovators in any discipline. I want to give them money so that they can continue their work without having any financial concerns for five-to-ten years. I want to liberate their minds so that they can concentrate on their good ideas."

"I hope to start with RMB 200 million, and then grow the fund to RMB 500 million or more. I will invite my friends to donate to this foundation as well. Then I can identify two-to-three people every year and give them independence and freedom from financial worry. They can do anything they want with the money, and they do not have to submit a plan. The whole idea is independence and freedom. This idea will be realized within the next two years."

Bao Fanyi

Yu Minhong and Bao Fanyi met at Peking University as freshmen. They were two of six students who shared a single room (today, according to Bao Fanyi, only four students share each room). According to Bao Fanyi, Yu Minhong was ridiculed by his fellow students (not Bao Fanyi) because he was from the countryside and lacked sophistication. His pants were worn and patched; he could not pay when classmates went to a restaurant for dinner; he was far behind the other students in terms of what they had read and in terms of what they knew about the world. Yu Minhong was hard working, but he lagged his classmates academically at first because of the poor quality of education that was available in his village. He also lost a year of school at Peking University because he contracted tuberculosis. Every year his mother raised a pig that she would sell in order to give Yu Minhong money for the expenses above and beyond tuition and living costs that were supported by the government.

"In the top universities in China, including Peking University of course, everybody is very smart and high achieving," Michael reflected. "One of the consequences of having all these smart kids packed together is that there is a lot of competition and criticism, especially if somebody makes a mistake. Everybody is posturing and trying to be the best, so attacking weakness is a favorite pastime. Bao Fanyi taught me that the truly confident people can mock themselves and take criticism without feeling bad. He also taught me that confident and generous people don't tolerate self-importance and pride. From Bao Fanyi I learned the value of humility and peacefulness, and that the one quality is a prerequisite for the other. I have learned to be unique and different, while not being better or worse than anybody. I am just myself."

Bao Fanyi is articulate, thoughtful, and soft-spoken. He smiles most of the time and laughs frequently, but it is a reflective chuckle rather than a belly-laugh. Bao Fanyi's mother was a high school teacher. Her father (Bao Fanyi's grandfather) was a painter who "had a mental illness and committed suicide during the Cultural Revolution."

Bao Fanyi confirmed that Peking University students were smart, elite, competitive, and highly critical of weakness of any kind. Bao Fanyi was well-prepared intellectually for the rigors of Peking University, but he suffered from shyness. Accordingly, he developed a diffident, self-mocking style to fend off the predators in the student body. This type of self-mockery defused the taunts of the predators. He advised Michael to adopt a similar form of self-mockery when he was criticized for being unprepared or unsophisticated. Yu Minhong learned this lesson well, and today he uses self-mockery with salutary effect as Chairman of New Oriental Education & Technology and the most famous teacher in China.

"I developed self-criticism and self-mockery to disarm people. It relaxes others when I make jokes about myself," Michael explained. "I guess that this is my natural personality, but I have consciously developed this style."

Ping Yi Jin Ren

One of the wellsprings of Chinese philosophy is a type of idiomatic expression called the "*chengyu*." There are thousands of *chengyu*. Dating from antiquity, they succinctly express wisdom, morality, and sometimes humor. *Chengyu* are generally four characters in length, and as often as not, completely unintelligible to the Western mind. My favorite in this category is "ma-ma, hou-hou," which translates literally as "horse-horse, tiger-tiger," but which means "so-so."

"My personal philosophy of life," Michael announced one night over dinner, "can be summarized by a Chinese chengyu, 平易近人 (pronounced ping yi jin ren). Ping means 'equal,' yi means 'easy,' jin means 'nearby' and ren means 'people.' As with all Chinese sayings, the words themselves are simple, but the meaning is deep. In this case, the meaning is that I think of all people as my equals. I am neither above anyone nor below anyone. This is not in the sense of being a Communist comrade, but more in the sense of respecting the worth of others and assuming they will respect me in return. Regarding 'easy,' this means that I am comfortable with other people. I like other people and get along with everybody. Regarding 'nearby,' and "people,' I like to be with other people. I guess this means I am a 'people person.'"

"In my company I follow some personal guidelines. First, respect everyone. Second, appreciate others. Third, build everybody into a team. Fourth, make sure everybody shares the same dream. Fifth, be very careful in choosing team members. Sixth, be open to criticism. I have a weekly session in which my subordinates are invited to make comments on my mistakes, weaknesses, and failings. Seventh, shift people to new jobs if they are not performing. Eighth, be prepared to fire people if they cannot perform. Ninth, stay friends with people even if you must fire them."

Who Is Yu Minhong?

As I conclude this chapter on Yu Minhong, I need to return to a scholar who has studied modes of human interaction (I do not say "leadership," since his research applies to interpersonal relations more generally than to leadership). Adam Grant, to whom I have previously referred, described Yu Minhong's personal style without ever having met him. Professor Grant, in his book *Give and Take*, took as his aim to "challenge traditional assumptions about the importance of assertiveness and projecting confidence." His research led him to the conclusion that gaining influence was possible through a "powerless communications style." He observed that this kind of person is:

> … *more inclined toward asking questions than giving answers, talking tentatively than boldly, admitting their weaknesses than displaying their strengths, and seeking advice than imposing their views on others.*

This description describes Yu Minhong in all his interactions with friends, family, employees, customers, the powerful, and the weak. He was once a miserable young man with no hope; today he is a U.S. dollar billionaire, and his face is known to 10s (maybe 100s) of millions of Chinese students. But he has not changed at all, and is still a compassionate man, full of humility, optimism, positivity, and enthusiasm. He wants to help as many people as he can by giving them the tools and the confidence to change their lives in the way he changed his life. And most of all, he wants everyone to have freedom and independence.

My journeys around the world in search of the common dispositions of the seventeen heroes and heroines have led me to a number of conclusions. One of the most valuable – to me at least – has been the redefinition of the word "leadership." I had for most of my life subscribed to the traditional sense of the word, but now I feel differently. Leadership to me can more accurately and broadly be defined as the 'enhancement of human flourishing.' Nobody exemplifies this redefinition more that Yu Minhong, a man, a friend, and a leader for whom I have the greatest respect and warm affection.

Moving on to Philadelphia

Let us now take the final journey of this book, from Beijing back to my home base in Philadelphia. This is another long journey of 6,867 miles that takes more than 13 hours, pushing the limits of even the largest airplane in anyone's fleet. Following a few days of rest and recuperation to allow for the stabilization of vital signs, we can begin to summarize the common dispositions and characteristics – the universal cell in the Venn Diagram – that have become more clear and salient with each passing mile and each passing day.

Part II
The Venn Diagram

I had finished my field research. I had identified and then interviewed 17 women and men whom I found to be uniquely interesting, admirable, and lovable; as well as 87 of their family members, friends, and business associates. I had accumulated several thousand pages of notes. I had read hundreds of relevant books, speeches, case studies, articles, and websites, and watched several movies. At this point, my inquiry into intercultural communication was ripening. I had concluded that my heroines and heroes most certainly did share common characteristics and that I would have no trouble drawing broader conclusions about intercultural communication from this correlation.

I identified 13 such common characteristics. These characteristics were all inherent qualities of mind and character. Some might be called moral dispositions or values. Others might be termed predilections which did not invoke moral judgments. Now my task was to name, summarize, give context to, and explain why I believe these characteristics can support, facilitate, and enable intercultural communication. My thinking had been provoked by Samuel Huntington and his article (and then book) on the "clash of civilizations." He concluded that the fundamental differences among civilizations – different value systems – cannot be reconciled. I think his analysis is ethnocentric, hypocritical, inflammatory, and pernicious. In short, I did not find his arguments persuasive. I have concluded that fundamental similarities in human dispositions make communication, and the resolution of differences, possible. My book, accordingly, is in part intended as a rebuttal to Huntington.

When I started my research, I made a personal commitment to avoid the overconfidence that has so often afflicted those who encounter and try to interpret different civilizations, and to make the effort to understand the point of view of strangers. An example of this type of hubris in action was described by Stephen Ambrose in his book on the Lewis and Clark Expedition from 1804 to 1806. When writing about the interaction of the leader of the expedition with a tribe of First Americans, Ambrose, although a great admirer of Meriwether Lewis, nonetheless concluded that he "... had no ability whatsoever to see the initial encounter from the Shoshone's point of view." My goal and commitment was to do my best to understand the unique point of view of each of these individuals. I knew if I wanted, as Nora Zeale Hurston believed, to "really see people, unvarnished and stripped of your own prejudices, you needed to love unselfishly."

To assist me, I decided to construct a Venn Diagram, which is a graphical method of illustrating the logical relationships among sets, by isolating those characteristics that are shared from those that are not. The following example of a Venn Diagram illustrates the intersection of three sets (Buddhism, Christianity, and Islam), segregates characteristics that are shared by two but not all three of the sets, and highlights the single characteristic which is shared by all three:

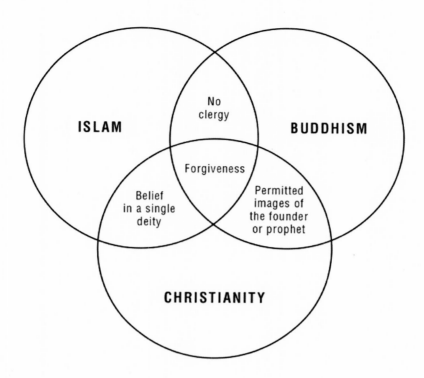

It would take a three dimensional and complex equation to expand the Venn Diagram to 17 sets represented by the men and women I have profiled in Part I. Although it is theoretically possible to draw a Venn Diagram of an unlimited number of sets, you will need to imagine it as a thought experiment. The number of partially overlapping cells and non-overlapping cells in a Venn Diagram with 17 sets is enormous: Muslims, vegetarians, speakers of Spanish, women, men, Cambodians, and so on. The differences were easy to identify. But in the end, I discovered that the center cell – that spot where all 17 sets coincided – contained at least 13 common dispositions and predilections shared by my heroines and heroes. Here the ones I have chosen to highlight:

Character. Each of the 17 individuals in my group has a glass front and a titanium back. They are all honest, open, and welcoming, with nothing to hide. And they all have the unbreakable courage of their convictions.

Standards. People who do more than they must and who are perfectionists when nobody knows. They are all committed to achieving a level "better than it has to be."

Resilience. Not all of them faced the same type of overwhelming odds, but all my heroes and heroines were subjected to trials and tribulations. They all bounced back, bloodied but unbowed, as stronger and more compassionate individuals.

Forgiveness. This characteristic has been a source of psychological nourishment and strength to all of the subjects of my book. If you want to be resilient, I learned, you must have the capacity to forgive.

Free Will. None of my heroes and heroines ever complained that their faults were in the stars, but each one has had at least one serendipitous turning point that changed everything. They may be agnostic about fate, but they are all willing to seize unexpected opportunities.

Money. They are not particularly motivated to accumulate financial assets, but they are unwilling to be poor. No Mohandas Gandhi in this group, but no Bernie Madoff, either. They have a unique and refreshing attitude about the role of financial success.

Tradition. All are respectful stewards of tradition, but no one is burdened by the past. This is a disposition that runs through the lives of all my heroes and heroines and is a key factor not only in their success but also in their sense of personal well-being and psychological stability.

Ambition. This may be difficult to accept, given the high rank and accomplishments of just about everybody in this book, but they are all surprisingly lacking in personal ambition. Nevertheless, this characteristic is central to an understanding of each of them.

Patriotism. They are all Citizens of the World. This one is easy to explain. There are no foreigners in this book. Everyone is a brother or a sister, although they have not met each other (yet).

Adventure. They all have the DRD4-7r gene and everyone has led an adventurous life. This is probably the strongest link among my heroines and heroes. This one was also easy to identify in everybody. How else would I have met them all?

Impact. Each one wants to leave the world a better place then they found it. This is the Mt. Everest Rule, which you will encounter soon. "So let us leave behind a country better than the one we were left with," as Amanda Gorman counselled.

H.O.P.E. This is a bundled thread, with humility leading quite naturally to optimism, positivity, and enthusiasm, with a natural immunity to cynicism.

Spirituality. Not many of these women and men ever enter a house of worship, nor do they generally seek the approval or validation of a religious hierarchy. And yet, they are all deeply spiritual.

Peter Singer captured an aspect of my process of discovery, revision, and refinement, when he wrote about the role of reason in helping humans to develop an ethical system. "Beginning to reason," Singer wrote, "is like stepping onto an escalator that leads upward and out of sight. Once we take the first step, the distance to be traveled is independent of our will and we cannot know in advance where we shall end." My friends, it seems, are all on the same escalator.

In learning about these individuals, the Venn Diagram helped me to sort out what characteristics made them so unusual, so personally outstanding, and so attractive to me. It was this collective set of dispositions and predilections that allowed me to formulate my hypothesis that there are universal human characteristics which are of greater importance than any number of superficial differences; and consequently that effective and productive intercultural communication is possible, regardless of the difficulties in translation.

Finding the characteristics that populated the center of the Venn Diagram did not give me a tool to predict success. But what it did give me was the confidence in my hypothesis that all the people I pulled from my card file share fundamentally important characteristics that permit and encourage fluent and mutually respectful intercultural communication. My findings led me to the conclusion that what I call superficial characteristics – language, form of government, cuisine, ethnicity, even history – might be the proximate and therefore mutable sources of behavior, while the dispositions at the center of the Venn Diagram might be the ultimate and therefore immutable causes of behavior. What we share is more powerful and meaningful than our differences.

Nature vs. Nurture

Before I enumerate these characteristics in the coming pages, I need to address the matter of "nature" and "nurture." As with many complex matters that have been debated for eons, I will not solve this question, which is still under review by scholars and scientists much more qualified than I. But since I am suggesting that there are universal dispositions, the question naturally arises as to their origin. Do we act a certain way because we are genetically predisposed to do so? Or do we make a cognitive decision to behave in accordance with what we believe are moral principles? While I willingly acknowledge the likelihood that genes play an important role in human behavior, I assert (with all the brave women and men profiled in Part I) that consciousness gives humans the power to overcome genetic programming should it be desirable and appropriate. I think that Edward O. Wilson, the American biologist and naturalist, got it right when he concluded that the ability to make choices and change the future constitutes the "meaning of human existence." My conclusion is that while it is interesting, the importance of resolving the question of nature vs. nurture is perhaps not quite irrelevant but certainly not crucial because we have will power and the freedom to decide. This conclusion is also supported by my reading of Jean-Paul Sartre. This conclusion will apply to all 13 dispositions that will be plotted on my gigantic Venn Diagram.

Character

To any officer or employee of the Government, please tell Mr. Lincoln Steffens anything whatever about the running of the government...and provided only that you tell the truth – no matter what that may be.

—U.S. President Theodore Roosevelt

Great nations don't ignore their most painful moments... They embrace them. Great nations don't walk away. We come to terms with the mistakes we made. And in remembering those moments, we begin to heal and grow stronger.

—U.S. President Joe Biden

Most of all, Lewis knew that Clark was competent to the task, that his word was his bond, that his back was steel. Clark knew the same about Lewis. Their trust in each other was complete...

—Stephen Ambrose
Undaunted Courage

You may have noticed that I have described many of the men and women you met in Part I by referring to their "glass fronts" and "titanium backs." What do I mean by these terms? How do they relate to the subjects of my book? I think it might help to start with some worthy individuals who display these characteristics. Three people – one a Malaysian Muslim woman, one an Indian Hindu man, and one an African-American Christian man – exemplify the glass front and the titanium back. Accordingly, I have chosen them to serve as good prototypes for the discussion of the first disposition. I will describe the first in more detail because she is less well-known; the other two are household names worldwide and need less introduction.

Zeti Akhtar Aziz

Tan Sri Dato' Dr. Zeti Akhtar Aziz is a gentle and soft-spoken Malaysian woman who commands respect and admiration because of her intellectual capabilities, knowledge, judgment, tenacity, calm demeanor, and grace under pressure. She was appointed Governor of Bank Negara Malaysia (BNM) in 2000, a post she held until 2016. Known as an expert on Islamic finance, she humbly and with humor acknowledges that when she was first publicly recognized for this wisdom, she knew nothing about the topic. She guessed that since she is Muslim and a central bank governor, everyone assumed that she would be an expert on Sukuk and other Sharia compliant financial instruments. Later, she conducted research and became knowledgeable. She also earned a global reputation for her expertise and success in policy-making regarding Malaysia's currency, money supply, and interest rates.

Governor Zeti believes in training, and in the value of gathering people together for the purpose of candid, mutually respectful discussion. She also is a booster of Malaysia and has done her part to publicize and enhance the reputation of her country, which for context has roughly the same population as either Peru or Saudi Arabia. In 2012, under Zeti's leadership Bank Negara Malaysia opened Sasana Kijang, a new "Centre for learning, knowledge management, development of thought leadership, and standard setting" in Kuala Lumpur.

During a visit to Kuala Lumpur, Zeti told me, with a twinkle in her eye, that the new build-ing was designed with "a glass front and a titanium back." She did not need to explain what this meant. Although she was ostensibly referring to construction materials – which allowed passers-by to view whatever was happening inside (the glass) and guaranteed struc-tural integrity (the titanium) – I knew that she was referring to moral dispositions that she hoped would be integral to the discussions that would take place in the new training center.

At the time Governor Zeti made this casual but deliberate remark to me, I was acquainted with all the people who would populate my book. I had not yet selected them, or even conceived of the book, but I had already begun thinking about the question of universal dispositions. Later, as I reviewed the characteristics of my special friends, I found them all to have glass fronts and titanium backs. I looked for this characteristic when I conducted the interviews for this book. By the time I reached the end of my first round of interviews, I concluded that this would indeed be one of the common dispositions. I was encouraged and motivated that I had identified the first of the common characteristics that would tie my disparate heroes and heroines together and give them powerful tools for intercultural communication.

Mohandas K. Gandhi

It would be difficult to write a chapter about glass fronts and titanium backs and not refer to Mohandas K. Gandhi. I do not intend to be guilty of such a lacuna, especially because his life is so rich in examples of the glass front and titanium back.

Gandhi set the bar so high that few have met his standard. In order to capture the meaning of his evolving philosophy, in 1906 he announced a competition through a newspaper in South Africa to come up with a word that captured its essence. The grandson of one of his uncles won the prize, and with slight modifications, "*Satyagraha*" became the rallying cry for Gandhi's movement.

Satyagraha derived from two Sanskrit words – "*Sat*," meaning "truth," and "*Agraha*," meaning "firmness." Not surprisingly, the texture was more complicated than a one word definition. Truth had three connotations: first, the opposite of falsehood; second, real, as opposed to illusory; and third, compassionate as opposed to evil. Firmness had the connotation of "polite insistence" as well as "holding firmly to." Essential to this concept was that there was nothing "passive" about *Agraha*. *Agraha* was assertive in the sense of being demanding, but in no instance could it be violent, evil, vengeful, or retributive. The practitioner of *Satyagraha* would love those who hated him.

"The glass front and titanium back" is my personal translation of *Satyagraha* from Sanskrit into English. First, the truth. Gandhi very much enjoyed teaching the children in his ashram and took pleasure in noting that "I got along merrily, because I never attempted to disguise my ignorance from my pupils. In all respects I showed myself to them exactly as I really was." Second, the firmness. In his first act of civil disobedience, Gandhi realized that he could inspire people to lose their fear of punishment through the force of *Satyagraha*. "When I come to examine my title to this realization, I find nothing but my love for the people. And this in turn is nothing but an expression of my unshakeable faith in *Ahimsa*."

Martin Luther King, Jr.

Like many of us, Martin Luther King, Jr. was inspired by Gandhi. Nowhere was this more apparent than in the Montgomery Bus Boycott. On December 1, 1955, Rosa Parks, an African-

American seamstress, was arrested for refusing to give up her seat on a bus to a white person. She was convicted of violating a law that enforced racial segregation and the subservience of Black people to orders from white people. Dr. King observed that the Black citizens of Montgomery had been passive in the face of these discriminatory measures and spoke this truth to his parishioners. He called on the Black citizens of Montgomery to resist this evil. His spark ignited a social and political protest led by Dr. King that centered on a boycott of the Montgomery public transit system.

The boycott was immediately effective and led to retaliatory measures from the white people. King was jailed for two weeks; his home was firebombed; churches were firebombed; a shotgun blast tore through the front door of his home; other Blacks were attacked; and other homes were fired upon by snipers. But nothing deterred King, and after 387 days, the boycott came to a successful conclusion when the U.S. Supreme Court ruled that Alabama's segregation laws were unconstitutional.

What had begun with *Sat* – telling the truth about the inequity of the segregation laws and the responsibility of the Black population to resist them peacefully – was fueled by *Agraha* – the resolute endurance to withstand more than a year of danger, hostility, and the determination of the white population never to surrender their privileges.

King held firmly to the truth through polite insistence and a refusal to be drawn into violence of any kind. He used a glass front to inspire the Black population and then needed a titanium back to endure the difficulties in persisting.

The Glass Front

A person with a glass front has nothing to hide. She is transparent, open, sharing, and frank. He seeks opportunities to clarify instead of to obfuscate. A person with a glass front does not fear revealing herself, with all her strengths and weaknesses. A person with a glass front also is willing to listen to the opinions of others and to take those opinions into consideration, including at those times when she or he is challenged by the opinions or beliefs of others. Openness by itself, however, is not enough. This kind of person is also truthful and does not prevaricate, exaggerate, or augment his own merits. Having a glass front also makes it correspondingly easier to distinguish principle from self-interest. Those with glass fronts hold themselves accountable for their decisions and actions because the reasons for their decisions and the consequences of their actions are readily apparent.

The person with a glass front does not need to offer subsequent clarifications, explanations, and flip-flops because she begins with the truth and no changes are necessary. No one with a glass front is clandestine, devious, or surreptitious. In my opinion, this is a laudable characteristic. I cannot assert that having a glass front is necessary for success, nor do I contend that an opaque front is likely to lead to failure, but I can confirm that it is a universal moral disposition among the individuals whom I chose to be the subjects of this book. I observed this to be a salient characteristic that transcended all the superficial aspects of culture and civilization.

The Titanium Back

A person with a titanium back has principles and he declines to retreat from matters of principle. This kind of personality has thought about and fully subscribes to a short list of absolutes (consistency, generosity, honesty, and compromise, for four examples) that form the basis for her decision-making, approach to human relationships, and response to challenge. This type of person is decisive and courageous, with no fear of the consequences of deciding. He understands the difference between compromise and capitulation, and never confuses the two. She also never worries about consistency, since each response emanates from the same set of principles. A person with a titanium back can feel fear, but courage is a stronger emotion than fear when it comes to deciding what actions to take. As with the glass front, I cannot assert that having a titanium back is necessary for success, or that its absence leads to failure. However, I can once again confirm that it is a universal moral disposition among my heroes and heroines. My point is that people who share this disposition find it easy to trust each other, across cultures, languages, spiritual traditions, and other superficial characteristics.

It All Comes Down to Trust

It all comes down to trust, and the fact that trust is a fundamental, bedrock component of intercultural communication. If we can trust people, we can communicate with them in meaningful ways, reach agreements, make peace, cooperate for mutual benefit, resolve differences, and even compete harmoniously. Having watched men and women from many cultures during a lifetime of travel and study, I conclude that starting with a glass front and a titanium back is a good way to establish and maintain trust. All the individuals you met in Part I have glass fronts and titanium backs. They have all enjoyed professional careers and personal relationships based on trust. As usual, I do not and cannot say that their success was determined by their glass fronts and titanium backs. Nor can I assert that a lack of a glass front or a titanium back predicts failure. But, as noted early in this book, prescribing ways to succeed or avoid failure is not my goal. My goal is to identify characteristics that facilitate intercultural communication, and there is no question in my mind that I have found a good place to start – character, and its components used by Governor Zeti to build her training center. As I think about the seventeen individuals I have profiled in Part I, it is clear to me that I have complete trust in all of them, the result, at least in part, of glass fronts and titanium backs.

Standards

...when we strive to become better than we are,
everything around us becomes better, too.
                                        —Paulo Coelho
                                        The Alchemist

Exceptional people strive to do more than is necessary, attain a level of excellence which is not required, and strive to be "better than it has to be (*btihtb*)." There is an upper boundary to this characteristic, past which it becomes obsessive behavior with no incremental value. This chapter is about those who approach but do not cross this boundary. As with the glass front and titanium back, I have concluded that *btihtb* is a universal disposition that transcends the superficial differences among the women and men in Part I.

I progressively developed the hypothesis that this would be one of the characteristics which would tie my friends together across language, nationality, cuisine, religion, and profession. But as I learned more about these people, and studied this concept both historically and across cultures, I realized that it is was more complicated than simply an endless striving to exceed standards. Let me explain my journey to this conclusion by introducing three examples – prototypes – from different cultures and times.

Steve Jobs

Steve Jobs was the legendary founder of Apple Computer. Paradoxically, one of the sources of his character was his father's approach to building things from wood: "It was important," Jobs said of his father, "to craft the backs of cabinets and fences properly, even though they were hidden. He loved doing things right. He even cared about the look of the parts you couldn't see."

This was not a chance comment or incident and reflected a fundamental philosophy of life. A "great carpenter," Jobs observed at another time, would know that "...to sleep well at night, the aesthetic, the quality, has to be carried all the way through." This attention to detail that exceeded any level that was necessary was an integral feature of Jobs' computer design, and to this day permeates the culture at Apple. I especially admire Jobs' inner-focused drive for perfection beyond what is needed. He did not lose sleep over metrics of market share and profitability. "To sleep well at night," he needed to know that the parts of the computer the customer never sees are as beautiful and as well made as the public face of the product.

Ise Grand Shrine

From a different culture and time, I draw another instance of this exemplary attitude from the Ise Grand Shrine in Japan, a Shinto shrine dedicated to the Goddess Amaterasu-ômikami in Mie Prefecture, located in the Kansai Region of the main island, Honshu. This shrine was first built in 692 CE by the Empress Jito. In homage to the tradition of standards higher than were necessary, it (technically "they" because there are two buildings) has been completely rebuilt every 20 years for the past 1,323 years on alternating, contiguous, sites. Ise Shrine is rebuilt every twenty years because of Shinto beliefs about death and renewal in nature, as well as rec-ognition of the impermanence of all things. It is also a way to teach new generations the tech-nique of building, since the shrine could undoubtedly last one hundred years or more, and in the absence of experienced carpenters, nobody would know how to rebuild it when it became necessary.

In addition to this reconstruction taking place every twenty years, certainly not necessary and clearly better than it must be, the construction techniques are also of a standard that exceeds what is required. The same care and attention to detail that is given to those parts of the shrine that are visible to the eye are also given to the parts that will be invisible to the eye, namely the beams, members, and joints that are covered, fitted to render them invisible, or otherwise obscured from sight. It is simply the devotion of the craftsmen to tradition, the respect they wish to show to the Goddess, and their own innate commitment to *btihtb* that results in this technically unnecessary but deeply emotional renewal of Ise Grand Shrine every twenty years. As Donald Keene, the eminent American Japanologist, wrote about his attendance at a ceremony marking the renewal of Ise Shrine, "Of all the religious ceremonies I have seen in Japan, this moved me the most."

Thomas Moser

I felt that my friends were worthy inheritors of Steve Jobs and the anonymous workmen of Ise Grand Shrine. But then I had the good fortune to discover another valuable dimension to this moral disposition. The discovery came about fortuitously because of an American cabinetmaker named Thomas Moser, based on the coast of Maine. Moser has had a lifelong love affair with wood, expressed through the design and construction of furniture made by hand. Moser shares the sentiment of Steve Jobs and the craftsmen of the Ise Grand Shrine regarding the importance of doing things better than necessary. Moser states, in a virtual paraphrase of Jobs, but with Yankee understatement, that "... we panel the backs of our case pieces to make them as presentable as the fronts."

When I read more about Moser's philosophy, however, I realized that *btihtb* is only the start. Exceeding standards by itself was necessary but insufficient. Moser expresses this more comprehensive understanding of Standards with three qualifications or modifications.

The first qualification is "no subterfuge or chicanery." In describing his approach to the design and construction of furniture, Moser wrote: "...we have dedicated ourselves to ... simplicity, integrity in construction, and a love and respect for materials...not only on the inside but on the exterior of a finished piece." Accordingly, Moser neither paints his furniture nor does he conceal or disguise the joints. *Btihtb* requires not simply higher quality of materials and workmanship, but also a Glass Front. Moser understands that the beauty of the furniture comes equally from quality and from simplicity revealed without concealment on the exterior as well as the interior. The hidden parts must be of a quality as high or higher than the parts that are on the exterior, but the exterior must also have the integrity to show itself without embellishment or dissimulation. Cunning and artifice may suffice for some but will not allow a true craftsman "to sleep well at night."

For the second qualification, Moser added another layer that I saw was vital to the central concept of Standards, but which addressed the human element. He artfully called it "the manufacture of risk:"

> ... the manufacture of risk... is characterized by any kind of technique ... in which the quality of the result is not predetermined but depends on the judgment, dexterity and care which the maker exercises as he works... Manufacturing becomes infused with humanity... literally thousands of challenges arise that require a reaction, and no two craftsmen will react in the same way.

What I concluded is that *btihtb* is insufficient without the manufacture of risk. With the infusion of humanity, the product, the performance, the article, the result of any kind is raised to a new and exalted level. My most immediate reaction to the description of Moser's manufacture of risk in wood was to compare it to Arantxa Ochoa's manufacture of risk in ballet.

The third qualification to the proposition of *btihtb* is what he calls "continuous challenge." At one point in the evolution of his business, Moser felt a gnawing concern that his furniture was derivative rather than original. His response was to launch a new, more complicated, and unique design that established his credentials as an artist and not merely as a craftsman with "sharp tools and quick hands." In this way, Moser rounded out his philosophy of cabinetmaking in a way that adds a level of valuable complexity to the concept of Standards: "Exploring new levels of difficulty is invariably fun...Success is not an end point. Thos. Moser Cabinetmakers has been a process rather than a static entity since the day of its founding. I expect that process to continue."

It all started to make sense to me. *Btihtb* was only the beginning. In order to be meaningful, the work performed cannot remain the same, so by definition it can never be better than it must be. The manufacturer, artist, writer, healer, igniter, conserver, or enabler will always operate in a dynamic mode. There will be no end point, and at its finest, the work will, in the manner of Ise Grand Shrine, endure for more than a thousand years by inspiring others to carry on the work and to take the product, performance, or service to even greater heights. Not so surprisingly, this aspect of endurance over generations recalled Kei Muratsu's commitment to Katoubushi, and also his concern that the chain might be broken in the next generation. In aspiring to achieve the highest possible standard, the exceptional individuals of my book do not expect to achieve their goals in the sense of stopping because they have reached the limit of what they are capable of accomplishing. The quality of the quest is as important as the achievement, which is always interim and never final.

Standards

I finally had a clear vision of the second disposition, Standards, which now included four elements. By itself, *btihtb* was an incomplete concept, but in combination with more textured thinking, it remained in the deep-water channel of my hypothesis. Everybody on my list had the highest expectations for themselves and held their performance, behavior, or decision-making to the most exacting set of expectations. But they also committed to "no subterfuge or chicanery." The highest standards can be achieved only when viewed through a Glass Front. All understand and live by this principle. They also insisted on "the manufacture of risk." The manufacture of risk is an essential element in achieving the highest standard because it expresses the uniquely human content of the activity. No two of Thomas Moser's chairs are the same. How could one be called perfect since they are all different by design? The work of all involves the manufacture of risk, infused with humanity. This is what makes them so compelling, memorable, and valuable. Finally, they are intrinsically motivated by "continuous challenge." No high standard is static, and must be challenged, renewed, and reinvigorated for it to remain meaningful. Once again, they all constantly reinvent themselves, always striving not only to achieve perfection, but also constantly to redefine perfection to keep them sharp, relevant, and above all, honest to themselves.

My observation is that this characteristic – *btihtb* – is shared by the people in Part I of this book. I am convinced that as a consequence of sharing this disposition, they are all able to communicate not only with each other but also with others who may exhibit very different, but ultimately superficial, characteristics shaped by culture, cuisine, religion, and climate.

Resilience

What might have been an act of reasonable caution to the average person was to Shackleton a detestable admission that failure was a possibility.

—Alfred Lansing
Endurance

When the ground rules changed, [he] shattered like glass.

—Nando Parrado
Miracle in the Andes

Just about everybody agrees that resilience is a desirable characteristic for individuals. But what is resilience? I define it in three parts, which correspond to the different stages of response to and engagement with the inevitable negative events or circumstances which we as humans encounter.

First, resilience is the ability to survive and respond appropriately during unexpected (e.g., a plane crash) or anticipated but chronologically unpredictable incidents (e.g., a hurricane). John Hudson, Chief Survival Instructor for the U.K. Military, has observed that taking a massive problem and breaking it down into smaller, achievable chunks, gives the survivor a sense of control, and with control comes hope. Once the immediate surprise has passed, to be resilient we must perceive (even if it is delusional) the possibility of escape from our predicament. Resilience requires that we retain the conviction of having a choice, even if the rules have changed. Otherwise, we can sink into what has been called, by John Leach, Senior Research Fellow in the Extreme Environmental Medicine and Science Group of the University of Portsmouth, "give-up-itis."

Second, resilience is the capacity to recover after negative events or circumstances are resolved, completed, or aborted, and not be defeated or overwhelmed by them. An individual needs to be able to hope, plan for the future, and maintain goal-directed behavior despite horrible and destabilizing memories. The alternative is post-traumatic stress disorder.

Third, resilience is the ability to learn, adapt, and grow from the negative events or circumstances. This has been termed, by Judith Rodin in her book of the same title, the "resilience dividend," the silver lining in the dark cloud of disaster. Our ability to embrace the experience, despite the fact that it was thrust upon us uninvited, and use it to grow stronger, is the payoff of resilience.

The individuals whom you have met in Part I of this book have endured and emerged from all three parts of this definition of resilience. My observation of their attitudes and responses to trauma and disaster led me to conclude that resilience is one of the dispositions that transcends language, culture, nationality, and all the other superficial attributes of humans.

There are three questions that follow from my definition, and we will explore them to attempt to understand the wellsprings of the resilience which is apparent in these women and men who come from diverse backgrounds, both geographical and cultural.

Where does resilience come from?

Why are some people resilient and other people not resilient?

Can anyone become resilient or is it an immutable characteristic?

I will attempt to answer these questions by looking at resilience from seven perspectives. There are many paths, I discovered, off the mountaintop. We make a mistake if we assume that resilience can only be obtained in "our" way.

Detachment or Non-reactivity

First, detachment, sometimes called non-reactivity. To the Buddha, pain and suffering were no more than illusions. If one could see pain and suffering as illusions, one could stop reacting to these unhelpful thoughts and be unaffected by them. Resilience, one might say, can be a by-product of detachment, although the Buddha might say that detachment renders resilience irrelevant because it is no longer needed. One of the Buddha's great ideas was to democratize enlightenment; detachment is available to anyone, without the need for intermediation by a civil or religious hierarchy. Most of us find the Buddha's path to be intriguing but challenging to follow. Nevertheless, we have found at least four Buddhists in Part I who survived trauma, recovered, adapted, grew, and found peace in detachment. My conclusion is that this is the most profound type of resilience although it is the most difficult to achieve.

Biology or Genetics

Second, biology. According to the findings of neuroscientists, there is evidence that the hormone/neurotransmitter dopamine plays a role in motivation and resilience. In the event a person is traumatized or encounters a challenge, dopamine is released into the brain and she feels motivated to solve the problem. We can label this motivation as resilience, in this case the chemically induced courage to fight back. Resilience is biologically generated in stressful conditions by the release of dopamine. There is a downside to this function, however. If we perceive that there is no escape from the trauma or problem, the amount of dopamine increases to the point at which it prompts passive, energy-saving, coping behaviors, and we will suffer from "give-up-itis." Does this mean that resilience (and under certain conditions, resignation) is unaffected by will power? Are we fooling ourselves to think that we can control our response to stress and trauma? Or is dopamine reinforced by will power? Or is will power reinforced by dopamine? At this point, these questions are unanswered, but some day science may help us to understand better the biological nature of resilience. What is clear is that while our control over biology is at best uncertain, we retain at least the illusion that we have an ability to make choices.

Meaning

Third, meaning. Many philosophers, economists, scientists, psychologists, and some baseball players have devised a "theory of everything." Adam Smith thought it was vanity, which was not much different from Francis Fukuyama, who thought it was recognition. Einstein went to his grave unable to figure it out scientifically, but he always believed that there was a theory of everything. Viktor Frankl believed that life was primarily a search for meaning. He based his conclusion on observations of prisoners (including himself) in Nazi concentration camps. He noticed that those who survived and retained their mental health invariably had meaning in their lives. Sounding like an early precursor to John Hudson, he observed that "…mental health is based on a certain degree of tension, the tension between what one has already achieved and what one still ought to accomplish, or the gap between what one is and what one should become." Similar to Hudson, Frankl believed that humans have the freedom to choose how they will respond to any given situation. Resilience, to Frankl who wrote before scientists discovered the function of dopamine, was a matter of choice, but depended to a high degree on having meaning in one's existence. All those profiled in Part I of this book had meaning in their lives, exemplified by a sense of purpose for what they "still ought to accomplish." There is no question that this strong sense of meaning contributed to their resilience, although I have never subscribed to the hubris of anybody's "theory of everything."

Defiance

Fourth, defiance. I suppose that defiance is a type of meaning, but I like it so much that I have decided to include it as a unique category. Defiance involves an unwillingness to give in or give up. It is the opposite of Buddhist detachment. Defiance tends to have a negative connotation, but this need not be the case. Defiance also tends to be associated with antagonistic, sometimes violent behavior, and this also need not be the case. Gandhi was defiant, and the philosophy of *Satyagraha* was defiant; but he was neither antagonistic nor violent. We have met at least one self-proclaimed "defiant optimist" (Durreen Shahnaz) who refused to be categorized, pigeonholed, or muzzled. Maybe adrenalin helps, if properly channeled.

Training

Fifth, training. If you train for emergencies, you may act by reflex rather than cognition when a problem arises. This is an example of Kahneman's "thinking fast." Although you are traumatized by the circumstances and unable to make conscious decisions, if you have trained for the particular type of event, your subconscious may take over and enable you to take the appropriate action without realizing what you are doing. This type of resilience is most applicable to predictable emergencies, such as smoke in an aircraft cabin or a fourth-and-one when the game is on the line. But many emergencies are Black Swans. If your training does not conform to the particulars of the emergency, you may collapse into inaction because the rules changed. For example, surviving a plane crash on a snow-covered mountain but having no food for the 72 days until being rescued. On the other hand, training about how to deal with the outcome of voluntarily entering into an emergency (for example, climbing Mt. Everest) may help with your ability to learn and grow from the experience. Training is different from habit (which comes next) because training is situational and not transferable outside of a small number of variations. Habit is global and transfers to every situation.

Habit

Sixth, habit. Fate, some people contend, is merely your expectations for yourself, defined by habit. If you respond positively and optimistically to every situation, it becomes a habit to respond with resilience. The habit kicks in whenever you have a trauma, an emergency, or a seemingly insoluble problem.

Niels Bohr, the Danish physicist, was an exemplar of this type of resilience. "For [Bohr] every difficulty, every conflict contains its solution. The greater the difficulty, the greater the step to surmount it, the greater is the reward that ensues…" One of the reasons I admire and respect my friends so much is that they are all inveterate optimists, and always assume that a problem can be solved. This type of resilience also involves accepting personal responsibility for one's physical and mental well-being. Resilience is much stronger when it does not depend on somebody else to solve your problem. If positive behavior and optimism are habits, and not contingent on anything or anybody, they are more likely to endure. Another of the benefits of inculcating the habit of positivity and optimism is that anybody can do it. We will revert to this particular thought in more detail when we get to the twelfth disposition, *H.O.P.E.*

Learning from Nature

Seventh, learning from nature. Nature is resilient, as described so eloquently by Columbia University Professor Ruth DeFries in her 2021 book entitled *What Would Nature Do?* How else could life have persisted for more than three billion years? Life has been resilient because it adapted to new conditions and challenges. Nature accomplished this adaptation through mutations. In human civilization, diversity of ideas, specialization of ideas, institutions, languages, and cultures serve the same function. We can learn from the experience of the natural world that successful adaptation is often inefficient. We live in an interdependent world where most decisions are based on identifying and selecting for the efficiencies of networks. While these networks are convenient and profitable, they are fragile and susceptible to collapse. By placing efficiency above all else, we are planning around a predictable future which is a chimera. Diversity keeps options alive when times change. Constant change and diversity of survival strategies hold the keys to life's resilience today as much as it did through geologic time. Evolution also favors redundancy in an uncertain world. The takeaway from nature is that we can contribute to resilience by building redundant, often inefficient and less profitable pathways, as communities and as individuals.

In Summary

Resilience comes from a variety of sources. Some are innate and some are acquired. All my friends have been remarkably resilient; they all faced adversity, survived it, recovered from it, and grew from it. It is difficult to determine why some people are resilient, and others are not, although the next wave of advances in brain science may give us some clues. And yes, anyone can become resilient, although nobody said it was easy. But the more you work at it, the better you get at it, whether through detachment, biology, meaning, defiance, training, habit, or learning from nature. There is no question in my mind that resilience either already is or can be (through choice and self-discipline) a universal human trait, valuable to the perpetuation of the human species, and highly satisfying to those who have it. Based on a lifetime of observations across a wide variety of cultures and civilizations, I have also concluded that we can adapt to the unusual, unsettling, uncomfortable, and even the catastrophic by being resilient.

Bad things happen. Those who can respond, recover, and gain strength from the bad things are able to recognize and share understanding with others who are similarly resilient. As Roberto Canessa learned through the observation of his fellow plane crash victims and the kids who recover from serious heart ailments, they are alike because they are survivors.

Forgiveness

[His anger] is a case of powder and spark; there is a
vivid flash and a deafening roar, but when the smoke
is blown away, that is the end.

—Written about Theodore Roosevelt
Francis E. Leupp, "Taft and Roosevelt"

…to live in bitterness and anger, would only keep me
from living any genuine life at all… I would try, every
day, to become more human and alive.

—Nando Parrado
Miracle in the Andes

According to some analysts, the airport at Lukla, Nepal, is the most dangerous in the world. Flying into Tenzing-Hillary Airport for the first time is not nearly as frightening as flying out for the first time. This is because when you arrive for the first time you are unaware of the fact that there is a vertical drop of 1,000 feet at the other end of the runway. When you depart, there will be no aborted take-off in the event of mechanical failure or second thoughts. Tenzing-Hillary Airport is not forgiving.

I arrived in Lukla on a November morning, accompanied by my friend Morris Cohen, a distinguished Professor of Operations and Information Management at the Wharton School. We were undertaking an adventure to celebrate our upcoming mutual fiftieth birthdays (actually, I am three days older than Morris, but I never pulled rank because of our age discrepancy).

Lukla is a small village of fewer than 300 permanent residents in Nepal, located at 9,383 feet, about 30 minutes by air from Kathmandu, the country's capital city. Lukla is the starting point for most people who visit Nepal to trek in the Himalayas. It is also the starting point for most people who attempt assaults on Mt. Everest. For our flight from Kathmandu, we had a choice of fixed-wing aircraft operated by Yeti Airlines or Buddha Air. The choice seemed obvious except for the fact that Buddha Air flew repurposed Soviet Air Force equipment. Nevertheless, we decided that The Buddha was a far more reliable inspiration for the pilots than a Yeti and made our choice accordingly. We learned after our arrival in Lukla that a third choice, a helicopter (a Soviet-era troop transporter), was available for the return flight to Kathmandu. We re-booked our return by helicopter to avoid the runway.

Our goals were modest in mountaineering terms, but ambitious for two novice mountain climbers: we planned to climb as far and as high into the Himalayas as we could go in ten days. This meant that we would be unable to summit Mt. Everest. This takes a minimum of three months, requires a US$60,000 permit plus hundreds of thousands of dollars for equipment, manpower, and supplies. It is also considerably more dangerous than the trek we planned. Earthquakes, landslides, and the "zone of death" above which there is insufficient oxygen to sustain human life for longer than a few hours, are only the most obvious challenges. Acrophobia, for example, is punished severely in the Himalayas. The people who live there call this mountain Sagarmatha ("Mother of the World" in Nepalese).

Sagarmatha is ruthless, relentless, all-powerful, and even more unforgiving than the airport at Lukla. There is no force on earth more powerful or more enduring than Sagarmatha. At night, the stars are unimaginably bright to city dwellers because of the lack of terrestrial light pollution. The solitude is both awe-inspiring and terrifying. The farther I climbed up this mountain range, the more I understood that I was undertaking the greatest physical and psychological challenge of my life and bearing witness to the primal strength of the planet earth. When I reached the highest point of our journey – Dingboche Peak at 17,322 feet – it

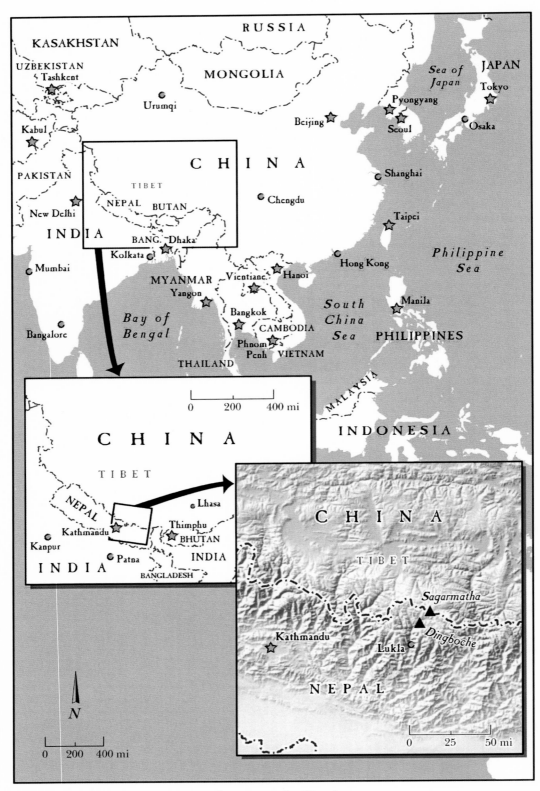

An Adventure in the Himalayas

248

was clear to me that all the other challenges of my life going forward would be less arduous. I felt an exhilaration that, having made this climb, nothing else would be impossible. This feeling was not hubris. Indeed, I felt utterly humbled – even humiliated – by the experience. I realized how puny and insignificant I was. Sitting at the top of Dingboche Peak, I could see what seemed to be forever in a 360 degree panorama, blocked only by Sagarmatha herself to the Northeast, still 11,707 feet higher at 29,029 feet and growing slightly every year, nudged upward by the inexorable clash of tectonic plates.

I learned several lessons from my adventure in the Himalayas, one of which was humility. We will discuss humility separately, in the twelfth disposition – H.O.P.E. I will mention two more lessons here. First, the experience left me sharply focused on forgiveness and how different people can view this disposition as either requiring a passionate act of will or as an effortless abnegation. Second, Sagarmatha is unforgiving but utterly dispassionate. The fourth of the dispositions shared by my friends is forgiveness, in a variety of formats.

Varieties of Forgiveness – Spiritual and Scientific

Although I do not subscribe to any particular religion, I have identified certain traits in several of the world's religions and spiritual philosophies that I find appealing. Perhaps that means that I have created my own religion or philosophy, or maybe I am just a syncretist. In any case, I was raised in the Christian "tradition," if not necessarily in the Christian "faith," because my parents were thoroughly secular. In this way, I at least became acquainted with Christian concepts and beliefs. I have always found the Christian concept of forgiveness to be valuable, although difficult to follow at certain times. We are all periodically insulted, ignored despite our self-perceived value, and often treated unfairly, so the best way to avoid feeling anger, confronting others, and carrying this burden is to forgive.

This concept is not exclusive to Christianity. I take comfort in the way this thought is also expressed in the first of the Analects of Confucius, which translates as "Not to be upset when one's merits are ignored: is this not the true mark of a gentleman?" Shabnam Shahnaz reflected on this concept as she learned it growing up Muslim, relating it to her sister, Durreen, who appeared in Part I: "If you can forgive, then you cannot be cynical. Cynicism is the curse of those who bear grudges. Forgiveness is a gift to those who truly feel it because it liberates you to be enthusiastic, and therefore happy." Mohandas Gandhi, raised as a Hindu, was in his own words, a prideful young man, quick to take offense. But he learned over time to "pocket the insult." He still felt the sting, but he learned, as one of his "experiments with truth," to forgive. This is part of what gave him the strength to change the world.

No discussion of forgiveness can exclude Nelson Mandela, raised as a Xhosa, whose religion was "characterized by a cosmic wholeness, so that there is little distinction between the sacred and the secular, between the natural and the supernatural." Surely no one has ever suffered as much and forgiven as much as Mandela, who must be considered one of the all-time world champions in this category. He said many memorable things after his release from prison on February 11, 1990, but my favorite refers to forgiveness. "As I walked out the door toward the gate that would lead to my freedom, I knew if I didn't leave my bitterness and hatred behind, I'd still be in prison." The Truth and Reconciliation Commission established in South Africa by Mandela soon after he was elected president in 1994 became the model for how post-conflict nations could chart their futures without revenge and the perpetuation of antagonisms.

Buddhism is a special case when it comes to forgiveness. The Buddha taught that what we perceive as reality is actually an illusion, and if we simply stopped reacting to the illusion (often referred to as 'detachment'), we would eliminate the causes of our suffering. Tenzin Gyatso, the 14th Dalai Lama, a well-known Buddhist, is no slouch when it comes to a life of perpetual conflict and unrealized aspirations. But he also understands the liberating quality of forgiveness. As noted by author Pankaj Mishra, "...the Dalai Lama appears wholly untouched by bitterness and self-pity...the sense of victimhood that fuels many contemporary battles for territory, resources and dignity."

Shiv Khemka introduced me (see page 106) to the work of Philip Zimbardo, a social psychologist and professor emeritus at Stanford University. Professor Zimbardo's research has focused on evil, its perpetrators, its victims, its prevention, its punishment, and its forgiveness – all from a secular, scientific perspective. Zimbardo observes that the foundations of psychiatry, psychology, law, and medicine – at least as practiced in most Western countries – are based on dispositional causes, namely the assumption that the individual is fully responsible for his or her own actions and condition. He disagrees with this commonly held assumption, based on his scientific experiments, and has concluded that dispositional explanations miss the equally or possibly even more important role played by the system within which an individual operates, and the situations that the system creates. While he still holds individuals responsible for their acts of evil, he argues that the situation should be taken into consideration during the sentencing of a convicted criminal. He believes that all people are usually good, but that anybody is susceptible to doing evil under the conditions of a situation. Forgiveness, in the form of sentence mitigation or conviction expungement, is often appropriate and desirable.

Another intriguing scientific basis for the empowering value of forgiveness comes from the medical field. Karen Swartz, a practicing psychiatrist and clinical programs director of the Johns Hopkins University Mood Disorders Center, has demonstrated that forgiveness can lower blood pressure, relieve anxiety and depression, and strengthen the immune system. Harboring grudges can have the opposite, medically undesirable, consequences. In her words,

"...your thoughts drive your feelings and emotions and can drive your behavior. So, if you think about it, if you stay on negative thoughts all the time, you're constantly in a negative, very tense state." Ultimately, according to Dr. Swartz, "... forgiveness isn't so much about the other person as [*it is about*] your own process of saying, I'm moving forward." I find it instructive that the modern, medical analysis of the value of forgiveness and the source of this forgiveness are so similar to what have been traditions of spirituality for millennia.

Easy to Agree; Difficult to Do

I mentioned earlier that for many people, forgiveness is a passionate act of will, not always successfully implemented. Others do not even feel the anger or betrayal caused by the disrespect, cruelty, injustice, or hardship that was inflicted on them and their families. In my study of this concept of forgiveness, I have found that it comes in many different formats and guises. But it always involves letting go of something within ourselves that is causing us anguish, pain, suffering, anger, or humiliation. One thing remains constant – we cannot make progress and live together peacefully without believing in and embracing forgiveness as a universal moral disposition. We are all humans.

After watching and studying many different forms of forgiveness, I conclude that my preference is for Buddhist detachment. It is the only form of forgiveness that is not a palliative. But it is also the most elusive because it requires rising above emotions that have been baked into the human genome for millions of years. I feel certain that in pocketing the many insults he felt, Gandhi still suffered. He just decided, as an act of will, not to react.

All of my friends profiled in Part I have suffered in their lives, and yet none of them carries anger in his or her heart. Not one of them is poisoned by this toxic chemical. Each one of them is filled with happiness and harmony because of and not despite the terrible wrongs from which they have suffered. Forgiveness can come from detachment, willpower, or a combination of the two. Regardless of its source, it is a valuable moral disposition. You are not a lesser person if you must force yourself to be forgiving; the test is whether the endpoint is forgiveness. Forgiveness is a strong, unbreakable part of the message of this book. The capacity to forgive is a common trait of all the individuals I admire and love so much. If we can forgive, we create the opportunity – the opening – to communicate with anyone, regardless of civilization, culture, language, or history. A forgiving heart knows no foreign lands.

Maybe we can all learn from Sagarmatha. Although she is unforgiving, hers is a dispassionate disposition. She has no anger or desire for revenge. Sagarmatha is most certainly detached, but very strong and unflinching. I think that she is a good role model for us humans. I know that when I feel anger welling up inside me, I try to remember Sagarmatha's perfect equanimity. Sometimes it works.

Free Will

Men at some time are masters of their fates:
The fault, dear Brutus, is not in our stars,
But in ourselves, that we are underlings.

> —Cassius to Brutus
> *Shakespeare, Julius Caesar*

… man is a creature with a conscience and capable
of attaining a higher and higher degree of truth.

> —Count Leo Graf Tolstoy
> *The Kingdom of God Is Within You*

For those who believe in this concept, fate is the unfolding of events, circumstances, or consequences that are not subject to human control. These circumstances are perceived by humans to be the results of the intervention (or non-intervention) of either a deity or another non-specific power whose decisions cannot be challenged. In some cases, humans believe that the performance of certain behaviors may have some influence on the power that decides, for example, prayer, sacrifices, or following the rules. Humans are not able to alter their own fates or the fates of others once these are decided by the controlling power. Fate is reassuring to people in the sense that it asserts that human existence has a predetermined meaning, and this belief can absolve humans of personal responsibility. Fate is, with a few minor exceptions, a passive belief. Fatalism prescribes policies of inaction, although in some cases it has served as the rationale for racism, colonialism, and imperialism. These "isms" depended on the assumption that "primitive" people either were not capable of becoming "civilized" or were capable of being civilized but were still in a state of "savagery" or "barbarism." Fate is a pre-scientific belief that has lost its credibility with many people, but certainly not all.

Free will, on the other hand, is the belief that humans can make their own decisions, choose between options, accept responsibility for the decisions they make, and change the future through actions that they decide to take. Or, as the Brazilian neuroscientist Suzana Herculano-Houzel writes, humans have developed "cognitive capabilities that depend on representing the past and learning to make predictions from it, forecasting different scenarios, and choosing one according to the best criteria at hand." Free will is disconcerting because it rejects the notion that there is a predetermined meaning of human existence, although it allows a person the opportunity to create meaning in his or her existence. Free will is an active belief, because it asserts both the possibility and the value of taking action to bring about change. The Enlightenment gave free will a dominance (at least in the Western world) which it has not lost in the succeeding three hundred years, although recently this supremacy has run into some scientific turbulence which will be discussed below.

Homo sapiens is apparently the only carbon-based life form which considers the concepts of fate and free will. It is one of the benefits (and the burdens) of our having an advanced level of consciousness. This ability gives humans the opportunity to define these concepts in different ways and to make (or accept) decisions based on their definitions. Having this capacity has been of enduring interest to our species.

The choice between an acceptance of fate and a belief in free will is seen by some people as binary, but actually a binary choice more often represents the extremes of a spectrum. My observations of multiple cultures, languages, religions, ethnicities, and civilizations around the world suggest that for most people – the broad middle of the spectrum – the choice embraces variations on the binary options. The choices are culturally determined, and therefore functionally unlimited.

Some Varieties of Human Interpretation of Fate and Free Will

Before examining the common thread that ties together the subjects of my book in their interpretation of the fate/free-will spectrum, it may be helpful to review (in appalling brevity) a few of its many different human (and now, non-human) permutations.

An example at the "fate end" of the spectrum is the ancient set of beliefs that was invented by the Greeks. Their mythology included many gods who were both immortal and all-powerful. These gods controlled everything from the weather to the underworld. Possibly even more powerful than the gods were the three "Fates," who controlled everyone's destiny. Astrology, which was probably invented by the Babylonians, was embraced by the Greeks, and added to the ways in which they, then the Romans, and even Galileo's tormentors lived under the illusion of knowledge that their lives were subject to sentient forces beyond human control. In modern times, the era governed by scientific inquiry and standards of evidence, these beliefs are interesting to study as historical artifacts but lack utility in any practical sense.

Ancient Chinese philosophy encompassed a broad spectrum of great thinkers, but most schools agreed that there was a "heaven" – although not an anthropomorphic "god" – that made the decisions. According to Confucius, one's fate is arbitrarily determined by heaven at birth. You have no choices, and you must accept what heaven has decided for you. This is the theory of "arbitrary divine fate" – it is random, accidental, and unpredictable. According to Mo Zi, by contrast, heaven rewards good behavior and punishes bad behavior. Your fate is contingent on what you do. This is the theory of "retributive divine fate." Humans subscribing to either philosophy believe that they lack control over what happens to them.

I find it difficult to accept these beliefs of the Babylonians, classical Greeks, ancient Chinese, and other believers in an unscientific fate which is not supported by empirical evidence. However, there is a modern, scientific hypothesis that asserts that human behavior is not entirely volitional and that the lives of humans may not be completely under their own control. In the twenty-first century, scientists have further developed the understanding that human behavior is at least partially determined by genes which evolved through natural selection. Genes, in this theory, are indifferent to human choice or preference; they merely follow the best genetically-mutated path to their reproduction and perpetuation. If a behavior emerged from a genetic mutation that resulted in a greater likelihood of successful reproduction, then more people will survive with that gene, which in turn will cause the population of people with that gene to expand. It has nothing to do with the preferences or conscious choices of the humans who carry the gene. The humans are just acting at the behest of the gene and have no choice in the matter.

Since these mutations and the genetic evolution took place hundreds of thousands of years ago, we may now carry predispositions for certain behaviors which are unneeded or even dysfunctional in modern society – vestigial genes. In a sense, this is an updated, non-supernaturally-determined definition of fate. We may be inclined to offer or accept bribes, for example, not because we are "immoral" (which is an imagined reality) but simply because bribery may have been a behavior that augmented the chances of surviving long enough to reproduce five hundred thousand years ago. It may be our genetic fate to be tempted to bribe and be bribed. However, in the Anthropocene we have elected to make it illegal in order to try to stop people from doing it because our current civilization works better when people do not engage in this form of activity. We might label this fate, differently defined.

Machine intelligence has created a new challenge for humans. We are now entering an age in which machines are already more knowledgeable and able more quickly and more reliably to retrieve information than the human brain. Some scientists are convinced that consciousness and sentience are not substrate-dependent, and that silicon-based machines will have the potential to become "life forms" which (who?) are able to develop consciousness, thereby freeing them from human control. All it will take is a computer with enough synapses to approach the number of cortical neurons in the human brain. If machines are sentient and are both smarter and faster than humans, will we have control over our lives? Already, machines have been programmed to make decisions which we cannot understand, and which the machines cannot explain. Our fates, in this hypothesis, are determined by mechanical omniscience. If all this is true, humans are probably doomed. This is fate again differently defined, and quite possibly many Enlightenment-based postulates are thereby exploded. Under this hypothesis, fate is not an outdated, non-scientific concept, but an immediate and provable reality.

Hindu belief is near the center of the spectrum we are considering between fate and free will. On the fate side, the Hindu believes that human lives are predetermined by the actions of their selves in previous incarnations. This is called Karma. We cannot alter the fact that what we did in our previous lives defines who we are in our current lives. However, we do have the option of making choices in our current lives that will have an impact on how we are reborn in our next lives. I have always thought that this was an ingenious method of social control. You may be miserable and angry, but if you behave well there is hope that next time around you will have a better life. We might label this incentive-based morality.

Calvin's Doctrine of the Elect is analogous to the Hindu concept, and virtually identical in terms of its goal of social control. According to Calvin, an individual has no control over whether they will be "saved." Only God can make that choice. Consequently, the meaning and purpose of human existence is to demonstrate, through virtuous acts (as defined by the church), that we have been chosen by God to be saved. In any case, our fate is sealed, and we are hoping that this fate will include salvation. The Calvinist did not expect to be reincarnated but did believe in an afterlife of either perpetual bliss or unending agony. We can label this another case of incentive-based morality.

I had been told repeatedly that Indonesians are particularly fatalistic. But then I had the good fortune to become acquainted with Dr. Boediono, whom you met in Part I. Boediono used a three-word Javanese proverb – *"Sabar, Sareh, Seleh"* – that summarized his personal philosophy. To recapitulate briefly: You should not get too agitated if you fail, and you should not get too excited if you succeed. Work hard but be at peace with any outcome. I would not call this fatalistic, although neither would I call it an affirmation of free will. Boediono was a paragon of action-oriented behavior as Vice President of Indonesia but was also steeped in Javanese tradition.

Gandhi, a Hindu by birth but a syncretist by choice, had something useful to say about this topic. He, too, placed himself dead center on the spectrum we are considering: "...how far a man is free and how far a creature of circumstances, – how far free-will comes into play and where fate enters on the scene, – all this is a mystery and will remain a mystery." He may have had internal doubts, but he certainly acted as if he believed in free will. His philosophy of *Satyagraha*, as I have noted previously, is a neologism which utilizes Sanskrit words for "truth" and "to hold firmly," neither of which has anything to do with a belief in surrendering to fate.

The Buddha was fundamentally unconcerned with fate (nor, as described in the third disposition, *Resilience*). His basic proposition was that there is no "self" and no "essence." Our suffering is caused by our reacting to these (and other) illusions. If we can detach ourselves from these unskillful misapprehensions, we are no longer influenced by the external world. There is no such thing as pain or hunger. We have the capacity to make the choice to detach from our desires for power and wealth, so as a practical matter free will is central to the Buddha's teachings. Both fate and free will become irrelevant to the individual who has understood that he has no "self' and that none of his desires or fears has any "essence." The Tao is in certain ways a Chinese counterpart to Buddhism in that it counsels detachment from passions such as desire, care, will, and intention as a way of avoiding suffering. Following the Tao means that you gain spiritual freedom by giving up worldly cares and expectations. Fate would become as irrelevant to the Taoist as it was to the Buddhist. Sensible advice, but exceedingly difficult to follow.

Despite what Confucius and Mo Zi thought about fate, there have been other strands of Chinese philosophy arguing for free will. Mencius, for example, shared some of the views of Confucius but allowed humans a measurable ability to determine their fates. Heaven, according to Mencius, did not have absolute power. Your destiny is determined by your actions. Moral integrity is the key to success. Mencius attributed poverty to sinfulness and prosperity to virtue. Fate had nothing to do with it.

Traveling down the road from fate to free will, we find another Chinese philosopher, Xun Zi, who was one of the first to conduct what might be called a rational examination of the human condition. Xun Zi believed that heaven created everything but rejected the notion that heaven had any interest in influencing the course of events on earth. He concluded that all human success and failure came from their own efforts. Luck plays a role, but humans govern their own destinies. This philosophy has an analog in the Western tradition of Deism, which was a belief shared by Thomas Jefferson, Benjamin Franklin, and other Founding Fathers of the American Revolution. The Deist believed that there was a supreme being who created everything but rejected the notion that this ultimate entity had any involvement (or even interest) in the world he (or she) created.

Jean Paul Sartre and the Existentialists are prominent members of the "free-will" end of the spectrum. While there are as many definitions of "Existentialism" as there are "existentialists," they tend to agree that humans are totally free and totally responsible. In Sartre's well-known expression, "Existence precedes essence." Humans create their own values and define the meaning in their existence because there is no prior meaning (essence) of existence. This is an unequivocal rejection of fate. There is no "truth" to be sought, no ultimate goal such as "heaven" to which to aspire, and no deity to whom humans must answer. We give meaning to our lives only by taking full responsibility and creating an identity with values that will be unique to each of us. In the interest of full disclosure (a glass front), this is the philosophy with which I am most comfortable. Peter Singer, whom I have used repeatedly as an exemplar of ethical thought and behavior, would probably reject the label of existentialist, but his thought clearly fits the template.

At the extreme end of the "free-will tail" is the belief that everything that happens is random and unpredictable. This is the opposite of fate, which is predetermined and (sometimes) predictable. The randomness hypothesis contends that the arbitrary nature of what happens to us does not proscribe free will (Taleb calls it responding "robustly") whereas Confucius prescribes the pre-scientific course of action, which is to accept the outcome since that is what heaven has chosen for us.

The Commonalities That Lead to Intercultural Communication

With this myriad of available positions on the spectrum of fate to free will, what choices do those who populate Part I make? Is there a common belief or form of activity that ties them together? It is a conundrum, since they were exposed to so many different cultures, religions, and historical influences. But I was not surprised to find a common thread.

My observation is that all created a similar, consistent meaning in their existence regardless of whether there are forces either supernatural, natural, or man-made that they felt might have influenced events outside of their control. Some of them retained the belief that fate is relevant and influences their lives; others denied any possibility of fate and took full responsibility for all their actions and outcomes; and the remainder were not certain and remained agnostic on the existence of fate. Operationally, all found meaning in their existence by following a common thread. This thread has two fibers, shared by all:

First, all shared an ability and a willingness to seize apparently random, unexpected opportunities and even disasters and to turn them to their advantage, to make positive use of them, or to defend themselves robustly from their untoward consequences. This required them to have an ability to adjust when the rules they had been following changed. Whatever the vicissitudes, nobody ever had lame excuses. They are all action-oriented problem-solvers. Nobody ever gave up.

Second, they all shared a deep sense of moral obligation to a common code of fairness, justice, compassion, honesty, and related virtues. They also all accepted personal responsibility for their actions and the outcomes of their actions, regardless of external conditions and the randomness, unfairness, or irrationality of events. Whether they were acting based on free will or refusing to submit to genetic imprinting, the consequences were the same. I think this is an important and desirable characteristic, since fate keeps rearing its ugly head across time, albeit in different forms.

All my seventeen friends share a firm resolve never to be thwarted or intimidated by fate, randomness, or karma. On the contrary, they celebrate the unavoidable, the "highly improbable," and the possible consequences of the good deeds, or misdeeds, of their souls in previous lives. This is part of what makes them so engagingly human, despite their superhuman characteristics. This is also the essence of the fifth of their common dispositions. In the case of each of these individuals, their ability to communicate interculturally has been augmented by their decision to act on the basis of a belief in free will, despite a wide variety of biological and cultural influences that may be embedded in their genomes and connectomes.

Money

The worth of gold is not in its utility; it contains no energy to sustain bodies or warm hearths. It is too scarce, heavy, and pliable to use for tools. It offers no shelter. Many people have died seeking it, but no person will die in its absence. The meaning and power of gold comes from the human mind, and how the human mind imagines gold's inertia....a monetary abstraction, valuable for its alchemic ability to become any other thing.

—Bathsheba Demuth
Floating Coast

I am, Sire, as rich as I wish to be.
—Michel de Montaigne

Money does not occur in nature. So why do we have money? Similar to many concepts, it is a product of the human imagination. To begin with, there was no commercial society and money did not exist because it had no purpose. Every hunter-gatherer did everything, regardless of the unnecessary duplication of effort. Jared Diamond points out that the division of labor and the rise of specialists all followed logically after the domestication of wild plants and large mammals about 13,000 years ago, actions which led to the creation of large, sedentary populations of humans.

Humans originally would obtain something from unrelated humans surreptitiously (stealing) or through violence. At some point, a turning point in human history, somebody came up with the idea that it was possible openly and peacefully to exchange goods or services of perceived equal or proportional value. This proved to be especially true if each side had a comparative advantage in the sourcing or production of the goods or services offered for exchange.

The next step was for someone to come up with the idea of denominating a small trinket (such as a cowrie shell) or a large object of value (such as a cow or a daughter) as a common unit of exchange. This evolved into "money." The number and value of goods and services that one could obtain using money was limited until the division of labor widened. The evaluation of wealth, and its correlation with status, has changed over the millennia. For example, when a powerful Russian had nothing to purchase (because he already owned everything), his wealth was calculated by the number of serfs in his domain. Eventually, money grew in importance as a mechanism for establishing status. Money also facilitated the exchange of goods and services, probably when "luxury goods" were created and commercial society came into being. The need to pay for war, an expensive and useless luxury, was another stimulus for the invention of money.

Later, nations valued their wealth by the quantity of specie (a form of trinket) they held. This policy led to all kinds of trouble, partly because it was an unreliable indicator of national wealth. For example, the Opium Wars can be traced back with a solid line to the drain of silver from the British treasury caused by the insatiable demand of English ladies and gentlemen for Chinese tea. This idea – mercantilism – was contradicted by Adam Smith starting in 1776 with the publication of *The Wealth of Nations*, thus launching capitalism, an economic system that depended on money.

In the modern era, money is of fundamental importance, although the trinkets exist increasingly in an electronic rather than a physical medium. There is an unfortunate paradox involving money in the twenty-first century. Hundreds of millions of people have climbed out of abject poverty in recent years because of capitalism and globalization. This is a good thing. But inequality of income and assets has sharply increased. This is an unsustainable and immoral trend.

While this chapter cannot address the reasons for any of these changes in the material well-being of humanity, it will attempt to consider the relationships that people have to money, and the meaning of these various relationships. This will involve making value judgments rather than expounding economic analyses.

The Materialistic Treadmill

Adam Smith, as noted above the father of capitalism, but a keen critic of the consequences of the system he espoused, wrote "Avarice overrates the difference between poverty and riches... The person under the influence of [*this extravagant passion*] is not only miserable in his actual situation but is often disposed to disturb the peace of society, in order to arrive at that which he so foolishly admires."

In the affluent societies of the twenty-first century, we are afflicted with this same extravagant passion that overrates the importance of the acquisition of material possessions to a degree that far exceeds what we require in order to have happy, healthy, and harmonious lives. I suppose that this propensity may have had some evolutionary value to our ancestors, but in any case, many of us are on what has also been termed a "materialistic treadmill." This treadmill is driven by an insatiable need to buy more things. We as individuals do not satisfy our wants with our next purchase because there is always something else we are convinced we "need" to buy. The treadmill never stops, and we keep purchasing things. When we run out of space in our homes, we rent storage bins and put the old things in them so that we can put the new things in our homes. The objects we buy give us pleasure for only a short period of time. Our pleasure soon abates, and we need to buy again. It is the act of buying that is the principal source of the pleasure, and that pleasure is very brief. If we feel pleasure only in the purchasing, then we must purchase again and again, and no purchase of any value will ever be enough. One of the great absurdities of the materialistic treadmill is that we pay more for an item – say, a tee-shirt or an automobile – only because of its logo. Its value increases because we pay to advertise its brand, which has nothing to do with its functionality.

Motivation for most people is based on money, a pat on the head, or other recognition. This is called extrinsic motivation. On the other hand, if we engage in some activity because we really like what we are doing, we find that our motivational system is quite different and that we do not need to be given money, praised, or otherwise recognized by someone else for what we achieve. This is called intrinsic motivation. Our reward will be the satisfaction of having done something for its own sake, without the expectation of reward or compensation. Altruism comes under this definition.

The government encourages our focus on the materialistic treadmill in ways that are sometimes insidious. One of the key statistics zealously maintained by the government that measures the 'improvement' in the economy is the growth of Gross National Product, which means the number of things and services that people and businesses produce (and presumably purchase). We all have been taught to believe that growth is an absolute good and non-growth (called 'stagnation') is an absolute bad, even if we already have enough of everything to satisfy our human needs.

To measure the quality of life by how much the economy grows every year destroys the quality of life in its wake. I have never been able to accept that the quality of life depends on maximizing profit for the sake of "shareholder value" (and the compensation of the senior staff) when it comes at the cost of job insecurity, insufficient wages, lack of basic human rights such as health care and a decent education, the suppression of the right to organize into unions, the exhaustion of natural resources, and the pollution and destruction of the natural world. One of the greatest public servants in American history was Robert F. Kennedy, who believed that GNP measured everything "except that which makes life worthwhile." It is interesting that both capitalism and communism share the belief that progress is defined as more, and faster, regardless of the long-term losses involved.

The Mountain Climbing Treadmill

Robert Pirsig wrote a book about a motorcycle trip he took with his son. His ruminations while riding his motorcycle roamed widely, and I found many of them intriguing. For example, Pirsig identified a character flaw that he called "ego-climbing" but that for our purpose I am going to re-name the "mountain climbing treadmill." His description of ego-climbing was based on an attempt to circumambulate Mount Kailas, a mountain sacred to the Hindu, the Buddhist, the Jain, and the Bon (a pre-Buddhist Tibetan religion). Despite his interest (high) and his physical conditioning (excellent), Pirsig failed in his attempt to complete the 32-mile trip around the mountain (it has never been climbed) and returned home exhausted and dispirited. The pilgrims he met along the way carried on and successfully completed the goal of their pilgrimage.

What Pirsig realized, after he considered his failure, was that he had adopted the wrong mind-set. Motivation and physical conditioning were insufficient, and even counterproductive. His approach had been to try to "conquer" the mountain, and consequently he perceived each step as a burden that must be borne to reach the goal. He never noticed where he was because he was always looking ahead to see the point that he had not yet reached. When he reached the new point, it was no longer enough, and he had to strive for yet another new point. In retrospect, he concluded that if you spend your time looking up the trail and wishing you were farther along in your journey, then you are not only missing the pleasure of the climb, but you are also adding to your chances of failure. You will never reach your goal because each subgoal, once achieved, loses its ability to satisfy you, which leads to discouragement and eventually to 'give-up-itis.' You are on a mountain climbing treadmill. The Hindus, Buddhists, Jains, and Bons were successful in their pilgrimages because they saw each step as an act of devotion, and never worried about how much farther they had to go. Completing the journey was incidental to their ultimate goal, which was spiritual renewal.

There is a link between the materialistic and mountain climbing treadmills. The link involves a comparison of intrinsic and extrinsic motivation. Both kinds of treadmills involve extrinsic motivation, which diminishes our personal freedom. However, when we become deeply involved in something that derives from intrinsic motivation, we do not worry about acquisitions or attainments. We are free and feel the greatest satisfaction a human can enjoy because we are defining ourselves and not depending on rewards or the approval of others to define us. We have created meaning in human existence.

While I am suspicious of the materialistic treadmill, I am also unconvinced by its antipode, namely asceticism and denial. I am not sure I can go as far as David Hume when he wrote that "celibacy, fasting, penance, mortification, self-denial, humility, silence, solitude, and the whole train of monkish virtues" were actually pernicious vices, but I do sympathize with his point.

The Middle Ground

If neither the materialistic treadmill of Jeff Bezos nor the asceticism of Mother Teresa is the answer, what can we say about the proper relationship of humans to money? Is there a middle ground? Yes, I believe there is a middle ground, occupied by the worthy individuals whom you have met in Part I. Here are some examples of what I believe are healthy relationships to money, regardless of its source or the amount accumulated by any individual.

Peter Singer, who has provided us with insight already, had what I consider to be useful thoughts on money. He did not demonize money, and even suggested that accumulating vast assets was perfectly acceptable. But his caveat was that if one accumulated these vast assets, one had an obligation to distribute the majority (80% was his suggestion) of them to those in need. His idea of philanthropy was focused on the poorest of the poor and was based on a simple equation: I must not value my interests as more important than the interests of anyone else, just because they are my interests. This is a demanding value judgment, and one which I find hard to implement, but it does provide a target. Nevertheless, we have met several individuals in Part I who have met or exceeded Singer's standard.

Another good use of money is through taxation to support government expenditures and regulation. I am worried about greed and its consequences in an unregulated marketplace. Humans seem to be genetically hard-wired to be greedy, and capitalism (as already noted by

Adam Smith) is prone to excess and corruption. Unfettered markets have repeatedly led to environmental and social disasters. I also pity those who decry taxation as a disincentive to innovation and hard work. They will never know the joy of intrinsic motivation. Despite the inefficiency and bumbling nature of government, I feel that some functions are best removed from the maelstrom of the free market – public education, infrastructure, food and drug safety, health care, the administration of justice, and the like. These, in my view, are all human rights that should not be apportioned through competition, but should be available to all, regardless of circumstances. We have met a variety of individuals in Part I who are engaging in these types of activities.

Another interesting and productive use of money is through what are called "public private partnerships." This is a type of investment in which a private citizen or corporation invests in a public work, such as a road or a port. The investor expects a return on the investment, but the consequence of the investment is that there is a benefit to the public without the immediate financial burden of additional taxation. We have learned about several such examples in Part I.

Impact Investing is a relatively new phenomenon in the field of investments but shows great promise for the future. This type of investment has two components, as previously discussed in our meetings with the Compassionate Capitalists. First, it supports social goals, such as the environment, poverty alleviation, women's empowerment, or public education. Second, it is also expected to provide an adequate return to the investors. Since the amount of money invested by individuals far outweighs the amount of money available through philanthropy or government aid programs, there is great potential for impact investing to change the dynamics of an individual's use of financial resources. In the future, investing and doing good need not be separate but can be an integrated whole. In Part I, we have met three of the pioneers of this new form of investing.

Venture Capital and Angel Investing are additional uses for money which have positive social consequences. While these two types of investing do not necessarily have social or environmental goals, they do represent important variations on traditional investing. Investing in early stages of businesses, when the risk is highest, must be done by individuals with the capacity to absorb losses. In this way, venture capital and angel investing combine hard-nosed investment strategy with the encouragement of entrepreneurship. In Part I, we have met several individuals who have entered this field of investing.

Capitalism seems to work the best of all the philosophies of organizing an economy. Accepting capitalism requires an acceptance of the existence of private businesses. But what is the proper purpose of a private business? There have been many attempts to rethink the purpose of running a business. Who matters more? Or most? Shareholders? Employees? Customers? Senior executives? Neighbors? To my way of thinking, Konosuke Matsushita, the founder of Matsushita Electric Industrial Co., Ltd., in Osaka, Japan, in 1932 (now called Panasonic), had the best definition. Matsushita-san decided that the purpose of a private enterprise was to make a high-quality product that could be sold at a reasonable price and which would improve the lives of people. Profit, in his mind, was not a proper goal of a company, but merely a by-product of the successful implementation of the purpose of the company. That worthy statement of purpose was gradually forgotten by succeeding generations but could well be a lodestar for the future.

I worked at a business school for thirty years, and in the course of this career, I had the opportunity to encounter (too) many individuals who acquired (too much) money. I did not earn a lot of money because this was never my aspiration. And never once did I feel the slightest envy of those who had so much money, or any regret that I had not amassed a fortune. The "pursuit of more" always struck me as an empty life. Growing up as a history professor's son, not exactly as poor as a church mouse, but certainly not in the "Top 1%," I lived with the pleasant delusion that I was already the wealthiest person on earth. I was always surrounded by books, ideas, and the support of parents who believed that true value was defined non-monetarily. Why would I need anything else? Maybe a new baseball glove, but I could count on Santa Claus for the fulfillment of that kind of need.

Please do not misunderstand me. Like Peter Singer, I don't demonize money. I agree with Tevye in *The Fiddler on the Roof*, who voiced his opinion that "It's no shame to be poor ... but it's no great honor either." And I have never been a Marxist, not even in the heady days of the student rebellion at Columbia University in 1968. I always thought this idea of an international proletariat rising in unison was silly, not likely, and risky.

I quoted Bathsheba Demuth in one of the epigraphs to this chapter. She wrote about gold and its allure, but she was worried about the impact that an obsession with money had on the area known as Beringia and its naturally occurring inhabitants – whales, walruses, fox, and caribou. I share this concern as do the women and men you have met in Part I.

Those I have chosen from my vast Rolodex of over thirteen thousand people from eighty-five countries share a disposition when it comes to money. They are all capitalists, but they all fear for the consequences of an unregulated marketplace in which the gap between rich and poor constantly widens and in which people lose sight of the "common good." Future global prosperity and equity will increasingly depend on the capacity of well-meaning individuals from around the world to communicate using the same moral standards and vision of the appropriate role of money in society. I believe my friends are all harbingers of this future.

Tradition

It is no wonder that high officials in Canton, whose respect for scholarship far exceeded that for navigation and commerce and whose criteria of judgment were taken from the classics, poetry, and calligraphy, should despise the European barbarians. It is equally natural that the Europeans, bred in the tradition of western democracy and nurtured in the spirit of the new mercantilism, should consider the mandarins as bigoted and ignorant tyrants.

—Hsin-pao Chang, Commissioner Lin and the Opium War

Explaining the inevitability of the First Opium War

Tradition often derives from ancient practices, the customs and beliefs that we pass down from generation to generation. It was not always so. But as humans evolved, they also acquired such characteristics as "…delayed maturation and increased longevity, and therefore increasing overlap between generations and, with it, growing opportunities for cultural transfer, learning, and systematization of knowledge." We now perform certain rites and rituals because our ancestors did. This is one of the ways we maintain continuity with our past and one of the ways we find the courage to face the uncertainty of the future. "Tradition transforms truth into wisdom," hypothesized Hannah Arendt, "and wisdom is the consistence of transmissible truth." Without tradition, this line of argument goes, truth by itself is ephemeral. Without tradition, and especially before writing was invented, we would have forgotten the truths that previous generations discovered. We would have been afflicted with the epistemological version of "Fifty First Dates." The predilection to formulate traditions is one of the characteristics of consciousness that made us human.

Paradoxically, tradition is also repeatedly invented. During times of political and social change, we create new traditions when the old ones no longer suffice. When monarchy and church were replaced by the "nation" (and, sometimes, democracy), the old traditions did not provide the same comfort that they formerly provided society. Benedict Anderson hypothesized that we had to invent new traditions, such as maps, flags, anthems, and museums to replace the traditions of allegiance and obedience to a lord and master. When a "middle class" emerged from the industrial revolution, its members required new traditions to define themselves and to distinguish themselves from the "lower class."

Tradition is also context-dependent and changing the context may result in unanticipated consequences. In the days before printing, photography, and the internet, there was a traditional form of communication called storytelling. In retrospect, we have determined that it had to meet several criteria, probably not articulated at the time but still central to its meaning. One criterion was that it was not derived from current events; its provenance was a mystical past with no news value and so it lacked the obligation to be believable. A second criterion was that the story carried a lesson – something useful in a timeless sort of way – such as a moral, a proverb, or a maxim that could be applied to situations independent of time or place. A third criterion was its oral transmission, which required others to be listeners. The listeners, in turn, would eventually be the storytellers, perhaps embellishing or gilding the lily. Homer was probably the best-known storyteller of all time.

Later, mechanical means of reproduction created another form of communication. This form was called "information," which contributed to the decline of storytelling. Information required a different set of criteria. One criterion was that it had to be true – or at least plausible – which made it substantially different from storytelling. A second criterion was that information was always current. As soon as it was old, it had no value and had to be replaced by new information which would subsequently lose its value as soon as it was not new. One consequence of these criteria was the predominance of communication without a didactic thrust, although information frequently included opinion.

Current events, accordingly, are sources of information, but are irrelevant to storytelling in the Homeric sense. While information is not interesting the second time (unless it is lurid) and needs updates to hold the attention of its audience, the traditional story gains strength, like a hurricane approaching landfall, with its retelling. With the advent of information, not only is this type of storytelling at risk, but so is the art of listening. The context changes, a tradition is lost, and unanticipated consequences follow.

Tradition, following this paradox and context-shifting, cannot be restricted to the old and hallowed. It may, but it does not necessarily, last forever. It may, but not necessarily, be exclusively new. How would this understanding apply to my inquiry into intercultural communication? Early in my interviews, I discovered that tradition played an important role in the life of every one of my friends. I knew this because paying attention to their traditions helped me better to understand them.

However, their concept of tradition was more complicated than the celebration of idiosyncrasies and the straightforward passing on of beliefs and customs to the next generation. Each of my friends was aware of his or her roots and a careful steward of tradition, but none was burdened by the past. They are all traditionalists but none was afraid or reluctant to break from a tradition that inhibited personal growth or was dysfunctional in the pursuit of the common good. Before we discuss this common disposition, let us take a brief look at some traditions around the world.

Some Varieties of Traditions

First, sports. Sports must appeal to something visceral in humans, because every human society engages in sports. Professor Michael P. Lombardo hypothesized a "Darwinian evolutionary explanation for sport." He argued that "sport began as a way for men to develop the skills needed in primitive hunting and warfare, then developed to act primarily as a lek where athletes display and male spectators evaluate the qualities of potential allies and rivals." As hunting and warfare became less than universal preoccupations of the males in a society, sports took on added importance as ways for males to evaluate each other. Sports proliferated, according to Professor Lombardo, because males would create new events to avoid competing in sports in which they were likely to lose. Traditions soon followed.

Traditions have clearly defined roles to play in sports and involve the spectators as well as the players. For example, in baseball it is traditional for the entire audience (the "fans" in American baseball slang) to stand up and stretch just before the start of the seventh inning, which is seven-ninths of the way through the game. This is known, comfortingly, as the "Seventh Inning Stretch." Another interesting sports tradition is in crew, where the coxswain (the diminutive person who steers the shell, but who also has the authority to berate the much larger oarsmen with impunity) of the winning shell is thrown into the river by the eight victorious oarsmen (perhaps in retribution for the berating). Traditions enliven sport, give it passion and provide the continuity of stories from one generation to another. Sports traditions can have a dark side, and I will describe one of them later in this chapter.

Food is a subject laden with tradition, and every civilization has its traditional foods. The surprising aspect to tradition in food is that so few of the traditions bear even a passing resemblance to any other. Japan has sushi, which is imitated elsewhere but is nowhere else indigenous. Borscht and piroshkies are distinctively Russian. Hummus, tabouleh, and falafel are Middle Eastern. Shark's fin soup and bird's nest soup are Chinese. The list is endless. How you eat your food is also governed by traditions. The English eat quietly, with highly formalized and rigid manners. The Chinese eat robustly, with cacophony and camaraderie. Muslims do not eat at all during the daylight hours of Ramadan, but then break their fast at sunset every day with the Iftar, a traditional meal. Steven Pinker credits some of the decline in global violence to the admonition not to use one's knife to move one's peas onto one's fork.

Academic institutions the world over have their traditions, as well. When a student earns a degree, she is entitled to wear a flowing black gown with a "hood" of many colors and a "mortar board" hat with a festive tassel (usually gold in color) at her graduation ceremony. Occasionally the hat takes a different shape, such as a lamp shade or a fedora. This get-up is called "academic regalia" and is common to most academic institutions in the world, although the gown is lighter weight in Thailand than in Belgium. Most universities also have a tradition called "tenure," through which professors are appointed "without limit of time," with the goal of guaranteeing freedom of thought and expression. Since all universities have sports, frequently the academic and sports traditions overlap. Universities are among the world's oldest continuously operating voluntary institutions, and traditions no doubt have contributed to their longevity.

Clothing is one of the most traditional of subjects. Think of the Sikhs and their "5 Ks," two of which are clothing items (but all of which are "worn"). The uniforms that are traditional for a sport are virtually universal throughout the world, although they sometimes evolve over time (e.g., basketball "shorts" were quite short a generation ago but now almost reach the ankles). Women and men are frequently the bearers of tradition through their forms of dress, which can be regional, religious, or national. The sari is instantly identified with women from South Asia. The hijab identifies Muslim women. The Barong Tagalog identifies a Filipino man. Clothing is an emblem of the in-group.

Not surprisingly, there are thousands of artistic traditions. I have personally witnessed a single rose being thrown onto the stage from the fifth balcony of the Bolshoi Theater in Moscow after a particularly moving performance by a ballerina in Swan Lake. The entire audience stands up (politely, of course) during live performances of the Hallelujah Chorus in Handel's Messiah. Women play all the roles (both male and female) in Takarazuka, a Japanese musical theater troupe. Beijing opera is always divided into four traditional roles (Sheng, Dan, Jing, and Chou). Every society in the world, at every stage in its history, has produced art forms that involve traditions.

There are political traditions. Some political traditions enrich society and protect its members. Other political traditions range from the silly to the shameful. Richard Hofstadter in 1948 published a landmark book in which he concluded that the United States of America had a "common ground, a unity of cultural and political tradition," that survived any regional or personal disagreement and held the American civilization together. Despite repeated assaults on this political tradition, it has endured to the present time. In fifteenth century Europe, there were ceaseless wars that lacked any economic impetus. Why, then, did France invade Italy? According to Barbara Tuchman, tradition was to blame: "…war was still the assumed activity of the ruling class."

Meriwether Lewis described the traditional political system of Native American tribes in the upper Missouri River in the early nineteenth century as the reason for the unending cycle of intertribal warfare. He recounted an interesting interchange with a teenage warrior who patiently explained that the rate of internal leadership turnover was high, and that without war, none of the contenders for succession would be able to establish his qualifications. Narayana Murthy, founder and former chief executive officer of Infosys Technologies in Bangalore, once told me that the best way to understand India's political chaos was to think of the country collectively as the "world's largest traditional debating society."

One might say that religion is a seething caldron of tradition, with each sect casting their beliefs and customs as "The Truth" in an effort to encourage the faithful to behave. Huston Smith noted, "In human beings it is tradition rather than instinct that conserves what past generations have learned and bequeath to the present as templates of action." But then he noted that the Buddha "…preached a religion devoid of tradition." Confucius, on the other hand, "was all but obsessed with tradition." So it seems that different people, different religions, and different cultures may take alternative routes to this universal aspect of the human condition.

Noah Yuval Harari concluded that myths and traditions, which accustom people almost from birth to "behave in accordance with certain standards, to want certain things, and to observe certain rules," are the basis for the ability of humans to live together cooperatively. He calls them "artificial instincts" or "imagined orders," since they have no objective reality. When networked together, these myths and traditions become "cultures."

In my experience, tradition is an important source of a secure, stable, and deep sense of self-esteem and self-confidence. How do I know this to be true beyond my personal case? I have observed at close range dozens of societies around the world. Each one has traditions, all different and perplexing to the outsider, but warm and comforting to the child who has grown up with the certain knowledge that as the day follows the night, a special food or song, or decoration or ritual, will mark the next phase of the next year of her life. These well-worn and predictable banalities occurring with numbing precision help to give her the confidence – and the refuge – to overcome the challenges of the Black Swans she will inevitably meet. Traditions require time – unproductive time to the hyperventilating pace of the twenty-first century. But the time spent on traditions is as important as the time invested in sleeping. Traditions cannot be rushed or contracted. A tradition deficit can be as destructive as a sleep deficit.

Problematic Traditions

Despite the fact that humans seem to need traditions and imbue every single facet of their civilizations with traditions, these same traditions can cause problems. It is to some of these problems that I now turn.

Texas A&M is an American university that has traditionally valued the role that football plays in enhancing its reputation and in strengthening the sense of community among its students and alumni. Many sub-traditions developed over the years to encourage the enthusiasm of the university's constituents for its football culture. One of these sub-traditions involved building a bonfire, to which all the members of the community would be invited, as part of the effort to stimulate support for the home team the night before its annual game against its archrival (another sub-tradition). Part of the tradition stipulated that each bonfire had to be bigger than the previous year's bonfire. In 1999, the bonfire was based on a pyre built from 59 wooden telephone poles, and attracted thousands of students, alumni, faculty, and townspeople. It was a spectacular fire, but then something went wrong. The flaming pyre collapsed. Twelve people were killed, and twenty-seven others were injured. Tradition run amuck and young lives squandered. We cannot assume that traditions are an unmitigated good.

The telephone pole disaster ended a tradition instantaneously. Other traditions are identified as harmful only incrementally. For many generations there was a traditional type of humor which mocked attributes of ethnicity, disability, gender, and other characteristics. Over time, people came to regard this type of humor as unacceptable because of the pain it caused the people it mocked. Today, this type of humor is not considered to be funny and in fact is proscribed in polite society. A new social context has made a tradition unacceptable.

We have already spoken of the illusions of knowledge. Traditions can also be barriers to changes that are necessary for progress to take place. This turns traditions into burdens. Daniel Boorstin has written at length about the painfully slow process of overcoming the illusions of knowledge concerning global geography that were part of traditional Christian theology. He observed that it was more complicated "to imagine the unknown than to chart the outlines of what people imagined they knew." Traditional concepts, based on imaginary but firmly-held beliefs, stood in the way of thinking that would lead to what was still not known but was actually real.

Herein lies one of the fatal flaws of tradition left to its own devices, namely the destructive consequences of an unwillingness to change a tradition despite the logic of doing so. This is the opposite of the bonfire tradition, which relied on constant change until the change over-whelmed logic and common sense. Is there a middle ground? I am convinced that the brave and kind people you have met in Part I of this book represent this middle ground.

Seventeen Traditions – The Underlying Purposes Are All the Same

The people who populate this book are all mindful of tradition. In fact, they celebrate it to a high degree as storytellers and listeners. They cultivate it, ensure its continuity into the next generation and revere the comfort and security that tradition gives them. Tradition is, without any doubt, one of the dispositions that they share. And yet, many of them are rebels who broke with tradition and managed to lead purposeful and productive lives in part by breaking with tradition. Gary Wills captures the essence of how and why this can occur. In his view, tradition does not mean that nothing changes. In fact, "only a dead thing is immobile." He uses the analogy of a post painted white. If it is left alone, it will eventually be weathered to black. To retain its whiteness, it must be repainted, which Wills dubs "repristination." The same goes for human traditions, which will not stay the same just because they are untouched.

I believe that each of the people profiled in this book repristinated their traditions by celebrating them without being burdened by them. This is a crucial part of my understanding of tradition. The choices they made in their lives sometimes disturbed those who wanted to keep the traditions "blackened by time," but this commitment to maintaining traditions while not being burdened by them is part of what makes them all so estimable. They took risks in stepping outside of tradition, but never lost sight of the valuable parts of their traditions. They knew, deep in their hearts, that they could have the best of both worlds – a full and knowledgeable commitment to tradition, and the exhilaration of discovery, dispelling the illusions of knowledge. "Respect precedent but reject dogma," was how Robert Canessa summed up the concept.

Every one of them grew up in a society saturated with tradition. What made my subjects' concept of tradition memorable and universal was that they examined these traditions rationally and made individual decisions to embrace, respect, modify, ignore, or forcibly reject the teachings of their ancestors. You have met a Japanese man with an MBA from an American business school, Keisuke Muratsu, who decided to embrace an "important intangible cultural asset" of his country by learning the three-century old traditional art of Katoubushi. You have also met a Bangladeshi women, Durreen Shahnaz, who rejected the passive, submissive role that was traditional for women from her country, but still wears a sari for important occasions.

My inquiry into tradition, in its various guises, led me to several conclusions pertinent to my original hypothesis about intercultural communication. First, tradition is central to the self-concept of all societies. In order to transform truth into wisdom, every society has needed tradition. This means that all humans have the same bedrock of understanding of what tradition means. Second, all my friends recognized the importance of appreciating, respecting, and celebrating the traditions of other societies, regardless of how strange or illogical they may seem. Once you see past the oddities and recognize the reasons for the traditions, you can see that the "other" is no different from you. The superficial differences need not separate us since the underlying purposes are all the same.

Ambition

The people of the United States do not owe me another election. I hope that I am properly grateful for the one term of the Presidency which they gave me, and the fact that they withheld the second is no occasion for my resentment or feeling of injustice.

—U.S. President William Howard Taft

Only those are worthy to govern who would rather be excused.

—Confucius

Ambition is a complicated characteristic embedded in our genomes that has intrigued and all too frequently corrupted humans over the millennia. Certain types of ambition are clear cut and laudatory. An ambition to end hunger in impoverished communities. An ambition to find a cure for cancer. But I am talking here about ambition as the quest for money, power, and glory. I felt certain that this type of ambition, or more precisely its absence, would figure in some way in the stories of my heroines and heroes, who are all so humble and self-effacing.

I have always been suspicious of ambition which can lead rational, generous people to engage in devious and unworthy behavior simply for ego gratification – another case of extrinsic motivation – often with lamentable consequences. Just ask Macbeth. Ambition, as I saw it, might be rewarded in the short-term, but was unlikely to end well. I think that Tolstoy got it right: "The good cannot seize power, nor retain it; to do this men must love power. And love of power is inconsistent with goodness; but quite consistent with the very opposite qualities – pride, cunning, cruelty." Accordingly, I have long admired those who had no ambition at all, or who at least stifled it. I had even greater respect for those who achieved greatness while at the same time eschewing ambition.

Ambition to me is synonymous with selfishness, and I always thought that the world needed less of it. Furthermore, ambition is most often motivated by the desire for reward or praise, and as we have discussed previously, extrinsic, reward-based motivation rarely leads to freedom and autonomy. Adam Smith, from whom we took succor in our discussion of money, also had some thoughts about ambition: "For to what purpose is all the toil and bustle? What is the end of…ambition?… To be observed, to be attended to, to be taken notice of with sympathy, complacency, and approbation, are all the advantages which we can propose to derive from it. It is the vanity, not the ease or the pleasure, that interests us." The Buddha had perhaps the best assessment of ambition, finding it neither good nor bad but a simply meaningless cause of suffering.

I decided to explore some historical examples to see if I could clarify my thinking and learn if it was possible to enhance the flourishing of others without succumbing to ego-based ambition. My plan was to compare my friends to four historical figures who I believe achieved greatness without ambition.

First, Solon. Solon was an Athenian statesman who lived in the sixth century BCE. This was pre-democratic Athens and the city-state was in the midst of a crisis involving inequities in society, unsustainable debt, and growing demands for change. The people of Athens called upon him to help. He accepted the assignment, which gave him great powers. In quick sequence, he took action to solve the debt crisis and laid the foundations for Athenian democracy (for which Pericles would get most of the credit a hundred or so years later). When Solon completed the restructuring of the state to make it more equitable, humane, and stable, he demanded that the members of the Athenian Council swear an oath not to make any changes to his reforms for ten years. Being satisfied with the commitment of those in charge to maintain his reforms, he sailed into voluntary exile, also for ten years, thereby preventing the inevitable petitions for revision as well as disclaiming any interest in maintaining or increasing his control of the government. His devotion to the good governance of Athens was proven by his lack of ambition.

Second, Cincinnatus. Cincinnatus was a full-time farmer and part-time statesman who lived in Rome a hundred or so years after Solon. He too was called upon by his fellow citizens to help the state during a time of political distress. His duty was necessary because of the ongoing warfare with the Aequi, a tribe that was in regular rebellion against Rome. Fearing defeat, the Roman Senate asked Cincinnatus to take the role of dictator, which he accepted. Fifteen days later, having defeated the Aequi and restored peace to the empire, he resigned and returned to his farm. Nineteen years later, he was once again appointed dictator to save Rome, this time from a conspiracy by Spurius Maelius, a Roman plebian. Once again, as soon as he completed his task, he voluntarily resigned his post and returned to his plow. His devotion to the peace and harmony of Rome was proven by his lack of ambition, not once but twice.

Third, George Washington. The most famous of all Americans and a name known throughout the world, Washington served a pivotal role in both the War of Independence and the discussion of "what sort of government would emerge in the aftermath of a successful war." There was no blueprint to follow, and the Americans had to make it up as they went along. Six months after the defeat of the British in late 1781, one of Washington's officers in the Continental Army, Colonel Lewis Nicola, wrote him a letter proposing that he become King of the United States. Washington replied, using the circumlocutions of the time, that "If I am not deceived in the knowledge of myself, you could not have found a person to whom your schemes are more disagreeable." He further stated "If you have any regard for your country, concern for yourself or posterity, or respect for me, banish these thoughts from your Mind and never communicate as from yourself, or anyone else, a sentiment of the like Nature." Seven years later, when he was unanimously elected President on February 4, 1789, and inaugurated on April 30th of the same year, he repeatedly expressed his trepidations at having the proper qualifications for this high office and disavowed his desire to found a royal dynasty. This modest man, who bore himself with great dignity and integrity, never wavered in his absolute commitment to the ideals of the American Revolution and to the rule of law as set forth in the new Constitution, which had been ratified in 1788. Another man lacking in ambition but achieving greatness.

Fourth, Lin Tse-hsü. A little closer to our time, Lin Tse-hsü, a Confucian gentleman, was an official in the court of the Tao-kuang Emperor in the late 1830s when the scourge of opium was destroying China. Despairing of the human and economic consequences that the sale and consumption of opium were having on the population, the Emperor ordered Lin to proceed to Canton (the port through which the British imported the opium) for the purpose of ending the trade and the use of the drug. As Commissioner, Lin destroyed all the opium he could locate in Canton, as well as tens of thousands of opium pipes, severely punished the Chinese involved in the trade, and inadvertently precipitated the First Opium War. In the words of his biographer: "Lin Tse-hsü's political activity cannot be explained as a striving for personal aggrandizement. He was more concerned with effecting reforms than with his own political career."

I felt that my friends were the intellectual and emotional descendants of the lineage that ran through Solon, Cincinnatus, George Washington, and Lin Tse-hsü. I decided, accordingly, that a lack of ambition would be one of the dispositions that I would locate in the center of the Venn Diagram. I realized my conclusion was imperfect in a conversation with John Rice, Vice Chairman of General Electric. I spoke with John because he and Chanthol Sun (both of whom you have met in Part I) had joined General Electric at the same time in 1978 and have been close friends ever since. When we discussed the dispositions I had identified, he observed that they all matched well with the criteria for success at GE – with one exception.

> I think #8 – Ambition – may underestimate the motivation of people of this caliber... people on your list don't lack ambition – in fact they have burning ambition – but it takes different, positive forms that benefit large numbers of people instead of themselves personally.

John was correct; I had missed the forest for the trees. My heroes and heroines lacked personal ambition, but they all had boundless ambition for matters of principle, the amelioration of the lives of others, the correction of injustices, and leaving the world a better place than they found it. Ambition need not be a negative.

This new approach helped to explain Solon's motivation. He was ambitious, but for the welfare of the Athenian people and not his personal power. The same applied to Cincinnatus, who was intensely interested in and motivated by the welfare of the citizens of Rome. Similarly, George Washington overcame personal reluctance at the idea of serving as the first President of the United States because of his knowledge of "how much was riding on this attempt at republican government." Lin Tse-hsü was committed to using his authority only for the betterment of the Chinese people but needed ambition to pass the highly competitive examinations that allowed him to reach the level of government at which he could make a difference. The common feature of these individuals was a burning inner mandate for service to others that was detached from personal ambition for money, power, and glory. Another way to phrase this would be to call their intrinsic motivation "altruistic ambition," namely ambition that unselfishly benefits others, with no personal benefit, and sometimes at a cost, to oneself.

Ambition, I also learned, must be an active characteristic. Solon, Cincinnatus, Washington, and Lin were never passive. Gandhi's *Satyagraha*, often mislabeled, was anything but passive. James Boswell, the Enlightenment biographer of Samuel Johnson, wrote of himself, "It is difficult to make my feeling clearly understood. I may say, I act passively. That is, not with my whole heart, and thinking this or that of real consequence, but because so and so things are established, and I must submit." Boswell's biographer, Leo Damrosch, in turn noted that this was "inauthenticity: going through the motions mechanically because other people expect us to." My friends, as you have seen repeatedly in Part I, lived authentic lives because they never submitted to "so and so things" or what "other people expect us to do."

With this new understanding of the disposition that I labeled Ambition, I discovered an undercurrent of altruism, manifested in seventeen different ways. In the same manner that I was spiritually refreshed when my friends taught me new ways to forgive, I felt spiritually refreshed after my indirect journey following ambition. I am no longer at odds with the concept of ambition, now that I have a better grasp of its altruistic dimension. Indifference, I realized, was unlikely to be the precursor to altruism, or making the world a better place.

I reviewed the personal biographies of the members of my improbable group...Luis Andrade, who gave up a lucrative career as a consultant to follow in the footsteps of Great Uncle Alberto, himself a reluctant hero with a burning ambition to serve the citizens of Colombia in their time of need...Boediono, who rose to the vice presidency of a nation of over two hundred seventy-five million people without ever having sought higher public office...Chanthol Sun, who three times declined his country's leader's request to enter the government as a minister...Jacob Wallenberg, who declined the opportunity to amass great wealth in favor of serving the common interest of the citizens of Sweden...Rosanna Ramos Velita, who resigned from a lucrative position in international banking to devote herself to the well-being and economic stability of the poorest citizens of Peru...Michael Yu, who improbably became a billionaire but who intends to give it all away to support education, entrepreneurship, and creativity among the poorest of China's citizens. The list goes on and the behavior is analogous in each instance – intense ambition to serve, have a positive impact on others, and refuse to accept the world as it is but with a determination to make it what it can be.

For the eighth time, I had stumbled upon a common characteristic that resonated across civilizations, cultures, ethnicities, languages, spiritual traditions, cuisines, and all the other reasons that we as humans find it so difficult to communicate. There is no question in my mind that the women and men you met in Part I are ready, willing, and able to communicate effectively. Traditional antagonisms and historical hostilities mean nothing to them, and they would find it easy to understand and support each other's burning ambition.

Patriotism

Our country is the world; our countrymen are all mankind. We love the land of our nativity only as we love all other lands. The interests and rights of American citizens are not dearer to us than those of the whole human race. Hence we can allow no appeal to patriotism to revenge any national insult or injury...

—*William Lloyd Garrison*

Nationalism is an infantile disease. It is the measles of mankind.

—*Albert Einstein*

For as long as I can remember, I have felt that I was a Citizen of the World, even growing up as I did in a small town of 30,000 inhabitants in the northeast of the United States. I loved my hometown, but I never felt that it was better than anybody else's hometown. I celebrated the Fourth of July, but not because I thought my country was in any way superior to anybody else's country. Fundamentally, I was unable to understand why people felt so separate, so foreign, so in conflict. As soon as I was cognizant of the world at large, which was very early in my life, I wanted to explore everywhere, meet everyone, and embrace global citizenship. Language to me was always a bridge, and never a barrier. Distance was a luxury in which to indulge, not an obstacle to be endured. I grew up as a patriot but not a nationalist.

There exists some confusion and substantial disagreement about the definitions of "patriotism" and "nationalism," although people use these words frequently and often with vehemence. I do not intend to settle the argument in this chapter, but I do need to make myself clear. This will involve defining the two words and some of their subcategories as I understand them and as they relate to my hypothesis. I acknowledge and respect Benedict Anderson's eloquent thesis on the origin of nations as a new form of imagined community. My purpose is not to revise the understanding of the origin of nations but to reflect on some of the many forms of imagined community which have evolved. My definitions will accept the existence and ubiquity of nations and suggest a preferred way in which citizens (and governments) may behave with respect to their neighbors, and in which the people in Part I of my book have already elected to behave.

Patriotism

I define patriotism as the love of one's native (either by birth or by adoption) land, expressed through a variety of both symbolic and substantive measures. It need not refer to a state, or even a political entity, although in the twenty-first century that is its most common usage. Patriotism, in my definition, is a positive, emotional response to those traditions and memories with which one feels most comfortable. It is not exclusionary nor is it aggressive, and it has a moral component that can readily expand beyond political boundaries. Being a patriot does not involve believing and acting on the belief that one's native land is better than anyone else's native land. Furthermore, patriotism does not involve the assumption that you lose whenever someone else gains. On the contrary, patriotism is global in the sense that the patriot understands the interconnectedness of the world and celebrates rather than fears the "other." I am not sure if patriotism as I define it is naturally-occurring like DRD4-7r or learned like a taste for durian, but either source will suffice.

Patriotism – and world citizenship – as I define it is a necessary condition for peace. In this regard, I am moved by the wisdom of Immanuel Kant, who was a Citizen of the World, although I cannot find anything he wrote that uses those words. Nevertheless, he did write that:

> ... *the right to visit, to associate, belongs to all men by virtue of their common ownership of the earth's surface; for since the earth is a globe, they cannot scatter themselves infinitely, but must, finally, tolerate living in close proximity, because originally no one had a greater right to any region of the earth than anyone else.*

There are various flavors of patriotism. One is called civic or constitutional patriotism. It describes a polity in which people come together based only on their acceptance of a set of pluralistic, liberal, democratic values, rather than real estate, culture, language, or ethnicity. It can be, but is not necessarily, a state, but whatever the polity, it is based exclusively on values. Civic patriotism is designed to promote collaboration and benevolence rather than greatness and domination. The European Union is an example (however flawed) of this type of polity. Another form of civic patriotism is known as municipalism, a political philosophy championed by Murray Bookchin and practiced at the time of the writing of this book by the City of Barcelona. Municipalism is centered around autonomy for sub-state polities such as cities and regions, coupled with the authority to form affiliations with similar polities regardless of their geographical locations. The idea behind municipalism is the desire to fix problems, especially the problems of the most vulnerable members of society, rather than to gain and exercise power.

Nationalism

Nationalism, again according to my definition, starts with a core of patriotism, namely a love of one's native land. However, it takes on the additional characteristic of exclusivity and distrust of the "other." Nationalism, a relatively recent phenomenon, is an imagined reality, and was created for the purpose of social control by despots and even some democrats as a replacement for the roles played either by religion or royalty prior to the creation of "states" in the modern sense. Nationalism is negative in the sense that it emphasizes the interests of those living within the nation regardless of the interests or even to the detriment of people living in other nations. If it has any moral content, concern for others stops at its borders. Nationalism is a source of competition rather than collaboration and left to its own devices ends up as a zero-sum game in which everybody is worse off. It appeals to fear, distrust, and hostility under the cloak of group solidarity. Albert Einstein, in comparing nationalism to measles, at least held out the possibility of a cure. Benedict Anderson wrote that nationalism in modern history is analogous to neurosis in humans, both of which he laments are "largely incurable."

Like patriotism, nationalism has variants. One such variant is liberal or civic nationalism.

This is a relatively benign form of nationalism in which the polity is not defined by language or culture but by its political institutions and liberal principles, such as freedom, tolerance, equality, and individual rights. If you accept the basic premises of the polity, you can come from anywhere, believe in your choice of god, and speak any language. The common history of this type of nation is what the citizens write together, not what they brought with them. However, despite some similarities, liberal nationalism is not the same as civic patriotism. For the liberal nationalists, national identity is important for the purpose of knowing who they are and explaining why they should stick together. As Samuel Huntington (a well-known liberal nationalist) wrote, "We know who we are only when we know who we are not and often only when we know who we are against."

Leaders of and apologists for this type of state build their case on the importance of giving priority to their citizens, who owe little to citizens of other states except for the forcible export of their political system. The USA is a variant of this type of polity. This type of nationalism comes under a magnifying glass during times of crisis. Consider, for example, the dilemma faced by President Joe Biden in 2021 when the United States had more than enough COVID-19 vaccines to inoculate its population but hesitated to give some of the surplus to poor countries which in some cases had no vaccines at all. An easy and morally responsible solution would have been to donate the vaccine patents to the poor countries so that they or others could produce vaccines for their populations. That the pharmaceutical companies refused to consider this is an example of unconscionable greed in the face of human misery and suffering. It would be difficult to imagine a more direct assault on Singer's imperative of moral impartiality. President Biden's decision to donate five hundred million doses of the vaccine to countries in need was an exemplary act of moral rectitude.

Exceptionalism, a pernicious belief that the people and the form of government of one polity are better than any other, is often the lamentable consequence of a successful state based on this philosophy. Too many American politicians subscribe to this belief.

Under stress or under the control of a charismatic despot, liberal nationalism can degrade into ethnic nationalism. Ethnic nationalism is a form of nationalism based on shared ethnicity, including language and religion. National identity is important, and the nation is confined to or reserved for those people who share characteristics and excludes those who speak different languages, believe in different gods, have different physiognomies, and practice different traditions. The common history of this type of nation is drawn from the common historical experiences of people who have lived there from the beginning of the current dominant group. There is no room for a new history based on the contributions of immigrants. It is an exclusionary political philosophy. This is the opposite of civic patriotism. Ethnic nationalism is based more on real estate than on values. Nazi Germany was an example of this type of nation. South Africa under apartheid was another example.

World Citizenship

There is no inconsistency between being a patriot and at the same time a Citizen of the World. It is just as clear that a nationalist cannot be a Citizen of the World. All those who have been introduced in Part I are self-proclaimed Citizens of the World, while at the same time self-proclaimed patriots of the countries in which they were born or which they adopted. So obvious to me and my friends as an admirable trait, this characteristic is not yet self-evident to most of the population of the world. In fact, this feeling of global citizenship is shared by only a small percentage of humankind.

Peter Singer, who has been a constant source of comfort and inspiration in the writing of this book, has spent his career thinking about the biological and cultural sources of ethics. He notes that in the early stages of human societies, it was prudent for groups (defined by language, culture, or genetically determined characteristics such as skin color) to fear and be hostile towards those who were different because they constituted threats. In modern, multi-ethnic societies such as the United States, this hostility is both atavistic and dysfunctional. Consequently, norms have evolved that are designed to override hostility to people who are different, regardless of whether these differences are culturally or genetically based. What can this evolution of attitudes teach us about the role, and quite possibly the dysfunctionality, of nationalism in a multi-ethnic world?

I believe that the time has come to acknowledge that nationalism is a behavioral vestigial organ. The world is too small, too interconnected, and too dependent on meaningful altruism by all humans to continue to fight over meaningless distinctions that are no longer necessary, desirable, or have the functionality that brought about their existence (whether biological through evolution or cultural by experience) in the first place. There are some enthusiasts of this proposition, including Yuval Noah Harari, who takes what to me seems to be a desirable but probably unrealistically optimistic view when he states that "nationalism is losing ground" and that "states are fast losing independence."

Benedict Anderson makes an interesting case that "print-capitalism" not only helped to create "nation-ness" but was essential to this process. Will it be the case that "digital-capitalism" will help to create "global-ness" and bring all world citizens together? It is true that print-capitalism also depended on a single vernacular to allow the citizens of a nation to feel this sense of community, and the global community of humans is unlikely ever to speak a single language. However, machine learning has already progressed to the point at which we can simultaneously and at no cost have any written or spoken language translated into any other language. Unfortunately, this does not yet seem to have accelerated global-ness, but at least mechanically it is now possible, and the access will only get increasingly seamless.

Steven Pinker got it right when he noted that "Many peaceable countries today are in the process of redefining the nation-state by purging it of tribalistic psychology. The government no longer defines itself as a crystallization of the yearning of the soul of a particular ethnic group, but as a compact that embraces all the people and groups that happen to find themselves on a contiguous plot of land." This sentiment is consistent with Singer's notion of the dysfunctionality of my definition of nationalism, and supportive of my definition of patriotism.

This disposition is entitled "Patriotism" for a reason. This is the type of political philosophy in which I, and all those profiled in Part I, believe. A number of them have suffered from nationalism in one or another of its variants. The world is less peaceful, less prosperous, and less just because of the abuses of nationalism. I do not share Huntington's description of the world and its civilizations. My conclusion is that there are universal dispositions, but that they are not inherent in ideologies, politics, economics, or cultures. They are inherent in humans. The thirteen dispositions that I describe in this book are, I believe, universal. The result, in my view, is that we are not the same, but neither are we necessarily in conflict. We can learn to get along with each other because we are human. I believe that the subjects of this book are the harbingers of a "global spring" that will someday replace the system we have now. They have gone beyond the illusion of knowledge that is an obstacle to discovery on twenty-first century earth.

Intercultural communication – this book's category on the bookstore shelf – is embraced by patriots and disdained by nationalists. For the brave and hospitable individuals whom you met in Part I and who form the database for my hypothesis, it is easy to communicate between and among cultures. They have no trouble conceiving of themselves as Citizens of the World and acting accordingly. This is undoubtedly one of the reasons I chose them for my inquiry, since I feel the same way. It is not an effort on my part or on their parts. However, I recognize that not everybody feels this way; in fact, most people do not. This is why I call my friends the harbingers of a new world. This, I feel, is humanity's best hope for the future, and I am counting on nationalism, exceptionalism, Huntingtonism, and all their variants to recede, perhaps not as quickly as Harari predicts, but perhaps as inevitably and inexorably as Pinker has discovered. It all comes back to my hypothesis, that intercultural communication – and all the benefits that derive from its effective implementation – can be facilitated and augmented by patriotism practiced as defined earlier in this chapter.

Adventure

We were setting out into terra incognita, marked only by blank spaces on the maps, magnetized by the ambition of the explorer.
—Henrich Harrer
Seven Years in Tibet

I think whatever I shall meet on the road I shall like; and whoever beholds me shall like me.
—Walt Whitman
Song of the Open Road

When I have been truly searching for my treasure, I've discovered things along the way that I never would have seen had I not had the courage to try things that seemed impossible...
—Paulo Coehlo
The Alchemist

The tenth disposition in the center of my Venn Diagram is adventurousness, which is not really a moral disposition since those without it are not reproachable. I once met a man who said that he had no time for adventures because he had to be home every day to feed his collection of scorpions, tarantulas, snakes, and lizards. I respect his choice but declined an opportunity to join him for dinner in his home.

Loving adventure is an unending joy to those who do. I have always been interested in adventure, both personally and vicariously. I was stimulated by what I read, and even more by what I dreamed. This interest, as far as I could tell, started at birth. It is a predilection and may even be genetically hard-wired. Back in the introduction to Luis Andrade (page 15), I wrote about DRD4-7r, the wanderlust gene. If the science behind the DRD4-7r theory is true, then there is no doubt that I have it, and in this sense I am very distantly related by blood to all the people whose lives I have chronicled in this book.

When I was very young, I read a book called *Seven Years in Tibet*, written by an Austrian adventurer named Heinrich Harrer who so enthusiastically adapted to Lhasa (where he lived from 1946 to 1952) that he became the confidante of, and tutor to, the teen-aged Dalai Lama. This book did not inspire me to be an adventurer because that was in my blood already. But the book did give me goose bumps. Sixty years later, I returned to the identical copy of this book that I had read when I was eleven years old and found the corner of one page turned down. I re-read the page and all my excitement was reanimated. Harrer had begun his book "All our dreams begin in youth…The men who went out to explore new lands or with toil and self-sacrifice fitted themselves to become … the conquerors of the great peaks – to imitate such men was the goal of my ambition." I have not yet visited Tibet, but as noted in the fourth disposition, I climbed into the Himalayas from the Nepal side, reaching 5,280 meters and just a few (but treacherous) kilometers short of Tibet itself. I sensed the spirit of Harrer everywhere I looked.

I read another book as a young boy: *Kon-Tiki* by a Norwegian adventurer named Thor Heyerdahl. This is the story of the author's 1947 voyage by raft in an attempt to verify his hypothesis that pre-Columbian South Americans could have crossed the Pacific and settled in Polynesia. Whether or not this voyage proved anything was to me beside the point. The adventure was what mattered. I never duplicated anything even close to this adventure, but it formed a central core of my attitude about the world and my role in it.

Another of the books that energized me as soon as I learned to read was *New Worlds to Conquer*, by an American adventurer named Richard Halliburton. This book described his journey around and through Central and South America in the early twentieth century. My favorite part was when he swam through the Panama Canal, insisting that he be charged a fair toll, based on his "tonnage."

Ernest Shackleton was a British adventurer who undertook his adventures during the

"Heroic Age of Antarctic Exploration" in the early twentieth century. Shackleton took three voyages to Antarctica, the most celebrated being his 1914 attempt to cross the continent of Antarctic from sea to sea, via the South Pole. The expedition failed; but in the act of failing, he lived through an adventure that lives on today. "The whole undertaking was criticized in some circles as being too 'audacious.' And perhaps it was. But if it hadn't been audacious, it wouldn't have been to Shackleton's liking." Shackleton and his men took great pleasure in their adventure, even when in the direst straits. This was written by one of his men in his diary when they were stranded on an ice floe, their ship having recently sunk, with no hope of rescue: "One of the finest days we have ever had…a pleasure to be alive."

These vicarious adventures when I was young allowed me to learn about myself. They constituted my apprenticeship in adventuring. By the time I graduated from high school, I was frothing at the bit to engage in my own adventures. There was never any doubt in my mind that this was the life I was meant to lead.

Ants in Their Pants

The DRD4-7r gene must have run rampant on every continent during the Age of Exploration that flourished from the fourteenth to the sixteenth centuries. What an exciting time to be alive! Risky, but exhilarating. When I have felt tired and discouraged waiting for a delayed plane in Jakarta or standing in a seemingly endless airport security checkpoint line in Buenos Aires, I consoled myself by remembering that I need not worry very much about sea voyages, disease, inaccurate maps, or the illusions of knowledge that created so many unnecessary impediments for adventurers.

What a thrill to be Muhammad Ibn Battuta on his first Hajj in 1325. Or to be Zheng He in 1405, commanding a vast navy that ventured out to bring new tributaries under the benevolent gaze of the Emperor of China. Or to be Bartolomeu Dias in 1488 and to discover that the continent of Africa does not end with a precipitous drop off the face of the earth but with a simple turn to the northeast. Or to be Amerigo Vespucci at the dawn of the sixteenth century and understand, for the first time, that the New World recently discovered consisted of two continents and not a land bridge to Asia. Or to be Vasco Núñez de Balboa, "silent, upon a hill in Darien…" Or to be Yuri Gagarin, the Russian Cosmonaut who was the first human in outer space in 1961. My first circumnavigation was from JFK to Paris to Seoul to JFK. It was before the collapse of the Soviet Union, so there were no polar flights. We went around the long way, but the entire trip was three segments of less than twelve hours each.

As President, Thomas Jefferson was committed to the concept of a nation stretching from the Atlantic to the Pacific. He found a man with "undaunted courage" to lead an expedition up the Missouri, across the Rockies and then down the Columbia to the Pacific.

His name was Meriwether Lewis, and he was the spiritual ancestor of every man and woman who was introduced in Part I of this book. Lewis was the archetypal adventurer, born into a "country that was a nursery of explorers." He had no choice but to be an adventurer. "His desire to see new lands, to explore, to roam was insatiable..." From Lewis' journal, written just at the moment of departure from the last outpost and as the expedition entered the true unknown: "I could but esteem this moment of my departure as among the most happy of my life." Lewis had come to a point that he had longed for, worked for, dreamed of all of his life. "He was ready, intensely alive..."

Returning one final time to the genetic mutation that may have occurred some 60,000 years ago and that may have made such an important contribution to the adventurousness of the subjects of my book, I will leave this topic with an intriguing hypothesis to consider. According to a study of a tribe in northern Kenya called the Ariaal, those individuals with the DRD4-7r gene tended to be better fed and stronger than those without the gene, but only if they were nomadic. By contrast, those with the adventure gene were weaker and more emaciated if they lived a sedentary existence in a settled village. "A restless person may thrive in a changeable environment but wither in a stable one." No wonder, I thought to myself, that the adventurous people I chose to illustrate the hypothesis of my book are all so healthy, strong, and well-fed.

Although my principal focus has been on adventure that involves travel, not all adventurers go somewhere; and I have equal respect for the adventurer who makes audacious intellectual journeys without ever leaving his parlor. Prince Henry the Navigator, after all, never left Portugal. Isaac Newton was another individual who went on adventures that changed the world, but which unfolded in the English countryside rather than in the South Atlantic during a storm. As described so well by Edward Dolnick, "with a trumpet flourish," Newton deduced Kepler, deduced Galileo, explained the planets, the moon, the tides, and central to it all – gravity. In short, the "System of the World," all from his mother's kitchen table. It is difficult to imagine a "nobler goal," or a "greater adventurous spirit."

Harmonious Joy and Hope

This same spirit lives in all those I have written about in Part I. You have met seventeen individuals who were all "ready" and "intensely alive," two of the essential characteristics of the true adventurer. The interesting – crucial – point is that they share this characteristic, despite the fact that they are representative of such wildly dissimilar ethnicities, cultures, religions, languages, and professions. Whether it is a Cambodian Buddhist man, an American lapsed Fundamentalist woman, a Peruvian Catholic woman, or an Ivoirian man with Animist roots, you have learned that each has been animated from birth with this spirit of adventure.

There is no question in my mind that a love of adventure helps to tie together all of humanity.

For me, and I suspect others, adventure is its own reward. Nothing else comes close – not recognition, not fame, not wealth, not power. There is something intoxicating about adventure. One passage from Dostoyevsky's *The Idiot* has stuck in my mind since I first read the book when I was a high school senior. Prince Mishkin, the protagonist of the novel, was an epileptic, and before each seizure, "…with extraordinary impetus all his vital forces suddenly began working at their highest tension. The sense of life, the consciousness of self, were multiplied ten times at these moments... His mind and his heart were flooded with extraordinary light; all his uneasiness, all his doubts. all his anxieties were relieved at once; they were all merged in a lofty calm, full of serene, harmonious joy and hope." This is the feeling that adventure always generates in me (although I never had an epileptic seizure).

My book's hypothesis is that there are common human dispositions and predilections, and that these common traits make intercultural communication not only possible but also accessible and fruitful. An adventurous spirit is one of these dispositions shared by those gallant individuals whom you have met in Part I. What they share is more important than what separates them, and this sense of adventure I have found in my friends demonstrates to me once again that there are no foreign lands. We can build strong bonds through sharing stories of our adventures. In this way we will understand each other better and ultimately build trust.

Impact

A life is not important except in the impact it has on other lives.
—Jackie Robinson
I Never Had It Made

It would be difficult to identify a human who did not have an impact on other humans. It is the nature of the beast. Originally this impact was determined by consanguinity. We care for, protect, and favor our children over all others. This is what has been termed "in-group bias" and at the most profound level pertains to those with whom we have blood relationships. This is also the nature of the beast. These in-groups are immutable. If we were not compelled biologically to do this, children would not survive, and our species would quickly become extinct. On an expanded dimension, mutable in-groups can include additional categories, ranging from baseball teams and religions to street gangs and nations, to which we have feelings resembling loyalty to blood relatives. Hence, "When you're a Jet, If the spit hits the fan, You got brothers around, You're a family man!" Attachment to in-groups, social scientists and geneticists have suggested, is something we cannot control as it has been selected genetically over hundreds of thousands of years.

This genetically determined in-group behavior can have dysfunctional impacts. In 1996, Samuel Huntington hypothesized that "Unless we hate what we are not, we cannot love what we are." This hypothesis troubles me a great deal, and I cannot subscribe to it. Twenty-three years later, with additional authority based on developments in the field of genetics, Nicholas Christakis wrote, "The capacity for making friends comes with a capacity for making enemies." The impact of this type of in-group behavior is catastrophic, as it has been for millennia. Although it is probably foolish on my part to disagree with these distinguished scholars, I think they are wrong. And even if they are right, they are wrong in assuming that we are in some kind of genetic jail and cannot escape.

As humans evolved and developed relationships outside their consanguineous in-groups, they discovered some advantages in having positive impacts on others to whom they were not related by blood. At times, the impact was inadvertent. In the mid-sixteenth century, Nicolaus Copernicus changed the world profoundly, and set in motion a series of scientific advances, when he posited a heliocentric system. But his revolutionary discovery was initially an unanticipated by-product of his efforts to improve the computation of planetary positions. There are many other examples of inadvertent impact, from Alexander Fleming (penicillin) and Wilhelm Conrad Roentgen (x-rays) to Antonie Philips von Leeuwenhoek (bacteria).

This chapter, however, deals with a third type of impact, namely deliberate impact motivated by altruism, behavior which unselfishly benefits others, unhinged to kinship, traditionally thought to be with no benefit to oneself, and sometimes at a cost to oneself. These are the conscious actions of individuals who feel a personal obligation to find a cure, correct an injustice, stamp out intolerance and bigotry, help others less fortunate than oneself – to make the world a better place – and then set in motion a process that achieves this goal. This is what Jackie Robinson had in mind. Auguste Comte, the nineteenth century French philosopher, coined the term "altruism" in reaction to the "egotism" that he perceived as being pervasive in the post-revolutionary era. This definition of the word accurately describes what I mean by impact in the context of the men and women you met in Part I of this book. Altruism is a vital and infinitely valuable concept that is accessible to anyone and can serve us all.

As with in-group behavior, we can ask if altruism is genetically predetermined or learned through culture. My conclusion is that the answer to this question is irrelevant. My examples come from a wide variety of cultures, regions, ethnicities, and spiritual traditions, but they all share an identical bias to be altruistic. Whether it is predetermined by natural selection, or invented by choice, or learned by training, there is no reason why we cannot be altruists. Since I have observed this characteristic across the seventeen cultures represented in this book, I conclude that there is no reason why this cannot be a universal moral disposition.

Peter Singer

In my ruminations on this disposition, as on so many other dispositions, I have found the work of Peter Singer to be helpful in clarifying my own feelings about altruism (which is an ethical doctrine) and its impact. Singer asks whether there is any universal ethical concept. He concludes in the affirmative, by stating that, when making ethical decisions, "my interests count no more, simply because they are my own, than the similar interests of others." One might argue that this concept is too simple. But on reflection, I find that it becomes more complex and often difficult to implement.

Having argued that one's own interests should have no greater value than the interests of anybody else, Professor Singer takes the next step, putting this universal ethical imperative into practical terms. He argues that ethical reasoning leads us "towards a more universal point of view... The circle of altruism has broadened from the family and tribe to the nation and race, and we are beginning to recognize that our obligations extend to all human beings." Ethics, then, requires us to be altruistic and, hence, to have a positive impact on others. Put in reverse order, impact which is motivated by altruism is both profoundly and universally ethical. The concept transcends borders. There are no foreign lands.

The Hindu

It is interesting to me how much this concept resembles one of the fundamental precepts of Hinduism. Huston Smith wrote about the third (of three) great limitations on human life as believed by Hindus: "A man who identifies with his family, finding his joys in theirs, would have that much reality," argues Smith. "A woman who could identify with humankind would be that much greater." To the Hindu, the greatest triumph of the human spirit is to identify with the greatest number of others, and then to have the most widespread impact.

The Mt. Everest Rule

Mt. Everest, whom we met during our pursuit of the third disposition, *Resilience*, has been under assault by mountaineers for almost a hundred years. In the modern era, climbers have brought with them enormous amounts of non-biodegradable equipment ranging from tents to oxygen tanks. Regarding Sagarmatha as their personal garbage pail, these thoughtless individuals have simply left behind their trash, which had turned the formerly pristine wilderness into a gigantic, high altitude dump. Offended by the disrespect of the litterers, the Nepalese government instituted a new regulation in 2014. Simply put, every climber who goes past Base Camp must bring back a minimum of eight kilos of garbage, in addition to their own trash. This has become known as the Mt. Everest Rule, and fits well with the definition of altruistic impact: behavior that unselfishly (they have been told to do it but let us assume that they concur with the imperative) benefits others, without any personal benefit and at a cost to oneself. Nobody knows whose trash they are bringing out, and they do not know who will enjoy the scenery more because of the reduction in garbage at the top. The interest of you as a summiteer is of no more importance than the interest of the next summiteer.

Pierre Leroux

One of my personal favorite examples of an altruistic impact is not well-known, but only gains in value because of its obscurity. Described in some detail by Professor John Tresch in his book on "romantic machines," this impact involved a nineteenth century French philosopher and inventor, Pierre Leroux, who developed the first mechanical process of setting type for printing newspapers, magazines, and books, called the "pianotype."

"How quaint!" you interject, as you glance up from your e-reader.

But listen to how Professor Tresch describes Leroux's philosophy of "freedom of information," and how the pianotype would have an impact on us all. Leroux believed that "printing was 'the one among all the industries which has the most to do with thought, and which is its most direct messenger,' and accordingly 'had a unique social destiny.'" Leroux declined to patent this device because "owning a monopoly over its use would run counter to this goal.... [to] make the censors' job impossible by vastly increasing the number of publishers." Leroux benefited many others, with no benefit and at some cost to himself.

Dramatic Altruism

There are some interesting, indeed dramatic, examples of altruistic impact that receive substantial publicity. Bill Gates has given away ("at a cost to oneself") more money, even on an inflation-adjusted basis, than anybody in world history. Of course he has accumulated more money, even on an inflation-adjusted basis, than almost anybody in world history. But the decision to make these donations was his. And he has given most of his money away to help save the lives of the poorest of the world's poor, who are disproportionately affected by diseases that no longer threaten people in the richer countries of the world. His foundation has awarded over US$6 billion for "global health." Two of his goals are to eliminate polio and malaria (to say nothing of a simultaneous effort to eliminate various "neglected" tropical diseases) from the category of illnesses afflicting humans. If he is successful, he will indeed have had an enormous impact. And it is beyond dispute that he receives no benefit from eradicating polio or malaria, other than the equal benefit that all 7.7 billion humans would enjoy. This is an excellent example of what Peter Singer calls "effective philanthropy."

Altruistic impact comes in different degrees of luminosity, some of them too intense for most of us. I once met a man named Zell Kravinsky, who exemplifies the extreme end of luminosity. Zell is a polymath who earned 2.5 doctorates, made a fortune in real estate, gave away all his money, and finally donated one of his kidneys to a stranger who was dying of kidney disease. His reasoning, as he relates the story, was mathematical: he had a 1 in 4,000 chance of dying from either the operation to remove one of his kidneys or the aftermath (such as losing functionality in his remaining kidney). Under the circumstances, "...to withhold a kidney from someone who would otherwise die means valuing one's own life at 4,000 times that of a stranger," a ratio Kravinsky termed "obscene." While Singer finds Zell commendable, I think that most mortals would find it difficult to follow his philosophy to its logical conclusion.

Surprisingly, although probably not directly as a result of Kravinsky's example, a new form of "out-group altruism" (not a contradiction of terms in this case) has arisen in so-called "kidney chains." One of the frustrations of family members of individuals who need kidneys is that they are frequently unable to donate one of theirs in support of their relative because of tissue or blood mismatch. In a kidney chain, a relative of an individual in need of a kidney donates a kidney which is used by a stranger. A relative of the stranger who receives the kidney then makes an anonymous donation of a kidney which is used by yet another stranger. Those who have donated kidneys to strangers receive priority in receiving kidneys from strangers. A fascinating example of in-group bias converted into out-group altruism.

The Rest of Us

Is there any hope for the rest of us who do not have a spare billion and who might not be ready to give up a kidney? Looking at this question from a less dramatic perspective, blood donations are a good example of out-group altruistic impact that can be undertaken by most people. The blood you donate is pooled (not literally) and used as needed. You will never know the name of the person who receives your blood. And the donation is certainly of no benefit to the donor and there is no question that it is "at some cost to oneself." The supply of donated blood rarely meets demand, and yet this simple, painless, act requiring about thirty minutes of our time can make each of us capable of saving another life.

Shorten the Distance Between the Heart and the Deed

In this book, we have been looking at acts of altruistically-motivated, out-group impact that are somewhat less dramatic than those of either Bill Gates or Zell Kravinsky, but that are commendable for their motivation and their consequences, and much more manageable for most normal humans. Importantly, I believe that they all meet the tests of Auguste Comte, Peter Singer, the Hindu, the Government of Nepal, and Pierre Leroux.

Anything we do counts, but we must be doers and not simply talkers. Matthieu Ricard wrote that "...compassion without action is hypocritical," and that "Altruism...remains limited if it is confined solely to its emotional component." Raphael Lemkin, who coined the word 'genocide,' and forced the world to outlaw its practice, called his effort a desire to "shorten the distance between the heart and the deed. To live an idea, not just to talk about it." I have found that each of my friends is an altruist with a bias for action. The route that each person has taken is quite unlike the route of any other, and for this reason, impact comes in many forms and intensities. But there is an endless number of ways that the world can be impacted for the better.

Some of my exemplars have elected to use great fortunes to have a positive impact on the world. Some started with no money at all, but starting poor is not an impediment to having an impact, and neither does starting rich make one's altruism less praiseworthy. Several of them contribute to an improvement in the lives of others through organizations and institutions they personally created. Others among the seventeen change the world very slowly, literally one person at a time. Still others have had an impact on the world by preserving cultural traditions through live performances. And there are three government officials who represent all that is desirable and praiseworthy in public service. The key to this attribute of impact, as far as I am concerned, is their choices to make the world a better place – to have an altruistic impact. They are all intrinsically good people who concluded that their "obligations extend to all human beings." Whether these decisions are genetically guided or culturally determined is, as I suggested above, irrelevant. My anecdotal survey of seventeen different countries and cultures found a common human interest in having an altruistic impact beyond their in-groups. If it arises independently in countries as geographically and culturally diverse as Cambodia, Sweden, and Uruguay (and fourteen other countries), then I am persuaded that any of the world's seven billion humans can make the same choice. It seems that the altruistic impulse exists in all cultures. If we can share this impulse, nurture it, and recognize it as essential to the future of human life, then there is hope. Intercultural communication can be facilitated through the implementation of this common moral disposition.

H.O.P.E.

The longer I live, the more I read, the more patiently I think,
and the more anxiously I inquire, the less I seem to know...
Do justly. Love mercy. Walk humbly.

—U.S. President John Adams

Their position was ..., a place where no man had ever been before,
nor could they conceive that any man would ever want to be again....
Still the men showed an astonishing optimism.

—Alfred Lansing
The Endurance

Nothing great was ever achieved without enthusiasm.

—Ralph Waldo Emerson

H.O.P.E. I know it may seem corny, but I am starting this chapter with an acronym. Humility. Optimism. Positivity. Enthusiasm. My friends share a disposition that is a homogenous mixture of these four characteristics. The qualities are not the same, but they are most often found together. One rarely finds an enthusiastic person who is a pessimist, for example. Like Nemo in the anemones, they do not cause each other harm. Consequently, I have titled this disposition, *"H.O.P.E.,"* and even the meaning of the word unintentionally created by the acronym is apt. Remember what President Snow said: "Hope is the only emotion stronger than fear."

By now the reader will have spotted certain recurrent themes in this book. One is intrinsic motivation, which is a characteristic shared by all of my friends. Intrinsic motivation, to recapitulate, is the motivation that comes from within and does not need a reward in the form of a pat on the head, remuneration, or the votes of an electorate. Another recurrent theme in this book is the conviction that while there is no meaning *of* human existence (in the sense of an ultimate goal that humans are supposed to attain); there is meaning *in* human existence (that is, goals defined and chosen – and perhaps attained – by each human). These two themes are also pertinent to this chapter, since H.O.P. and E. all derive from intrinsic motivation and create meaning in human existence.

Many people, unfortunately, do not intrinsically exhibit H.O.P. and E. You can fake these qualities for a while, but since these characteristics are all the result of intrinsic motivation, you cannot dissimulate for long. But you can also develop them, over time, by an act of will. It is possible that H.O.P. and E. (or a lack thereof) have genetic roots or components, but in my moral universe, no one can use genetics as an excuse to avoid them.

Humility

What is humility? Traditionally, humility was self-denigration, thinking of oneself as unworthy or unimportant. This is an attitude central to the theology of certain monotheistic religions and is based on deference to an omniscience. This was a wasted emotion, in my opinion, as it was dependent on what I believe is a fiction. In modern psychology, humility is described as "an ability to accurately acknowledge one's limitations and abilities and an interpersonal stance that is other-oriented rather than self-focused." Humility is a core attitude of "givers." In his book *Give and Take*, which has already proved relevant to several of the chapters in this book, Adam Grant makes this same distinction, repeatedly citing the behavior of humble givers as great catalysts of the enhancement of human flourishing.

I prefer the current definition and Grant's distinction, both of which focus on the avoidance of aggression, pride, bigotry, intolerance, and arrogance. A person with humility can feel worthy and even important but does not insist on making himself the center of attention. The humble person listens more than talks and empathizes more than asserts. Shyness is a form of humility that is often associated with low self-esteem. I believe that this is unfair to the person perceived as shy. Gandhi was cripplingly shy but learned to think of his shyness as his "shield and buckler." He concluded that his shyness was of assistance to him in his search for truth. The individual with humility facilitates rather than orders and brings out the best in people rather than searches for the worst. Humility at its best is generated by a respect for all others rather than a fear of one.

Aggressive behavior was once necessary for survival, and natural selection favored the transmission of this trait. Modern civilization has reduced the need for aggression, while increasing the need for collaboration. Accordingly, humility has increased in value. In this way, culture may be influencing genes and accelerating genetic evolution, if humility is now more linked to reproductive success than aggression. Let's hope this is true, while remembering that genetic evolution is painfully slow (from the human perspective).

The humble person is likely to be harder on himself than on others. Michael Yu, whom you have met in Part I, built a multi-billion-dollar company with tens of thousands of employees, with a leadership style based on humility. He wrote: "[*humble people are*] not afraid of self-negation or self-criticism because they know they will reach a higher level of being. Being modest, tolerant, generous, disciplined, and gentle to others, they are lenient towards others, but harsh on themselves."

Although all the dispositions and predilections I have described in this book are important, I believe that humility may be the secret code word that unlocks the vault. The reason is that a special kind of humility – cultural humility – is the foundation of intercultural communication. I have been constantly reminded that every interaction I have with the men and women who constitute my research pool is an intercultural negotiation. My ability to work with them, celebrate our commonalities, and communicate effectively depends to a high degree on my willingness to recognize and override my biases, accept their differences without judgment, and remember the importance of cultural humility.

Optimism

What is optimism? When I was younger, I thought that Dr. Pangloss was an optimist: "This is the best of all possible worlds." Now that I am older, I am not sure about this interpretation. In fact, I think that Pangloss may have been a pessimist. If this is the best of all possible worlds, then he denies the possibility of progress and improvement. I am not a Pollyanna, and I accept that there is much that needs improvement in our world. But we are making progress. I am convinced by Steven Pinker's conclusion that we are living in the least violent period in human history. I am a child of the Enlightenment: I believe that through science and reason, things can and do get better; not that we are already in the best of all possible worlds. The improvement will take constant effort paired with constant vigilance, and there will be setbacks and disasters.

Princeton Professor Sebastian Seung studies the "connectome," which he defines as the "totality of connections between the neurons in a nervous system." He has written that "... the genomic worldview is pessimistic...", but "your connectome changes throughout life, and you have some control over that process. The connectome bears an optimistic message of possibility and potential." We can choose the meaning in our existence. If we choose optimism, we are happier and more likely to be satisfied with our existence. We will also be busy, because there is still much to be done. Predicting success is a mindset. We may not always be successful, but the chances are much greater if we are convinced of at least the possibility of success.

The optimist lives in a world characterized by self-fulfilling assumptions. Some people may cynically suggest that these assumptions are dangerously naïve, and it is possible that these prophecies at the outset may not even be true, but they can become self-fulfilling. Optimists, moreover, are pronoiacs.

When one has the good fortune to be a pronoiac, whether genetically or by choice, there is no time wasted on worry, disharmony, envy, or any of the other negative emotions. Pronoiacs truly believe that optimism is realism. This is how mountains are moved and ridiculous dreams are achieved. "I never seriously considered the possibility that I would not emerge from prison one day," wrote Nelson Mandela. "I am fundamentally an optimist."

Positivity

What is positivity? Positivity is a companion emotion to optimism. A positive person is one who focusses on the present and is determined to find the good (or at least the humor) in most situations that we face every day. My mother's definition of rain was "liquid sunshine," and I have never heard a better example of positivity.

Life has challenges. Things go wrong. There is no meaning of human existence. We are all alone. But if we choose to be positive, we know that, with Bobby McFerrin, "This too will pass." Positivity resembles resilience, but it has additional characteristics. You can be positive even when things are going well. Positivity does not require a problem, but it may involve a challenge. Nirmal Purja Magar climbed all 14 of the world's 8,000-meter peaks in a seven-month period, a feat that had previously been considered impossible. "... I hope to have proven that anything is possible with determination, self-belief, and positivity," wrote Mr. Purja after reaching the top of the fourteenth and final peak.

This attitude derives from intrinsic motivation and does not require a reward of any kind. The acid test is contingency. True positivity cannot depend on circumstances being supportive; on the contrary, it is when circumstances are the worst that the person with positivity is most treasured. The positive person carries on and fixes the problem. Roberto Canessa (who you have met in Part I) nearly died in a plane crash but solved innumerable problems and saved the lives of seventeen others. He went on to a career as a pediatric cardiac surgeon and expressed his enduring positivity when he described his approach to his patients: "I can't help it. I identify with any living being who has to overcome impossible odds." In this instance, Roberto is expressing neither optimism (his patients sometimes die) nor humility (he is confident in his ability to help his patients); in this case he is expressing the irresistible urge within him to be positive. His friend Juan Berchesi confirms his fundamental attitude about life: "Nothing can stop him. There is nothing he believes he cannot do. Roberto is the most positive person you will ever meet."

Enthusiasm

What is enthusiasm? Enthusiasm is usually characterized as intense, energetic interest in something. It is distinct from humility, optimism, and positivity, but related to all three. Enthusiasm can be the source of H.O. and P., or enthusiasm can be the result of H.O. and P. This is the fourth of the characteristics that are likely to create meaning in human existence, and it always derives from intrinsic motivation. You cannot force anyone to be enthusiastic. Each of us must take personal responsibility for our own enthusiasm. But the consequences of being enthusiastic are manifold. The Beatles got it right: "...the love you take is equal to the love you make." The more enthusiasm (love is the strongest and most widespread version of enthusiasm) you put into any effort, the more you benefit. Indifference or hostility never generated health or happiness. The acid test, again, is contingency. Enthusiasm must not be allowed to dissipate in the face of a problem.

An important feature of enthusiasm is that it does not acknowledge boundaries. One of my favorite examples of an enthusiastic person is Steve Jobs' collaborator in the early days of the development of Apple Computer, Bill Atkinson. Bill understood that they never would have invented such cool stuff if they had known it was impossible to do so. Atkinson said, "Because I didn't know it couldn't be done, I was enabled to do it."

Various thinkers already cited in the present study have spoken about this concept. Steven Pinker summarized the concept quite well when he wrote, "...outstanding thinkers ... are troubled by the boundaries that custom places on their reasoning, for it is in the nature of [enthusiasm] that it dislikes notices saying, 'off limits.'"

A Flame That Leaps

H.O.P. and E. are all characteristics that must be intrinsic. You can force people to be obedient, but you cannot force someone to have these characteristics. The best you can hope for was described by Plato: "... after much converse about the matter itself and a life lived together, suddenly a light, as it were, is kindled in one soul by a flame that leaps to it from another, and thereafter sustains itself." This flame of H.O.P.E. has been kindled in all seventeen of the men and women that you have met in Part I. Their biographies introduced those from whom the flames leapt – mothers, fathers, teachers, and others. H.O.P.E. defines the attitudes of people who are curious, open-minded, and exhibit cultural humility. They are also non-judgmental, and despite the mistaken reputation of humble people, not easily manipulated. They have the titanium backs described in the first disposition. These are people with whom you want to associate because they make you a better person. And returning once again to my hypothesis, H.O.P.E. is a universal disposition, shared by people of every civilization, enabling fluent and peaceful intercultural communication.

Spirituality

Religion did not create morality.
—Brian Hare
A Most Interesting Problem

"What I believe in is spirituality. Not the rituals or trappings of one religion or another, but the spirituality that comes from knowing yourself and understanding your relationship to the external world," said Gowri Ishwaran, speaking with conviction on a temperate December New Delhi evening that corresponded to a very cold Philadelphia morning. "Honesty. Generosity. Tolerance. Integrity. Courage. Love. Hope. Forgiveness. And so on. These are the simple values that define spirituality for me."

At first, these words seemed to me almost banal, and yet this may be the most important message of the entire book, which is why I saved this Disposition for last. We will need to explore this concept in some detail because the 17 women and men you have already met exude the spirituality that I have come to believe is such an important asset in the effort to communicate interculturally.

"We need to teach children to incorporate these values into their habits and into their reflexes," continued Mrs. Ishwaran. "They will all be tested, and when they are tested we want to be sure that their instincts guide them in the direction of making decisions based on good spiritual values."

Mrs. Ishwaran, a Hindu by birth, was the founding principal of the Sanskriti School in New Delhi. She now serves as President of the Global Education & Leadership Foundation (tGELF), created and funded by Shiv Khemka. You met both Gowri and Shiv in Part I.

For most of the research for this book, I was reasonably certain that my dispositions would be limited to twelve. I had not originally intended to have a thirteenth disposition, or a disposition labeled "Spirituality." In fact, I started with what I now believe was the foolishly self-limiting assumption that most of my subjects would be atheists or, at the extreme end, agnostics, thereby rendering spirituality irrelevant. But as I conducted interviews, this thirteenth disposition became increasingly apparent. I learned from a number of my interviewees that the harsh word "atheist" was an indication only of an incomplete understanding of the concept of spirituality. I now understand that all humans embrace spirituality, but there may be as many people in the world who do not include an omniscient being in their concept of spirituality as who do. Much to my delight, I discovered that a "devout atheist" is not an oxymoron. Arguing about whether there is an omniscience is, I came to feel, a pointless distraction from considering what really matters. Arguing about "right" or "wrong" contaminates the quest for wisdom and compassion, as the Buddha helpfully pointed out to those who gathered to learn from him.

Just because neither Guru Nanak nor Confucius believed in a god does not make Sikhism or Confucianism any less spiritual than the Islam of Mohammed or the Christianity of Jesus. It is irrelevant to spirituality how the values are derived or communicated, and whether or not these values are discussed in a so-called "house of worship." Indeed, by 2015 the Dalai Lama himself had "turned away from organized religion…and started to emphasize the secular values of compassion." The French philosopher Michel Terestchenko referred to the need for "complete conformity and fidelity to [self]." Mohandas Gandhi, one of the most spiritual humans who ever lived, defined his religion as "self-realization or knowledge of the self." He read the Gita, the Bible, and the Koran – each with an open mind – as part of his "experiments with truth."

Let us consider for a moment a crucial aspect of this disposition of spirituality, which is truth. I do not mean truth in the sense of what your mother told you always to tell, but truth in the metaphysical sense, the goal of science, morality, and consciousness. In the predominant Western spiritual traditions (Christianity, Islam, and Judaism) people are taught that there is a true account of everything and that everything has a true plan. This is self-evident because each of these three religions specifies an all-powerful, all-knowing creator, who had a plan for everything. From the time of the formation of these religions and their respective set of beliefs, the faithful have assumed that humans are at the top of God's totem pole, the ultimate truth of the hierarchy of plants and animals. This is called anthropocentrism and it is a fallacy.

Charles Darwin threw a monkey wrench into anthropocentrism when he "replaced the intentional creator(s) with a purposeless natural force." He concluded that there was no plan and that the best we could do would be to describe from whence we came, and to observe what advantages (and therefore more likely reproductive opportunities) the process of natural selection had so far conferred on humans. If there was no divine plan, there was no ultimate truth for which to strive, and we were left at the side (not the top or the bottom) of the totem pole without any guidance as to what to do next. We would be required to synthesize our own values, ethics, and spirituality, based on what seemed to work best for the perpetuation of the species and flourishing in the lives of all. I think that Mrs. Ishwaran was describing the outcome of this quest for meaning. Jean-Paul Sartre was, in my evaluation, a very spiritual person. His philosophical conclusions are not different from Charles Darwin's scientific findings.

Some Viewpoints from Religious (Not Spiritual) Perspectives

The Pew Research Center interviewed 40,080 people in 40 countries between 2011 and 2013 with the goal of determining global attitudes about the relationship between a "belief in God" and perceptions of morality. In 22 of the 40 countries, "clear majorities" felt that it was necessary to believe in God in order to be moral and to have "good values."

According to the Pew Survey Report, most people in the world believe that you cannot be moral unless you believe in God. This gives me some cause for anguish, although not for the reason that you might think. Since there are many different entities referred to as "God" (remember that the survey was conducted in 40 countries world-wide), this means, implicitly, belief in "My God" and not belief in "The God" or "Your God." If you believe that one cannot be moral unless one believes in My God, then you believe that most of the people in the world are not moral, because no single religion or god is the faith of a majority of the world's people. I cannot share the conviction that most people are not moral. How can you engage in intercultural communication if you think the majority of your interlocutors are immoral? This is Huntington's thinking, and I believe he is mistaken.

Do you find this an unfair judgment of organized religion? Please recall that "Over the last two millennia, monotheists have repeatedly tried to strengthen their hand by violently exterminating all competition." Mini- and micro-aggressions provide interesting datapoints in the absence of overt physical violence.

After having been cornered by a Christian evangelist, Gandhi wrote, "Mr. Coates… wanted to convince me that, no matter whether there was some truth in other religions, salvation was impossible for me unless I accepted Christianity which represented the truth, and that my sins would not be washed away except by the intercession of Jesus, and that all good works were useless…." Intolerance wrapped in bigotry.

Members of the Mormon religion hold a biannual conference in Salt Lake City. At one of these conferences held on April 4, 2015, L. Tom Perry, a member of the faith's "Quorum of the Twelve," made a speech in which he asserted that a marriage must be between a man and a woman. "We want our voice to be heard against all of the counterfeit and alternative lifestyles that try to replace the family organization that [our] God Himself established," Perry stated. All I can see in that statement is bigotry wrapped in theological hocus-pocus, unrelated to spiritual themes of compassion and tolerance.

Bobby Jindal, the elected governor of the state of Louisiana in the United States and (briefly) an announced candidate for the presidency of the United States in 2016, made a trip to Europe and on his return declared (without any factual basis for the declaration) that he discovered that there were "no-go zones" in Europe for non-Muslims. He made a speech about this alarming "discovery" in which he reassured his audience that in the end, "Our God wins!" The group to which he made these remarks was the "American Family Association," a 500,000-member group which operates a radio network hosted by Bryan Fischer, who wrote, on August 1, 2014, "I have contended for years that the First Amendment [to the U.S. Constitution], as given by the Founders, provides religious liberty protections for Christianity only." More intolerance wrapped in theological hocus pocus, unrelated to spirituality.

"The full story of religion," wrote Huston Smith, "is not rose-colored; often it is crude. Wisdom and clarity are intermittent, and the net result is profoundly ambiguous." Smith's observation was particularly illuminating because it encouraged me to look at the ideas of religions rather than at the means of holding the attention of the faithful, proselytizing the unconverted, and encouraging financial donations to support the hierarchies.

Steven Pinker was not as circumspect as Smith in his evaluation of the facts of religious history. Writing at the end of his book on the decline in human violence over the centuries, he concludes that the world's religions were not helpful in the civilizing process: "The scriptures…were used to rationalize the massacre of infidels, the ownership of women, the beating of children, dominion over animals, and the persecution of heretics and homosexuals ….The theory that religion is a force for peace…does not fit the facts of history."

How can the world communicate and cooperate if most people believe that most of the other people in the world are not only immoral but also condemned to eternal damnation (whatever that is)? What role can spirituality play in a world divided into walled enclosures of religious bigotry?

True Spirituality

I observed that all my subjects are spiritual in Mrs. Ishwaran's sense of the word. There was no question in my mind that spirituality was a common disposition, but it expressed itself so differently in each case that I had been at risk of missing it. Now I had to double back from this dead-end and work to understand how each of the 17 arrived at what was clearly a common notion of spirituality, as so artfully and passionately expressed by Mrs. Ishwaran.

I observed that few (most never did, some did so in a perfunctory manner, only a few did so with unvarnished enthusiasm) of them regularly entered a house of worship, but they all talked of spirituality as a driving force in their lives. In fact, I eventually concluded that each of the other twelve dispositions had its origin in this thirteenth. However expressed, even by the most ardent atheist, spirituality was the ultimate source of all the characteristics that I found so appealing in them. Through self-knowledge, expressed with "complete conformity and fidelity to self," they were able to be true to their fundamental natures and to act with compassion.

Another key factor in the spirituality of my heroes and heroines is that they cherish and practice these values independently of the instructions, approval, or validation of the hierarchy of the religious traditions in which they were raised. One of my favorite descriptions of the role of the rituals they no longer need is from Vassily Sidorov, a Muscovite whom you met in Part I. "Some say," wrote Vassily, "that the choice of Orthodox Christianity in the 10th century was made on the back of costume design and the attractiveness of ceremonies rather than a fundamental, ideological, spiritual, popular analysis or process." Vassily and my other 16 friends expect neither reward for good works, nor punishment for moral failings. Their actions are motivated by self-knowledge and the determination to live with authenticity.

Religion, I concluded, is at best an "ambiguous" source of the high moral character of the individuals whom you have met in Part I. Their spirituality, on the other hand, is not in the least ambiguous. All my friends, I believe, have achieved a high level of self-knowledge and consequently, understand quite clearly their "relationship to the external world." The outcome is compassion, with which they can serve others without expectation of personal benefit, achieving the elusive goal of altruistic love. The way they behave is a true reflection of their inner selves and an accurate expression of what they believe in their hearts. This, to me, is the essence of spirituality. For all my friends, their spirituality is defined as the expression of their freedom and autonomy. They have all shortened the distance between their hearts and their deeds.

We will most probably never know for sure who is right and who is wrong, since faith is what Yuval Noah Harari calls a "subjective reality," which exists only if people believe it. My conclusion is that "right" and "wrong" are irrelevant, and anyone who insists on using these terms is merely misunderstanding spirituality's true nature.

The Venn Diagram Is Now Complete

This is the last of my dispositions – moral and otherwise. The reader has met 17 individuals from almost as many spiritual traditions, including several Buddhists, at least one (and probably two) Animists, a small collection of Christians (including a lapsed Fundamentalist), a Hindu, a Sikh, some Muslims, a smattering of Confucians, an avowed atheist (who recently built a chapel on his farm), and quite a few syncretists. There is some overlap here, since all have taken spiritual journeys during their lives and several have been the offspring of interfaith marriages.

They are all, despite their differing traditions, deeply spiritual in the sense that Gowri Ishwaran stated, namely "the spirituality that comes from knowing yourself and understanding your relationship to the external world." My conclusion – not so different from the Hmong and not so different from the Buddhist– is that everything is a spiritual problem, spirituality is the solution to every problem, and we all have control over our own spirituality if we are true to our authentic selves. I like the way Hazel Rowley described Jean-Paul Sartre's defense of Existentialism, which I believe is as spiritual a philosophy as any religion imagined by humans:

> In truth, existentialism was neither a pessimistic nor a negative philosophy, Sartre told the audience. Its doctrine was that since God does not exist, man makes himself... "Man is responsible for what he is... We are alone, without excuses. This is what I mean when I say that man is condemned to be free."

My conclusion is that intercultural communication is facilitated when you are free, but conscious and respectful of spirituality. And by "free," I do not mean without responsibilities to others, which is selfishness. Religion often gets in the way of intercultural communication because it is exclusionary. The freedom of spirituality opens up the possibility of communication.

Part III
Concluding Thoughts

Concluding Thoughts

Men often hate each other because they fear each other; they fear each other because they do not know each other; they do not know each other because they cannot communicate; they cannot communicate because they are separated.

—Martin Luther King, Jr.
Stride Toward Freedom

The belief that there are foreign lands is an illusion of knowledge, as persistent and incorrect as the pernicious belief that humans are divided into different races identifiable by skin pigmentation. But my believing that there are no foreign lands was not enough. Did anybody else share this belief? I am an empiricist; I need some evidence other than my naïve idealism that this belief might be widespread. I have always felt sure that there are universal characteristics and dispositions that would facilitate intercultural communication, and which would establish a common basis for all of us to perceive the humanity of all others. My life's mission, I found, was to make inquiries into this topic, in the hope of finding clarification, if not proof.

My observations over a lifetime of global travels, combined with the qualitative data provided by the 17 close friends I made around the world, supported the idea that others shared this belief. This evidence did not prove anything, as I have repeatedly reminded myself. But it did answer – at least to my satisfaction and I hope to yours as well – the four questions I raised in the Preface to this book: Why had I chosen these 17? What moved me to respect and have affection for them? Were there characteristics that they shared? And if they did share characteristics, were there broader conclusions that could be drawn from that discovery? I decided to be satisfied with answers, if not proofs.

We have come a long way together. Adding up the journeys from one city to the next, we have taken a virtual voyage of 107,160 miles, or roughly four times the earth's circumference of 24,901 miles. We have now visited and become acquainted with 17 individuals born in 17 countries, speaking 13 mother tongues, deriving from a variety of spiritual traditions, representing many of the world's ethnic groups, and engaging in a rainbow of professions. I have learned through painstaking study that they are all, in the aggregate, really the same person. This composite person could provide, I believe, a promising way of dispelling the illusion of knowledge that there are foreign lands.

The concept of imagination is worth considering here. As far as we can tell only humans can imagine. Pigeons do not have a concept of justice and salamanders do not use money. Neither human rights nor *renminbi* exist in nature, but they have proven to be useful ways of describing imaginary realities that enhance the flourishing of human lives. Both concepts depend on shared belief, which itself is made possible by imagination, which in turn has proven to be advantageous to *Homo sapiens*.

I believe in the value and importance of being able imaginatively to enter the mental worlds of others who are initially significantly, but ultimately only superficially, different from oneself. A leopard cannot enter imaginatively into the mental world of an antelope and feel sympathy. But any member of the human race can do this. I am convinced that because we can do this (even if it requires an act of will), we will be better able to imagine "what could be" and in this way define a world in which *Ahimsa* is the dominant force, replacing thermonuclear weapons.

One of my goals in writing this book has been to stimulate the imaginations of as many people as read it by describing in detail the mental worlds of my friends, many of whose cultures, languages, and histories may be unfamiliar to my readers. I suspect that few people have had the good fortune I have had to become so well-acquainted with such a variety of people, and I felt an obligation to share what I discovered. The reader will know by now that I find these individuals to be worthy of emulation, and I believe that by entering into their mental worlds, even if only partially, the rest of us can benefit in many ways.

In my own lifetime of global peregrinations, without any specific plan to do so, I have stumbled upon seventeen brave individuals who have used their imaginations to dispel many illusions of knowledge that still exist in the world. Despite the fact that a number of the people in this book are citizens of nations with which my nation has had or continues to have substantial disagreements, the participants in this book told me their stories openly and honestly, without dissimulation, disingenuousness, or exaggeration. I sat at their tables and we had no clashes, disagreements, or misunderstandings. They were all willing to admit ignorance, and to take the leap of faith to acknowledge that some of the things they had been taught were not true. As they gained knowledge and examined their deepest and most authentic values, they all became free and autonomous. I have learned a number of essential truths from these people. The following is just a sample:

- Intercultural communication is aided by being transparent and having the courage of your convictions.
- Striving to be better than you need to be is never wasted.
- We all need resilience because the world, while better than it used to be, is still turbulent and occasionally dangerous.
- Forgiveness is a powerful asset that helps us as much as it helps others.
- Acknowledging the free will of others, as well as accepting responsibility for ourselves, unleashes opportunities.
- Money is less important than many people think, except when it can empower others to achieve what we already have.
- Tradition turns truth into transmissible wisdom, although we need to watch out for dogma, which is sometimes mistaken for wisdom.
- Ambition is an important attribute, as long as it is focused on the common good instead of personal gain.
- Patriotism is a life-affirming disposition, but we must guard against its evil twin, nationalism.
- Altruism is the source of impact that affirms the moral imperative of the equal consideration of interests.

- The quartet of humility, optimism, positivity, and enthusiasm are values that are inherent in all languages, civilizations, histories, and spiritual traditions.
- Spirituality is a necessary ingredient in intercultural understanding, but religion is neither necessary nor sufficient to be moral.
- And, to bring my book full circle, there are no foreign lands.

A Walk Along the Schuylkill

I live in Philadelphia – the Kyoto of America – and every other morning at 6:00 am, rain, snow, or shine, I take an 8-mile walk along Martin Luther King, Jr. Drive, which follows the Schuylkill (please do not try to pronounce this word unless you are Dutch) River, which itself separates West Philadelphia from Center City Philadelphia. During every season of the year, it is a beautiful and peaceful refuge in the middle of a congested and noisy city.

As I walk along the river, I pass under seven bridges – some towering a hundred feet over me, some just a few feet above my head; some designed for trains, others for automobiles, humans an afterthought. To me, the salient feature of all the bridges is the type of construction, which varies among stone, reinforced concrete, and steel. The bridges built from stone are the most impressive. Gigantic bocks of granite in original condition, hand-hewn more than a century ago, are better than they have to be, especially in comparison with the more recently constructed, but already rusting steel and crumbling concrete with its exposed rebar. The stonemasons of these sturdy bridges would have felt an affinity that transcends language and culture with the woodworkers who have patiently rebuilt the Ise Grand Shrine in Japan to such a high and unnecessary standard for more than a thousand years.

On my walks I am also constantly reminded of the inefficiency and the redundancy of nature. Deer, rabbits, bullfrogs (heard but not seen), woodchucks, squirrels, robins, sparrows, crows, at least half-a-dozen varieties of duck, turtles, and flocks of Canada geese (with goslings in the spring) have brightened many of my mornings. We certainly do not need as many species of birds as exist; nor as many different species of mammals that call the slim forests home. But I also reflect on the fact that nature, because of (and not despite) its inefficiency and redundancy, is profoundly resilient, and has survived and evolved for billions of years. Meanwhile, human society, which strives endlessly for efficiency and constantly tries to eliminate redundancies, is fast hurtling towards an apocalypse of its own making as it assassinates the resilience of nature.

Frequently on these walks, I have ideas, flashes of inspiration, insights into problems, or solutions to complex sentences. I usually forget these moments of *satori* by the time I return home, or if I remember them, they are hopelessly corrupted. But there is one idea I had repeatedly that I remember with crystal clarity. It occurred to me on mornings when the sun poured down like honey on the forest and the water, and on mornings when the snow fell softly but relentlessly. This idea involved an observation about which I wrote on the first page of this book. In the Introduction, I stated my regretful conclusion that the wealth and power that certain countries amassed gave their inhabitants the idea that they were morally and cognitively superior – not just richer and more capable of killing people – to others they encountered.

This hubris came about in large part because of a characteristic that I have repeatedly observed in this book, namely the love of adventure. And it made a certain kind of sense. If you had the money and technology to encourage those among you with the DRD4-7r gene, then they would go out and discover people who were poorer in physical assets and less well-armed. Since these explorers rarely had any interest in communicating with the people they encountered, it was not a big stretch of the imagination for them to decide that exploiting or exterminating them would be an easy way to solve problems, amass more wealth, and prove their superiority. The result was a long arc of history – 400 years – characterized by reprehensible behavior. Slavery proved to be an irresistible source of inexpensive labor. When slavery became less respectable, colonialism replaced it with attitudes and behaviors that were little changed. Imperialism fed the egos of the rich and powerful.

After the Second World War, and especially in the early 1960s, colonialism came to a close, although like the freed slaves in the United States, the citizens of the newly independent countries were manipulated, excluded from the economy except for the most menial tasks, and left a legacy of abject poverty, abysmal education, and rotting infrastructure. The world still suffers from this towering moral failure, and a challenge for the next generation is to rectify the intolerable inequities perpetrated by our ancestors and inexplicably tolerated by us.

Farewell

President John F. Kennedy met with the White House gardener soon after he was inaugurated on January 20, 1961. The gardener asked President Kennedy what flora he would like to see in the grounds of the White House. The President responded with a request for a specific type of tree. "But," the gardener responded with some concern, "that species does not flower for many years."

"In that case," Kennedy replied, "you had better plant it today."

Acknowledgments

Tennyson is a wonderful poet, and his "Ulysses" is an inspirational poem. I will begin my acknowledgments by quoting him, that "I am a part of all that I have met." My acknowledgment list, no matter how long, cannot hope to thank all those who have, directly and indirectly, contributed to this book, which has been a lifetime in the making.

I am deeply indebted to the heroines and heroes who shared so much of themselves with me, and I will once again thank Luis, Boediono, Chanthol, Dawn, Eric, Rosanna, Durreen, Shiv, Jacob, Anthony, Kei, Arantxa, Leslie, Vassily, Roberto, Jim, and Michael. I feel very close – almost like family – with these 17 individuals whom I have come to know so well and for whom I have such respect and affection.

I also want to thank the many family members, ancestors (posthumously), friends, business associates, enemies, rivals, and spiritual advisors who consented to speak with me (in some cases indirectly) about my heroines and heroes, and about life in general. They include Tan Sri Dato' Dr. Zeti Akhtar Aziz, Alberto Lleras Camargo, Donald Lim, Andres Maldonado, Hugo Baquerizo, Yopie Hidayat, Farid Harianto, John Riady, Abdilla Toha, John Rice, Sotha Sun, Ratavy Sun, Nyny Sun, Mony Sun, Anvanith Gui, Ruben Hines, Ann Daverio, Aimé Bwakira, Rob Henning, Cristina Velita Labourieux, Dina Weitzman, Maya Chorengel, Johanna Posada, Shabnam Shahnaz, Sue Suh, Jorge Born (Jr.), William Engels, Jorge Born the 4th, Mario Fernandez, Gowri Ishwaran, Urvashi Khemka, Yngvar Berg, Peter Wallenberg, Beatrice Bondy, Sputte Baltscheffsky, Olive Hamilton Russell, Curtis Brashaw, Anthony Ogilvie Thompson, Masumi Muratsu, Ken Muratsu, Midori Muratsu, Hur Kwangsoo, Kozo Yamamoto, Beatrice Affron, Rosemary Ogle, Emilia G. Ayala, José Ignacio Ochoa, Charles Tseng, Lin Tse-hsü, Gary Burnison, Nancy Garrison Jenn, Ken Jarrett, Lamia Boutaleb, Youssef Boutaleb, Kenza Boutaleb, Hicham Qadiri, Koo Chen-fu, Chester C.Y. Koo, Cecilia Yen Koo, Lydia Chao, Victoria Sidorov, Veronika Sidorov, Dmitry Razumov, Irackly Mtibelishvily, Larissa Vassilievna Ivkina, Mohammed Ali Ettehadieh, Fadi Arbid, Ammar Al Khudairy, Romain Benoist, Kaia Arbid, Laura Surraco, Juan Berchesi, Maria Isabel Varela, Sergio Abreu, Pablo

Vierci, Nando Parrado, Alberto Gari, Louis Siani, Bao Fanyi, Wang Xiao Wen, Zhou Chenggang, and Jamie Yu.

Although the cultural mistakes and unintended insults on these pages are my personal responsibility, I owe a great debt of gratitude to many people (in addition to those profiled in this book) who patiently introduced me to other countries and cultures. They were my teachers and taught me, above all else, the value of tolerance and understanding. These include Sehoon Lee (Korea), Bong Suh Lee (Korea), Wang Xi (China), Phillip Wu (China), Kohei Takubo (Japan), Minako Shimanuki (Japan), Kaneyoshi Saitoh (Japan), Angel Corcostegui (Spain), Sebastian Escarrer (Spain), Felipe Oriol (Spain), Roberto Mestre (Argentina and Cuba), Jean Louis Goma-Ballou (La République Centrafricaine), Manu Chandaria (Kenya and Africa), Anil Ambani (India), Narayana Murthy (India), Keshub Mahindra (India), Miran Sarkissian (Greece and Armenia), Claudio Engel (Chile), Harvey Chang (Taiwan), Kongkiat Opaswongkarn (Thailand), Anant Asavabhokin (Thailand), Olarn Chaipravat (Thailand), Roberto Civita (Brazil), Odemiro Fonseca (Brazil), Julio de Quesada (Mexico and Cuba), Tono Baltodano (Nicaragua), Joe Harari (Panama), Larry Moh (China), Meng Jian Zhu (China), Mirzan Mahathir (Malaysia), Joey Cuisia (Philippines), Manny Pangilinan (Philippines), Anthony Salim (Indonesia), Benny Santoso (Indonesia), Mehmet Habbab (Turkey), Mohammed Alshaya (Kuwait), Corrado Passera (Italy), Guy Detrilles (Belgium), Frédéric Dubois (France), Daouda Thiam (Côte d'Ivoire), Tomas Aleman (Cuba), and Barry Wilson (Zimbabwe).

I need to thank some of my classroom teachers, including Miss McGinty (6th grade), Colin Dobson (8th grade physics), and Alfred Rubin (graduate school international law) for guiding and inspiring me in one way or another..

Many Wharton and Penn colleagues and friends have given me excellent guidance and inspiration (sometimes unknowingly), and I want to thank Brenda B. Casper, Morris Cohen, George Day, Steve Kobrin, Sheila Murnaghan, Dan Raff, Skip Rosoff, Harbir Singh, Jitendra Singh, Mike Useem, and John Zhang. A special thanks to my good friend Mukul Pandya for his encouragement, advice, unfailing support, and gentle corrections of my errors in Sanskrit.

Strangers, with whom I connected only by email or phone, were the biggest surprises to me. The global feeling of scholarly collegiality was endlessly encouraging, and I want to express my deep appreciation to Neville Rubin, Damien Evans, John Leach, and Elizabeth Fergus-Jean.

I thank Lara Andrea Taber, who designed the book and guided it through the production process. Erin Greb proved to be a cartographer in the grand tradition of Visscher and Bellin and created every map in the book. Eve Lehmann and then Melissa Flamson labored tirelessly and meticulously to obtain the permissions from publishers for my quotes. Thank you also to Jean Taber, who reminded me of grammar and punctuation rules that I had apparently missed in the 5th grade.

Paula Roberts played a special role in this book, both as a cheerleader and a sounding board. Her editorial suggestions improved the content, although I retain responsibility for any remaining infelicities.

Injay Tai, my spiritual brother, has been my best friend for more than 30 years, and has saved my life more than once. I owe him a debt of gratitude that can never be repaid, but of course you do not need to thank your brother.

Sehoon Lee is also my spiritual brother and also my best friend, in his case for 33 years. He gave me my most important lessons in intercultural communication. And now in old age we share identical ailments and take comfort in comparing both symptoms and treatments, which is yet another case of effective intercultural communication.

This book was, not incongruously, published first by Shanghai University Press (SUP), and enjoyed a two-month run on the best-seller list in China. The editorial team at SUP worked tirelessly and patiently to prepare the Chinese version for publication. I am grateful to the members of the team for their successful effort to turn a complicated, multicultural work of analysis into a book which is not only accessible to Chinese readers but also completely faithful to the author's spirit and intent.

Endnotes

Epigraph
The first epigraph is drawn from my favorite poem, Tennyson's *Ulysses*, lines 50-52.

Preface
and by name: I will forever be indebted to my faithful assistant, Kathy Overton, who patiently and with meticulous attention to detail maintained these card files for many years. Her diligence greatly facilitated my book.

Introduction
1   *others did not*: I learned by reading his books that Benedict Anderson, my senior by 12 years, is my spiritual and intellectual older brother. I am standing on his shoulders to write my book. I will refer to his work and thought more than once in the pages ahead. See, for example, his **Imagined Communities**, p. 68.

1   *to fill it*: Jared Diamond's **Guns, Germs, and Steel: The Fates of Human Societies** makes a similar point. His book, however, is focused on how and why some societies modernized and others did not. My book acknowledges that this happened but offers no new insights into the origins of the differences.

1   *They also invented*: I am not suggesting that modernized societies produced nothing of value. On the contrary, I am grateful for vaccinations, air conditioning, strawberries in February, and many of the other positive attributes that paralleled the negative ones I am describing here.

1   *First Opium War*: Lin Tse-hsü (now transliterated Lin Zexu) was a Chinese public servant in the early 19th century. He is a role model for all those who aspire to public service. Professor Chang Hsin-pao wrote a biography of Lin entitled **Commissioner Lin and the Opium War**. This quotation is found on p. 49 of this excellent book. We will meet Commissioner Lin again later in my book.

1   *minister, wrote that*: Fred A. Ross, **Slavery Ordained of God**. The first quote is from p. 25; the second quote is from the Preface, which is unnumbered.

1   *called the "West"*: Even the geographical terms are loaded. "West" of what? It is difficult to think of San Francisco as being West of Shanghai. The "Middle East" and the "Far East" of what? London, of course. The Chinese never thought of themselves as being in the "Far East." They always assumed they were at the "Center."

1   *that different "races"*: Anthropologists formerly divided the world into three races – Caucasian, Mongoloid, and Negroid. American draft cards in 1940 listed as possible racial options "White, Negro, Oriental, Indian, or Filipino." The United Nations, in the modern era, declines to use "race" as a category and has adopted "ethnic groups," of which there are more than 5,000 according to a Research Note published by Rodger Doyle in the **Scientific American**. See Dorothy Roberts, **Fatal Invention**, for a thorough debunking of the myth of the biological basis for "race." David Reich has recently (2019) upset the applecart with his **Who We Are and How We Got Here**. I am not qualified or predisposed to try to settle the dispute that his research generated. Suffice it to say that the field changes on a daily basis, with new evidence from both fossils and ancient DNA. The argument will continue, perhaps never to be resolved. My personal opinion is that the efforts to divide humans into "races" is a misguided idea. There is only one human race.

2   *apartheid*: Nelson Mandela wrote in his autobiography that "The premise of apartheid was that whites were superior to Africans, Coloreds, and Indians, and the function of it was to entrench white supremacy forever" (p. 111).

2   *their historical journeys*: The concept of the "latitudes of time" figures prominently in this book and will reappear more than once in the pages ahead. The term was coined by Daniel J. Boorstin in his **The Discoverers** and is elucidated in chapter 74, pp. 596-603. He introduces the concept on p. 596: "...what I will call the latitudes of time, vistas of contemporaneity, a sense of what was going on all over the world at the same time." Walter Benjamin used a different, more esoteric phrase to describe the same concept. He called it "homogeneous, empty time." Benjamin coins the phrase and develops its meaning in **Illuminations**, pp. 261-264: "The concept of historical progress of mankind cannot be sundered from the concept of its progression through homogenous, empty time." We will return to this most interesting book in Part II, when we consider Hannah Arendt's introduction to Benjamin's thought and writings.

2   *and distant sites*: This is the conclusion not only of Boorstin but also of Yuval Noah Harari in **Sapiens**, pp. 126-130. It is interesting that Jared Diamond, in **Guns, Germs, and Steel**, takes the same facts and reaches a different conclusion, namely that the paucity rather than the profusion of sites at which writing was invented is remarkable.

His thinking on this topic is contained in chapter 12, pp. 215-238. He takes his most pointed swipe on p. 232: "It would be a remarkable coincidence if, after millions of years of human existence without writing, all those Mediterranean and Near Eastern societies had just happened to hit independently on the idea of writing within a few centuries of each other," which is the point of the latitudes of time/homogenous, empty time, just introduced above. I side with Harari and Boorstin, at least on this point.

2   *of kinship systems*: Lewis Henry Morgan, **Systems of Consanguinity and Affinity of the Human Family.**

3   *be considered civilized*: Charles King wrote an excellent book entitled **Gods of the Upper Air,** which focuses on the revolutionary ideas and research of Boas, Mead, and the other founding cultural anthropologists.

3   *so-called civilized ones*: King, **Gods of the Upper Air**, p. 9.

3   *had to strive*: **On the Origin of Species** had been published only in 1859 and was still meeting headwinds of its own when Boas was active.

3   *share certain behaviors*: Nicholas A. Christakis, in his book **Blueprint: The Evolutionary Origins of a Good Society**, argues that there is a "social suite" of eight behaviors that are shared by all humans and that have evolved to enable us to cooperate and build decent societies.

3   *getting better*: Steven Pinker is another thinker and author who has had an influence on this book. He argues, persuasively to me, in his **The Better Angels of Our Nature**, that we are now living in the most peaceful and civilized era in human history.

3   *Former U.S. Senator Rick Santorum*: On April 23, 2021, former U.S. Senator Rick Santorum addressed the Young America's Foundation (yaf.org), a conservative youth organization which has earned a reputation for being both influential and controversial. The topic of his speech was "The Fight for Religious Freedom." A transcript of Santorum's speech, and a link to a video of the speech, are available on newsweek.com in an article by Samantha Lock dated April 27, 2021.

3   *human rights violations*: The full report, entitled "Global Trends: Forced Displacement in 2018," is available on the website of the United Nations High Commissioner on Refugees (unhcr.org).

4   *clash of civilizations*: I am referring here to Samuel Huntington's use of this phrase, first in an article in **Foreign Affairs** and later in a book-length version. I will use him as my foil when we return to his concept more than once in the coming chapters.

4   *superficial characteristics of civilizations*: This is a variant of Christakis's hypothesis, although his focus is on behaviors rather than dispositions. The two hypotheses are mutually supportive.

4   *which includes meeting*: When I say "meeting," I mean that I had enough to do with them that we exchanged business cards. I do not include restaurant waiters and taxi drivers in the category of "meeting."

4   *As a species*: I do not suggest that knowledge is an illusion. I use the phrase as formulated by Daniel J. Boorstin to describe the certainties that later turned out to be illusions, for example, the "knowledge" that the sun revolved around the earth. Boorstin introduces this concept on the first page of text in his **The Discoverers** (p. xv), and it is a continuing theme throughout the following 684 pages of this long and deeply satisfying book. I have already introduced Boorstin above through his concept of the "latitudes of time." Albert Einstein did not read very much because he thought that imagination and creativity were more important than knowledge. Boorstin is a paragon of the synthesis of creativity and knowledge. His erudition is staggering and his creativity is life-changing. I hope it is not unpardonably pretentious to call him my role-model as an author.

4   *mother tongue*: An earlier version of this book was translated into Chinese and published on August 8, 2019, by the Shanghai University Press.

4   *loyalists or mutineers*: The founders of Elevar Equity, an impact investing firm in Seattle, call themselves and their staff "mutineers." You will learn more about this admirable company later in the book.

5   *middle of either one*: Anne Fadiman, **The Spirit Catches You and You Fall Down**, p. x.

5   *confirm my conclusions*: I conducted 104 interviews in total.

5   *are capable of resisting evil*: Philip Zimbardo, **The Lucifer Effect**, p. 461. Professor Zimbardo is another thinker who has had a positive impact on my thinking. This is not the last time I will refer to his work and observations.

6   *transfusion of courage*: Huston Smith wrote a book initially called **The Religions of Man**. After his feminist wife reprimanded him, he entitled subsequent editions **The World's Religions**. This quote is from p. 105 of the expurgated version.

6   *draft of this book*: Email dated November 11, 2014, to the author from Jitendra Singh.

6   *the people I profile*: Telephone conversation on January 12, 2015, with John Zhang.

6   *reasons for success*: Diamond, **Guns, Germs, and Steel**, p. 157: "We tend to seek easy, single facts or explanations for success. For most important things, though, success actually requires avoiding many separate causes of failure."

6   *social science research*: Although I do share some of Nassim Nicholas Taleb's feelings about what he calls the "ludic fallacy," I do not know enough to talk about it in public.

Part I – The Heroines and Heroes

Introduction

10   *encountered a crusty*: That is, a hard surface covering a soft interior.

10   *"Long Legacy of Echo"*: Lehman, **Dublin School**, pp. 257-261.

11   *other-directed "givers"*: I am using this term as defined and elucidated by Adam Grant in his book **Give and Take**. I think he makes an important point in his book. We will return to Professor Grant several times as my book progresses.

Luis Fernando Andrade Moreno

15   *poetically called DRD4-7r*: It is a controversial theory and may be true. For the purposes of my book and its hypothesis, I find it useful to identify a common thread that explains the propensity of many individuals, including all 17 of the subjects of my book (plus myself) to act the way they do. The wanderlust gene is a logical choice, and I am assuming that it is true. Although I am walking out on a limb here, there is an ample supply of articles on this topic which support my assumption and which are all accessible through a Google search. See, for example, David Dobbs, "Restless Genes," in **The National Geographic** (nationalgeographic.com), January 2013, for an intriguing look at this uniquely human characteristic and how it may have shaped human civilizations. The evidence supports the central conclusion that *Homo sapiens* emerged from Africa. Certain humans today exhibit the propensity – even the compulsion – to explore, to embrace the new and unusual, and to treasure the rewards of intercultural communication. Why did *Homo sapiens* undertake this journey out of Africa and why do some humans exhibit the same propensity today? DRD4-7r is a good explanation and an intriguing storyline. I will refer to the DRD4-7r gene periodically over the course of this book.

15   *indigenous means*: merriam-webster.com.

15   *Luis laughed*: I first met Luis in 2004. We became well acquainted when he was the leader of the organizing committee for the Wharton Global Forum in Bogota in 2009. We have spent time together in many cities around the world. Much of the information in this chapter comes from an interview I had with him in Philadelphia on October 24, 2013, and another discussion I had with him, also in Philadelphia, on May 19, 2015.

15   *land bridge*: In 2014, archeologists found new (new to them, but quite old in archeological terms) evidence that the land bridge hypothesis may have at least one competitor, artfully entitled the "Beringian Standstill Hypothesis." This new hypothesis holds that humans on their march from Siberia to North America were actually marooned for about 15,000 years in "Beringia," a broad plain that spread between what are now two distinct continents. This may have slowed down but did not stop the migration. See Nicholas Wade, "Linguistic Light on a Continent's Peopling," in **The New York Time**s, March 13, 2014, p. A6.

16   *an empty territory*: The reader will kindly take note of this matter of Spanish colonization of the New World, since it will reappear later when we meet both Rosanna Ramos Velita *(Compassionate Capitalist)* and Arantxa Ochoa *(Long Legacy of Echo)*.

16   *Latin America's independence movement*: Benedict Anderson describes in some detail how the creole populations of Latin America were radicalized and fought for independence. See his **Imagined Communities**, pp. 47-65.

17   *Pinilla, in 1953*: Alberto Lleras was the Secretary General of the Organization of American States, and its predecessor organization, from 1948 to 1954, a recusal which is reminiscent of Solon of Athens, who will figure prominently in *Disposition – Ambition*. By the mid-1950s, Lleras was drawn back to save his country once again.

17   *overthrow the dictator*: Sounding very much like Cincinnatus of Rome, who will also figure prominently in *Disposition – Ambition*.

17   *commitment to the rule of law*: Henry Kissinger, in his book **World Order**, p. 143, writes: "When states are not governed in their entirety, the international or regional order itself begins to disintegrate."

21   *boost to the economy*: James McKeigue: "If this man succeeds, he'll transform Colombia's economy," in **MoneyWeek Online** (moneyweek.com), October 15, 2013.

22   *12,323 miles*: The circumference of the earth is 24,901 miles, so an antipode is 12,450.5 miles. This flight is as close to an antipodal journey as we will encounter in this book, although Montevideo to Seoul will come close.

Boediono

25   *Pancasila*: "Five principles" in Bahasa Indonesia, which enumerate the country's foundational philosophy, encompassing belief in God, humanity, unity, democracy, and social justice.

25   *first meeting with Dr. Boediono*: I have known Boediono for more than 30 years, and much of the information in this chapter is based on the accumulation of knowledge obtained through many conversations. I also conducted two formal interviews with him in Jakarta, on June 20, 2012, and on February 14, 2014.

25   *never changing part*: A significant percentage of the people in this book describe their places of birth as "never changing" or "static." But Charles King, in his **Gods of the Upper Air**, brought me back to reality when (on p. 134) he wrote: "Modern societies might be literate and history-conscious, reveling in their own complexity, but that did not imply that premodern ones were therefore simpler and change-free. Primitive societies had histories, too. They did not exist in a timeless state of nature, like a stuck wristwatch, awaiting the arrival of civilized people to tap them into life. Researchers should not go into the field with the assumption that they were looking at a society more or less unchanged since the dawn of time." I think that Boediono, who is adept at intercultural communication, was reflecting what Westerners thought and said about Indonesia. I found Indonesian society and culture to be infinitely complex, dynamic, and instructive. We will return to this point repeatedly in the coming pages.

26   *the next day*: Vietnam became independent from France two weeks later; Cambodia became independent, also from France, on September 11, 1953; The Philippines became independent from the United States on July 4, 1946. Thailand has been independent since 1238 CE and has never been colonized.

26   *their first language*: Papua New Guinea, which is geographically contiguous with Indonesia although an independent country, is home to more than 800 languages. The reasons for this linguistic diversity are fascinating, but we have no time to explore them here. Jared Diamond takes a stab at this topic in **Guns, Germs, and Steel**, pp. 306-307.

26   *the first Black Swan*: I am referring here to the concept as introduced and developed by Nassim Nicholas Taleb in his book of the same name. Taleb's Black Swan has three characteristics: first, it is unpredictable. Second, it has an enormous (either beneficial or catastrophic) impact when it occurs. Third, people tend in hindsight to rationalize that it was predictable. Taleb urges us to respond "robustly" to such occurrences, which are inevitable. His concept is concurrent although not identical with Boorstin's idea of the "illusions of knowledge." Both warn us to be humble about our assumptions. In Taleb's words, we have a "blindness with respect to randomness, particularly the large deviations." (Taleb, **The Black Swan**, p. xxiii.). Everybody in this book has been subject to multiple Black Swans. Sometimes they call them "inflection points," or "lightning strikes," but regardless of the terminology, each of the women and men profiled in this book has been defined in large part by how they responded to such moments in their lives. Many Black Swans will appear in the pages ahead.

27   *the bongo drums*: Conversation with Abdillah Toha in Jakarta on Febuary 14, 2014.

27   *was never acknowledged*: The irony was not lost on him when many years later he was elected Governor of Bank Indonesia, his stepping-stone to the Vice Presidency.

27   *the Rockefeller Foundation*: An interesting but unintentional discovery I made in the research for this book was that the Rockefeller Foundation has played a role in four of the lives I chronicle. In addition to this scholarship for Boediono, the Rockefeller Foundation was also an original champion of impact investing, which is discussed later when we meet the Compassionate Capitalists. The Rockefeller Foundation has had long-term, positive impacts on people who make a difference in the world.

27   *development in Indonesia*: The title of his thesis is "Econometric Models of the Indonesian Economy for Short-Term Policy Analysis."

28   *a career teaching and researching*: Another spiritual descendant of Cincinnatus of Rome.

29   *Biden in 2020*: For the fact-checkers among my readers: in 2012, the Obama-Biden team received 62,615,406 votes, which was still far behind the SBY-Boediono team in 2009. In 2015, Joko Widodo was elected President of Indonesia with 70,997,859 votes, or 2,876,703 fewer that SBY-Boediono in 2009. Trump/Pence garnered 62,984,828 in 2016.

29   *Sabar, Sareh, Seleh*: Conversation with Yopie Hidayat in Jakarta on February 13, 2014.

29   *Peter Singer's conclusion*: Peter Singer is a moral philosopher who teaches at Princeton University. I first encountered his thought when I read his **The Expanding Circle**, which I still believe is his best book although he is more famous

for **Animal Liberation** and **The Most Good You Can Do**. I have great respect for his thought as expressed in all three of these books and refer to his thinking about ethics repeatedly in my book. My respect for him as a person, however, was rattled because of an interview with Singer conducted by Daniel A. Gross and published in **The New Yorker** on April 25, 2021. In this interview, he expressed blatantly racist views, which contradicted his fundamental philosophical teachings. This interview challenged my high regard for Professor Singer, although I still respect and try to follow the ethical imperatives as expressed in his books.

30 *mastery of nature*: This comment of Boediono is consistent with the thought expressed by Ruth DeFries in her 2021 book, **What Would Nature Do?** We will return to this concept again later.

32 *influential advisors*: I met Farid at the same time that I met Boediono, in 1992. He has been my cultural guide to Indonesia ever since that time. I am deeply grateful to him for his patience with my halting attempts to understand Javanese culture and for his willingness to arrange for my meetings with Boediono.

Chanthol Sun

37 *Dien Bien Phu*: I have known Chanthol Sun for almost 25 years and have had dozens of conversations with him in my home in Philadelphia, in his homes in Bangkok and Phnom Penh, and in various other locations around the world. I also know his wife and three daughters and have seen Chanthol interacting with them on many occasions. This portrait is a composite of information acquired in conversations, phone calls, and email messages and during breakfasts, lunches, and dinners. I conducted two formal interviews with him, in Phnom Penh on August 21, 2011, and in Philadelphia on November 19, 2013, that added many details to the narrative. I also had the good fortune to spend a week with him in Phnom Penh, during which time I observed him interact with a number of government executives in his official capacity.

37 *static, peaceful, and unchanging*: Chanthol said these words and I dutifully wrote them down. However, similar to my previous comment about Boediono's description of his hometown, I think that Chanthol, who is adept at intercultural communication, was reflecting what Westerners thought and said about Cambodia.

37 *This secret war rained death*: Kissinger claimed that the bombing was necessary because the North Vietnamese were using Cambodia as a sanctuary from which to launch attacks against American troops. Forty-six years later, Kissinger justified the bombing this way: "We had suffered, one month after coming into office, over 2,000 casualties, mostly from sanctuaries in Cambodia. They had to be reduced....We come to power, the North Vietnamese start an offensive within two weeks, we have 500 casualties a week – the bombing of Cambodia was a way not to resume the bombing of the North." (Goldberg, Jeffrey. "World Chaos and World Order: Conversations with Henry Kissinger." theatlantic.com, November 10, 2016.) This was realpolitik to Nixon and Kissinger. To me, killing a quarter of a million innocent civilian Cambodians was not justified and was an immoral and heinous war crime.

38 *Each time a man*: MacAfee, **The Gospel According to RFK**, p. 178. Bobby Kennedy was a bright, shining light of compassion and common sense to me and my generation. I often wonder how our world would have been different and much improved had he lived and had he been elected President of the United States.

39 *known as the "Killing Fields"*: Nobody knows or will ever know how many Cambodians were killed by the Khmer Rouge. As an order of magnitude, it was about 30% of the population, which if it occurred in the United States in 2021 would result in the murders of almost one hundred million men, women, and children.

39 *granted "Green Cards:"* Senator Edward Kennedy was a tireless advocate for the helpless and a champion of immigration reform. The efforts he made on behalf of refugees was doubly impressive. Not only did he save lives, but he did so with no political benefit to himself. Refugees had no constituency. Kennedy defended and protected refugees because it was the morally responsible thing to do. Ted Kennedy literally saved Chanthol's life.

40 *Vice Chairman of General Electric*: Phone call with John Rice on November 26, 2013. I had an opportunity to meet him in person at Ratavy's wedding in 2014.

42 *chief of staff*: Phone call with Anvanith Gui on November 22, 2013. I met Anvanith in Phnom Penh and renewed my acquaintance with him at Ratavy's wedding in 2014.

45 *you contend that*: Goodwin, **The Bully Pulpit**, p. 540.

46 *Cambodia needs not one*: Kamm, **Cambodia: Report from a Stricken Land**, pp. 249-250.

46 *Rift the hills*: From Alfred, Lord Tennyson, **Locksley Hall**, fifth couplet from the end of the poem.

Dawn Hines

49   *Genetic mutation DRD4-7r*: As discussed above in the chapter on Luis Andrade, I am referring to the genetic mutation that may have created the bias for movement in modern humans.

49   *largest antiwar protest*: "Anti-Vietnam War Demonstration Held," **The New York Times**, November 16, 1969, p. 1.

50   *Bellagio on Lake Como*: Rodin and Brandenburg, **The Power of Impact Investing**, p. 4.

50   *with respect and affection*: I first met Dawn in Philadelphia in 2006. This chapter is based on meetings, telephone conversations, email exchanges, and all manner of communication since that time, in cities as far away as Cape Town, South Africa. I conducted one formal interview with her in New York City on January 10, 2013, and another in Ann Arbor, Michigan on July 9, 2014. She also participated in a group discussion with two of the other *Compassionate Capitalists* in New York City on October 1, 2014.

51   *October 30, 1929*: The day after the stock market crash that induced the worst financial panic in the history of the United States and precipitated the Great Depression.

52   *Gordon was Dawn's*: Meg Meeker wrote a book called **Strong Fathers, Strong Daughters**, which explains this phenomenon. Any father who has a daughter needs to read this book.

55   *August 20, 1960*: Thirteen days after the independence of the Côte d'Ivoire, which we will visit in the next chapter. The year 1960 was a watershed in the demise of colonialism. A total of seventeen African countries achieved independence in this year.

55   *religious and ethnic tolerance*: It was interesting to me how similar her description of Senegalese Islam was to the nature of Islam in Indonesia, where it is tempered by the Hindu and animist roots of Indonesian society, and which we visited two chapters ago when we met Boediono.

56   *Ann Daverio*: I had several telephone conversations with Ann on March 10 and 11, 2014.

58   *he (The Buddha) would say*: Armstrong, **Buddha**, p. 64.

Eric Kacou

61   *just past Cap Bojador*: At 26 degrees north latitude, Cap Bojador is only a few miles south of present-day Morocco. The trepidations of the European explorers were another example of the "illusions of knowledge."

61   *most linguistically diverse*: See Claire Felter, "Why does Africa have so many languages?" in **The Christian Science Monitor**, April 21, 2015.

61   *led by a strong and determined*: Information on the legend of Queen Pokou comes from a book by Véronique Tadjo, **Queen Pokou: Concerto for a Sacrifice**, which recounted several versions of what happened, including one in which Queen Pokou refused to throw her son into the river.

62   *despite what the Marxists*: In 1973, Professor Benjamin J. Cohen wrote a book on this topic entitled **The Question of Imperialism**. His arguments are detailed in Chapter 2: Classical Imperialism, pp. 19-82. Almost fifty years later, the cogency of his thesis holds fast.

62   *50 European colonies*: The one exception was the Congo, which King Leopold II of Belgium had already claimed as his personal property.

62   *geographical absurdities*: See, for example, Agyemang and Ofusu-Mensah, "The People the Boundary Could Not Divide: The Gyaman of Ghana and Côte d'Ivoire in Historical Perspective," **Journal of African Studies and Development**.

63   *step backward a few paces*: I first met Eric in 2007 during the planning for the Wharton Global Forum in Cape Town, and I have met him in a variety of cities around the world since that time. Most of the information in this chapter, unless cited separately, is based on interviews with him in Philadelphia on September 11, 2012, and October 12, 2012, and on telephone calls with him on February 21, 2014, and April 20, 2015.

66   *a seminar in high school*: Noguera, Francisco, "NexThought: Eric Kacou on Mindsets and 'Survival Traps' at the Base of the Pyramid," **Next Billion** (nextbillion.net), April 18, 2011.

66   *a unique informant*: Telephone conversation with Aimé Bwakira on May 2, 2015.

66   *founded by Michael Fairbanks*: Fairbanks is a charismatic apostle of market solutions to poverty, entrepreneurship, and the positive impact of competition. He has observed that the strongest correlation to economic development is the punctuality of the population.

67   *The nation's biggest innovation*: Kacou, **Entrepreneurial Solutions for Prosperity in BoP Markets**, p. 35.

67   *Upon graduation from Wharton*: He applied to McKinsey and was unsuccessful. I can only conclude that McKinsey realized that their universe was not big enough for Eric and his plans.

68   *Entrepreneurial Solutions for Prosperity (ESP) Partners*: espartners.co.

68   *The reason we started*: Telephone conversation with Rob Henning on April 27, 2015.

68   *Understanding the unique nature*: Kacou, **Entrepreneurial Solutions for Prosperity in BoP Markets**, p. 18.

68   *The Survival Trap is a vicious cycle*: Ibid., p. 12.

68   *Focusing solely on 'operating reality'*: Ibid., pp. 21-22.

69   *In an era in which no one*: Ibid., p. 39.

Rosanna Ramos Velita

73   *static for generations*: Once again, I dutifully transcribed her words. But, as in the cases of Boediono and Chanthol Sun, who used similar words, not everybody agrees with this characterization. Rosanna is, similar to the others, adept at intercultural communication and knows that this is the typical way that North Americans refer to small towns in Peru.

73   *Rosanna began, dispassionately*: I first met Rosanna in 2007 during the preparation for a Wharton Global Forum in Lima (that took place on March 12-14, 2008,) and we have encountered one another in various cities around the world since that time. Most of the material for this chapter comes from interviews I had with her on December 2, 2013, May 23, 2014, and October 1, 2014, all in New York City.

73   *Spanish blood in our line*: This makes Rosanna the genetic inverse of Luis Andrade, who is predominantly Spanish and slightly Amerindian.

74   *This was a lightning strike*: "Black Swan" in the argot of the present study, but "lightning strike" will certainly suffice.

75   *Maoist guerrilla group*: The reader will recall from the chapter on Luis Andrade a similar challenge faced by Colombia in the same time period and for roughly the same reasons.

76   *the Lauder Institute*: The Lauder Institute for Management and International Studies at the University of Pennsylvania offers a joint degree program through the Wharton School (an M.B.A.) and the School of Arts and Sciences (a Master of Arts in International Relations).

76   *immediately became best friends for life*: Conversation with Dina Weitzman on May 14, 2014, in Montvale, New Jersey.

77   *articulate his concept of micro-finance*: muhammadyunus.org

77   *"Bottom of the Pyramid markets"*: Prahalad and Hart co-authored an article on the topic. Prahalad was the sole author listed on the book, **The Fortune at the Bottom of the Pyramid**. The concept has been enormously influential.

77   *the phrase "Impact Investing"*: The term was coined by Bugg-Levine at the Rockefeller Foundation gathering on Lake Como, previously referenced on p. 50.

78   *an altitude of 12,556 feet*: To put this altitude in perspective, the U.S. Federal Aviation Agency requires pilots who operate unpressurized aircraft above 12,500 feet to use supplemental oxygen.

78   *the shores of Lake Titicaca*: The largest navigable fresh-water lake in Latin America. Peru forms (mostly) the western shore and Bolivia (mostly) the eastern shore.

78   *I spoke with Maya Chorengel*: Telephone conversation with Maya Chorengel on June 10, 2014.

78   *Elevar Equity*: elevarequity.com.

79   *Banca de Inclusión Social*: "Social Inclusion Bank"

79   *I also spoke with Johanna Posada*: Telephone conversation with Johanna Posada on June 10, 2014.

Durreen Shahnaz

84   *The Peace Corps*: Founded on March 1, 1961.

84   *less money to make peace than war*: Quoted in Vaughn's obituary in **The New York Times** on November 4, 2012, p. 32.

84   *summer as a volunteer*: I also wrote a book, **My Year of Living Adventurously**, which includes an extensive description of my time in Africa and the Middle East.

84   *I had to meet Durreen Shahnaz*: I have known Durreen for fifteen years and we have had many conversations, both in person in many countries and over Skype, Zoom, and other apps. Much of the material for this chapter was gathered in a discussion in Singapore on June 18, 2012, and in another discussion in New York City on October 1, 2014.

85   *"defiant, optimistic, and self-sufficient"*: She explains this with conviction and humor in a TED Fellows Talk, posted on YouTube on November 2, 2010.

85   *her father had written*: The information on Durreen's ancestors that follows comes from a five-page, hand-written history authored by her father, which she sent to me in PDF format. The history is not dated but is considered authentic by Durreen.

85   *Mir Kasem (the Nawab)*: Nawab was an honorific title bestowed on semi-autonomous Muslim rulers by the Mughal Emperor.

85   *daughter of a Kazi*: A Kazi was a chief judge and magistrate.

86   Nawab of Bengal appointed this ancestor: The genealogy, interestingly, does not speculate whether this Nawab was Mir Kasem, with whom Durreen's mother's ancestor had allied himself in an unsuccessful effort to expel the British from Bengal.

87   *between her heart and her deed*: This is my first – but not my last – reference to a great man named Raphael Lemkin. Lemkin coined the word "genocide" and then single-handedly and eventually successfully fought, through an international convention, to declare it a crime and to provide for its prevention and punishment. Like so many of the women and men in this book, Durreen's intrinsically motivated goal matches the ambition of Lemkin. Lemkin's autobiography, **Totally Unofficial**, was published posthumously by Donna-Lee Frieze. He described his ambition succinctly on page 2: "I always wanted to shorten the distance between the heart and the deed. To live an idea, not just to talk about it, or to feel it, was my slogan. Thus my basic mission in life was formulated: to create a law among nations to protect national, racial, and religious groups from destruction."

87   *providing all instruction in Bengali*: Durreen was four years old at the time. Her proud native tongue is Bengali.

87   *too many Bangladeshis died*: There is no verified and official death count. Estimates range from 300,000 to over 3,000,000.

87   *to condemn these [human rights] violations*: A good source of information on this callous calculation are Kissinger's own words in an interview with Jeffrey Goldberg, Editor-in-Chief of **The Atlantic** (Goldberg, Jeffrey. "World Chaos and World Order: Conversations with Henry Kissinger." theatlantic.com, November 10, 2016.) This is my second reference to this interview with Kissinger, the first having been in the chapter on Chanthol Sun.

88   *... the results require no apology"*: Ibid.

89   *ironically, I had grown up*: My parents, also socially conscious, had no such compunction and unleashed me into the cauldrons of change, as noted at the start of this chapter.

89   *Smith was remarkable*: The reader will note here the similarity of Durreen's religious evolution to that of Dawn Hines, *Compassionate Capitalist*.

90   *her sister Shabnam*: Skype call with Shabnam Shahnaz on November 15, 2013.

91   *'development jobs' with USAID*: United States Agency for International Development, formed in 1961, ten months after President John F. Kennedy was inaugurated. Although created with well-meaning intent, this is exactly the type of organization that Durreen (and Dawn Hines) sees as a cause and not one of the solutions to many of the problems of the developing world.

92   *the business plan for Impact Investment Exchange*: iixglobal.com.

92   *impact investments are intended*: Rodin, **The Power of Impact Investing**, pp. vi-viii.

92   *"I met Durreen in Singapore in 2009"*: Telephone conversation with Sue Suh on November 21, 2013, and refined in subsequent email exchanges.

Shiv Khemka

97   *astonishingly brutal and sadistic*: I find it helpful when discussing violence to refer to Steven Pinker's **The Better Angels of Our Nature** that both catalogues and explains the remarkable but statistically verifiable drop in violence worldwide over the span of human history.

97   *what drew people to the Sikh faith*: Singh, **The Sikhs**, pp. 236-237.

98   *serve a strife-torn society*: Ibid., p. 23.

98   *India had for centuries prior*: The maharajas continued to rule their kingdoms well beyond the time when the British colonized India. Their status was abolished by Indira Gandhi in 1971 through a constitutional amendment.

98   *Guru Har Raj succeeded*: Singh, **The Sikhs**, p. 42.

98   *Phul had six sons*: When I quoted Patwant Singh's reference to Phul as a "poor young lad" to Shiv, he was quick to note that Phul was not from a poor family, but quite to the contrary traced his lineage back to Rao Jaisal from Rajasthan, who lived during the 12th century and claimed descent from Lord Krishna himself. Suffice it to say that Phul was in straightened circumstances and, inspired by the seventh Sikh Guru to reinvigorate his line, he did so successfully.

98   *"one of the ablest of Nabha rulers*: thesikhencyclopdeia.com.

99   *The source of the disagreement:* The British Government had assumed dominion over India on August 2, 1858. Under this arrangement, the British had suzerainty but not sovereignty, a tricky balance to maintain for both sides, although the Brits never acknowledge any ambiguity.

99   *Shiv proudly stated that Ripudaman:* According to Shiv, maharajas were opportunistic, and eventually they all supported independence. While it would be impossible to prove or disprove Shiv's claim, it is indisputable that Ripudaman supported independence and was penalized severely by the British for this support.

99   *Ripudaman suddenly "died":* Without in any way excusing the behavior of the British, it is worth noting the complex environment in which this nation was operating in late 1942. Engaged in a world war against the Nazis, Fascists, and Japanese, Britain relied on Indian manpower, financing, and industrial production as part of its war effort. At the same time, the "Quit India" movement had begun in August of the same year. While Gandhi had denounced Nazi Germany, he had also refused to support the Allies unless India was given its independence. *Satyagraha* in action.

100   *commodity-based businesses:* Jagannathan, "Marwari Businesses: Leveraging Social Capital," in **Forbes India** (forbesindia.com), March 21, 2014.

100   *Money will come in the long-term:* Quoted in **Forbes India**, March 21, 2014, p. 50.

101   *language, customs and names:* Ibid., p. 54.

101   *eat only vegetarian food:* GD Birla, quoted in Margaret Herdeck and Gita Piramal, **India's Industrialists Vol. 1.**, p. 97.

101   *humility, simplicity, goodness:* Gandhi, **Autobiography**, p. 408.

102   *namely the Sikh and the Marwari:* I first met Shiv in 1987 when he was applying to the Wharton School. We have engaged in conversations in many countries (Russia, Chile, France, the U.K., Singapore, and China, among others) around the world in the ensuing years. Much of the content of this chapter comes from interviews I had with Shiv in Singapore on February 18, 2012, in Washington, D.C. on February 5, 2014, and in my office in Philadelphia on April 1, 2014.

102   *Shiv was wild in college:* Telephone conversation with Yngvar Berg on December 12, 2013.

103   *the Lauder Institute:* The reader will recall that Rosanna Ramos Velita, *Compassionate Capitalist*, is also a graduate of this program. (lauder.wharton.upenn.edu)

103   *Taleb's Extremistan:* Extremistan refers to a phenomenon where a single, curve-distorting event or person can radically skew the distribution. Imagine including Bill Gates in an average of executive net worth.

103   *They elected to conduct:* Information on the Khemka family's activities in Russia from 1990 to 2004 was obtained from discussion with Shiv, and from two Harvard Business School cases, **SUN Brewing (A)** and **SUN Brewing (B)**, both authored by Belén Villalonga and Raphael Amit, and both published in revised form on July 10, 1991.

103   *By mid-1991 the new Russian:* Boris Yeltsin was the first freely-elected President of Russia and assumed office on July 10, 1991.

104   *He lived in Russia for twenty years:* When I was in Moscow, Shiv assigned his personal driver Igor to me. I asked Igor if Shiv's Russian was understandable. Igor's response was, "Shiv is a Russian man." True Marwari adaptability.

106   *Philip Zimbardo, a professor:* Zimbardo, **The Lucifer Effect**.

Jacob Wallenberg

110   *Departing from Stockholm:* It was not until 1652 that Sweden gained political control (from the Dutch) of the port of Gothenburg on the west coast, which reduced but did not eliminate the complications.

110   *a narrow channel:* The width at its narrowest point is 2.5 miles.

110   *out from Sagres:* Technically, Henry was active in the first half of the 15th century, so the chronology is a bit misaligned here. But his intellectual and emotional descendants were still active in the mid-17th century.

110   *"Catherine" Street:* Named for the foster mother of Queen Cristina, who lived from 1626-89 and reigned from 1632-54.

110   *"Queen" Village:* Named in recognition of Sweden's queen at the time of the neighborhood's initial settlement.

111   *enter the Lutheran:* Martin Luther posted his 95 theses on the door of the Wittenberg Castle Catholic Church in 1517, and his doctrine had found a receptive audience in Scandinavia.

111   *an eponymous foundation:* The historical record reveals that this was a fertile time for the creation of charitable foundations in Western Europe and the United States. The Nobel Foundation had been established in Sweden in

1900. By 1911, Andrew Carnegie had established five charitable organizations in the United States and three in the United Kingdom. The Rockefeller Foundation was founded in 1913.

111 *assets also grew*: The obituary for Peter Wallenberg (Jacob's father), published in the **Financial Times** on January 19, 2015, reported that the assets of the foundation were SKr 85 billion or approximately US$10.3 billion.

111 *father lived abroad*: Most people, including his father, underestimated Peter's capabilities. He was sent abroad to get him out of the way of his brother Marc, who was being groomed to take over the family dynasty but who committed suicide in 1971. As reported in his obituary in the **Financial Times**, already cited above, Peter "confounded his critics, who failed to appreciate the gritty determination to prove himself that lay behind the rumpled appearance and bluff, self-deprecating humor."

111 *"Surprisingly, yes"*: I first met Jacob in 1984 in Singapore, and we have been friends ever since. Our paths have crossed repeatedly, in Philadelphia and in Stockholm. I conducted two interviews with him, on September 24, 2012, and on September 18, 2014, both in his office at Investor AB in Stockholm.

112 *a straight-talking and self-assured*: I had a telephone conversation with Beatrice on Monday, October 13, 2014, and subsequent email exchanges to clarify and expand on the topics we discussed.

113 *Jacob brings to mind*: Singer, **The Expanding Circle**, p. 151.

113 *I asked him about Raoul*: No one will ever know how many lives were saved by Raoul Wallenberg's personal heroism. The figure of 100,000 is at the upper end of the estimates. Raoul would most definitely be called ethical under Singer's definition.

114 *Peter, Jr. is Chairman*: Peter, Jr. was appointed Chairman of the foundation one week before their father's death on January 19, 2015.

114 *Chairman of Investor AB*: Jacob was named a Director of Investor AB in 1988, Vice Chairman in 1999, and Chairman in 2005.

114 *Wallenberg-controlled*: The family no longer holds a majority share in any of the businesses, but through the legal structure, which includes several classes of shares with different voting rights, its "reach is greater than its grasp."

114 *our influence can also*: Interview with Göran Sandberg in **Research Media Ltd.**, "Europe's Leading Portal for Scientific Dissemination," August 2011.

115 *a cardinal virtue*: After I first wrote the term "cardinal virtue," I realized that I was invoking Western values as originally defined in classical antiquity and later echoed in the Christian tradition. The first cardinal virtues were prudence, justice, temperance (which included modesty), and courage. But on second thought, I realized that Confucius would not have felt uncomfortable with the concept.

115 *giving more interviews*: See, for example, Richard Milne, "Jacob Wallenberg, Investor Head with More Influence Than Money," in the **Financial Times** (FT.com), June 30, 2014, and Richard Milne, "Election Hopeful Stefan Löfven Aims to Return Sweden to the Left," in the **Financial Times** (FT.com), August 21, 2014.

115 *128 billion Swedish Kroner*: Not surprisingly, the Knut and Alice Wallenberg Foundation has a highly transparent and helpful website (kaw.wallenberg.org/en.)

115 *It is ironic*: Again, quoting from Peter, Sr.'s obituary in the **Financial Times**, "…Jacob Wallenberg is one of Sweden's most powerful businessmen…"

116 *the small size of the Swedish*: Keynote speech by Jacob Wallenberg at the Wharton Global Forum in San Francisco on June 23, 2011.

116 *price was insufficient*: An interesting, consequential, and little remembered fact during the search for a vaccine occasioned by the COVID-19 pandemic. What would have been the consequences to the development of vaccines if Pfizer and Astra Zeneca had no longer been separate companies?

118 *Jacob is a joyous person*: I spoke with Sputte by telephone on October 14, 2014.

118 *mutual unselfishness*: Pinker, **The Better Angels of Our Nature**, p. 182.

118 *defined by Zimbardo*: Please go back to the Introduction (p. 5) to re-read Zimbardo's definition of heroism.

119 *Stockholm is separated*: Fewer than 23 minutes of longitude separate Stockholm from Cape Town.

Anthony Hamilton Russell

122 *The master of his college*: Sir Michael was a distinguished educator who studied under Arnold Toynbee and John Ruskin and counted Wassily Kandinsky among his friends. He was what we would now call a liberal, and one can only speculate what impact his thinking had on the young James Hamilton Russell.

122   *the United Nations*: He also drafted the preamble to the UN Charter and performed a wide assortment of other tasks in support of global peace and tranquility.

123   *voting rights of Coloreds*: While this term in American usage is highly charged and never used in the United States in the twenty-first century, in South Africa it has no political connotation and is used without causing discomfort.

123   *broke up families*: There were hundreds of apartheid laws. Leslie Rubin prepared a study for the United Nations in 1971 entitled **Apartheid in Practice**, which listed two hundred practical effects of apartheid laws.

123   *The state had grown stronger*: Mandela, **Long Walk to Freedom**, pp. 438-439.

123   *the golf course*: Email message to the author from Neville Rubin, dated October 25, 2014. Neville is the son of Leslie, cited above.

123   *was called apartheid*: An Afrikaans word meaning "the state of being apart."

124   *"detention without trial" laws*: According to Mandela's rendition, "…the Ninety-Day Detention Law, waived the right of habeas corpus and empowered any police officer to detain any person without a warrant on grounds of suspicion of a political crime. Those arrested could be detained without trial, access to a lawyer, or protection against self-incrimination for up to ninety days." Mandela, **Long Walk to Freedom**, p. 338.

124   *Mike and his wife*: Martin Jarvis, "Michael Russell: Pioneer of effective treatments to help people stop smoking," in **The Guardian**, August 4, 2009.

124   *Originally committed to peaceful*: Nelson Mandela followed the same path from non-violence to violence. "For fifty years, the ANC had treated nonviolence as a core principle, beyond question or debate. Henceforward, the ANC would be a different kind of organization. We were embarking on a new and more dangerous path, a path of organized violence, the results of which we did not and could not know…. Our mandate was to wage acts of violence against the state…" **Mandela, Long Walk to Freedom**, p. 274.

125   *while possessing a social conscience*: Once again from Neville Rubin: "I also knew Tim as a rather conservative contemporary—his conversion to liberalism came about in Oxford, and he joined the Liberal Party on his return to Cape Town in the mid-1960s."

125   *Their second child was a son*: I first met Anthony, incongruously, in Santiago, Chile, in 2005. We have been together in many cities around the world since that time, including Philadelphia and Hermanus, South Africa. I conducted interviews with him on May 23, 2013, in Philadelphia, on October 20, 2014, in Cape May, New Jersey; and on March 4, 2015, by Skype from his home in Hermanus.

125   *To start with, though*: Email message to the author from Neville Rubin, dated October 25, 2014.

126   *While highly successful in advertising*: Jane Broughton, "Tim Hamilton Russell, South African Wine Pioneer, Dies at 79," in **Wine Spectator** (winespectator.com), August 6, 2013.

126   *The English-speaking universities*: **Mandela, Long Walk to Freedom**, p. 90.

127   *"Anthony is the kind of person*: Conversation with Curtis Brashaw in Cape May, New Jersey, on March 29, 2015.

127   *after completing his responsibilities*: I had originally written "shortly thereafter." Anthony asked me to make this small adjustment because he did not want anyone to think that he was irresponsible to his employer.

127   *his first thirty-two years*: It is a curiosity of the heroes and heroines of this book that most (not all) of them spent many years of wandering in the wilderness before they started their true life's work.

130   *understanding of the whole*: Email message to the author from Anthony Hamilton Russell dated November 27, 2014.

131   *higher 'E.Q.'*: Emotional Quotient, the soft counterpart to I.Q., or Intelligence Quotient.

131   *I think he recognized*: This theme will echo later in this book when we meet James Joo-Jin Kim, who, with his father, struggled to find the appropriate response to the Japanese colonization of their native Korea.

Keisuke Muratsu

135   *Kato-bushi is an area*: Kojuro, Miyama, "An Introduction to one of the oldest styles in Kabuki: Kato-bushi," in **DooBeeDooBeeDoo NY** (doobeedoobeedoo.info), a cross-cultural, online music magazine, September 21, 2010.

135   *My earnest attempts*: At one point my tutor was a Japanese woman. She taught me "feminine" Japanese, which is quite different from "masculine" Japanese. Fortunately, a good friend explained this to me in time to avoid excruciating embarrassment in public.

135   *While these comparisons*: Takarazuka, another traditional Japanese performance art, by comparison, is only one hundred years old.

136   *His father was descended*: I have known Muratsu-san for more than 37 years. We have visited each other's homes, shared triumphs and tragedies together, and have played golf more than two dozen times in at least eight countries.

This chapter also draws heavily on an interview that I had with him in his office in Tokyo on January 19, 2012, and my attendance at his performance in the role of Yuya on February 3, 2013.

137 *from your observation*: Email message to the author from Keisuke Muratsu on May 31, 2015.

137 *Wanting to learn*: Telephone conversation with Kwangsoo Hur on December 10, 2013.

137 *Asian Pacific Golf Confederation*: apgc.online.

138 *static environment of his youth*: Once again, these are the words of my informant, and may understate the complexity of the society in which he lived in his youth.

138 *The year 1968 was confusing*: We have already discussed this era and the profound effect it had on men and women in their youth at the time in the chapters on Dawn Hines and Durreen Shahnaz.

138 *eleven months between 1968 and 1969*: With the benefit of many years of hindsight, I am intrigued to have lived long enough to observe the unique nature of what happened at that time. Never in the decades since has there been a truly global student movement. The "Arab Spring" which crossed many borders was analogous but limited to a single world region. The revolutions of 1968 spread from the United Sates to Europe and Asia. The fact that students from all around the world shared our concerns gave us hope that we could forge a new world order.

138 *One of Kei's closest friends*: Telephone conversation with Yamamoto Kozo on December 16, 2013.

138 *We disapproved of their tactics*: This sentence is evidence of yet another similarity in the student rebellions in the United States and Japan. At Columbia University at the same time, where I was a student, I was also among those who disapproved of the radicals' tactics but supported their goals. I remember being vilified and criticized by the radicals for not having sufficient revolutionary zeal.

139 *the negotiations were unsuccessful*: This is the same tragic consequence that unfolded at Columbia University in 1968, when I was an undergraduate student.

139 *in Minami Azabu*: A district in the central part of Tokyo.

141 *called "Naigai"*: The literal translation is "inside" (nai) and "outside" (gai.) Kei explained that the implication is "home" and "foreign," but he thinks that his father "just named it" and the words are not particularly meaningful.

141 *Muratsu-san filed a lawsuit*: Yoshiro Miwa and J. Mark Ramseyer wrote a case study in 2005 based on Kei's lawsuit.

143 *learning the shamisen*: The three-stringed instrument used to accompany Katoubushi singers.

144 *a delectable mountain*: I use this phrase in the sense used by e.e. cummings in **The Enormous Room**.

144 *In Katoubushi, by contrast*: Classical ballet is probably the closest analogue to Katoubushi in Western culture.

145 *resilience sustained by an indomitable*: Kissinger, **World Order**, p. 189. In this passage, Kissinger was referring to post-World War II Japan, but this response is no different from its response to Perry's Black Ships in 1853, or to the "Lost Decade" from 1991 to 2001.

Arantxa Ochoa

149 *guns, germs, and steel*: As described at length and so eloquently in Jared Diamond, **Guns, Germs and Steel**.

149 *ordered the conquests*: Boorstin, **The Discoverers**, p. 632.

150 *Not merely the Spanish*: Ibid., p. 635.

150 *Ochoa is marvelous*: Janet Anderson, "Debuts," **Citypaper** online edition, October 18, 2001.

150 *an athlete like Ochoa*: Jim Rutter, "When the Artists Are Athletes (and Vice Versa), **Broad Street Review** (broadstreetreview.com), April 16, 2011.

151 *But the performer*: I knew about Arantxa for several years before I actually met her. I attended many of her performances and admired her from afar. Later, I watched her as a teacher when my daughter Angie was her student. I interviewed her twice, on April 4, 2013, and on January 15, 2014, both times in Philadelphia. After the formality of our two interviews, we became close friends.

151 *I later met Arantxa's parents*: Meeting with Emilia G. Ayala, Jose Ignacio Ochoa, and Arantxa in Philadelphia on July 3, 2014.

153 *The Academy of Music*: I have attended performances at La Scala in Milan and The Bolshoi in Moscow and stand by my judgment about the Academy of Music in Philadelphia. Of course, I have a 'tin ear' and no artistic qualifications, so I am only speaking from the perspective of a civilian.

153 *the Music Director of Pennsylvania Ballet*: Conversation with Beatrice Affron in Philadelphia, on May 10, 2014.

153 *close friend of Arantxa*: Everybody who is a friend of Arantxa is a close friend. She is a passionate woman who has no casual acquaintances.

153 *The Principals at Pennsylvania Ballet*: Conversation with Rosemary Ogle in Berlin, New Jersey, on July 29, 2014.

155 *Materialism derives*: Tim Kasser, **The High Price of Materialism**, p. 76.

157 *by opening yourselves*: Riccardo Muti, Commencement Address at the University of Pennsylvania, May 19, 1987.

Leslie Koo Cheng Yun

161 *His fifth son*: This made him a dragon, according to the Chinese zodiac. The dragon is the only animal in the Chinese zodiac that is imaginary. Consequently, it is considered the most powerful of all. Dragons are thought to be courageous, intelligent and tenacious, with enthusiasm and confidence. Dragons do not fear risks and welcome challenges. They also have a soft side, and are generous, warm and giving. Deng Xiao Ping and Vladimir Putin are both dragons. Please note that I do not believe in this unscientific method of character analysis, but many Chinese do, so it is important.

162 *his father trained him to be trilingual*: Japan was also profoundly influenced by Confucianism. The Japanese embraced many of the same principles as the Chinese, such as reverence for education, respect for hierarchy, strict adherence to the rules of propriety in interpersonal relations, and a monarchical political tradition.

162 *Hitler invaded Poland*: Formerly historians dated the start of World War II from the Nazi invasion of Poland on September 1, 1939. More recently, there is a growing consensus that the Double Seven Incident between Japan and China on July 7, 1937, is an equally valid measurement of the start of the global conflict.

162 *Where they established the Republic of China*: I am fully aware of the fact that the People's Republic of China claims Taiwan as one of its regions. I am also aware of the fact that very few countries in the world recognize the R.O.C. as a country (none recognize "Taiwan"). Nevertheless, the PRC does not exercise political or military control over Taiwan, nor does it command the obedience of the population of Taiwan. Consequently, Taiwan is a "de facto" if not a "de jure" sovereign nation. When the Shanghai University Press published an earlier version of this book in Chinese in 2019, the editor insisted that I refer to Taiwan as a "region." I agreed to this compromise because it had no impact on the description of the moral dispositions of Leslie Koo, who was born and raised in Taiwan. This book is not about politics, and I have attempted to preserve my neutrality on political matters in each jurisdiction in which it has been published. Professor Jacques deLisle of the University of Pennsylvania Law School is an articulate and authoritative commentator on the topic of cross-straits issues. He wrote an excellent "E-Note" on this topic for the Foreign Policy Research Institute (fpri.org), published on July 1, 2011. Although it is now a decade old, not much has changed, and his E-Note is still a good source of information on the international legal and organizational issues involved in this seemingly intractable dispute.

162 *Their second son*: This makes Leslie a horse, again according to the Chinese zodiac. Horses are energetic, active, and involved with matters. They are optimists and enthusiasts and display an excellent sense of humor. Horses are known to be good leaders, with the capability of making good decisions and leading groups of people to accomplish goals. Not surprisingly, they are extroverted, easy-going, and comfortable with others. Genghis Khan and Zhang Daoling (the founder of Taoism) were both Horses.

163 *Leslie, as we will learn*: Leslie passed away on January 23, 2017. This book, as a snapshot of an era that ended in 2015, will not cover that tragic and untimely event.

164 *Leslie was educated*: I have known Leslie since 1989 and have met him in at least a dozen cities around the world, both by planning and by chance. One of our most interesting conversations took place when by happenstance I sat next to him on a bus going from downtown Tokyo to Narita International Airport. Most of the information in this chapter, and all the quotes, derive from two interviews I conducted, the first in my office in Philadelphia on May 16, 2014, and the second in his office in Taipei on November 3, 2014.

167 *so-called QFII investors*: "Qualified Foreign Institutional Investors."

169 *We must do much more*: "Corporate Social Responsibility," was coined to describe efforts by companies to enforce self-regulation in the areas of ethics and compliance in response to public expectations about responsible corporate behavior.

170 *I have real doubts*: This is an interesting echo of what both Dawn Hines and Durreen Shahnaz, the *Compassionate Capitalists* you have already met, had to say about the limitations of government largesse and philanthropy.

Vassily Vassilievich Sidorov

175 *About three million Russians*: Nobody knows how many Russians died in the First World War, the Civil War, the Red Terror, Stalin's Gulag, the Second World War, and the proxy wars of the Cold War. Entire books have been written on the subject. I include round numbers here as points of departure. An historian who disputes my numbers is missing the point. It is the order of magnitude – the number of zeroes after the first number – that matters.

175 *Stalin killed tens of millions*: Robert Conquest, in his book **The Great Terror**, concludes that Stalin killed 20,000,000. R.J. Rummel, in his book **Lethal Politics**, increases the estimate to 43,000,000. Nobody contests the assertion that he killed "tens of millions."

176 *The consequences of Stalin's policies*: The reasons for this have something to do with Stalin's control of information, something to do with American and European indifference to the suffering of the Soviet peasantry, and something inexplicable. Donald Rayfield discusses this conundrum at length in his book **Stalin and His Hangmen**. In retrospect, Western attitudes about the Show Trials, Gulag, and Red Terror are challenging to understand. Not having lived through this period, I cannot judge; I can only wonder what my response would have been.

176 *John Steinbeck's novel*: It was still a best-seller in 1940, although it slipped to #8.

176 *the USSR was, theoretically*: The Soviet-Nazi Non-Aggression Pact of 1939 lasted only 22 months and ended precipitously when Hitler invaded Russia in June 1941, six months before Japan bombed Pearl Harbor.

176 *hostility set in*: See Williams, **The Tragedy of American Diplomacy**, Chapter Seven, The Impotence of Nuclear Supremacy, pp. 276-293, and Chapter Eight, The Terrifying Momentum Toward Disaster, pp. 294-304, for an analysis written in 1959 that still rings true in 2021.

177 *Vassily Sergeyevich Sidorov*: There will be two men named Vassily Sidorov who play important roles in this chapter. I will use the patronymic as necessary to avoid getting them confused.

177 *the Battle of the Bulge*: Estimates of casualties are in the 100,000 range for Germany and in the 80,000 range for the United States. Such a tragic human waste.

177 *Siege of Budapest*: We have already briefly touched on the life of this great man, in the chapter on Jacob Wallenberg.

177 *All alike carry*: Freeman Dyson, **Weapons and Hope**, p. 181.

178 *who was named for his father*: I first met Vassily on March 31, 2003, when he was First Vice President for Finance and Investments at Sistema Telecom. We have met many times since then, including in my home in Philadelphia. Most of the material in this chapter is based on interviews I had with him in New York City on July 28, 2012, and at his dacha in the suburbs of Moscow from April 1-3, 2015.

178 *an "unusual" birthplace*: Conversation with Larissa Sidorov in Moscow on April 1, 2015

179 *first intelligence officers*: Donald Rayfield, in his book on Stalin to which we have already referred, catalogues horrifying statistics as well as anecdotes about the atrocities committed by non-Russian Jews who served in the Cheka. There is no information available that I have been able to find about Isidore's work, so I do not insinuate anything by mentioning this. My only purpose is to add to the admiration I have for his son.

179 *interview conducted on his 90th birthday*: Andrei Zolotov, Jr., "I Revel in What I Have Grown: Russian Teacher and Principal Turns 90," in **Expatru** (expat.ru), "The virtual community for English-speaking expats and Russians," March 15, 2011. I originally found this interview on a site called Russiaprofile.org. When I was checking footnotes, I discovered that, although Russiaprofile.org still exists, this article no longer exists on the website.

179 *I wanted the kids to become*: Ibid.

179 *The most important thing*: Ibid.

179 *the school's Komsomol*: The equivalent of the president of the student council.

180 *Citigroup Global Markets*: Conversation with Irackly Mtibelishvily in Moscow on April 2, 2015.

180 *a Faustian bargain*: A Christian legend about negotiating with the Devil, in which one sacrifices one's soul in exchange for great knowledge or power. The Devil always wins.

180 *decided to attend the Wharton School*: Unknown to either of us, I may have played a small role in enabling him to attend the University of Pennsylvania. I earned my graduate degrees at the Fletcher School of Law and Diplomacy at Tufts University in 1977 and worked at the school for a time after graduation. One of the projects in which I was involved was the creation of the Association of Professional Schools of International Relations (APSIA.) This organization grew, prospered, and in 1991 launched an initiative to enable students from the Moscow State Institute to attend universities in the United States, and vice versa.

181 *When I was at Svyazinvest*: At the time the largest Russian telecommunications company, state-owned until the end of the decade.

182 *When I asked Vassily*: I met with Dmitry in his office in Moscow on April 3, 2015. He had a large photo of his three sons hanging on the wall. They looked to be the same ages, more or less, as my two daughters. We agreed that this next generation would be needed to bridge the gap between our countries.

182 *one of the richest men in Russia*: The ever-changing ratio between Russian rubles and U.S. dollars makes it challenging to calculate his net worth at any particular moment. Suffice it to say that he has multiple billions of U.S. dollars and equivalents.

183 *I am not a revolutionary*: I know I am repeating myself. Vassily said this so many times that it needs to be noted accordingly.

184 *He cited "recent evidence"*: Dyson, **Weapons and Hope**, p. 193.

Roberto Canessa

188 *in the 13th row*: The absurdity of this superstition (all superstitions are absurd) is proven by the fact that Chinese are certain that the number four is unlucky, Japanese are convinced that the number seven is unlucky, and Thais are sure that the number three is unlucky. None of these civilizations has any fear of the number 13, which terrifies superstitious Americans.

188 *no limit to how long they can whirl*: My personal experience with Whirling Dervishes took place at the Ciragan Kempinski Hotel during the Wharton Global Forum in Istanbul on June 9, 2006.

188 *But this is not a performing art*: I am indebted to Mehmet Gun Calika for explaining the religious aspect of the Whirling Dervishes.

189 *I had heard Roberto speak*: In Santiago at the Wharton Global Forum on July 1, 2005, and in Madrid at the Wharton Global Forum on June 24, 2010. Most of the content of this chapter consists of material acquired during my visit to Montevideo and through numerous follow-up phone calls and email messages.

189 *In preparation for my visit*: Read, **Alive**.

189 *Roberto's fellow survivors*: Parrado, **Miracle in the Andes**.

190 *second smallest country*: Suriname is the smallest.

191 *Roberto employs a number of people*: Skype conversation with Juan Berchesi on December 30, 2013.

192 *perspective of a Sartrean hero*: This is my first mention of Jean-Paul Sartre, the French Existentialist, but it will not be the last. Sartre contributed a great deal to my thinking and helped me to clarify my values. His writing can be challenging. **Being and Nothingness**, his magnum opus, is very long (634 pages in the English translation) and convoluted. I found Sartre's short essay "Existentialism Is a Humanism" to provide an accessible entry point into his thinking. His play, **No Exit**, is also a good starting point. **At the Existentialist Cafe: Freedom, Being and Apricot Cocktails with Jean-Paul Sartre, Simone de Beauvoir, Albert Camus, Martin Heidegger, Maurice Merleau-Ponty and Others** by Sarah Bakewell is an excellent introduction to the philosophy and its origins. For a sympathetic and compassionate description of the relationship between Sartre and de Beauvoir, see **Tête-à-Tête: The Tumultuous Lives & Loves of Simone de Beauvoir & Jean-Paul Sartre** by Hazel Rowley.

192 *I was fascinated by surgery*: Canessa and Vierci, **I Had to Survive**, p. 166.

193 *They were exemplary human beings*: I cannot let the moment pass without calling attention to the perfect correspondence of this thought with the Confucian concept of the source of successful leadership, and with Gandhi's philosophy of leadership.

194 *Don't be afraid, Roberto*: Canessa and Vierci, **I Had to Survive**, p. 15.

194 *I know that he misses his mother*: Conversation by Skype with Alberto Gari on July 15, 2013.

194 *first cousin or sister:* This distinction is meaningful to North Americans but not to South Americans.

197 *Instead, that person desperate for help*: Canessa and Vierci, **I Had to Survive**, p. 256.

197 *This does not mean*: Slightly adapted from Edmund Morris, writing about Roosevelt in **Time Magazine** on April 13, 1998.

James Joo-Jin Kim

201 *This question was brought to my attention*: I have known Kim Joo-Jin (he uses "Jim" as his given name in the United States) for almost three decades (based on the first business card I received from him, which I dated January 15, 1992), and have encountered him in many cities around the world, from Seoul and Manila to Philadelphia and

Chandler, Arizona. I interviewed him three times during the summer of 2014, on June 30th, July 14th, and August 4th, and once in the summer of 2015, on June 8th. I also had the unusual advantage of reading the elegant English translation of his father's 285-page autobiography.

201 *Benjamin Lee Whorf*: We have already encountered Professor Boas and his coterie in the introduction to this book.

201 *Next, I picked up a book*: McWhorter, **The Language Hoax**.

202 *My ancestry goes back*: Kim, **A Small Key Opens Big Doors**, p. 20.

202 *seventy-two generations*: One thousand, eight hundred years, if a generation is calculated as twenty-five years.

202 *There are many Kim families*: Family names are more concentrated in Korea than in the United States. This is probably the result of a country with few immigrants compared to a country that is a global melting pot. It is estimated that 20% of Koreans have the family name "Kim." Lee and Park together represent another 20% of Korean surnames. Smith, by contrast, the most common surname among Americans, is shared by less than 1% of the population.

203 *eventually reached Cheonan*: Jim repeatedly cautioned me that his recollection of chronology was distorted after so many years. It would not have been possible for him and his mother carrying a new-born to walk 52 miles on a railroad track in one night. But he distinctly remembers the incidents, regardless of when they actually took place.

203 *and Christmas morning*: This poignancy was not meaningful to them at the time since they had not yet been exposed to Christianity.

204 *From the start of the war until 1953*: The armistice that ended the fighting went into effect on July 27, 1953, three years, one month and two days after it began. No one will ever know for certain how many people were killed and wounded in this war, but the average estimate is that more than a million people perished and more than another million people were wounded. According to Pinker, **The Better Angels of Our Nature**, p. 320, "…about 4.5 per cent of the population died from disease or starvation in every year of the four-year conflict."

205 *named his business "Anam"*: In Korean, "An" means "Asia" and "Nam" means "South." To this day, Jim is not quite sure why his father chose this name.

205 *Forever confident in my powers*: Kim, **A Small Key Opens Big Doors**, p. 171.

206 *His father officially retired*: Kim Hyang-Soo was 80 years old at the time of his retirement.

206 *Anam, a shrimp in comparison*: This aquatic comparison is discussed in an article in **Forbes Magazine** (forbes.com), December 19, 1994, issue, entitled "A Shrimp Among Whales," written by Gale Eisenstadt.

207 *Jim Kim has lost $3 billion*: "Amkor Founder's Relentless Push," by Bob Fernandez, in **Philly.com** on April 1, 2001.

207 *Jim is consistent*: Conversation with Louis Siani in Conshohocken, Pennsylvania on August 13, 2014.

209 *This is philanthropy in the sense described by Peter Singer*: Peter Singer describes his theory of ethical philanthropy in his book **The Most Good You Can Do**.

Michael Yu Minhong

214 *Mao Tse Tung's Great Leap Forward*: A radical economic and social campaign created by Chairman Mao to transform China into a communist utopia. It failed spectacularly.

214 *Yang concludes, therefore*: Yang, **Tombstone**, Table 11.7, pp. 411-414.

214 *I noted that Jiangyin*: I have had many conversations with Yu Minhong in Beijing and in Philadelphia, in person, by telephone, and on Skype; and in many circumstances, ranging from dinner at his home in Beijing to dinner in my home in Philadelphia. I conducted one formal interview with him in my office in Philadelphia on October 8, 2013, another by Skype on June 23, 2014, and a third again in Philadelphia on December 8, 2014. Most of the quotes in this chapter are taken from the three interviews. I also had the good fortune to get to know his daughter Jamie, who attended the Wharton School as an undergraduate. She provided most interesting insights into her father's personality and life philosophy.

215 *accused of being a spy for the Kuomintang*: The Kuomintang is the Chinese political party led by Chiang Kai-Shek that fought (and lost) the civil war with the Communist Party led by Mao Tse Tung.

216 *"Gang of 4" was crushed*: A political faction that included Mao's last wife, Jiang Qing, and that was accused, after his death, of causing the worst excesses of the Cultural Revolution.

217 *I didn't lose by helping others*: A "giver" as defined by Professor Adam Grant in his book, **Give and Take**, pp. 4-5.

218 *Michael is the same person today*: Conversation with Zhou Chenggang in Beijing on February 12, 2014.

219 *I donate several million RMB*: More than US$300,000 at the current exchange rate.

220 *donated RMB 500 million*: About US$80 million at the current rate of exchange.

220 *Wang Xiao Wen*: Since I cannot communicate in Chinese, I needed to have this conversation translated. I wish to express my deep appreciation to Fu Qi Qi, known as Michelle in English, Michael's assistant at the time, for her excellent and nuanced translation of my conversation with Wang Xiao Wen, who was not comfortable speaking in English.

220 *My mother attended*: Conversation with Weng Xiao Wen in Beijing on February 11, 2014.

220 *and committed suicide*: I am quoting verbatim all the references to "mental illness" that led to suicide, but I cannot accept that people who were tortured and took their own lives during the Cultural Revolution had mental illnesses.

221 *new ideas for businesses that help people*: Professor Zhang Weiying of the Guanghua School at Peking University has written extensively on his belief that entrepreneurship, not the growth of the domestic economy by itself, is what will propel China into its next stage of prosperity. See his book, **The Logic of the Market**.

221 *I hope to start with RMB 200 million*: Over US$30 million at the current rate of exchange.

222 *articulate, thoughtful, and soft-spoken*: Conversation with Bao Fanyi in Beijing on February 11, 2014.

223 *challenge traditional assumptions* and *more inclined toward*: Grant, **Give and Take**, p. 131.

Part II – The Venn Diagram

Introduction

226 *a rebuttal to Huntington*: Although I was inspired to write this book in part because of my disagreement with Professor Huntington's thesis, my argument with his reasoning is tangential to my thesis, so I will not spend a lot of time refuting him. I will take the opportunity of this endnote, however, to provide a single illustration of where our reasoning differs. In 2019-2021, the world endured a terrible pandemic, the overcoming of which necessitated vast numbers of individuals around the world to change their personal behavior to lessen the risk of infection to themselves and others. In China, the government mandated and enforced these behavioral changes, and the pandemic was quickly extinguished, with a minimal loss of life. In the United States, the government (at the federal and state levels) had a bewildering diversity of weak responses, none of which matched the comprehensive nature of the Chinese response. The consequence was that the pandemic spread in the United States and over 700,000 perished. Huntington praises American "individualism" and "freedom" as human rights, while at the same time pointing out that Asian culture does not respect human rights. What about the human rights of the 700,000 Americans who died because of the "freedom" that allowed Americans to ignore basic safety measures? In my view, American insistence on "freedom" is too often a smoke screen for selfishness. If the common good requires some mandatory measures, this is not a violation of human rights; on the contrary, it is for the protection of human life, which is the ultimate human right. China believes in human rights; sometimes the common good requires the surrender of individual preferences to protect a larger number of people. Huntington's thesis is not only ethnocentric but also incorrect.

226 *had no ability whatsoever*: Ambrose, **Undaunted Courage**, p. 256.

226 *really see people*: Zora Neale Hurston was one of Franz Boas's students. This quote is from King, **Gods of the Upper Air**, p. 300, referring to her book **Dust Tracks on a Road**, p. 231.

228 *Amanda Gorman counselled*: This line is from Amanda Gorman's poem which she recited at the inauguration of U.S. President Joe Biden on January 20, 2021. Gorman, **The Hill We Climb: An Inaugural Poem for the Country**.

228 *beginning to reason*: Singer, **The Expanding Circle**, p. 88.

229 *meaning of human existence*: "...the capacity to decide, and how and why the capacity came into being, and the consequences that followed, are the broader, science-based meaning of human existence. Premier among the consequences is the capacity to imagine possible futures, and to plan and choose among them." Edward O. Wilson, **The Meaning of Human Existence**, p. 14.

Character

230 *To any officer or employee*: Goodwin, **The Bully Pulpit**, p. 484.

230 *Great nations don't ignore*: Extract from a speech delivered by U.S. President Joe Biden on June 17, 2021, at a ceremony in which he signed a bill into law making Juneteenth a national holiday.

230 *Most of all, Lewis*: Ambrose, **Undaunted Courage**, p. 97.

231 *Tan Sri Dato' Dr.*: Malaysians celebrate heritage, achievement, and respect through a formal, complex system of titles and honorifics. Some of these titles are inherited (by members of a royal family, for example) and others are awarded for merit. "Tan Sri" is a very senior title conferred on a strictly limited number of Malaysians who have served the country with great distinction. "Dato'," while honorable, is more common and is held by numerous Malaysians. Zeti, lacking royal ancestry, earned both her titles. The "Dr." attests to an earned Ph.D. from the University of Pennsylvania.

231 *expert on Sukuk*: An Arabic term describing financial instruments that comply with Islamic law forbidding the charging or paying of interest.

231 *other Sharia compliant*: The Islamic canonical law, derived from religious sources regarded as divine (although it has been supplemented over time through legislation).

231 *In 2012, under Zeti's leadership*: Sasana Kijang translates as "The meeting place of the barking deer," which begs for some explanation. The barking deer, native to Malaysia, long ago became the symbol for Bank Negara Malaysia and is featured on its logo. My thanks to Donald Lim for explaining the derivation of the logo to me.

231 *During a visit to Kuala Lumpur*: Conversation with Tan Sri Dato' Dr. Zeti Akhtar Aziz at Bank Negara Malaysia in Kuala Lumpur on August 16, 2011. I have known Governor Zeti for over twenty years, and we have had conversations in cities ranging from Jakarta to Tokyo.

232 *Satyagraha derived from two*: Gandhi discusses the derivation of this word in Chapter XXVI, "The Birth of Satyagraha," on pp. 318-319 of his **Autobiography**.

232 *I got along merrily*: Ibid., p. 336.

232 *When I come to examine*: Ibid., p. 412.

232 *Like many of us*: This epochal struggle is described in detail in his book **Stride towards Freedom**.

Standards

235 *When we strive*: Coehlo, **The Alchemist**, p. 155.

236 *It was important*: Isaacson, **Steve Jobs**, p. 6.

236 *A "great carpenter"*: Ibid., pp. 133-134.

237 *Of all the religious ceremonies*: Keene, **On Familiar Terms**, pp. 162-164.

237 *construction of furniture made by hand*: Moser, **Thos. Moser: Artistry in Wood**.

237 *We panel the backs*: Ibid., p. 74.

237 *We have dedicated ourselves*: Ibid., p. 97.

238 *the manufacture of risk*: Ibid., p. 160.

238 *Exploring new levels of difficulty*: Ibid., p. 170.

Resilience

240 *What might have been*: Lansing, **Endurance**, p. 103.

240 *When the ground rules changed*: Parrado, **Miracle in the Andes**, p.112.

241 *Just about everybody*: Corporations, organizations, cities, countries, ethnic groups, and baseball teams also need resilience. The focus of this discussion is on resilience as it is manifested in individuals.

241 *John Hudson, Chief Survival Instructor*: johnhudsonsurvival.com.

241 *"give-up-itis"*: This section draws on the work of John Leach, PhD, Extreme Environmental Medicine and Science Group, University of Portsmouth, U. K. See John Leach, "'Give-up-itis' Revisited: Neuropathology of *extremis*," **Medical Hypotheses**, vol. 120, November 2018, pp. 14-21, and John Leach, "Coping in Captivity: A Cognitive Perspective," in **Advances in Psychological Research**, vol. 66, 2010.

241 *the "resilience dividend"*: See Rodin, **The Resilience Dividend**.

241 *off the mountaintop*: I have learned from experience that, counterintuitively, the climb up a mountain is easier than the climb down.

242 *According to the findings of neuroscientists*: Leach, "'Give-up-itis' Revisited," pp. 18-20.

243 *Mental health is based to a certain degree*: Frankl, **Man's Search for Meaning**, pp. 104-105.

243 *This is an example of Kahneman's*: Kahneman, **Thinking Fast and Slow**.

244 *For [Bohr] every difficulty*: Palevsky, **Atomic Fragments**, p. 230.

244 *Nature is resilient*: Ruth DeFries, in her book **What Would Nature Do?**, discusses this strategy in detail.

Forgiveness

246   *[His anger] is a case*: Francis E. Leupp, "Taft and Roosevelt: a Composite Study," *Atlantic Monthly* (November 1910), p. 649. Quoted in Goodwin, **The Bully Pulpit**, p. 69.

246   *to live in bitterness and anger*: Parrado, **Miracle in the Andes**, p. 251.

249   *growing slightly every year*: Approximately 2.5 inches annually, or about one mile every 26,000 years.

249   *Not to be upset when*: Leys, **The Analects of Confucius**, p. 3.

249   *If you can forgive*: Skype conversation with Shabnam Shahnaz on November 15, 2013.

249   *pocket the insult:* On pp. 98-99 of his autobiography, Gandhi relates how he learned to "pocket the insult." He later recounts, over an entire chapter (pp. 259-261), how difficult it was to maintain this form of self-control. Gandhi was not a perfect man, but he sought the truth unceasingly.

249   *characterized by a cosmic wholeness*: Mandela, **Long Walk to Freedom**, p. 13.

250   *As I walked out the door*: Clinton, **Living History**, p. 236.

250   *the Dalai Lama appears wholly untouched*: Mishra, "The Last Dalai Lama?" in **The New York Times Magazine**, Sunday, December 6, 2015, p. 44.

250   *He believes that all people*: A belief shared by Confucius.

251   *Your thoughts drive your feelings*: Quoted in **Johns Hopkins Health: Insight and News from Johns Hopkins Medicine** (hopkinsmedicine.org), Summer 2014, pp. 6-9.

Free Will

252   *Men at some time*: Shakespeare, **Julius Caesar**, 1, 2, 146.

252   *man is a creature*: Tolstoy, **The Kingdom of God is Within You**, p. 188.

253   *Free will, on the other hand*: I have already referred to Edward O. Wilson's take on this matter, which I find sensible and persuasive. Jean-Paul Sartre also had some useful things to say on this topic, and I will refer to them in a few pages.

253   *Suzana Herculano-Houzel write*s: DeSilva, ed., **A Most Interesting Problem**, p. 58.

254   *lack utility in any practical sense*. Not everybody agrees with me on this point. Professor Peter T. Struck has written a book called **Divination and Human Nature**, which argues that oracles, omens, and dreams were all early chapters in the "cognitive history of intuition," which he asserts is real.

254   *Ancient Chinese philosophy encompassed*: In the preparation of the following discussion of Chinese philosophy, I have been guided by an excellent book entitled **The Chinese Philosophy of Fate** by Yixia Wei.

254   *In the twenty-first century, scientists*: Sebastian Seung, in his book **Connectome**, argues that what we learn and how it is processed by our brains' synapses is also of critical importance to how we behave. We will return to this point in *Disposition – H.O.P.E.*

255   *We may be inclined*: See Robertson and Nichols, eds., **Thinking About Bribery**, for a thoughtful discussion of this question.

255   *which is an imagined reality*: Following Yuval Noah Harari's taxonomy.

255   *machine intelligence has created*: This is another fast-changing field (the first such field I mentioned being ancient DNA research conducted by David Reich and associates), and whatever we read today will be out-of-date by tomorrow. One book I found especially helpful is **Life 3.0** by Max Tegmark.

255   *some scientists are convinced*: The substrate in this case consisting of carbon-based life forms, a random mutation that resulted in a sequence of mutations that, on one tiny branch, included a species we now call *Homo sapiens*.

256   *how far a man is free*: Gandhi, **Autobiography**, p. 24.

256   *The Buddha was fundamentally unconcerned*: An excellent source of knowledge about Buddhism can be found in **Why Buddhism Is True** by Robert Wright. Matthieu Ricard has written extensively on the subject and is a good interpreter of Buddhism for the unenlightened.

257   *Jean Paul Sartre and the Existentialists*: See the note to page 192 for some suggestions on becoming acquainted with the thought of Sartre.

257   *The randomness hypothesis:* We have encountered Nassim Nicholas Taleb before, and we will engage with him again before we are done.

Money

259   *The worth of gold*: Bathsheba Demuth, **Floating Coast**, p. 200.
259   *I am, Sire*: **Montaigne, The Complete Works**, Letter to King Henry IV, September 2, 1590 (?), p. 1336.
260   *Jared Diamond points out*: This concept is central to the thesis of Diamond, **Guns, Germs, and Steel**.
261   *this will involve making value judgments*: There is a robust field of study which concerns itself with the economic and ecological wisdom and feasibility of unfettered economic growth. In the modern era, it began in 1972 with the Club of Rome and **The Limits of Growth**. The debate continues to this day. I list in the Bibliography relevant work by Giorgos Kallis, Vaclav Smil, Tim Jackson, Abhijit Banerjee and Esther Duflo, Dietrich Vollroth, Alex Bowen, Kate Raworth, Wilfred Beckerman, Donella Meadows, and Robert Pollin. I am neither inclined nor qualified to comment on this side of the question. My book, and this chapter in particular, is more concerned with the moral questions that must be answered on an individual basis, in part inspired by Henry David Thoreau's **Walden**.
261   *avarice overrates the difference*: Adam Smith, **The Theory of Moral Sentiments**, Part III, sec. III, pp. 31, 149.
261   *a "materialistic treadmill"*: Tim Kasser does a creditable job of skewering this illusion of knowledge in **The High Price of Materialism**.
262   *except that which makes life worthwhile*: Kennedy, Robert F., Speech delivered at the University of Kansas on March 18, 1968, in MacAffie, ed., **The Gospel According to RFK**, p. 45.
262   *Robert Pirsig wrote a book*: Pirsig, **Zen and the Art of Motorcycle Maintenance**.
263   *celibacy, fasting, penance*: Rasmussen, **The Infidel and the Professor**, pp. 58-59.
263   *He did not demonize money*: Singer developed his ideas about money and philanthropy in his book **The Most Good You Can Do.**
264   *Impact Investing is a relatively new*: Rodin and Brandenberg, **The Power of Impact Investing** is a good introduction to this concept.
264   *To my way of thinking, Konosuke*: Matsushita, **Not by Bread Alone**.
265   *It's no shame to be poor*: Stein, Joseph. **Fiddler on the Roof**, p. 24. New York: Pocket Books, 1965. Music by Jerry Bock, lyrics by Sheldon Harnick.

Tradition

266   *It is no wonder that high officials*: Chang, **Commissioner Lin**, p. 11.
267   *delayed maturation and increased longevity*: Suzana Herculano-Houzel in DeSilva, ed., **A Most Interesting Problem**, p. 61.
267   *Tradition transforms truth*: Benjamin, **Illuminations**, p. 41. In this section I draw on some of the ideas articulated by Hannah Arendt in her introduction to this anthology as well as on Benjamin's writing. I have already cited Benjamin in the Introduction, p. 2.
267   *In the days before printing*: Benjamin, **Illuminations**, pp. 83-109.
268   *Sport began as a way for men*: Michael P. Lombardo, "On the Evolution of Sport," in **Evolutionary Psychology**, 2012, vol.10, no. 1, pp. 1-28.
269   *Steven Pinker credits*: Yes, he did write this. See the **Better Angels of Our Nature**, p. 59, and the penultimate paragraph on p. 72 if you do not believe me.
269   *Think of the Sikhs*: Uncut hair, wooden comb, iron bracelet, sacred shorts, and iron dagger.
270   *common ground, a unity of*: Hofstadter, **The American Political Tradition and the Men Who Made It**, p. x.
270   *war was still the assumed*: Tuchman, **March of Folly**, p. 78.
270   *He recounted an interesting interchange*: Ambrose, **Undaunted Courage**, p. 189.
270   *In human beings it is tradition*: Huston Smith, **The World's Religions**, p. 93.
270   *a religion devoid of tradition*: Ibid., p. 96.
270   *all but obsessed with tradition*: Ibid., p. 168.
270   *behave in accordance with certain standards*: Harari, **Sapiens**, p. 163.
272   *to imagine the unknown than to chart*: Boorstin, **The Discoverers**, p. 99.
272   *Wills dubs "repristination"*: I have had the pleasure of encountering a number of neologisms in the course of writing this book, and one of my favorites is "repristination," coined, as best as I can tell, by Gary Wills in his book, **Certain Trumpets**, pp. 143-144.
272   *Respect precedent but reject dogma*: Canessa and Vierci, **I Had to Survive**, p. 195.

Ambition

274 *The people of the United States*: Goodwin, **The Bully Pulpit**, p. 740.

274 *Only those are worthy*: Huston Smith, **The World's Religions**, p. 178.

275 *The good cannot seize power*: Tolstoy, **The Kingdom of God Is Within You**, p. 133.

275 *For to what purpose is all the toil*: Adam Smith, **The Theory of Moral Sentiments**, Part I, Sec. III, Chap. II, 1, p. 50. It is interesting that this description of ambition corresponds so closely to the word for recognition – Thymos – used by Francis Fukuyama in **The End of History and the Last Man** as a metaphor for the "fundamental source of human evil" (p. 181).

276 *what sort of government*: Chernow, **Washington: A Life**, p. 428.

276 *If I am not deceived*: Ibid.

276 *If you have any regard*: Ibid.

276 *which had been ratified in 1788*: It is interesting that Washington was hailed as the "new Cincinnatus" at the time. See Wills, **Certain Trumpets**, p. 152.

277 *Lin Tse-hsü's political activity*: Chang, **Commissioner Lin and the Opium War**, p. 123.

277 *I think - Ambition*: Conversations with John Rice on November 26, 2013 (by phone), and on June 28, 2014 (in person).

277 *how much was riding on this attempt*: Chernow, **Washington: A Life**, p. 569.

278 *It is difficult to make my feeling*: Damrosch, **The Club**, p. 80.

278 *inauthenticity: going through the motions*: Ibid.

Patriotism

279 *Our country is the world*: William Lloyd Garrison, Declaration of Sentiments Adopted by the Peace Convention, Boston, September 18-20, 1838 (appearing in **The Liberator**, vol. VIII, no. 39, on September 28, 1838).

279 *Nationalism is an infantile*: Attributed to Albert Einstein by George Sylvester Viereck in an article, based on an interview, entitled "What Life Means to Einstein," in the October 1929 edition of **The Saturday Evening Post** (saturdayeveningpost.com), p. 117. An interesting coincidence with a catastrophic month.

280 *I define patriotism as the love*: Peter Singer, with whom I agree completely on this subject, uses the word "patriotism" in the same way that I use "nationalism." This is an example of how these words get misunderstood and cause confusion. On the other hand, Jill Lepore's definition of patriotism (and argument against nationalism) corresponds with mine without qualification. See Lepore, **This America: The Case for the Nation**, for a brief but succinct exposition of her views on this topic. It is a short book (138 pages), and every page is a treasure on this important topic.

280 *I am not sure if patriotism*: I hate to quarrel with Benedict Anderson, but his definition of patriotism conflicts with mine in several ways. He asserts that patriotism consists of "something to which one is naturally tied" (I think that patriotism can be acquired); "something unchosen" (I think that patriotism can be transferred by choice); and has a "halo of disinterestedness" (I agree with this part). I think he conflates two issues when he ascribes a "purity through fatality" (in other words, the willingness to die for your country) to patriotism. While I would hope that I would have been willing to die to prevent Hitler from dominating the world, I would not be willing to die, for example, to protect my country's access to the fossil fuels that are destroying the earth. Anderson discusses this definition of patriotism in chapter 8, Patriotism and Racism, in his **Imagined Communities**, pp.141-154.

281 *the right to visit*: Kant, **Perpetual Peace**, p.118.

281 *championed by Murray Bookchin*: See Biehl, **Ecology or Catastrophe**, for an introduction to his thought and life.

281 *relatively recent phenomenon*: Recent research has suggested that humans are biologically wired to fear the "other," and that antagonism to out-group individuals is genetic. See "This Is Your Brain on Nationalism," by Robert Sapolsky in the March/April 2019 issue of **Foreign Affairs** for an interesting discussion of this question.

281 *"largely incurable"*: Tom Nairn originally wrote these words in **The Break-up of Britain**, p. 359; Anderson quotes Nairn in **Imagined Communities**, p. 5.

282 *We know who we are only*: Huntington, **The Clash of Civilizations**, p. 21.

282 *comes under a magnifying glass*: Beaton, et al., "Crisis Nationalism," is an interesting take on this controversial, but morally relevant, question.

283 *In fact, this feeling of global citizenship*: I should note here that I do not include "netizens" as patriotic Citizens of the

World, because this is a sterile and hollow existence. I share with Edward Said his lament that "It seems a common human failing to prefer the schematic authority of a text to the disorientations of direct encounters with the human." (Said, **Orientalism**, p. 93). I favor world citizens who eagerly seek out and relish the abrasion of new textures, the assault of new and intriguing fragrances on the nostrils, the sadness of sunsets in new places, the extremes of temperatures, the pungent taste of *hongeo*, the chaos into which jet lag throws body rhythms, the nervous excitement of discovery, the consumption of previously unimagined animal body parts, the propinquity of alligators in the Ubangi River, the community and ultimately, the compassion of altruistic love that allows cherished friendships to ripen over time, unexpectedly. My heroes and heroines are all Citizens of the World, a designation earned over time, through travel and because of their enthusiasm for direct human interaction.

283   *nationalism is losing ground*: Harari, **Sapiens**, p. 207.

283   *"print capitalism"*: In **Imagined Communities**, Anderson introduces his theory of print-capitalism and its role in the origins of national consciousness in chapter 3, pp. 37-46.

283   *Many peaceable countries today*: Pinker, **The Better Angels of Our Nature**, p. 525.

Adventure

285   *We were setting out*: Harrer, **Seven Years in Tibet**, p. 103.

285   *I think whatever I shall meet*: Walt Whitman, "Song of the Open Road." Originally published in his collection **Leaves of Grass** in 1856.

285   *When I have been truly*: Coelho, **The Alchemist**, p. 135.

286   *All our dreams begin in youth*: Harrer, **Seven Years in Tibet**, p. xiii.

286   *based on his "tonnage"*: Halliburton, **New Worlds to Conquer**, p. 93.

287   *The whole undertaking was criticized*: Lansing, **Endurance**, p. 11.

287   *One of the finest days*: Ibid., p. 87.

287   *There was never any doubt*: As previously noted, I wrote a book about what happened next for me. It is titled **My Year of Living Adventurously – 1966-1967**.

287   *The DRD4-7r gene must have run rampant*: Yet another example of what Daniel Boorstin metaphorically called the "latitudes of time," when humans without contact with each other simultaneously began exhibiting certain behaviors, such as writing, war, and adventure.

287   *silent upon a hill in Darien*: John Keats, "On First Looking into Chapman's Homer," last line.

288   *country that was a nursery*: Ambrose, **Undaunted Courage**, p. 20.

288   *His desire to see new lands*: Ibid., p. 37.

288   *I could but esteem*: Ibid., p. 212.

288   *He was ready, intensely alive*: Ibid., p. 216.

288   *A restless person may thrive*: Dobbs, "Restless Genes."

288   *with a trumpet flourish*: Dolnick, **The Clockwork Universe**, pp. 294-295.

289   *with extraordinary impetus*: Dostoyevsky, **The Idiot**, pp. 203-204.

Impact

290   *A life is not important*: Jackie Robinson said this. For those readers who are not familiar with the history of professional baseball in the United States, Jackie Robinson is an American icon, the first African-American to play in baseball's Major League. When he broke the color barrier in 1947, he set in motion a chain of events that is still unfolding. His enthusiasm and resilience are legendary. He was a thoroughly admirable man and remains a model of excellence. This quote is drawn from page 268 of his autobiography, **I Never Had It Made**.

291   *When you're a Jet*: Leonard Bernstein and Stephen Sondheim, "Jet Song" from *West Side Story*.

291   *Unless we hate what we are not*: Huntington, **The Clash of Civilizations**, p. 20.

291   *The capacity for making friends*: Christakis, **Blueprint**, p. 261.

291   *an unanticipated by-product*: Kuhn, **The Copernican Revolution**, pp. 1-2.

291   *This chapter, however, deals with a third type*: The definition of this word formerly maintained that the altruist must derive no benefit from the act. There exists a new and intriguing form of altruism that benefits both parties. This requires a slight modification of the traditional definition of the word. Impact Investing, as espoused by Durreen

Shahnaz, Dawn Hines, Rosanna Ramos, Eric Kacou, and increasing numbers of others, is a good example of a new form of altruism.

291 *Auguste Comte*: John Tresch discusses this concept, and many others developed by Comte, in chapter 9, "Comte's Calendar," of his book, **The Romantic Machine**, pp. 253-286.

292 *my interests count no more*: Singer, **Expanding Circle**, p. 109.

292 *towards a more universal point*: Ibid, pp. 119-120.

292 *A man who identifies*: Huston Smith, **The World's Religions**, p. 24.

293 *the one among all the industries*: Tresch, **The Romantic Machine**, p. 245.

294 *I once met a man named Zell Kravinsky*: Jitendra Singh, already cited in the Introduction for his role in improving this book, was the person who introduced me to Zell.

294 *to withhold a kidney*: Quoted in an article by Peter Singer entitled "What Should a Billionaire Give – and What Should You?" published in **The New York Times** on December 17, 2006.

294 *While Singer finds Zell*: While I find Professor Singer to be a source of much wisdom, I cannot follow him blindly into the many extreme positions he takes. But he certainly does provoke discussion, regardless of whether you agree with him, and for that we should all be grateful.

295 *compassion without action is hypocritical*: Ricard, **Altruism**, p. 7.

295 *Altruism… remains limited*: Ibid., p. 32.

295 *shorten the distance*: Lemkin, **Totally Unofficial**, p. 2.

H.O.P.E.

297 *The longer I live*: McCullough, **John Adams**, p. 650.

297 *Their position was*: Lansing, **Endurance**, p. 84.

298 *hope is the only emotion*: President Snow is the evil leader of Panem in the movie version of **The Hunger Games**. Ross, Gary, dir. *The Hunger Games*. Performed by Donald Sutherland. Lionsgate and Color Force, 2012.

298 *an ability to accurately acknowledge*: Daryl R. Van Tongeren, Don E. Davis, Joshua N. Hook, and Charlotte vanOyen Witvliet, "Humility," **Current Directions in Psychological Science** 10 2019; vol. 28, no. 5, pp. 463-468.

298 *In his book, Give and Take*: Adam Grant, **Give and Take**, p. 131.

299 *"shield and buckler"*: Gandhi, **Autobiography**, pp. 59-62.

299 *In this way, culture may be influencing*: This intriguing idea is discussed in some detail in Christakis, **Blueprint**, pp. 360-388.

299 *[humble people are] not afraid*: Yu, **The Relentless Pursuit of Success**, p. 67.

299 *This is the best*: Dr. Pangloss is a character in the novel **Candide**, published by Voltaire in 1759. Pangloss is the tutor to the novel's protagonist. The novel is a satire and Voltaire ridicules everything, including optimism. The book was banned after its original publication. Dr. Pangloss is reported to have proven this belief on the first page of Candide and is quoted repeatedly thereafter reaffirming this belief, although at the end of the novel he admits to some difficulty in believing his own philosophy. Voltaire, **Candide and Other Stories**, p. 5.

300 *totality of connections*: Seung, **Connectome**, p. xiii.

300 *the genomic worldview*: Ibid., p. 116.

300 *Optimists, moreover*: Pronoia is little used and less known but holds the power to change everything. Pronoiacs harbor the ridiculous belief that other people are secretly plotting to do kind and thoughtful things for them and also saying positive and complimentary things behind their backs.

300 *I never seriously considered*: Mandela, **Long Walk to Freedom**, p. 391.

300 *"This too will pass"*: Bobby McFerrin. "Don't Worry, Be Happy" lyrics. ©1988 ProbNoblem Music.

300 *Nirmal Purja Magar*: "Nepal climber makes history speed climbing world's tallest peaks." **National Geographic**, May 24, 2019.

300 *I hope to have proven*: Megan Specia, "Climbing World's Highest Peaks in 6 Months, Breaking a Record by 7 Years," in **The New York Times**, October 30, 2019, p. A7.

301 *I can't help it*: Canessa and Vierci, **I Had to Survive**, p. 172.

301 *Nothing can stop him*: Conversation with Juan Berchesi in Montevideo, Uruguay, on March 3, 2013.

301 *the love you take is equal*: John Lennon and Paul McCartney, "The End" lyrics.

301   *Because I didn't know*: Isaacson, **Steve Jobs**, p. 100.
301   *outstanding thinkers*: Pinker, **The Better Angels of Our Nature**, p. 649.
302   *after much converse*: Plato, **The Seventh Letter**, p. 49.

Spirituality
303   *Religion did not create*: Brian Hare in DeSilva, ed., **A Most Interesting Problem**, p. 81.
304   *What I believe in is spirituality*: Conversation by Skype with Mrs. Gowri Ishwaran on December 18, 2013.
304   *turned away from organized religion*: Pankaj Mishra, "The Last Dalai Lama?" in **The New York Times Magazine**, Sunday, December 6, 2015, p. 43.
305   *complete conformity and fidelity*: Quoted in Ricard, **Altruism**, p. 117.
305   *self-realization or knowledge*: Gandhi, **Autobiography**, p. 31.
305   *This is called anthropocentrism*: Spiritually, on some days I am a pantheist, on others a deist, on others an atheist, and on still others a Hmong. As I write this sentence, I am a Buddhist, but I am still a pilgrim when it comes to my spiritual beliefs.
305   *replaced an intentional creator*: Brian Hare in DeSilva, ed., **A Most Interesting Problem**, p. 63.
305   *The Pew Research Center interviewed*: Pew Research Center (pewresearch.org), March 2014, "Worldwide, Many See Belief in God as Essential to Morality."
306   *Over the last two millennia*: Harari, **Sapiens**, p. 218.
306   *Mr. Coates...wanted to convince*: Gandhi, **Autobiography**, pp. 123-124.
306   *We want our voice to be heard*: "Mormon Leaders Outline Support for Marriage for Man–Woman," by Brady McCombs, AP (apnews.com), April 4, 2015.
306   *I have contended*: "Bobby Jindal Wants to Fistfight Your God," quoted online in **The Daily Beast** (thedailybeast.com), January 27, 2015, and updated on April 14, 2017.
306   *First Amendment [to the U.S. Constitution]*: The First Amendment, in full, reads as follows: "Congress shall make no law respecting an establishment of religion or prohibiting the free expression thereof; or abridging the freedom of speech, or of the press, or the right of the people peacefully to assemble, and to petition the Government for a redress of grievances."
306   *The full story of religion*: Huston Smith, **The World's Religions**, p. 4.
307   *the scriptures... were used*: Pinker, **The Better Angels of Our Nature**, pp. 676-677.
308   *In truth, existentialism*: Rowley, **Tête-à-Tête**, p. 154.

Concluding Remarks
310   *Men often hate each other*: King, **Stride Toward Freedom**, p. 20.

Bibliography

Agyemang, Joseph Kwadwo, and Ababio Emmanuel Ofosu-Mensah. "The People the Boundary Could Not Divide: The Gyaman of Ghana and Côte d'Ivoire in Historical Perspective," **Journal of African Studies and Development**, vol. 5, no. 7, pp. 177-189, November 2013.

Allison, Graham. **Destined for War: Can America and China Escape Thucydides's Trap?** Boston and New York: Mariner Books, Houghton Mifflin Harcourt, 2018. First published in 2017.

Ambrose, Stephen E. **Undaunted Courage**. New York: Simon & Schuster, 1996.

Anderson, Benedict. **Imagined Communities: Reflections on the Origin and Spread of Nationalism**. London: Verso, 2016. First published in 1983.

———. **A Life Beyond Boundaries: A Memoir**. London: Verso, 2016. First published in 2009 in Japanese.

Apollodorus. **The Library of Greek Mythology**. Translated by Robin Hard. Oxford University Press, 1997.

Armstrong, Karen. **Buddha**. London: Phoenix Books, 2000.

Bagrow, Leo. **History of Cartography**. Revised and enlarged by R.A. Skelton, 2nd edition. Chicago: Precedent Publishing, Inc., 1985.

Bandura, Albert. "The Psychology of Chance Encounters and Life Paths," **American Psychologist** (July 1982) vol. 37, pp. 747-755.

Banerjee, Abhijit, and Esther Duflo. **Good Economics for Hard Times**. New York: Public Affairs Publishing Company, 2019.

Batchelor, Stephen. **After Buddhism: Rethinking the Dharma for a Secular Age**. New Haven: Yale University Press, 2015.

Beaton E, Gadomski M, Manson D, Tan KC. "Crisis Nationalism: To What Degree Is National Partiality Justifiable during a Global Pandemic?" in **Ethical Theory and Moral Practice**. 2021 Feb 14:1-16.

Beckerman, Wilfred. **In Defence of Economic Growth**. New York: Vintage/Ebury, 1976.

Benjamin, Walter. **Illuminations**. New York: Shocken Books, 2007. Originally published in German in 1955.

Bezruchka, Stephen. **Trekking in Nepal: A Traveler's Guide**, 6th edition. Seattle: The Mountaineers, 1991.

Biehl, Janet. **Ecology or Catastrophe: The Life of Murray Bookchin**. Oxford University Press, 2015.

Bird, Kai, and Martin J. Sherwin. **American Prometheus: The Triumph and Tragedy of J. Robert Oppenheimer**. New York: Vintage Books, 2005.

Boorstin, Daniel J. **The Creators: A History of Heroes of the Imagination**. New York: Vintage Books, 1993.

———. **The Discoverers: A History of Man's Search to Know His World and Himself**. New York: Vintage Books, 1985.

————. **The Image: A Guide to Pseudo-Events in America**, 50th Anniversary Edition. New York: Vintage Books, 2012. First published in 1962.

————. **The Seekers: The Story of Man's Continuing Quest to Understand His World**. New York: Vintage Books, 1999.

Bowen, Alex, ed. **Improving Incentives for the Low-Paid**. London: Palgrave Macmillan, 1990.

Bradbury, Ray. **Fahrenheit 451**, 50th Anniversary Edition. New York: Simon & Schuster, 2013.

————. **The Martian Chronicles**. New York: Bantam Books, 1979. First published in book form in 1950.

Breyer, Stephen. **The Court and the World: American Law and the New Global Realities**. New York: Alfred A. Knopf, 2015.

Buckley, Brendan M., Kevin J. Anchukatis, Daniel Penny, Roland Fletcher, Edward R. Cook, Masaki Sano, Le Canh Nam, Aroonrut Wichienkeeo, Ton That Minh, and Truong Mai Hong. "Climate as a Contributing Factor in the Demise of Angkor, Cambodia," **Proceedings of the National Academy of Science**, April 13, 2010, vol. 7, no. 15, pp. 6748-6752.

Canessa, Roberto, and Pablo Vierci. **I Had to Survive: How a Plane Crash in the Andes Inspired My Calling to Save Lives**. Translated by Carlos Frías. New York: Atria Books, 2016.

Carroll, Sean. **The Big Picture: On the Origins of Life, Meaning, and the Universe Itself**. New York: Dutton, 2016.

Chang, Hsin-pao. **Commissioner Lin and the Opium War**. New York: W.W. Norton & Co., Inc., 1970.

Chang, Iris. **The Rape of Nanjing: The Forgotten Holocaust of World War II**. New York: Basic Books, 1997.

Chernow, Ron. **Alexander Hamilton**. New York: Penguin Books, 2005.

————. **Washington: A Life**. New York: The Penguin Press, 2010.

Choate, Pat. **Agents of Influence: How Japan's Lobbyists in the United States Manipulate America's Political and Economic System**. New York: Alfred A. Knopf, 1990.

Christakis, Nicholas A. **Blueprint: The Evolutionary Origins of a Good Society**. New York: Little, Brown Spark, 2019.

Christopher, Robert C. **The Japanese Mind**. New York: Fawcett Columbine, 1983.

Clinton, Hillary Rodham. **Living History**. New York: Simon & Schuster, 2003.

Coburn, Broughton. **Everest: Mountain Without Mercy**. Washington, D.C.: National Geographic Society, 1997.

Coelho, Paulo. **The Alchemist**, 25th Anniversary Edition. Translated by Alan R. Clarke. New York: HarperCollins Publishers, Inc, 1993.

Cohen, Benjamin J. **The Question of Imperialism: The Political Economy of Dominance and Dependence**. New York: Basic Books, Inc., 1973.

Cohen, Stephen Philip. **The Idea of Pakistan**. Washington, D.C.: Brookings Institution Press, 2004.

Coleman, Graham, and Thupten Jinpa, eds. **The Tibetan Book of the Dead**. Translated by Gyurme Dorje. New York: Penguin Classics, 2005.

Conquest, Robert. **The Great Terror: Stalin's Purge of the Thirties**. London: Macmillan Publishers, 1968.

Damrosch, Leo. **The Club: Johnson, Boswell, and the Friends Who Shaped an Age**. New Haven: Yale University Press, 2019.

Darwin, Charles. **The Descent of Man, and Selection in Relation to Sex**. New York: D. Appleton and Company, 1871.

———. **On the Origin of Species**, 150th Anniversary Edition. New York: Signet Classics, 2003.

Day, Mary Beth, David A. Hodell, Mark Brenner, Hazel J. Chapman, Jason H. Curtis, William F. Kenney, Alan L. Kolata, and Larry C. Peterson. "Paleoenvironmental History of the West Baray, Angkor (Cambodia)," **Proceedings of the National Academy of Sciences**, January 24, 2012, vol. 109, no. 4, pp. 1046-1051.

de Bli, Harm J., Peter O. Muller, and Jan Nijman. **Geography: Realms, Regions, and Concepts**. New York: Wiley, 2014.

de Soto, Hernando. **The Mystery of Capital: Why Capitalism Triumphs in the West and Fails Everywhere Else**. New York: Basic Books, 2000.

DeFries, Ruth. **What Would Nature Do? A Guide for Our Uncertain Times**, New York: Columbia University Press, 2021.

deLisle, Jacques. **Taiwan: Sovereignty and Participation in International Organizations**. Foreign Policy Research Institute E-Note, July 1, 2011.

Demuth, Bathsheba. **Floating Coast: An Environmental History of the Bering Strait**. W.W. Norton & Co., New York, 2019.

DeSilva, Jeremy M., ed. **A Most Interesting Problem: What Darwin's Descent of Man Got Right and Wrong about Human Evolution**. Princeton University Press, 2021.

Diamond, Jared. **Guns, Germs, and Steel: The Fates of Human Societies**. New York: W.W. Norton & Company, 2005. Originally published in 1997.

Dobbs, David. "Restless Genes," **The National Geographic**, January 2013.

Dolnick, Edward. **The Clockwork Universe: Isaac Newton, the Royal Society and the Birth of the Modern World**. New York: Harper Perennial, 2011.

Dostoyevsky, Fyodor. **The Idiot**. Translation by Constance Garnett. London: Wordsworth Editions, 1996. Originally published serially in the journal *The Russian Messenger* in 1868-69.

Doyle, Rodger. "By the Numbers: Ethnic Groups in the World," **Scientific American**, vol. 279, no. 3 (1998), p. 30.

Dyson, Freeman. **Weapons and Hope**. New York: Harper Colophon Books, 1984.

Evans, Damian, Christophe Pottier, Roland Fletcher, Scott Hensley, Ian Tapley, Anthony Milne, and Michael Barbetti. "A Comprehensive Archeological Map of the World's Largest Preindustrial Settlement Complex at Angkor, Cambodia," **Proceedings of the National Academy of Sciences**, September 4, 2007, vol. 104, no. 36, pp. 14277-14282.

Fadiman, Anne. **The Spirit Catches You and You Fall Down: A Hmong Child, Her American Doctors, and the Collision of Two Cultures**. New York: Farrar, Straus and Giroux, 1997, 3rd printing, 1998.

Ford, A. G. "Capital Exports and Growth for Argentina, 1880-1914," **The Economic Journal of the Royal Economic Society**, vol. 68, no. 271 (September 1958), pp. 589-593.

Frankl, Viktor E. **Man's Search for Meaning**. Boston: Beacon Press, 2006.

Friedman, George. **The Next 100 Years: A Forecast for the 21st Century**. New York: Anchor Books, 2009.

———— and Meredith Lebard. **The Coming War with Japan**. New York: St. Martin's Press, 1991.

Fukuyama, Francis. **The End of History and the Last Man**. New York: The Free Press, 1992.

————. **Trust: The Social Virtues and the Creation of Prosperity**. New York: The Free Press, 1995.

Fulbright, J. William. **The Arrogance of Power**, 50th Anniversary Edition. Fayetteville: The University of Arkansas Press, 2018.

Gandhi, Mohandas K. **An Autobiography: The Story of My Experiments with Truth**. Boston: Beacon Press, 1993. Originally published in 1957.

García Márquez, Gabriel. **One Hundred Years of Solitude**. New York: Harper Perennial Modern Classics, 2006. Translated from Spanish by Gregory Rabassa. First published in 1967.

————. **The General in His Labyrinth**. Translated from Spanish by Edith Grossman. New York: Vintage International, 1990.

Goldberg, Jeffrey. "World Chaos and World Order: Conversations with Henry Kissinger." theatlantic.com, November 10, 2016.

Golding, William. **The Lord of the Flies**. New York: Penguin Group (USA) Inc., 2006. First published in 1954.

Goodwin, Doris Kearns. **The Bully Pulpit: Theodore Roosevelt, William Howard Taft and the Golden Age of Journalism**. New York: Simon & Schuster, 2013.

Gorman, Amanda. "The Hill We Climb," **The Hill We Climb: An Inaugural Poem for the Country**. New York: Viking Books, 2021.

Grant, Adam. **Give and Take: A Revolutionary Approach to Success**. New York: Viking, 2013.

Greider, William. **One World, Ready or Not: The Manic Logic of Global Capitalism**. New York: Simon & Schuster, 1997.

Gross, Daniel A. "Peter Singer Is Committed to Controversial Ideas." In **The New Yorker** (newyorker.com), April 25, 2021.

Hallahan, William H. **The Day the American Revolution Began: 19 April 1775**. New York: HarperCollins Publishers, 2000.

Halliburton, Richard. **New Worlds to Conquer**. Garden City: Garden City Publishing Company, 1929.

Harari, Yuval Noah. *Homo Deus:* **A Brief History of Tomorrow**, New York: Harper, 2017.

———. **Sapiens: A Brief History of Humankind**. New York: Harper Collins Publishers, 2015.

———. **21 Lessons for the 21st Century**. New York: Spiegel & Grau, 2018.

Harrer, Heinrich. **Seven Years in Tibet.** Trans. Richard Graves. New York: E.F. Dutton & Company, Inc., 1954.

Henrikson, Alan K., ed. **Negotiating World Order: The Artisanship and Architecture of Diplomacy**. New York: Scholarly Resources, 1986.

Herdeck, Margaret, and Gita Piramal. **India's Industrialists, Volume I**. Washington, D.C.: Three Continents Press, Inc., 1985.

Hilton, James. **Lost Horizon.** Singapore: Pansing Distribution, 2004. Originally published in 1933.

Hobsbawm, Eric, and Terence Ranger, eds. **The Invention of Tradition**. Cambridge University Press, 27th printing, 2018. First published in 1983.

Hoffecker, John F., Scott A. Elias, and Dennis H. O'Rourke. "Out of Beringia?" **Science**, published by the American Association for the Advancement of Science, vol. 343, no. 6174 (February 28, 2014), pp. 979-980.

Hofstadter, Richard. **The American Political Tradition**. New York: Vintage Books, 1948.

Huntington, Samuel P. **The Clash of Civilizations and the Remaking of World Order**. New York: Simon & Schuster, 1996.

Hurston, Zora Neale. **Dust Tracks on a Road: An Autobiography**. New York: Harper Perennial, 2006. First published in 1942.

Huxley, Aldous. **Brave New World**. New York: Harper Perennial Modern Classics, 2006. First published in 1932.

I Ching: The Ancient Chinese Book of Changes. Author unknown. New York: Chartwell Books, Inc., 2012.

Isaacson, Walter. **Steve Jobs**. New York: Simon & Schuster, 2013.

Jackson, Tim. **Prosperity Without Growth: Foundations for the Economy of Tomorrow**. London: Routledge Press, 2016.

Jacques, Martin. **When China Rules the World: The End of the Western World and the Birth of a New Global Order**. New York: The Penguin Press, 2009.

Jaynes, Julian. **The Origin of Consciousness in the Breakdown of the Bicameral Mind**. Boston and New York: Houghton Mifflin Company, 1976.

Kacou, Eric. **Entrepreneurial Solutions for Prosperity in BoP Markets: Strategies for Success and Economic Transformation**. Philadelphia: Wharton School Publishing, 2011.

Kahneman, Daniel. **Thinking, Fast and Slow**. New York: Farrar, Straus and Giroux, 2011.

Kalck, Pierre. **Central African Republic: A Failure in Decolonization**. New York: Praeger Publishers, 1971.

Kallis, Giorgos. **Degrowth – The Economy: Key Ideas**, Agenda Publishing, 2018.

Kamm, Henry. **Cambodia: Report from a Stricken Land**. New York: Arcade Publishing, 1998.

Kant, Immanuel. "To Perpetual Peace: A Philosophical Sketch," in **Perpetual Peace and Other Essays**. Translated by Ted Humphrey. Indianapolis and Cambridge: Hackett Publishing Company, 1983. The essay was first published in 1795.

Kasser, Tim. **The High Price of Materialism**. Cambridge, Mass.: MIT Press, 2002.

Keene, Donald. **On Familiar Terms: A Journey Across Cultures**. Tokyo and New York: Kodansha International, 2004.

Kennedy, John F. **Profiles in Courage: 50th Anniversary Edition**. New York: Harper Perennial Modern Classics, 2006.

Kennedy, Robert F. **Thirteen Days: A Memoir of the Cuban Missile Crisis**. New York: W.W. Norton & Company, Inc., 1969.

Kerouac, Jack. **Mexico City Blues (242 Choruses)**. New York: Grove Press, Inc., 1959.

———. **On the Road**. New York: Penguin Books, 1999. Originally published in 1957.

Kiernan, Ben. **Blood and Soil: A World History of Genocide and Extermination from Sparta to Darfur**. New Haven: Yale University Press, 2007.

Kim, Hyang-Soo. **A Small Key Opens Big Doors**. Translated by John H. Cha. Seoul: Seoul Selection, 2013.

Kim, Woo-Choong. **Every Street Is Paved with Gold: The Road to Real Success**. New York: William Morrow and Company, 1992.

King, Charles. **Gods of the Upper Air: How a Circle of Renegade Anthropologists Reinvented Race, Sex, and Gender in the Twentieth Century**. New York: Doubleday, 2019.

King, Martin Luther, Jr. **The Autobiography of Martin Luther King, Jr.** New York: Grand Central Publishing, 2001.

———. **Stride Towards Freedom: The Montgomery Story**. Boston: Beacon Press, 2010. Originally published in 1958.

Kissinger, Henry A. **On China**. New York: The Penguin Press, 2011.

———. **World Order.** New York: Penguin Books, 2015

Kotter, John P. **Matsushita Leadership: Lessons from the 20th Century's Most Remarkable Entrepreneur**. New York: The Free Press, 1997.

Krakauer, Jon. **Into Thin Air: A Personal Account of the Mt. Everest Disaster**. New York: Villard, 1997.

Kuhn, Thomas S. **The Copernican Revolution**. Cambridge, Mass.: Harvard University Press, 1957.

———. **The Structure of Scientific Revolutions**, 50th Anniversary Edition. University of Chicago Press, 2012.

Lambert, Andrew. **Nelson: Britannia's God of War**. London: Faber & Faber, 2005.

Lansing, Alfred. **Endurance: Shackleton's Incredible Voyage**. New York: Basic Books, 2007.

Leach, John. "Coping in Captivity: A Cognitive Perspective." **Advances in Psychology Research**, vol. 66 (2010).

————. "'Give-up-itis' Revisited: Neuropathology of *Extremis*." **Medical Hypotheses**, vol. 120 (November 2018), pp. 14-21.

Lederer, William J., and Eugene Burdick. **The Ugly American**. New York: W.W. Norton & Company, Inc., 1958.

Lee, Yew Kuan. **The Singapore Story**. Singapore: Prentice Hall, 1998.

Lehman, Paul W. **Dublin School, 1935-1970**. Dublin, N.H.: William H. Bauhan Publisher, 1975.

Lemkin, Raphael. **Totally Unofficial: The Autobiography of Raphael Lemkin**. Edited by Donna-Lee Frieze. New Haven, Conn.: Yale University Press, 2013.

Lepore, Jill. **This America: The Case for the Nation**. New York: Liveright Publishing Corporation, 2019.

Leys, Simon, ed. and trans. **The Analects of Confucius**. New York: W.W. Norton & Company, 1997.

Liao, Yiwu. **For a Song and a Hundred Songs: A Poet's Journey Through a Chinese Prison**. Translated from the Chinese by Wenguang Huang. Boston and New York: Houghton Mifflin Harcourt Publishing Co., 2013.

Lim, Kieng Sieu. **Red Undertow: From Khmer Rouge's Cambodia to Freedom**. Stamford, Conn.: Mirror Books, 2006.

Lombard, Louisa. **State of Rebellion: Violence and Intervention in the Central African Republic**. London: Zed Books, 2016.

Lombardo, Michael P. "On the Evolution of Sport," **Evolutionary Psychology** (2012) vol. 10, no. 1, pp. 1-28.

MacAfee, Norman, ed. **The Gospel According to RFK: Why It Matters Now**. New York: Basic Books, 2004.

MacAskill, William. **Doing Good Better: How Effective Altruism Can Help You Make a Difference**. New York: Gotham, 2015.

MacFarquhar, Larissa. **Strangers Drowning: Grappling with Impossible Idealism, Drastic Choices and the Overpowering Urge to Help**. New York: Penguin Press, 2015.

MacMillan, Margaret. **Paris 1919: Six Months That Changed the World**. New York: Random House Trade Paperback Edition, 2003.

————. **War: How Conflict Shaped Us**. New York: Random House, 2020.

Mandela, Nelson. **Long Walk to Freedom: The Autobiography of Nelson Mandela**. New York: Little, Brown & Co.,1994.

Matsushita, Konosuke. **Not for Bread Alone: A Business Ethos, A Management Ethic**. Kyoto: PHP Institute, Inc., 1984.

————. **Quest for Prosperity: The Life of a Japanese Industrialist**. Kyoto: PHP Institute, Inc., 1988.

McCullough, David. **John Adams**. New York: Simon & Schuster, 2001.

———. **The Path Between the Seas: The Creation of the Panama Canal 1870-1914**. New York: Simon & Schuster, 2001.

———. **The Wright Brothers**. New York: Simon & Schuster, 2015.

McGregor, Richard. **The Party: The Secret World of China's Communist Rulers**. London and New York: Allen Lane, 2010.

McWhorter, John H. **The Language Hoax: Why the World Looks the Same in Any Language**. Oxford University Press, 2014.

Meadows, Donella H., et al. **The Limits to Growth**. New York: Signet Books, 1972.

Meeker, Meg. **Strong Fathers, Strong Daughters: 10 Secrets Every Father Should Know**. New York: Ballantine Books, 2007.

Mehta, Harish C., and Julie B. Mehta. **Strongman: The Extraordinary Life of Hun Sen**. Singapore: Marshall Cavendish International, 2013.

Meredith, Robyn. **The Elephant and the Dragon: The Rise of India and China and What It Means for All of Us**. New York: W.W. Norton & Company, 2008.

Metcalf, Franz. **What Would Buddha Do? 101 Answers to Life's Daily Dilemmas**. Berkeley, Calif.: Seastone Press, 1999.

Mishra, Pankaj. "The Last Dalai Lama?" **The New York Times Magazine**, December 6, 2015, pp. 40ff.

Miwa, Yoshiro, and J. Mark Ramseyer. "Toward a Theory of Jurisdictional Competition: The Case of the Japanese FTC," **Journal of Competition Law and Economics** (June 2005) vol. 1, no. 2, pp. 247-277.

Montaigne, Michel de. **The Complete Works**. Translated by Donald Frame. New York: Everyman's Library, 2003.

Morgan, Lewis Henry. **League of the Iroquois**. Secaucus, N.J.: The Citadel Press, 1972. Originally published in Rochester, New York, by Sage & Brother, Publishers, in 1851.

———. **Systems of Consanguinity and Affinity of the Human Family**. Lincoln: University of Nebraska Press, 1997. Originally published in Washington, D.C., by the Smithsonian Institution in 1870 as Volume 218 in the Smithsonian Contributions to Knowledge.

Moser, Thomas F., with Brad Lemley. **Thos. Moser: Artistry in Wood**. San Francisco: Chronicle Books, 2002.

Mostert, Noel. **Frontiers: The Epic of South Africa's Creation and the Tragedy of the Xhosa People**. New York: Alfred A. Knopf, 1992.

Nairn, Tom. **The Break-Up of Britain**. London: Verso, 1981. First published in 1977.

Nietzsche, Friedrich. **The Portable Nietzsche**. Edited and translated by Walter Kaufmann. New York: Penguin Books, 1982.

Ohmae, Kenichi. **The Borderless World: Power and Strategy in the Interlinked Economy**. New York: Harper Business, 1990.

Orwell, George. **1984**. New York: Signet Classics, 2017.

Palevsky, Mary. **Atomic Fragments: A Daughter's Questions**. Berkeley: University of California Press, 2000.

Park, Keun. **Hibiscus: The Journey of a Korean Man through the Rise of His Country**. Tokyo: Random House Kodansha, 2009.

Parrado, Nando. **Miracle in the Andes: 72 Days on the Mountain and My Long Trek Home**. New York: Three Rivers Press, 2006.

Patten, Alan. **Equal Recognition: The Moral Foundation of Minority Rights**. Princeton University Press, 2014.

Paul, E. Jaiwant, and Pramod Kapoor. **The Unforgettable Maharajas: One Hundred and Fifty Years of Photography**. New Delhi: Lustre Press, Roli Books, 2012.

Pinker, Steven. **The Better Angels of Our Nature: Why Violence Has Declined**. New York: Penguin Books, 2011.

——. **Enlightenment Now: The Case for Reason, Science, Humanism, and Progress**. London: Allen Lane, 2018.

——. **How the Mind Works**. New York: W.W. Norton & Company, 1997.

Pirsig, Robert. **Zen and the Art of Motorcycle Maintenance: An Inquiry into Values**. 25th Anniversary Edition. New York: William Morrow, 1999. First published in 1974.

Plato. **The Seventh Letter**. Translated by J. Harward. Written 360 B.C.E.

Pollin, Robert. **Greening the Global Economy**. Cambridge, Mass.: The MIT Press, 2015.

Pomerantsev, Peter. **Nothing Is True, and Everything Is Possible: The Surreal Heart of the New Russia**. New York: Public Affairs, 2014.

Prahalad, C. K. **The Fortune at the Bottom of the Pyramid: Eradicating Poverty Through Profits**. New York: Pearson Publishing, 2004.

Rasmussen, Dennis C. **The Infidel and the Professor: David Hume, Adam Smith, and the Friendship That Shaped Modern Thought**. Princeton University Press, 2017.

Raworth, Kate. **Doughnut Economics: Seven Ways to Think Like a 21st Century Economist**. White River Junction, Vt.: Chelsea Green Publishing, 2018.

Rayfield, Donald. **Stalin and His Hangmen: The Tyrant and Those Who Killed for Him**. New York: Random House, 2005.

Read, Herbert. **Education Through Art**. New York: Pantheon Books, 1954.

Read, Piers Paul. **Alive: Sixteen Men, Seventy-Two Days, and Insurmountable Odds: The Classic Adventure of Survival in the Andes**. New York: Harper Perennial, 2005. First published in 1974.

Reich, David. **Who We Are and How We Got Here**. New York: Vintage, 2019.

Reid, T. R. **Confucius Lives Next Door: What Living in the East Teaches Us About Living in the West**. New York: Random House, 1999.

Ricard, Matthieu. **Altruism: The Power of Compassion to Change Yourself and the World**. New York: Little, Brown and Company, 2015.

Roberts, Dorothy E. "Abolition Constitutionalism," **Harvard Law Review**, vol. 133 (November 2019), no. 1, pp. 1-122.

————. **Fatal Invention: How Science, Politics and Big Business Re-Create Race in the Twenty-First Century**. New York: The New Press, 2011.

Robertson, Diana C., and Philip M. Nichols, eds. **Thinking about Bribery: Neuroscience, Moral Cognition, and the Psychology of Bribery**. Cambridge University Press, 2017.

Robinson, Jackie. **I Never Had It Made: An Autobiography of Jackie Robinson** as told to Alfred Duckett. New York: Harper Collins, 1995. Original publication New York: Putnam, 1972.

Rodin, Judith. **The Resilience Dividend: Being Strong in a World Where Things Go Wrong**. New York: Public Affairs, 2014.

———— and Margot Brandenberg. **The Power of Impact Investing: Putting Markets to Work for Profit and Global Good**. Philadelphia: Wharton Digital Press, 2014.

Rodríguez, Elena M. **Global Vision: How Tohmatsu and Co. Serves Clients Worldwide**. Port Ludlow, Wash.: Pacific Press International, 1995.

Ross, Rev. Fred A., **Slavery Ordained of God**. Canton, Ohio: Pinnacle Press, 2017. First published in 1857.

Rowley, Hazel. **Tête-à-Tête: The Tumultuous Lives & Loves of Simone de Beauvoir and Jean-Paul Sartre**. New York: Harper Perennial, 2006.

Rubin, Leslie. **Apartheid in Practice**. New York: United Nations, 1976.

Rubio-Pueyo, Vicente. **Municipalism in Spain: From Barcelona to Madrid, and Beyond**. New York: Rosa Luxemburg Stiftung, 2017.

Rummel, R. J. **Lethal Politics: Soviet Genocide and Mass Murder Since 1917**. Piscataway, N.J.: Transaction Publishers, 1990.

Said, Edward W. **Orientalism**. New York: Vintage Books, 1994.

————. **Representations of the Intellectual**. New York: Vintage Books, 1996.

Sandel, Michael J. **The Tyranny of Merit: What's Become of the Common Good?** New York: Farrar, Straus and Giroux, 2020.

Sartre, Jean-Paul. **Being and Nothingness**. Trans. Hazel E. Barnes. New York: Grammercy Books, 1994.

————. **Existentialism Is a Humanism**. Trans. Carol Macomber. New Haven: Yale University Press, 2007.

————. **No Exit and Three Other Plays**. Trans. Stuart Gilbert. New York: Vintage International Edition, 1989.

Schell, Orville, and John Delury. **Wealth and Power: China's Long March to the Twenty-First Century**. New York: Random House, 2013.

Schiller, Friedrich. **On the Aesthetic Education of Man**. Trans. Reginald Snell. Mineola, N.Y.: Dover Publications, Inc., 2004.

Schlender, Brent, and Rick Tetzeli. **Becoming Steve Jobs: The Evolution from Reckless Upstart into a Visionary Leader**. New York: Crown Business, 2015.

Schuman, Michael. **Confucius and the World He Created**. New York: Basic Books, 2015.

Seligman, Martin E. P. "Building Resilience," **Harvard Business Review**, April 2011.

Seung, Sebastian. **Connectome: How the Brain's Wiring Makes Us Who We Are**. New York: First Mariner Books (Houghton Mifflin Harcourt Publishing Company), 2012.

Shropshire, Kenneth L. **Sport Matters: Leadership, Power, and the Quest for Respect in Sports**. Philadelphia: Wharton Digital Press, 2014.

Singh, Patwant. **The Sikhs**. New York: Doubleday, 1999.

Singer, Peter. **Animal Liberation: The Definitive Classic of the Animal Movement**. New York: Harper Perennial Modern Classics, 2009. First published in 1975.

———. **The Expanding Circle: Ethics, Evolution, and Moral Progress**. Princeton University Press, 1981.

———. **Marx: A Very Short Introduction**. Oxford University Press, 2nd edition, 2018. First published 1980.

———. **The Most Good You Can Do: How Effective Altruism Is Changing Ideas about Living Ethically**. New Haven: Yale University Press, 2015.

Sleigh, Dan. **Islands**. London: Vintage Random House, 2005.

Smil, Vaclav. **Growth: From Microorganisms to Megacities**. Cambridge, Mass.: MIT Press, 2019.

Smith, Adam. **The Theory of Moral Sentiments**, ed. D. D. Raphael and A. L. Macfie. Indianapolis: The Liberty Fund, 1982. First published in 1759.

———. **The Wealth of Nations**. New York: Penguin Classics, 1982.

Smith, Huston. **The World's Religions**. 50th Anniversary Edition. New York: Harper One, 2008. First published in 1958.

Soyinka, Wole. **The Open Sore of a Continent: A Personal Narrative of the Nigerian Crisis**. Oxford University Press, 1996.

Steinbeck, John. **East of Eden**. Steinbeck Centennial Edition. New York: Viking Press, 2003. Originally published in 1952.

———. **The Grapes of Wrath**. New York: Viking Press, 1939.

———. "To a God Unknown," in **John Steinbeck: Novels and Stories, 1932-1937**. New York: The Library of America, 1994.

Stewart, Katherine. **The Power Worshippers: Inside the Dangerous Rise of Christian Nationalism**. New York: Bloomsbury Publishing, 2019.

Struck, Peter. **Divination and Human Nature: A Cognitive History of Intuition in Classical Antiquity**. Princeton: Princeton University Press, 2016.

Tadjo, Véronique. **Queen Pokou: Concerto for a Sacrifice**. Translated from the French by Amy Baram Reid. London: Ayebia Clarke Publishing Limited, 2009.

Taleb, Nassim Nicholas. **The Black Swan: The Impact of the Highly Improbable**. New York: Random House, 2007.

———. **Skin in the Game: Hidden Asymmetries in Daily Life**. New York, Random House, 2018.

Tegmark, Max. **Life 3.0: Being Human in the Age of Artificial Intelligence**. New York: Alfred A. Knopf, 2017.

Tharoor, Shashi. **Inglorious Empire: What the British Did to India**. London: Scribe Publications, 2018.

Tobin, James. **The Man He Became: How FDR Defied Polio to Win the Presidency**. New York: Simon & Schuster, 2013.

Tolstoi, Count Leo. **The Kingdom of God Is Within You**. Translated by Constance Garnett. Gearhart, OR: Watchmaker Publishing, 1951.

Tresch, John. **The Romantic Machine**. University of Chicago Press, 2014.

Tuchman, Barbara W. **The March of Folly from Troy to Vietnam**. New York: Ballantine Books, 1984.

Van Tongeren, Daryl R., Don E. Davis, Joshua N. Hook, and Charlotte vanOyen Witvliet. "Humility," **Current Directions in Psychological Science** 10 2019; vol. 28, no. 5: pp. 463-468.

Villalonga, Bélen, and Raphael Amit. **SUN Brewing (A)**. Harvard Business School Case 9-207-022, rev. June 2, 2010.

———. **SUN Brewing (B)**. Harvard Business School Case 9-207-039, rev. June 28, 2010.

Vogel, Ezra. **Japan as No. 1: Lessons for America**. Cambridge, Mass.: Harvard University Press, 1979.

Vollroth, Dietrich. **Fully Grown: Why a Stagnant Economy Is a Sign of Success**. University of Chicago Press, 2020.

Voltaire. "Candide," in **Candide and Other Stories**. Boston: digireads.com, 2019. Originally published as The Works of Voltaire: Romances, ed. George Smollett, trans. William F. Fleming. Paris: E.R. Du Mont, 1901.

Wilder, Thornton. **The Bridge of San Luis Rey**. New York: HarperCollins Publishers, 2004. Originally published by Albert & Charles Boni, Inc., in 1927.

Williams, William Appleman. **The Tragedy of American Diplomacy, Fiftieth Anniversary Edition**. New York: W.W. Norton & Company, 2009.

Wills, Gary. **Certain Trumpets: The Nature of Leadership**. New York: Simon & Schuster, 1994.

Wilson, Edward O. **Consilience: The Unity of Knowledge**. New York: Vintage, 1999.

————. **The Meaning of Human Existence**. New York: Liveright Publishing Corporation, 2014.

————. **On Human Nature**. Cambridge, Mass.: Harvard University Press, 1979.

————. **The Origins of Creativity**. New York: Liveright Publishing Corporation, 2017.

Woodward, Colin. **American Nations: A History of the Eleven Rival Regional Cultures of North America**. New York: Penguin Books, 2011.

Wright, Robert. **Why Buddhism Is True**. New York: Simon & Schuster, 2017.

Wright, Quincy. **A Study of War**. University of Chicago Press, 1942.

Yamashita, Toshihiko. **The Panasonic Way: From a Chief Executive's Desk**. Translated by Frank Baldwin. Tokyo: Kodansha International, 1989.

Yang, Jisheng. **Tombstone: The Untold Story of Mao's Great Famine**. London: Allen Lane, 2008.

Yu, Minhong. **The Relentless Pursuit of Success**. Singapore: Thomson, 2007.

Zhang, Weiying. **The Logic of the Market: An Insider's View of Chinese Economic Reform**. Washington, D.C.: The Cato Institute, 2015.

Zimbardo, Philip. **The Lucifer Effect: Understanding How Good People Turn Evil**. New York: Random House, 2008.

Zimmer, Carl. "Darwin's Junkyard," **The New York Times Magazine**, March 8, 2015, pp. 60ff.

Credits and Permissions

Index

A page number followed by "en" (e.g. "16en") signifies a reference to an endnote.

A Note on the Type

This book has been composed in Arno, a
calligraphically-inspired humanistic Old-style serif
typeface designed by Robert Slimbach at Adobe. This
typeface is named for the Arno River, running through
Florence, and combines the Aldine and Venetian styles.
It also draws on the work of Ludovico Vicentino
degli Arrighi, a sixteenth century papal scribe and
type designer, for its italics.